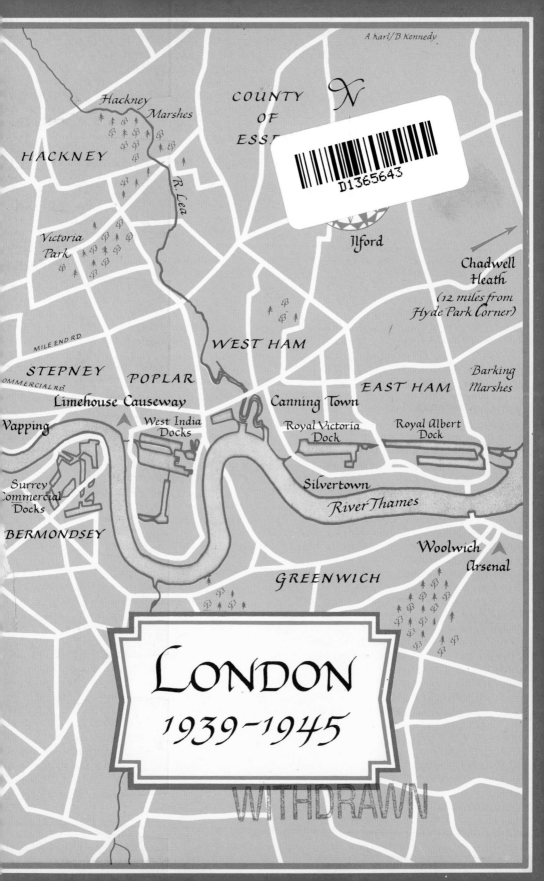

A. harl/B. Kennedy

Hackney Marshes

COUNTY OF ESS[...]

N

HACKNEY

R. Lea

Ilford

Victoria Park

Chadwell Heath
(12 miles from
Hyde Park Corner)

MILE END RD.

WEST HAM

STEPNEY

POPLAR

COMMERCIAL RD.

EAST HAM

Barking Marshes

Limehouse Causeway

Canning Town

Wapping

West India Docks

Royal Victoria Dock

Royal Albert Dock

Surrey Commercial Docks

Silvertown

BERMONDSEY

River Thames

Woolwich Arsenal

GREENWICH

LONDON
1939-1945

WITHDRAWN

D1365643

Also by Leonard Mosley

Backs
to the
Wall

Backs

RANDOM HOUSE

New York

to the *Wall*

THE HEROIC STORY
OF THE PEOPLE
OF LONDON
DURING
WORLD WAR II

by

Leonard Mosley

Copyright © 1971 by Leonard Mosley

All rights reserved under International and Pan-American Copyright Con-
ventions. Published in the United States by Random House, Inc., New York.
Originally published in Great Britain by George Weidenfeld & Nicolson,
London.

ISBN: 0–394–46080–4

Library of Congress Catalog Card Number: 74–159359

For permission to quote, the author would like to thank the following:

The British Broadcasting Corporation, for two recordings about the Blitz from
its archives;

Editions de la Table Ronde, Paris, for extracts from Robert Mengin's *De Gaulle
à Londres,* published in England by Michael Joseph Ltd., and in the United
States by Farrar, Straus & Giroux, Inc., under the title *No Laurels for De
Gaulle;*

Messrs. Wingate for extracts from *The Blitz,* by Constantine FitzGibbon, a
new edition of which was issued in 1970.

Manufactured in the United States of America
by The Book Press, Brattleboro, Vermont

Painting on Part Titles by Edith Dreikurs
Book design by Mary M. Ahern

9 8 7 6 5 4 3 2

FIRST AMERICAN EDITION

ACKNOWLEDGMENTS

In addition to those who have been named in the Foreword, I should like to express my thanks to many people in all parts of the world who were in London during World War II and have taken the trouble to search their memories or their records for facts, figures and anecdotes. They include the following:

Lt. Comm. Kenneth W. Allison, USNR, *Washington, D.C.*

Dr. W. Babinski, *Montreal*

Mrs. Elsie M. Banister, *St. Andrews, Fife*

Mrs. S. T. Brown, *Pittsburgh, Pennsylvania*

Commander L. J. Burt, *London*

Richard Collier, *Burgh Heath, Surrey*

Colonel John J. Christy, *Fort Benjamin Harrison, Indiana*

Mrs. Rita Cheren, *New York*

Mrs. Tania Long Daniell, *Ottawa*

Rodney Dennys, *Steep, Sussex*

B. J. Enright, Librarian, *University of Sussex*

Mrs. P. Foster, *London*

Major Carl R. Greenstein, *Sacramento, California*

Irving Gerdy, *Penndel, Pennsylvania*

Admiral John Godfrey, *Wilmington, Sussex*

Colonel Gerald M. Holland, *Washington, D.C.*

Mrs. Leland Hayward, *Connecticut*

Howard W. Johnson, *Brookline, Massachusetts*

A. H. Ketley, *Romford, Essex*

Eric Mandell, *Philadelphia, Pennsylvania*

Staff Sergeant Wilford B. Marshall, *San Diego, California*

Mrs. J. Nestor, *Forest Hills, New York*

General Carl A. Spaatz, *Chevy Chase, Maryland*

David A. Shephard, *New York*

H. S. Taylor, *Pakenham, Suffolk*

Mrs. Joyce Webb, *Hastings, Sussex*

Reverend C. Williams, *London*

To **D.**

FOREWORD

On a visit to England in 1847 Ralph Waldo Emerson made a speech in Manchester in which he expressed his thoughts about an England riddled by doubts, pressed by her competitors, struggling to adjust herself to the changes of the new machine age. Although it was a land in the throes of a great upheaval, Emerson, an unabashed Anglophile, had no doubt of her survival. For him, London was "the epitome of our times," a capital he described as—

> Not dispirited, not weak, but well remembering that she has seen dark days before; indeed, with a kind of instinct that she sees a little better in a cloudy day, and that, in the storm of battle and calamity, she has a secret vigor and a pulse like a cannon.

This book is the story of how that secret vigor and cannonlike pulse kept the great city of London alive through the six most painful and difficult years of its existence, from 1939 to 1945. It is not a statistical study of how the capital survived the years of war; it is not even a blow-by-blow account of London in World War II. It is, rather, an attempt to show a great city struggling to survive during a particularly agonizing and—it sometimes seemed—endless war through the experiences, aches, pains, tragedies, deprivations, fears, fulfillments and joys of the people who were there. In other words, it is many kinds and conditions of London seen by many kinds and conditions of its citizens and visitors, and I hope it comes to life through their eyes as the great, sprawling, palpitating, suffering but magnificent monster that it was during the dire days of World War II.

If I have succeeded in bringing it back to life, I have many people to thank for helping me.

First of all, there are those who gave me precious hours of their time to talk to me and remember. They include Lord Snow, better known as C. P. Snow, who recalled with wit and sagacity the days when he was a denizen of the corridors of power; Lord Boothby, better known as Robert Boothby, who readily talked about life at Westminster and his own heartbreaking moments there; Henry Moore, O.M., whose artistic life was catalyzed in the Underground railways of London; Commander Reginald K. Smith and his experiences with the Metropolitan Police in the East End; my old friends Jack Davies and Harold Conway, with their memories of the world of the London theatre; Geoffrey Page, who not only talked about his experiences in the RAF but also lent me his unpublished account of his adventures; Joan St. George Saunders, who told me of her own experiences and also found others who could tell theirs; and a host of others whose anecdotes and recollections have helped to add circumstantial details to the story. It will become apparent to those who read the narrative (particularly those sections dealing with Free French operations in London) why some of these are not named here.

There are also those who lent me their diaries or responded in other ways to my inquiries. I would particularly like to mention Mr. Donald Ketley, who spent his boyhood in wartime London; Mr. David Meade, who was then a policeman in Limehouse; and scores of others, soldiers-in-passage as well as natives, upon whom wartime London left its mark.

There is one diarist I must single out: Miss Vere Hodgson. A social worker in Holland Park and Notting Hill from 1940 onward, she faithfully and spiritedly recorded the life of her community and of her beloved city through all the triumphs and disasters of the war. It is a remarkable record, and I am in her debt for allowing me to use extracts from it.

I should also like to thank the British Broadcasting Corporation for allowing me to quote from two recordings in their archives dealing with the Blitz in London.

Finally, and most important, Mr. Tom Harrisson gave me access to the *Mass-Observation Papers*. In the 1930s Tom Harrisson pioneered a method of sounding public opinion and public feeling which probed the minds of ordinary citizens much more deeply than any of the forms of opinion-canvassing which have since been developed. In communities all over Britain he picked observers of both sexes and from all walks of life who "listened in" on their friends and reported what they said, how they felt, what they liked, what they resented. But these observers were not merely reporters. They were urged to express their own likes and dislikes and to do so in the most forthright fashion, whether they were criticizing the government, politicians, regulations, policies, fashions, trends or (when it came) the war itself. It is a tribute to Tom Harrisson's guidance and the trust his observers placed in him that they recorded what they felt and overheard with complete frankness. The result is a fascinating picture of Britain through the 1930s and World War II that is a treasure trove for historians.

A sample of the gold that the *Mass-Observation Papers* contain will be found in this book. The *Papers* have been deposited with the University of Sussex, and it is good news that Tom Harrisson himself will be working on them over the next two or three years. The books he distills from these remarkable documents cannot fail to be exciting, absorbing and invaluable. In the meantime, I have used extracts from the records of some of the observers who were in London during the war, and though I have quoted only a fraction of the material available, I believe it gives a flavor of the riches to come. My thanks to Mr. Harrisson and his observers for allowing me to do so.

In an appendix, "Where Are They Now?," will be found a list of all those who have helped me with facts, figures or anecdotes. They have my deep appreciation.

L.M.

CONTENTS

Part One

THE RUDE AWAKENING

1

The Last Days of Peace

On the evening of September 3, 1939, as dusk settled over the rooftops of the great city, a strange hush fell upon London such as no man had known since the days of the Great Plague. It was as if most of the capital's seven million souls had suddenly died. An observer who strolled in the gathering dark from Hyde Park Corner to Piccadilly Circus passed only three people on his mile-long journey. Even the prostitutes who in those days plied their trade along the sidewalks between the Park Lane Hotel and Half Moon Street had vanished.

In Piccadilly Circus the lights of the animated signs that made this the brightest and gayest spot in the British Empire had been doused. No flower girls sat beneath the statue of Eros at its hub, for there were no passers-by to buy favors from them. The winged figure of Eros himself had been boarded up, as if to emphasize the disappearance of love from the capital. It was so quiet that the honking of the geese on the St. James's Park lakes a mile away was plainly audible.

Farther east, on the other side of the city, Police Constable David Meade walked his beat along Limehouse Causeway and reflected that he had never felt so lonely in his life. September 3, 1939, was a Sunday, and in this part of the East End, Sunday night was the time when everyone came out for a beer and a sing-along. The pubs filled up with Cockney couples, and their kids played hopscotch on the sidewalk outside. Often there was trouble and strife when closing time neared, but there was life too.

Tonight, however, Limehouse was dead. The pubs had closed early because their blackout curtains weren't yet up, and it was now a criminal offense to show a light. The chalk marks on the flagstones with which the kids marked out their games were old and smudged. David Meade suddenly realized how they must have felt in Hamelin Town after the Pied Piper passed by, for here too in London the children were gone. As he turned down a narrow street toward the river, the darkness finally closed in and no lights came on to relieve it. The men who had walked the East End streets each evening at dusk, turning on the gaslights, had put away their poles for the duration. The road ahead was suddenly the arena for a game of blind man's buff, with a sandbag, a pothole or a broken curb waiting to waylay him. Meade had practiced walking in the dark for several months in preparation for this night, but he shied in alarm when a cat squawked in an alleyway.

From across the housetops of an eerie, silent London whose citizens stayed locked behind their doors, the great bell of Big Ben began chiming eleven o'clock, and the sound was taken up by church towers all across the blacked-out city.

Eleven o'clock on a Sunday night, and, David Meade told himself wryly, all was not well. There was a war on. Twelve hours earlier Britain's ultimatum to Germany had expired, and for the people of Britain the first night of World War II was upon them. How long would it be before the horrors that had been forecast came raining down upon their heads?

Only four weeks earlier, it had still been possible to hope that war could be avoided. On August 3 the nation's spirits had risen at the news that Parliament was adjourning for the summer recess and would not be back on their benches until October 3. If MPs could go away for that long, surely things weren't as bad as they seemed.

True, many Members on both sides of the House of Commons (Tory supporters of the government as well as Labour party opponents) had pleaded or exhorted the Prime Minister, Neville Chamberlain, to keep the summer session going, or at least curtail the recess to two or three weeks. The times were too dangerous for holidays, said one MP, a backbencher named Winston Churchill. In Germany the Nazi dictator, Adolf Hitler, was mobilizing the German armed forces and getting ready to march upon Poland, Britain's ally in Eastern Europe, and the government was pledged to come to Poland's aid in the event of an attack. The German dictator had a habit of grabbing countries while the democracies were vacationing. Was this the time for the nation's watchdogs to disperse?

With the bland superiority which infuriated his opponents, Neville Chamberlain had brushed all the objections aside. The destinies of Britain could safely be left in his hands, he said smoothly. One of his most fervent supporters, Henry ("Chips") Channon, had rushed out to the Libraries to check on some dates while Churchill was speaking. On returning, he pushed a note across to Chamberlain, who read it, smiled at him in thanks, and then pointed out that Hitler had invaded Austria and occupied Prague while the House was in session, while his fellow dictator, Benito Mussolini, had taken over Albania a few hours after Parliament adjourned for Easter. Apparently the dictators did not worry about whether the Commons was on holiday or not. MPs could rest assured that the situation was in good hands, and neither they nor the country at large should allow themselves to be panicked by the alarmist speeches of some of his friends behind him. Chips Channon swung around and grinned in triumph at Churchill and these friends, who were bunched on the benches behind him. He called them the Glamour Boys, and loathed every one of them: Churchill himself, "always howling for war"; the wild young Scot, Robert Boothby; the equally uncontrollable redheaded Irishman, Brendan Bracken, his faithful henchmen; and all the other opponents of Chamberlain's policies— among them Anthony Eden, Leopold Amery, Harold Nicolson, Alfred Duff Cooper—who were trying to drag the country into what Channon believed was a quite unnecessary war.

He was delighted at their discomfiture. "The PM used [my] notes with devastating effect," he wrote in his diary later. "By the very brilliance of his performance, and it was his third in one week, he infuriated the House, as everyone hates the truth about himself. When he sat down there were roars of delight and approval, but also some of rage."

The House stood adjourned until October 3, but would be recalled, the Prime Minister said blandly, "should the need arise."

If many an MP walked home from the House that night with fear in his heart for what lay ahead, most Londoners heard the news with joy and relief. War might not come, after all, in which case they could get back to what every decent Cockney was concerned with the first week in August: planning where to go and what to do over the Bank Holiday weekend.

PARLIAMENT IS TAKING A HOLIDAY—WHY NOT YOU? said an advertisement in the *Daily Express* that weekend. "Visit the Belgian Coast, where everyone is happy, peaceful and smiling."

The Hardiman family did not venture so far afield, but the fact that they went anywhere at all was an indication of the way their circumstances had changed by 1939. For the past four years, ever since the clothing factory in Aldgate closed down, George Hardiman had been out of a job, and no amount of standing in line at the employment agency or hanging around factory gates had found him another. The Hardimans hadn't been too surprised; in their Canning Town street of forty-four small houses, eighteen men, fourteen youths and twelve women had been out of work for more than two years. Two million people were living on welfare in Britain.

Every day when she went to work in the West End of London and looked at the fashionable shops, saw all the smart women and shiny cars, and heard money clinking in people's pockets, Ellen Hardiman used to wonder bitterly how the other half was living. It was a different world, a world where they had Empire Shopping Weeks in Bond Street, and banners saying *Be Proud of Our Glorious Empire*. Did anyone in Bond Street guess that in Canning Town—which, after all, was part of the glorious Empire—the Hardiman family of four was living on thirty-four shillings a week and a diet consisting mainly of bread, potatoes and scrag ends of meat? Did they know what slum houses were like, with the rats and roaches from next door and holes in the roof? Did they know that though the Hardiman children, John and Sheila, were scrubbed from head to toe twice a week in the kitchen, they brought nits back in their hair from school which Ellen had to comb out with a dog comb? Did they know about the Means Test, with those welfare snoopers coming around to keep an eye on you to be sure you didn't take a job on the side without reporting it? Ellen Hardiman had taken a job just the same, as a charwoman in a bank two hours' journey away in the West End. That distance away, no one knew you, and she didn't have to declare the extra ten shillings a week: ten shillings with which she could get the kids' shoes repaired, buy them the clothes they were always wearing out or growing out of, and give George the odd shilling for a pint of beer and a bit of company at the pub. She had to get up at four o'clock every morning, it took eight hours out of every day of her life, and she was always dog-tired. For four years Ellen Hardiman hadn't had a drink or bought a new dress, or been to a movie. She was twenty-nine years old.

But now, suddenly, things were better. There was a war coming, and it had changed their lives. The government had voted for conscription and all the young men were being called up. That meant uniforms, so the factory in Aldgate had reopened and George was back in his old job. There were still rats scratching in the back lavatory, the landlord still wouldn't mend the roof, even though they had paid the rent, and the kids still came home with nits in their hair. But the furniture, bought on the installment plan, had been paid for, there were new shoes for the kids and a pair of flannels and a jacket for George and a dress for herself. She had even been to the movies to see Gracie Fields in *Shipyard Sally*.

"You can thank old 'Itler for it," George said, on the bus back from the Granada on Mile End Road.

"George," Ellen said, "d'you think there'll be a war?"

"What's it matter, so long as I'm working? And what can we do about it, anyway?"

"Dad, where are we going for Bank Holiday?" asked his nine-year-old daughter, Sheila.

There were plenty of choices, and a record number of Londoners set off to enjoy them: a track meet at the White City, cricket at Lords and the Oval, the great fair on Hampstead Heath, Tyrone Power making a personal appearance at a movie theatre in Leicester Square, a parade of Empire troops in Hyde Park. But in the end, like a quarter of a million other Cockneys, the Hardimans went thirty-five miles down the river to Southend, London's very own seaside resort. Outside a pub on the promenade they lunched on stewed eel, fish-and-chips and stout, with lemonade for the kids. Afterward, as George and Ellen were dozing in deck chairs and watching the ships plow out to sea from the Thames Estuary, the thud of guns suddenly shook the sultry heat of the afternoon. The coastal batteries at Shoeburyness, just around the corner of the estuary, were starting their regular practice firing.

Ellen Hardiman shivered. "D'you think 'Itler'll bomb us if there's a war?" she asked.

Before George could answer, a man in the next chair thrust a newspaper toward her. "Look, missus," he said, "we're on 'oliday 'ere. D'you mind not bringing up unpleasant subjects? 'Ere, read this!"

It was an editorial in a morning paper, and the Hardimans read it together. "Don't let Hitler spoil your holiday," it said. "Don't talk about crisis news. Change the subject if others bring it up. Don't brood. Take plenty of exercise. Slack livers cause most of the world's gloom."

Ellen Hardiman angrily handed the newspaper back. "Cheek!" she said.

"'E's right, love," George Hardiman said. "Come on, let's forget about it."

It was midnight when they got home, exhausted but content. There was an envelope lying on the doormat, with the West Ham Council stamp on the outside. Inside was a mimeographed form:

EVACUATION

In the event of an Emergency, arrangements have been made to evacuate school children from the London area to safe places in the country. It is hoped that your child/children will participate in this scheme. On receipt of further instruction, he/she/they should report to Elm Road School bringing with him/her/them hat, raincoat, haversack containing night-clothes, towel, soap, tooth brush and tooth paste, and he/she/they should wear a card round his/their neck(s) giving his/her/their full name(s), age(s), School, home address and names of next of kin.

Ellen Hardiman found it hard to sleep that night, but she told herself that she was simply overtired from such a lovely outing.

It so happened that the MP for Southend-on-Sea was Chamberlain's perfervid admirer and supporter, Henry ("Chips") Channon. A more unlikely representative of that gamey Cockney seaside resort could hardly have been found, for Chips was considered by most of his fashionable London friends the biggest snob of all. It was a title he would not have thought of as pejorative; he was proud to be a snob. He had inherited his Southend seat in Parliament from his rich in-laws, who controlled the local Tory party, and he had proved to be a conscientious MP to whom no constituent in trouble ever appealed in vain. But that did not mean that he wanted to mix with them, much less with the crude characters who swarmed to the resort from the East End every weekend to gorge themselves on beer and fish-and-chips.

Henry Channon was quite content to accept England as it was in 1939, a land divided into Them and Us, those who were ruled and those who had been chosen to rule them. He was a firm believer in the right of breeding, background and money, and he considered London the center of the earth. "One of those London days," he once wrote,

8

"when one's blood surges within one, and one is madly desperately happy, when one is tempted to spend a quarter's income on flowers, and something puckish impels one to a thousand capers. Oh, this London!" To Channon, the British Empire was the greatest institution in the history of man, and he could find no fault with it. One of his great fears was that if war came, class barriers would be destroyed and the Empire would break up. Equality was the last thing he wished to see in England.

Ironically enough, Chips Channon was an American. Born in Chicago on March 7, 1897, the only son of a rich Midwestern businessman, he had come to Europe in World War I and never went back, except for visits. It was to escape egalitarianism that he gave up his U.S. citizenship in the 1920s and became a naturalized Englishman. Since then he had been elected to Parliament, made secretary to R. A. Butler at the Foreign Office (at that time Undersecretary of State for Foreign Affairs), married into the aristocracy, and become indistinguishable from the princes, dukes, duchesses and powerful Tory businessmen and politicians in whose circles he now moved. "Oh, land of freedom," he wrote of England, "where women are all sirens and men are all gods!" He meant upper-class women and men, of course.

After Parliament went into recess that August, Chips had refused an invitation from friends of Neville Chamberlain's to go north to the Scottish grouse moors; he retired instead to Kelvedon Hall, the estate in Essex which he shared with his wife, Honor, daughter of Lord Iveagh. Mrs. Channon was the heiress to the millions her family made from Guinness stout, the favorite tipple of Chips's Southend constituents.

"I woke up at 6, got up and went for a long walk in the woods with Bundi," he wrote in his diary on August 6. "There were yokels working, clearing out the debris, and the Essex sun shone through the trees. The noise of chopping and of boughs dragged over the turf was like a Grimm fairy story . . . We lazed all day . . . Honor and I intend to spend the rest of the month quietly here, if events in the outside world will let us."

Three days later, however, a telephone call summoned Channon back to London. His superior, Mr. Butler, was already there and so was Neville Chamberlain. The Foreign Office had secret information that Hitler was planning a spectacular move on August 15, but Channon was warned not to let a word of it get out either to his fellow MPs or to the public. "I am genuinely apprehensive," he wrote that night at his mansion in Belgrave Square. But he was also "quite childish in my fanatical worship of the PM," who he was sure would save them yet.

So was the British public. In a snap poll, a group of Londoners on holiday at Margate were asked whether they thought that Hitler would get his territorial demands from Poland: the Free City of Danzig and the Polish Corridor. Five replied yes, six no, and four were undecided. "Do you think we should go to war to defend Danzig?" they were asked. Seven said yes, four no, and three were undecided. "Do you think there will be a war?" Eight said no, four yes, and three were undecided. "Do you think Hitler wants war—or is he bluffing?" All fifteen thought that he was bluffing.

Neither did George Bernard Shaw, the Irish playwright and the public's favorite gadfly, think there would be a war. "The Jews will be Hitler's ruin in the long run," he said, "even if they perish with him, especially if enough perish with him. Has war become more imminent? No, the peace at present is maintained by funk. Anything that intensifies funk makes for peace . . . A lasting peace is a dream, but any statesman who is not desperately afraid of starting a cannonade should be sent to a mental hospital."

On the night of August 9 there was a practice blackout in London. Chief Superintendent Reginald K. Smith of Scotland Yard, in charge of A Division, which was responsible for the West End of London, climbed to the top of Marble Arch to look at the result and afterward remarked that there were so many lights showing that "London looked like a Gruyère cheese with a candle behind it." A number of drunks gathered in Trafalgar Square to splash in the fountains and sing "Show Me the Way to Go Home."

That night William Hutchins, a London bus driver, came back red-eyed to his municipally owned apartment in Hammersmith and said to his wife, "Blimey, if that's what driving in the blackout's going to be like, I'd be better joining up and driving a tank."

There had been traffic tie-ups all over London as cars, buses and trucks tried to pick their way through the streets using only their side lights.

Amy Hutchins shook her head. "You stick to your bus, love," she said. "At least they won't be firing things at your bus, even if there is a war."

Thirteen months later she and her husband were to learn how wrong she had been.

*　　*　　*

The Last Days of Peace

Around mid-August even the most optimistic ostriches in London were beginning to take their heads out of the sand. By then great lolloping, elephantine shapes—the barrage balloons that would, it was hoped, scare away low-flying raiders—were ringing London and flying out of parks and playgrounds inside the city. Many of the crews were inexperienced and had trouble anchoring them; since the balloons were apt to behave like unruly bulls in changing temperatures or high winds, a number broke loose and went nodding off across the North Sea. "It's not like flying a kite," said one disconsolate balloon commander.

The Home Secretary, Sir Samuel Hoare, was forced to take to the airwaves on the BBC to reassure the public about the efficacy of the street bomb shelters which were now being erected around London. One of them, in South Wales, had been hit by lightning in a storm, and five people sheltering inside had been killed. This, said Sir Samuel, was just a fluke. People were skeptical, and quietly made up their minds to avoid street shelters if and when air raids came. As it turned out, they were quite right.

For the superstitious there was more bad news a few days later. In the middle of August the Minister for Air, Sir Kingsley Wood, left a Cabinet meeting to fly to Belfast to launch a new, 23,000-ton aircraft carrier, the *Formidable*. His wife went with him. Lady Wood was standing talking to the other guests on the launching platform, her hand resting on the bottle of Empire wine she was to smash across the *Formidable*'s bows, when a massive groan made her turn around. At the same moment the bottle was gently pulled out of her hand and bounced, unbroken, against the aircraft carrier's side. Underneath, where spectators were gathered along the slipway, someone cried, "She's moving!" There was half an hour still to go before the official launching, but the big ship had decided not to wait.

Hastily someone handed Lady Wood another bottle, and mumbling a blessing, she hurled it desperately toward the moving ship. It was a hit and the bottle smashed. But the cheers which greeted her marksmanship mingled with the screams coming from below. As the *Formidable* lumbered toward the water, she scattered struts and planks in all directions. One of them hit a woman and killed her; others broke limbs among the crowd struggling to get out of the way. Slowly the great carrier groaned her way to the end of the slip and sidled into the water. But would the tugs, still thinking they had half an hour to wait, reach the hulk's side in time to halt her before she crashed into the opposite bank? They managed it. Britain's newest and biggest carrier was afloat, but behind her she left a trail of blood (one woman died and twenty-two people were seriously hurt) and debris, along with dire prophecies that she was bound to be a ship with a jinx.*

The call-up of reservists and members of the Territorial Army into the regular forces had been going on quietly ever since the middle of August. The newspapers made light of this by concentrating attention on those who had joined the all-voluntary women's branch of the army, the ATS (Auxiliary Territorial Service), the previous autumn, during the Munich crisis, and were now being summoned for training.

> Rock-a-bye baby, or Daddy will spank,
> Mother's at Aldershot, driving a tank.
> When the camp's over, Mum will return
> And oh! what a lot of new words you
> will learn!

So wrote one newspaper columnist, and an alarmed magistrate wrote to the *Times* expressing his hope that "the girls now going into the Forces will not be encouraged to wear masculine trappings like trousers on active service."

There were pictures of pretty girls smiling and waving good-bye to their husband and boy friends off to the army. But there were others who wept. Jimmy Martin, an ex-driver in the Royal Army Service Corps, returned on the night of August 18 from the garage in Pimlico where he was now working and found a letter from the War Office which instructed him to report to Chelsea Barracks in twenty-four hours. The day after that his wife, Jenny, saw him off on a train for Southampton and a troopship for the Mediterranean. She was twenty-seven years old, the mother of three small children, and the Army would pay her an allowance of thirty-eight shillings a week while Jimmy was away. In fact, she was not to see him again for five years.

For administrative purposes, the constantly expanding metropolis of London was divided into a number of boroughs and townships, but

* In fact, the carrier emerged from the war unscathed after operations in the Mediterranean and the Pacific.

the overall control of this great agglomeration of people and the facilities that kept them going were the responsibility of the London County Council. The headquarters of the LCC was in County Hall, a sprawl of pillared, turn-of-the-century buildings on the south bank of the Thames, facing the Houses of Parliament.*

Unlike the government (which was Tory-controlled), London in 1939 was in the hands of the Labour party, and its leader was a small, fiery, one-eyed Socialist from the East End named Herbert Morrison. " 'Erbie," as his Tory opponents never failed to remind him, had been a conscientious objector in World War I; he had, in fact, gone to jail for his beliefs. Now his attitude was different; he believed that Britain should stand up to Hitler even if it meant war. In August 1939 his main concern was not what Britain should do to Hitler but what Germany might do to London. As he repeatedly told his permanent officials at County Hall, "You see before you a frightened man. Frightened at what's going to happen to this capital if we aren't ready in time to face up to what they will do to us."

Morrison always had a report in front of him on his desk at County Hall. A terrifying document, it had been prepared for the government by the Imperial Defence Committee. It purported to give considered projections of what the Germans could do to Britain, and what they almost certainly would do, once war began. At the outset it claimed that Germany was so overwhelmingly superior in bomber and fighter planes that they would be masters of the sky. Once war was declared, these formidable fleets of planes would sweep across the North Sea and rain down their fire and high-explosive bombs upon London, and it was estimated that they would continue to do so for sixty days and nights. The committee felt that no matter what planes and antiaircraft fire were turned against the German bomber fleets, they would get through, that approximately six hundred thousand people would die, three quarters of them Londoners, and that the capital would die with them. Moreover, there would be more than a million wounded people in the ruins in need of hospitalization. But the hospitals would have been hit too.

'Erbie Morrison believed every word of this scarifying report. He had to; it would have been criminal folly to ignore it. For the past year, ever since the Munich scare of 1938, he had been harrying his officials to make preparations for the great rain of death which might descend

---

* It is now the headquarters of the GLC (Greater London Council).

on London at any moment, and he had worked in close co-operation with the Home Office and its experts on air-raid precautions. Now, as the crisis grew worse through the sunny August days, he could persuade himself that he had done almost all that was humanly possible to prepare for the horror to come. All over London, emergency first-aid and ambulance stations had been organized. Auxiliary fire-service workers had been called up to strengthen the London Fire Brigade. Air-raid wardens walked the streets. There were water tanks ready for fire hoses in every district. Hospitals had raidproof wards and operating theatres. There were blood banks and medical flying squads to take them where they were needed. For the hundreds of thousands of dead that London could expect, he had requisitioned vast numbers of papier-mâché coffins. Swimming pools were closed "for repairs," irate little boys were told, but in fact to store all these coffins, and all around the city, huge holes were being dug for the mass graves into which the victims would be placed.

There was only one other thing which haunted 'Erbie Morrison, and that was London's children. There were a million of them, and he vowed that they should not be among those killed or maimed when the bombs started falling. The LCC's evacuation scheme had already been drawn up, and trains and buses and trucks requisitioned, ready to spirit the children off to the country, away from the terror of the bombs. In Morrison's opinion, they should have been sent away in mid-August, when the situation began to get really serious. "So long as the children remain in London," he said, "so long can Hitler blackmail us by threatening them. Let's get them out of the way, to places of safety, so we can stand up to the Nazis without worrying about what will happen to our tots."

The trouble was that the government would not let the children go. Morrison was the MP for an East End constituency whose children would be most vulnerable once war began, for it was near the docks, and each time he crossed Westminster Bridge to Whitehall from County Hall he would call at 10 Downing Street and say to Sir Horace Wilson, Neville Chamberlain's aide, "Let the children go."

"My dear fellow," Sir Horace would reply, with all the smoothness of his master, "surely that would be a policy of panic, wouldn't it? Think what Mr. Hitler would say if we did a thing like that? No, the PM is against all such panic measures—for the moment, anyway."

"I wouldn't like to have your conscience," Morrison said, "if you leave it too late."

The Last Days of Peace

On the morning of September 1, 1939, shortly after the BBC announcement that the German army had invaded Poland, Herbert Morrison burst into Sir Horace Wilson's office at Downing Street.

"I know," said Sir Horace. "You want the children out of London. But we're not at war yet, and we wouldn't want to do anything to upset delicate negotiations, would we?"

"Look, 'Orace," said Morrison, "go in there and tell Neville this from me: if I don't get the order to evacuate the children from London this morning, I'm going to give it myself—*and* tell the papers why I'm doing it. 'Ow will 'is nibs like that?"

Half an hour later Morrison was on his way back to County Hall with the necessary permission. That very day the great evacuation began.

For the next twenty-four hours, all over London, people turned to watch the long processions of children making their way to railway and bus stations. Most of them had handed their haversacks over to their teachers, but each child wore a small square cardboard box around his neck containing a gas mask, and a card with his name pinned to the lapel. Brothers and sisters clung to each other's hands like grim death, and refused to be parted.

Ellen Hardiman had given Sheila and John a bath in the kitchen that morning, after the message came around, and at two o'clock in the afternoon she brought them to Elm Road School. Most of the children were laughing and playing, as if it were a great adventure, but some looked frightened or were crying, as were a lot of their mothers. Sheila and John said nothing; they simply held hands and looked up reproachfully at their mother.

"Why can't you come with us, Mum?" Sheila said at last.

"I just can't, love," Mrs. Hardiman said. "Who'd look after your father? You know he can't even boil an egg. It won't be long, anyway. We'll soon polish off Hitler, and then you can come home again."

She made sure that they each had the half crown she had sewn into the lining of their raincoat pockets, and told them to keep together no matter what. Then the teacher called them together, formed them into a long line and they went off down the road to the buses that were to take them to Suffolk.

Ellen Hardiman stood there watching them as they filed across the intersection. A policeman marched out into the road and lifted up his hand to halt the traffic, and as the children marched past him two tots ran over to him, and she could hear them shouting out, "Bye-bye, Daddy." He looked down for a moment, smiled at them and said, "Now be good, kiddies." As the line went on, she noticed that tears were rolling down the policeman's cheeks, but his hands were too busy directing the traffic to wipe them away.

One million children and two hundred thousand mothers left London in the great evacuation. Suddenly the capital was a very empty place. There were no more nursemaids and baby carriages in the parks, no more shouts and screams from the playgrounds, no more small boats on the ponds in Hyde Park and on Hampstead Heath. In the East End, particularly, something appeared to be wrong with the acoustics of the streets, and people seemed to be cocking their ears for the missing sound of childish cries and laughter. No one talked about it much, but everyone noticed it and was sad.

While the children of the poor poured out of London to the reception areas in Norfolk, Suffolk and the Midlands, many a better-off parent was sending his offspring farther afield. Not even when it was announced from Moscow and Berlin on August 22 that Russia and Germany were concluding a nonaggression pact had Chips Channon entirely given up hope that peace might still be snatched from the fire. The pact meant that Germany no longer had to worry about an attack from the rear and could go ahead with her plans to invade Poland. Channon shared Neville Chamberlain's loathing for the Russians, and his indignation against them boiled up. "The Russians have double-crossed us," he wrote. "They are the foulest people on earth." He added: "Perhaps we have a few more days, even weeks, of peace, but a partition of Poland seems inevitable. For if Poland resists we automatically go to war. But I cannot bear to think that our world is crumbling to ruins. I refuse to admit it . . . Everyone secretly or openly, whatever they may say, hopes that the Poles will climb down."

So Chips Channon was still hoping against hope for a last-minute "arrangement" that would bring the engines of war to a grinding halt, and he ignored friends who urged him to send his son and heir, Paul, to the safety of relatives in the United States. Channon knew that those who were doing so were being bitterly attacked in the columns of the *Daily Worker*, the Communist organ, for "using their wealth to buy funk-holes for their pampered offspring." But in fact, few blamed any parents for using what money they could scrape together to send their children to safety, and many middle-class couples sacrificed their savings to ship their youngsters overseas. It was the flight of well-to-do grownups from the capital which aroused most resentment and contempt. Shipping offices were full of people desperately trying to buy or bribe tickets from clerks for the United States or Canada. The roads to the West Country were already jammed with big cars packed with trunks and boxes of food. The search was on among the panic-stricken rich for what soon came to be known as "safe hotels," where they proposed to stay for the duration. Many were in for painful shocks. What seemed to be peaceful havens in 1939 later became prime targets, as the fortunes and directions of the war fluctuated.

By the night of September 2, the German army had already been fighting inside Poland for thirty-six hours and Luftwaffe bombers were raiding Warsaw, Gdynia and Lwow. But Britain, which was pledged to come to Poland's aid, still had not declared war on Germany. Neville Chamberlain was waiting to coordinate his ultimatum with that of Britain's main ally, France, and in Paris they were dithering and pleading for time.

A restive House of Commons received Chamberlain's explanations of his procrastination with such hostility that the PM was white in the face when he sat down, and old hands whispered that had it come to a vote, he would have been forced to resign. Even his Cabinet was in revolt against him. When he got back to 10 Downing Street at the end of the night's session he found his ministers waiting for him around the table; they were not going to move, they told him, until he sent an ultimatum to Germany.

Chamberlain finally nodded his head. "Right, gentlemen," he said. "This means war."

When the news reached the House of Commons, Chips Channon rushed up to a fellow MP, Alec Dunglass (now Sir Alec Douglas-Home). "Are we all mad?" he asked. He turned to David Margesson, the government Chief Whip, and urged him to wait for a few more hours.

Margesson shook his head. "It must be war, Chips, old boy," he said. "There's no other way out."

It was raining in London that night. As a precaution, all streetlights and public signs had been turned off. "I creep carefully," Harold Nicolson, MP, wrote in his diary, describing his journey home. He foresaw a recrudescence in London of footpads and highway robbery.

* * *

At 11:15 A.M. on September 3, 1939, Neville Chamberlain informed the nation over the BBC that there had been no reply to the government's ultimatum, and that Britain and Germany were now at war. Twenty minutes later the air-raid sirens sounded over London.

There was no cheering, only a sad, silent acceptance of the state of war, and there was no panic as the sirens wailed the warning that bombers were approaching. The crowds outside 10 Downing Street and the Houses of Parliament walked swiftly, pretending not to hurry, to the nearest place of shelter, some to the underground urinals by the river, others to the cloisters of Westminster Abbey, but most to the street shelters in Whitehall. Farther east, in St. Paul's Cathedral, the unusually large congregation had just finished singing

"O God of love, O King of Peace,
Make wars throughout the world to cease!"

when the warning came, and the Bishop of Willesden led the worshipers down to the crypt. The people of the East End were to know that crypt very well indeed in the months to come.

There was little panic anywhere. There was hardly time, for the sirens sounded the all clear a quarter of an hour later. It had been a false alarm, and people emerged into the Sunday morning sunshine looking sheepish.

But that night it was different. The sirens sounded again at two o'clock, stopping Police Constable David Meade in his tracks as he marched down Limehouse Causeway. When the final wails had died down, it seemed to him as if all London were holding its breath and listening for a sound in the sky. He felt the skin crawling on the back of his neck.

Then the sounds came. Shouts, screams, moans, cries of "Jim, oh Jim!" and "For God's sake, Maggie, shut up and get dressed!" Then doors began to open and there were people in the streets, muttering and sobbing and cursing as they hurried toward the shelters. They were frightened, and David Meade did not blame them; he was frightened himself. Had they not been told that from now on they must expect an avalanche of bombs? He did not believe that anyone could not be frightened.

But he did not know Chips Channon. Now that his world was about to collapse in ruins, Channon had become fatalistic. Of that terrifying 2 A.M. alarm, all he wrote was: "In the night there was another air raid alarm but I did not awake until called by the butler. Then I joined the servants in the cellar, where I found everyone good-tempered and funny. The Duke of Kent sent me a message asking me to go to his shelter next door, but I was too sleepy, and declined."

It turned out that this was a false alarm too. World War II had begun for the capital with a wail and a whimper, but ordeals were to come that would change the face of London and the nature of the world.

2

The Phony War

Mr. and Mrs. Arthur Ketley and their son, Donald, lived in a small terrace house on a dead-end street in Chadwell Heath, on the fringe of the East End of London. Since that first day of war was a Sunday, Mr. Ketley was not working at the docks, where he had a job as an overseer in the office, but for once he was not pottering with his plants in the back garden, either. When Donald, who was playing in the yard, came in, he found both his parents sitting around the radio listening to Neville Chamberlain telling them that the war had begun.

Donald noticed that his father and mother looked strained and worried. His mother glanced up as he entered the room and said, "Is it all right for him to be outside?"

"Don't be silly," Mr. Ketley answered.

So Donald went back to the yard, and twenty minutes later, when the siren sounded, his mother dashed out of the door and bustled him inside. They all squeezed into the broom closet under the stairs. Mr. Ketley had read in the papers that in the Spanish Civil War, when buildings collapsed under bombing, the stairs nearly always remained standing, so he had converted the closet into a temporary shelter: cushions on the floor, candles, and a bottle of 100-proof rum from the docks.

Donald watched his father pour rum into a couple of glasses, and saw that his hand was shaking so that the bottle rattled against the rim of the glass. He knew then that both his parents were frightened.

"We should have sent him away," Mrs. Ketley kept saying.

"No, we shouldn't," Arthur Ketley said firmly. "He's better off here with us."

When the all clear sounded, Donald could tell that his parents were both surprised and baffled, even a little disappointed that nothing had happened. Presently they all went out to the backyard and talked across the fence to their neighbors, wondering what it was all about.

Donald Ketley was eight years old at the time, and he never forgot the first morning of the war. "It was all a wonderful adventure," he recalls, "a sudden release from boredom." Mostly he remembers it, however, because his father was frightened, and he had never seen this before.

That night he was carried downstairs still asleep for the second alarm and didn't know anything about it until it was over. He was disappointed and kept saying to his mother, "Why didn't you wake me, Mum? I missed it, I missed it!"

It was especially annoying because thereafter, no more air-raid warnings sounded; what came to be known as the "phony war" began.

It was not, of course, a phony war so far as the Poles were concerned. Their country was bombed and ravaged, and then divided up between Germany and Russia, and the Poles themselves were turned into a nation of slaves. Nor was it phony for the Royal Navy. Their pride was dented considerably in the first few weeks of war by a daring Nazi submarine raid on the Royal Navy base at Scapa Flow, which cost them the battleship *Royal Oak*. That humiliation was wiped out when the German pocket battleship *Graf Spee* was trapped off the coast of Uruguay and put out of action for good. But by then the Royal Navy was engaged all over the North and South Atlantic in a bitter war with German U-boats, which now lay athwart all shipping lanes leading to Britain.

It was a war which the First Lord of the Admiralty told Parliament and people the Royal Navy was winning during the winter of 1939–40. This was not true. The First Lord was falsifying the figures; far fewer submarines were being sunk than he claimed. But it was the first government job this particular First Lord had held after many long years in the political wilderness, and he did not wish it to appear that his department was unsuccessful.

The First Lord of the Admiralty during this phase of the war was Winston Churchill. He had joined the Administration of Prime Minister Neville Chamberlain on the day war was declared, after years of bitter opposition to Chamberlain's policy of appeasing Hitler and Nazi Germany. Now that Chamberlain was willing to fight the Germans, Churchill was more than eager to help him, and he was delighted to be the head of the only service that was in action against the enemy during this period. The Royal Navy, in turn, was glad to have him as their chief, but they did wish he would tell the truth about the U-boats.

What changed the look of London most of all were the barrage balloons flying above the rooftops like Disney elephants; but except for these and for the increasing number of uniforms worn in the streets, it was hard to tell that there was a war on. At first everyone carried a gas mask over his shoulder, for there were dire warnings about mustard gas. There were gas masks for babies and even for dogs, and couples who wandered down lovers' lanes in the evening dutifully took their gas masks with them. But after a month or two people became blasé and began leaving them at home. Finally they were discarded in odd corners of the house, except by those who had had gas-mask covers made of snakeskin or colored cloth, and continued to use them as convenient handbags.

Lovers in London quickly discovered that private nooks were no longer necessary, because after dark, privacy could be found anywhere. It was possibly the only virtue—if that is the word—of the blackout which had fallen over the capital. Soon there were shocked yelps from outraged puritans that the tarts along Piccadilly, determined that blacked-out streets should not keep them hidden from their customers, were actually opening their coats and shining flashlights on themselves; and that young lovers, on a dare, were coupling in shop doorways within a few feet of passers-by. If so, they were the only ones enjoying the Stygian darkness covering London by night. Blackout curtains had gone up in every home, and there were heavy fines for anyone who showed a crack of light or flashed a cigarette. If lights were left on in uncurtained homes where owners were away for the evening, police broke in or shot them out with air guns. For persistent offenders there were heavy fines and even imprisonment. The blackout was certainly the most trying and infuriating aspect of the phony war. It made driving by night laborious and dangerous because only small slits of light were allowed as headlights; it made walking murderous, because motorists couldn't see pedestrians and pedestrians couldn't see obstacles.

One of the additional trials of the blackout was that it begat a smug mythical character named "Billy Brown of London Town" whose face was to be seen on posters all over the capital urging people to emulate him and become a model citizen who never did anything wrong. Londoners loathed the self-righteous little man, who exhorted them in verses such as:

> *Billy Brown's own highway Code*
> *For blackouts is "Stay off the Road."*
> *He'll never step out and begin*
> *To meet a bus that's pulling in.*
> *He doesn't wave his torch at night,*
> *But "flags" his bus with something white.*
> *He never jostles in a queue,*
> *But waits and takes his turn. Do you?*

Theatres had closed at the outbreak of war, but soon opened again; however, curtain time was now moved forward to six or six-thirty. There was minor food rationing, but so far, canned goods and tea weren't affected and there were no real shortages of anything. Restaurants continued to serve meals adequate for all but the gourmand, and they were crowded. It was considered helpful toward the French ally to continue consuming as much French wine as possible.

Not all Londoners were complacent about the war, or bored by it. There were perceptive people who worried about the future, knowing in their bones that the lull couldn't last. There were others, especially those of military age, who worried about conscription, some because they were pacifists, some because of their jobs, some because of their women. "I am trying to get a job before conscription," Dylan Thomas wrote to a friend on September 11, "because my one-and-only body I will not give. I know that all the shysters in London are grovelling about the Ministry of Information . . . and all I have managed to do is have my name on the crook list . . . So I must explore every avenue now . . . because along will come conscription and the military tribunal, and stretcher-bearing or jail or potato peeling or the Boys' Fire League. And all I want is time to write poems and enough money to keep two and a bit alive."

Personal problems preoccupied most people, and there was no detectable feeling of participation, of a population united by a common danger or of being part of a crusade against the dark forces that Germany represented. It was business as usual, and let someone else get on with the war. Life in London seemed safe, if dull. Even crime dropped, not because the criminal population had suddenly become patriotic but because the armed forces were taking all kinds, thieves among them.

The Phony War

It was not until the spring of 1940 that the faint taps of doom, which had so far been inaudible to the British public, began to sound in more sensitive ears. The Germans invaded Denmark and Norway on April 9, at a moment when Neville Chamberlain was boasting that "Hitler has missed the bus." Subsequent ministerial statements were of such fatuous optimism that the British public cheered the dispatch of an expeditionary force to Norway—it landed at Narvik on April 15—and waited confidently, like the audience at a Western, for the good guys to wade in and force the bad guys to bite the snow. Only, it didn't happen that way. The good guys had heart, but they didn't have good leaders, good plans or good planes to protect them, whereas the bad guys had all of these. By the end of April the optimistic statements emanating from the government could not conceal the fact that the Norwegian campaign was being lost and that defeat was looming.

The vague uneasiness which more percipient people had felt during the idle days of the phony war now spread. As British troops in Norway began to die in the snow or retreat toward the sea, a hitherto complacent Parliament at last turned upon the Prime Minister and his Administration and demanded an explanation. Neville Chamberlain, the "man of peace," had failed in his first attempt to prove himself a man of war, and the people wanted to know why—and what he was going to do about it.

On May 7 Parliament assembled in London for a debate on the situation in Norway. At least that is what it was intended to be: the Opposition would complain; the government's friends would ask the right questions; and then Neville Chamberlain would rise to explain, make excuses and promise to do better in the future, after which he would duly be given a vote of confidence by his supporters. That was the plan, and the Cabinet worked out its strategy accordingly.

But there were men in Parliament who saw the defeat of British troops by the German army in Norway as only a symptom of the crisis in which the nation found itself. The real danger to Britain, they believed, was much closer to home—in the government itself and its leaders, incompetent, fatuously complacent, deaf to the drums of doom on the other side of the Channel. They were not planning to listen to explanations from Neville Chamberlain. They wanted a change of leaders, and they were prepared to rebel in order to get it.

On May 7, 1940, they did so, and on that day the phony war ended.

3

The Buds of May

At 9:45 A.M. on Tuesday, May 7, 1940, the policeman on duty at the main gate of Buckingham Palace marched out into the road and raised his arm to halt the thin stream of London's midmorning traffic. A gleaming black horse clip-clopped into the Mall from the Palace yard, drawing behind it a small, elegant maroon-red brougham of the kind once used by Victorian dandies for discreet assignations with their ladies. But this carriage's doors were outlined in gilt and emblazoned with a small royal cipher, and two grooms in royal livery sat side by side on the outside perch. Inside, a young man in army uniform leaned back against the leather, staring vacantly at the pale blue sky. One of the grooms flourished and cracked his whip; the black horse broke into a smart trot and the brougham moved smoothly down the Mall in the direction of Trafalgar Square.

Of all the curious pedestrians and motorists who watched the carriage, probably only one of them could have known where it was going and the nature of its errand. Robert Boothby had decided not to drive to the House of Commons, for he had much on his mind and he wanted time to think; he was in a bitterly angry mood, and the fact that it was a lovely May morning and that the tulips splashed color over the flower beds along the Mall did nothing to soften his feelings. Staring at the high-stepping horse and the brougham, he reflected that if anything mirrored Britain's attitude toward the war, there it was. It was eight months since Britain had declared war on Germany, and how did

His Majesty George VI, King of England, Emperor of India, crowned head of the greatest empire the world had ever known, acquire the dispatches from the heads of his armed forces which told him how the war was going? Why, he sent a horse and brougham to fetch them from military headquarters down the road.* Dammit, Boothby muttered to himself, the way things were going in Norway at the moment, the British army would be on its way home while the King was still reading about their arrival!

Robert Boothby, forty years old, had come up to London from Scotland at the age of twenty-four to become the youngest Member of Parliament in the House of Commons at Westminster. Though a Tory, and therefore expected to toe the party line, he had been fighting authority ever since—and no one more fiercely than Neville Chamberlain when he tried to appease Hitler through the humiliating months of 1938 and 1939. When the Prime Minister at last declared war on Germany, Robert Boothby had returned to the Tory fold. Like that other rebel against appeasement, Winston Churchill, he had let Chamberlain know that henceforth he would be his loyal supporter. He had been regretting it ever since.

As a war leader, Chamberlain was proving even more inept than he had as a man of peace. Everything was going wrong, and he did not seem to realize it. As for his Administration, with the exception of Churchill, they were boobies and incompetents. Boothby winced as he remembered the telephone call he had received that very morning from Leslie Burgin of the Ministry of Supply. A week earlier Boothby had been in Holland and Belgium on a mission for the government to buy up rifles, of which the British army was desperately short. He had secured firm offers of two hundred thousand rifles for immediate delivery, provided the British were prepared to pay in dollars.

But what had Burgin said? "My dear Boothby, we are most grateful for your efforts, but I have to tell you that the Cabinet Committee has decided that the rifles are not, after all, required. In any case, the Treasury has categorically refused to pay for them in dollars."

It was infuriating because anyone with an ounce of sense knew that a crisis was imminent; soon every rifle that Britain could procure would be vital for the safety of the country.

As he strode through St. James's Park toward Whitehall and the Houses of Parliament, Boothby could feel in his pocket the letter he had

---

* He continued to do so for the rest of the war.

just written to Churchill: "I was sent over to Belgium at the shortest notice and as a matter of the greatest urgency, ten days ago, in order (in Burgin's written words) to 'find and secure rifles.' I found them. This morning I was told by Burgin that no rifles are required; and that, even if they were, the Treasury would not pay for them. It would be incredible if it were not true."

It would also be incredible if not true, Boothby reflected, to realize that he was walking through a London which had been at war for eight months. The roads were still busy with private cars (there had been traffic jams on all roads leading out of London that Easter); rationing hardly mattered and every restaurant in London was booming; you were safe from being drafted provided you were a gardener, a recreation-ground attendant, a jockey or a chauffeur. Office buildings and movie houses were still going up in the city, and in one of the newspapers that morning one of the employment ads read:

> WANTED. By gentleman (titled), handyman about house, London, S.W. 1. Wages £90 and uniform. Twelve servants, three pantry, kept.

There were plenty of other advertisements for such utterly unnecessary and out-of-date jobs. It was as if the war had never happened, and life in England persisted in its old, class-conscious way. Meanwhile, in Norway, British and French soldiers and sailors were dying and the Allied Expeditionary Force sent to help the Norwegians fight the Nazis was being forced back into the sea by an enemy better equipped, better led and ruthlessly determined.

Boothby's pace quickened as he approached the House of Commons. So far as he and his friends were concerned, there was only one solution: get rid of Chamberlain and his inept hangers-on before they lost the war. There was no time to waste; today was the day to do it.

There was a long queue outside the public entrance to the House of Commons. The debate was to be on the military situation, and the crowds had come to see the political fireworks. Some of them raised a small cheer for the MP when they saw him and a man shouted, "Gi' it 'em guid and hot, Bob," in a strong Scots accent. Boothby raised his hand in greeting and hurried inside.

iss Vere Hodgson had had a busy day at her office in Holland Park, but the prospect of going to the theatre on the evening of May 7 refreshed her, even though there was no time to go home and change. The fact that the curtain now rose at six o'clock meant she had to rush straight from the office. But oh, she decided, as the house-lights went down, it was worth it, how it was worth it, just to be transported for a little while out of the drab routine of wartime London.*

Miss Hodgson felt slightly guilty nowadays when she confessed to herself that so far she had found the war disappointing. ("As if wars are run for your entertainment. You ought to be ashamed of yourself, Vere Hodgson!") Nevertheless, for some time now the war had both bored and depressed her. It worried her too; she felt a nagging anxiety that something was wrong, that this wasn't the way a war should be run if it was to come out all right in the end.

Vere Hodgson was a brisk, good-looking woman in her mid-thirties of an English type no one except official registrars would ever call a spinster, even though she was unmarried. She had left the university in her early twenties to go to Italy to teach English to young ladies a year or two her junior (among them Mussolini's daughter, Edda) and one got the feeling that she had left her love, if not her whole heart, there when she came home. Subsequently she had been a teacher in Birmingham, where she was born, until shortly before the outbreak of war, when she decided to go into welfare work in London. Ever since then, she had been a secretary, consultant and general dogsbody at the Sanctuary, in Holland Park Road, not far from Notting Hill Gate in West London. The Sanctuary was the headquarters of the Greater World Federation, a philosophical and charitable trust, and it gave shelter, money, food and general advice to the poor of Notting Hill and North Kensington, and ran a mission for the needy in the East End as well.

But how little eight months of war had changed the nature of her work! She remembered that first night when the air-raid warnings sounded at two in the morning, and everyone braced themselves for the ordeal to come. But nothing had happened. For two hours that first night Vere Hodgson, like millions of other Londoners, crouched under the stairs and waited for death to descend. She did not mind confessing later that she had been terrified, and she believed that anyone who was not must be an unimaginative dolt.

But death had not come; it was too busy on the other side of Europe helping the German air force slaughter the Poles. Ever since, Vere

---

* Miss Vere Hodgson kept a daily diary of her experiences and observations on life in London during World War II, and it is from this, from her letters and from her conversations with the author that quotations are drawn in this book.

Hodgson had felt cheated, and the feeling of anticlimax had persisted all through the winter. Poland was battered into defeat and occupied by the Germans and Russians while the British and French did nothing to help their gallant ally. They remained safe in their defenses behind the Maginot Line and stared at the Germans on the other side of the Rhine, but made no effort to engage them.

As far as her life in London was concerned, Vere Hodgson decided, there might be no war at all. If it hadn't been for the blackout, which she loathed, and the government posters exhorting you to "Join Up or Shut Up," it could have been peacetime. There were still two million unemployed men living on the dole; every morning there were still queues of hunched, ragged, defeated souls waiting for jobs outside the Labour Exchange at Notting Hill. Surely there was something wrong with a nation which claimed it was fighting Germany to end tyranny and injustice and still let able-bodied men and women half starve in enforced idleness? Didn't a war change anything? After all these months, shouldn't it have brought to an end the old relics of peacetime inequality which she still saw everywhere around her? Shouldn't it mean that in face of a common enemy, they should all share the burden and help one another?

Yet everywhere she looked she saw examples of inequity and injustice. Take the three young women who had come to see her that day at the Sanctuary. All three were young, with young children, and all of them were foolish, she knew that. They had been evacuated from London in September, along with nearly a quarter of a million other young mothers, to escape the impending slaughter. When it didn't come they had drifted back to the "Big Smoke" because they hated the loneliness of country life, the unfamiliarity of green fields, the inhospitality of the unwilling hosts on whom they had been thrust, and because they missed the warm friendliness of London's back streets. But now they were in trouble. Their husbands had been drafted, and all they had to live on were the allotments from their army pay.

Vere Hodgson boiled with indignation when she thought of what that meant to these three young wives. In London they had about twenty-eight shillings (roughly $7.50 at the then rate of exchange) a week to keep themselves and their children fed, clothed and the rent paid. Their husbands were either in France or in the north in training camps, called up for the duration. They were harassed for money and bored with their own company and that of their children, and all around them were temptations, for there were plenty of free-spending troops in London. Why not go out and have a good time and perhaps pick up a bit of money? "After all," one of them had said, "there's a war on, isn't there?"

All one could do was to tell them to think of their husbands and children, slip them clothes for the kids and a few shillings for an extra bit of food or a movie, and hope for the best—though Vere Hodgson feared that in at least one case, the prettiest and most resentful one, it would be for the worst. What right did the government have to call men into the army and pay them such appalling wages for serving their country? By what right did soldiers' wives have to be faced with poverty or temptation, when all around them fashionable restaurants were full, when chauffeured cars still drove through the street with fat businessmen in the back, when some people were obviously still making fortunes? She felt that the Americans were right to call this the "phony war." Something *was* false about it; she had a sneaking feeling that the government was not really taking it seriously.

As the curtain rose, Miss Hodgson forgot her uneasiness and settled back to enjoy the show. She and her friend from the office had chosen to see a revue called *New Faces*, which was typical of London entertainment that spring. No one seemed to want anything serious, particularly anything that reminded them of the war. Movie theatres had streamers across their posters informing the public that "This Is Not a War Film." The biggest hits in town were Flanagan and Allen and the Crazy Gang at the Palladium, in a series of slapstick gags and with a line of chorus girls; a Cockney revue called *Me and My Gal*, in which the big number was "Doing the Lambeth Walk," a sort of Cockney conga; a nude revue at the Windmill Theatre, where show girls on pedestals were permitted by the Lord Chamberlain, the official censor, to bare their breasts and pose in G-strings as long as they kept perfectly still ("If it moves it's rude," was the current gag about the show); and *New Faces*. The big moment of the evening came when a tall brunette named Judy Campbell strolled onstage, and against a backdrop of London's West End, sang a haunting song called "A Nightingale Sang in Berkeley Square." Vere Hodgson had been told that there was something so nostalgic about the song, so evocative of the good old days gone by, that every night members of the audience wept. It was true; she found the tears welling in her own eyes as she listened, and was ashamed of herself. Why should she weep over a love song about peacetime London? What was there to lament about a city so full of slums, poverty and unemployment? Yet she wept.

The mood changed as the spotlight picked out the master of ceremonies walking to the footlights. "Ladies and gentlemen," he announced. "During rehearsals, authors were constantly sending in sketches. Unfortunately, most of them turned out to be *war* sketches— and we did feel that audiences nowadays are getting just about enough about war. However, it was suggested that for patriotic reasons we should have at least one war sketch, so here it is, presented with due apologies to our good friends in His Majesty's forces!"

The sketch, called "Awfully Quiet on the Western Front," was set in a gun battery somewhere in France. A dartboard hung from the barrel of one of the guns, some laundry from the others. Downstage three British soldiers were sitting at a table, on which there was a silver teapot and a milk jug, and plenty of pastries and sandwiches. One of the soldiers was knitting; the other two were drinking tea.

FIRST SOLDIER   One or two lumps, Foulkes-Foulkes? I never can remember.

SECOND SOLDIER   Two, please. Thenk you!

THIRD SOLDIER   Knit one, purl one, knit three, drop three.

FIRST SOLDIER   Look here, Harrington, I do think you might stop knitting while we're having tea. After all, you've been at it all day.

THIRD SOLDIER   I know, I know. But you seem to forget there's a war on. Back home in England hundreds of poor Service girls are freezing to death. They need these little things I'm doing for them.

As usual, the sketch was a huge success with the audience. There had been too much in the newspapers about the well-heated billets and home comforts of the troops in France for those at home not to lap up every comic jab. And when a general strode onstage and asked the soldiers where the enemy was and they, astonished, cried in unison, "*What enemy?*," the whole house burst into applause.

Vere Hodgson laughed with them. Yet when she returned home and thought about it, uneasiness overwhelmed the humor. A month ago, perhaps, it would all have been an enjoyable skit. But this evening on the midnight news there was a report of the row in Parliament over the debacle in Norway. The British soldiers there had known who the enemy was, all right, and they had been killed, wounded and captured by him. The British Expeditionary Force was in retreat and the German conquest of Norway was all but complete.

Added to which, there was a small item tucked away in one of the evening newspapers under the headline WESTERN FRONT OFFENSIVE?:

Neutral sources in Berlin report that the German Army is now turning its eyes westward. There are strong rumours that Hitler has made up his mind to bring Holland and Belgium, which he considers pro-Allied rather than neutral, into the Nazi orbit and will use force if necessary to do so. This could well be the first move in an offensive in the west.

If so, those British boys in France wouldn't be enjoying their creature comforts much longer, and it would be a mockery to laugh at them, as she and the audience had that night.*

enry Moore turned away from the man at the desk to whom he had been talking and came across the gallery floor toward his wife, Irene. Balancing a picture frame against her thigh, she was watching a workman hammering a nail in a packing case. She was a slim, shapely woman with a narrow, lively Slavic face and shining eyes; there was a slight touch of concern in her look of affection as her husband approached her.

Moore's round face was smiling but she knew him well enough not to be deceived. As if in answer to an unspoken question, he said, "We calculate I should make about ninety pounds [$440] out of the exhibition." His voice had not quite lost its flat Yorkshire accent, but the tone was cheerful. "That's with commissions and expenses knocked off. It isn't too much—but then, there's a war on."

As they went out into Leicester Square, one of the workmen was taking down the poster reading EXHIBITION OF PAINTINGS AND SCULPTURES BY HENRY MOORE. Neither Moore nor his wife looked at it; their eyes were caught by two other posters which a newsstand was brandishing. CHAMBERLAIN: VITAL DEBATE said one, and CHAMBERLAIN FIGHTS BACK said the other.

They climbed into the car they had parked around the corner, loaded some canvases in the back, and started off for Hampstead.

"It will pay the rent, at least," Irene said.

Yes, it would do that all right, thought Henry Moore, and still leave them fifteen pounds over. With that and the £240 a year he was getting from teaching at the Arts School in Chelsea they could continue to go on living quite comfortably. There was nothing they really lacked, he thought. And if Barbara Hepworth did have twins† and went off to

---

* The sketch was, in fact, taken out of the show by its author a week later. It was written by Jack Davies, now a well-known screen writer but at that time an officer in the RAF.

† She had triplets, not twins, and did depart for Cornwall that summer.

Cornwall, as she threatened to, she would let them take over her studio, and then they would really be saving. It only cost £50 a year.

But what if the war really got hot and teaching became difficult? During the previous summer, when it looked as if war was inevitable, he had received a telephone call from Sir Kenneth Clark, director of the National Gallery, asking him to come over for a drink. It had turned out to be more than a social occasion. Clark had been asked by the government to draw up a panel of artists who, when hostilities came, would move among the armed forces and record a picture of Britain at war. He wanted to put Moore's name on the list; would he accept?

It was a temptation, of course. There would be no more worrying about the scarcity of buyers and commissions in wartime. Yet Moore shook his head. "No," he said. "What interest could there possibly be for me in drawing successions of guns and soldiers and tanks? I did enough of that in the last war. There's nothing new I could possibly say."

He didn't add that he had reached a climactic moment as an artist, and that both in his drawing and in his sculpture he was beginning to visualize everything in abstract terms. It would do too much violence to his development if he were to start making illustrations for wartime propaganda. He just couldn't face it.

Artistically, Moore had never doubted the rightness of his decision. But now as he read the war news, he wondered whether he could continue to remain aloof. He was no pacifist, but until this time he had not felt involved. Now, however, he smelled something in the air.

"I think the war is getting serious," Irene said. As usual, she had been reading his thoughts.

On May 7, 1940, Chips Channon wrote in his diary: "A dreadful day. The political crisis overshadows everything; one cannot eat, sleep or concentrate."

Channon was still a Chamberlain man heart and soul. In his view, Neville Chamberlain had saved the British nation once, at Munich, and he was convinced that he would do it again. He loathed Winston Churchill and had been downcast when Chamberlain brought him into the War Cabinet as First Lord of the Admiralty. His beloved Neville could do no wrong, and it was Winston whom Channon unhesitatingly blamed for the military disaster in Norway; it was Winston too whom he now suspected of intriguing behind the scenes to saddle Chamberlain with Norway and replace him as Prime Minister. In fact, Churchill was innocent of political scheming (though not so innocent of military bungling over the Norway campaign), and the events of May 7 and the next forty-eight hours were neither initiated nor encouraged by him. But Channon and his friends believed otherwise.

When the MPs took their seats in the House of Commons that afternoon, it had been apparent for twenty-four hours to England and the world that Germany had completed the conquest of Norway, and save for a small group of gallant troops fighting and dying in Trondheim, had driven the Allied Expeditionary Force into the sea. It had been an ineptly planned and amateurishly handled operation from which no one except the soldiers fighting on the spot had emerged with any credit, and it had demonstrated only too ominously, in view of what was to come, how short the British armed forces were on leadership, battle experience and equipment. But the British public and many members of Parliament had little doubt that the guilty men were not the soldiers in the field but the government which had sent them there; and their anger was only compounded by the sunny optimism which government spokesmen had displayed right up until the final humiliation.

At Westminster that afternoon, observers sniffed blood. The debate would be an opportunity for which Chamberlain's enemies had been waiting—to criticize his Administration not merely for its inefficiency in Norway but for its war policy in general, its failure to galvanize the nation, and its inability to face up to the hard facts of war and legislate accordingly. Since before dawn, Londoners had been lining up to enter the House, and now the public galleries were crowded. So were those for the peers of the realm and ambassadors from Allied, friendly and not so friendly nations. Diplomats already in their seats included U.S. Ambassador Joseph P. Kennedy, who only an hour earlier had told Lord Halifax, the Foreign Secretary, that he was disgusted by Britain's performance so far, that the armed forces in particular and England in general were bumbling ("even degenerate"), and that he and his military attachés were convinced, and had so reported to Washington, that England was going to lose the war.*

Listening to the opening speech of the debate by Neville Chamberlain, one would have had to acknowledge that Kennedy had not reported wrongly. Almost from the time he arrived in England, the American

---

* Channon's opinion of the ambassador is perhaps best summed up by his diary entry "I talked to Mr. Kennedy, the new American ambassador, whose chief merit seems to be that he has nine children."

ambassador had conceived an admiration for the British premier. The reasons were simple; they were both men of peace who were terrified of war and its consequences. It was with Kennedy's wholehearted support that Chamberlain had tried and failed to make a deal with Hitler that would keep Britain (and, Kennedy believed, the United States) out of war. But now that the lines had been drawn and the fighting begun, Kennedy had to admit that there could scarcely have been a man less fitted to lead a nation at war than his friend Chamberlain. He reported later that the PM's speech in the House was "lamentable and lacking in grip."

Even Channon, biased though he was toward his hero and eager to gloss over any of his flaws, could not disagree. As he wrote in his diary: " . . . he spoke haltingly and did not make a good case: in fact he fumbled his words and seemed tired and embarrassed. No wonder he is exhausted; who would not be? All day and all night he works, while the small fry criticise. I realised at once that the House was not with him, and though he warmed up a little towards the middle of his speech, the very crowded House was restive and bored and the Egyptian ambassador even slept."

Chamberlain's lackluster delivery and the coolness of his reception made some observers think that, after all, there would be no real fireworks in the debate. The critics would make their points, some of which would be wounding, but in the end (so the old hands in the press gallery were saying) the Prime Minister would emerge relatively unscathed. He might agree to some changes in the make-up of his War Cabinet—he might even appease his critics by dumping Churchill, thus implying that he was responsible for the Norway disaster—but it would all work out in the end. The dissident MPs of the Tory party were known to number not more than thirty, and since two former members, Churchill and Eden, had been tempted into joining Chamberlain, the rebels had lost both drive and the appeal of glamorous leadership. The present leader of the group was a former Cabinet member named Leopold Amery, and his chief lieutenants were Alfred Duff Cooper, Harold Nicolson and Robert Boothby, opponents all but so far content to complain about Chamberlain rather than try to drive him out of his office. So though the PM sat down to only dutiful cheers from his most fervent supporters, he had no qualms.

There was a hiss of excitement in the public galleries when into his seat clanked the Member for Portsmouth North. Clanked is the word. Portsmouth is Britain's chief naval base on the Channel, and its representative—a Tory, of course—was a naval man, Sir Roger John Brownslow Keyes, a much-decorated veteran of World War I and still an active officer. He had, in fact, just returned from Norway where, at considerable personal risk, he had watched the last stages of the British defeat at Narvick, and he was seething with anger at the bungling and lack of preparation he had seen there. He had decided to come to the House in the full uniform of Admiral of the Fleet, wearing all his medals, to give weight to his indignant condemnation of the government and ministers he held responsible for the debacle.

Sir Roger was not an articulate man, but at that moment he did not need to be. His uniform and his face spoke for him. "Roger Keyes, an ex-hero, but a man with a grievance, was damning," Channon had to admit, though he observed that the uniform and medals were of "questionable taste, but it lent him dignity. The atmosphere was intense . . ."

Chamberlain was still not really worried, though his supporters were beginning to whisper. At six o'clock that evening he drove to Buckingham Palace to see the King. "He said smilingly that he had not come to offer his resignation and that he had not yet abandoned all hope of reconstructing his Government on the basis of a national coalition in which the Labour Party would join."*

George VI, who liked Chamberlain and certainly did not relish the thought of having to deal with a rambunctious Winston Churchill in his place, offered to call in Clement Attlee, leader of the Labour party, and tell him that he hoped he and his Socialist colleagues "would realize that they must pull their weight and join the Nat'l Govt." Chamberlain didn't think that Attlee's help was necessary at this stage, but thanked the King for his sympathy. "I told the P.M.," wrote the King in his diary, "that I did not like the way in which, with all his worries & responsibilities he had to bear in the conduct of the war, he was always subject to a stab in the back from both the H. of C. and the Press."

Chamberlain seems to have been comforted by these words, and to be still less unaware that his control over events was steadily slackening. Had he returned to the House, his euphoria might have suffered a jolt; instead he went off to dinner.

In the Chamber, Leopold Amery, the leader of the dissidents, was on his feet. In normal circumstances, Amery spoke like the chairman of a family company reading the annual report in an unspectacular year; he was worthy but dull. When he rose most of the House bolted and went off for *their* dinners, and there were rows of empty benches around

---

* John Wheeler-Bennett, *King George VI: His Life and Reign.*

him as he launched into his attack on government policy. But for this supreme occasion Amery had prepared hard, rehearsed repeatedly, and for once was able to project the passion and concern he felt. The public galleries remained jammed, since the visitors knew they would lose their seats if they went out to eat, and the rustling and the restlessness among them stilled to an attentive silence as the import of the words reached them. Soon word spread to the bars and the restaurant of the House that "Amery is stirring things up," and first Labour MPs and then the Tories began to slip back into their seats. They did not, however, include the Prime Minister or any members of his Cabinet. As Amery continued, it became apparent that his strategy was to take the argument away from the immediate cause of concern—the disastrous defeat in Norway—because that involved the responsibility of Churchill for many of the most serious mistakes, and Amery wanted the nation rid of Chamberlain, not Churchill. Instead, his arguments drifted toward a general indictment of the government's attitude and lack of resolution in its war efforts, spheres in which Churchill could not be blamed.

By the time Amery reached his peroration, he had a well-filled House hanging on his words; even Tory MPs had begun to applaud some of his sallies. Then came the passage which was to make all the front pages in Britain the following morning. Quoting Oliver Cromwell's famous words to John Hampden, "Your troops are most of them old, decayed serving men and tapsters and such kind of fellows," he pointed out that with one or two exceptions, it was a good description of Chamberlain's Administration. Then Amery paused. Afterward he was to say that until that moment he had not decided how he would continue. He had another quotation in mind, a much more devastating one, also from Cromwell, but it depended on the mood of the House whether he would use it. If they were in the wrong temper, any sympathy they might feel for the speaker would turn to resentment, and his arguments would be dismissed.

But Amery felt waves of sympathy from all parts of the House, and they emboldened him. Taking a deep breath, he went on, "I have quoted certain words of Oliver Cromwell. I will quote certain other words. I do it with great reluctance because I am speaking of those who are old friends and associates of mine, but they are words which, I think, are applicable to the present situation. This is what Cromwell said to the Long Parliament when he thought it was no longer fit to conduct the affairs of the nation: 'You have sat too long here for any good you have been doing. Depart, I say, and let us have done with you. In the name of God, go!' "

There was a moment's silence, and then members of the Labour Opposition took up the cry: "In the name of God, go!" Squirming, the Tories sat back in uneasy silence.

Channon had not been in the House to hear the slashing attack on his beloved Prime Minister, but he was soon aware of what had happened and rushed into the smoking room to rally the Tories behind Chamberlain. "I am most uneasy now about tomorrow," he wrote in his diary, "as it is rumoured that the Opposition will challenge the Government with a division."

Some of his Tory friends in the Lobbies of the House were already betting that if it came to a vote, at least fifty government supporters would be against the regime. Channon was outraged and shattered. So long as Chamberlain remained in power he was one of the charmed circle. "Political life will lose much of its fascination for me if Neville goes," he wrote, "as I shall no longer be in the inner councils of the racket."

Arthur Ketley looked up from his morning paper and said to his wife, "Looks like Chamberlain's in trouble. They're after his blood, it says here. Can't say I'm surprised. Fat lot of good his lot have done since the war started."

"Oh, I don't know," said Mrs. Ketley mildly. "We can't grumble. At least we haven't had any air raids. We haven't heard a siren sound since last September—and that was a false alarm!"

Their son, Donald, chimed in, "I remember that false alarm, Mum. You weren't half scared!"

His mother smiled. "I was not!" she said.

"She was scared for you, not for herself," his father said.

But Donald knew this was only partly true. His mother *had* been scared, and so had his father. He remembered the scene exactly, because he had enjoyed every moment of it. But on this May morning there were no more sirens and everything was a bore again. If getting rid of silly old Chamberlain was going to change that, then Donald was in favor of it. All you heard people talking about was the war, and yet nothing ever happened. Why couldn't he be in a real bombing raid, like the soldiers over in Narvick?

"I can't see what people have to complain about," said Mrs. Ketley. "Not that I'd hang his picture on the wall, but old Chamberlain hasn't done so badly so far. At least he's kept things quiet."

"Not in Norway, he hasn't," said her husband. "He's made a right mess of it there."

"You can blame Winston for that," said Mrs. Ketley. "You know Winston—always rushing in and starting trouble. It's Gallipoli all over again."*

Mr. Ketley sighed. Perhaps he didn't have any reason for feeling dissatisfied. The months of the phony war had probably been better for East Londoners than they had for years. Take Tom Foster, their next-door neighbor; he had been unemployed for so long that no one could remember when he had last had a job. His wife used to come around and borrow enough to buy some fried potatoes from the local fish-and-chips shop, and that would be dinner for four. But when the war came Tom had joined the ARP (Air Raid Precautions) and become a warden, and now his family had started eating properly. He had changed in every way, especially in self-respect.

No, they couldn't grumble, really. But there was something wrong with the setup, and Mr. Ketley felt that somehow they were all going to have to pay for the peace and comparative security of the past eight months. Yet he couldn't see how Chamberlain's departure would make any difference to him or his neighbors or his workmates. What did the war have to do with them, when you got down to it? They didn't feel any real antagonism to the Germans. It wasn't their war; it was the bosses' war.

Robert Boothby had received no reply to the letter he had left at Winston Churchill's office, and when he passed him in the Lobby of the House of Commons on the afternoon of May 8 the old bulldog growled an unfriendly acknowledgment to his greeting and hurried on. Boothby decided that Winston was deliberately avoiding any contact with the dissidents in order not to compromise his own political position, which was, to say the least, embarrassing.

If the rebels could get rid of Chamberlain, the man they were intriguing to put in his place was Churchill. Yet the attack on Chamber-

---

* When World War I began, Churchill was the First Lord of the Admiralty. It was mainly on his insistence that the Allies sent an expeditionary force to the Gallipoli Peninsula in 1915 in order to gain control of the Dardanelles. Because of poor Allied co-operation, the expedition was a disaster; since Churchill had been the prime promotor of the undertaking, he was given all the blame for its failure.

lain was being made as a result of the disaster in Norway—and Churchill's responsibility for that was at least as great as his premier's. Moreover, during his speech to the House the day before, Chamberlain had made no attempt to shift the blame for the debacle from his own shoulders to those of the First Lord of the Admiralty; if anything, he had sheltered Churchill from blame.

In these circumstances, Churchill was in a difficult position. As a loyal member of the government, he was bound to support Chamberlain and fight the men who were out to get for him the office he dearly wanted for himself. As Boothby ordered a drink at the bar of the House, he could hear the buzz of speculation all around him. Everyone seemed to be asking the same question: What will Winston do? His enemies in particular were enjoying the situation, for they relished Churchill's dilemma. The better he performed in the House that afternoon, the worse it would be for his ambitions. Would he be tempted not to give his best?

Yesterday there had been a chance that the great debate would come to a stalemate, that the Labour Opposition would yield to pressures and not bring the issue to a vote. But Clement Attlee and Herbert Morrison, the two leaders of the party, had finally been persuaded that even the Tories were swinging against the Chamberlain Administration, and that they had a good chance of winning on a vote of confidence. In a sharp attack on the government's weakness and lack of policy, Morrison announced that the Opposition would challenge the government to a division. After a hurried conference the Tory party managers immediately dispatched a three-line whip to all their members.* This meant that all Conservative MPs would be required to be in the House and to vote with the government—or be disciplined for insubordination.

Morrison's speech had not only challenged Chamberlain to a vote but goaded him to anger with its sly Cockney barbs and half-humorous insults. The Prime Minister's thin face flushed with the ominous red that all Members knew was the danger signal. Boothby leaned over to Duff Cooper and whispered, "My God, he's going to accept the challenge. What a bloody fool!"

The Prime Minister had risen and was moving to the dispatch box, and the House fell silent as they waited for him to speak. It was as if they all instinctively realized that what he said in the next few seconds would settle the issue once and for all.

---

* With their fringe supporters, the Tories had a clear majority (286 votes) over their Labour party opponents.

Chamberlain spoke slowly and precisely, but the dry tones had an unusual undercurrent of anger. A man less sure of himself would have angled for the sympathy of the House, but Neville Chamberlain was not one to lose his arrogance in a moment of crisis. A Churchill would have dodged the issue and temporized, but the Prime Minister was not that kind of man; he was too sure that the Tories would never let him down.

" . . . I do not seek to evade criticism," he said crisply, "but I say this to my friends in the House—and I have friends in the House. No government can prosecute a war efficiently unless it has public and parliamentary support. I accept this challenge. I welcome it, indeed. At least I shall see who is with us and who is against us, and I call on my friends to support us in the Lobby tonight."

It was a fatal error of judgment. It was the Labour Opposition which had brought the debate down to a party political level by challenging the government to a division, but the Conservatives expected more of their Prime Minister. They had anticipated an appeal to put politics to one side in the interests of the nation, a call for unity in the face of outside peril; instead, Chamberlain was waving his political big stick—his parliamentary majority. When he used the words "I call on my friends to support us in the Lobby tonight," his tone had made it quite clear that this was not a request but a command, and that the Tories had better obey or face reprisals.

There was a small cheer from the faithful, but the rest of the House, Tories among them, sat back in astonished silence, like schoolboys appalled at a headmaster's indiscretion. Boothby glanced across to see the reaction on Churchill's face, but the bulldog's head was bowed and his face carefully hidden by his papers.

Chips Channon felt a premonitory shudder, and he moved to sit behind his Prime Minister, "hoping to surround him with an aura of affection." Chamberlain had need of it as the debate reached its culmination, because there was little comfort elsewhere. Speaker after speaker turned on the government and assailed it. Channon looked up at the gallery; "several times I caught the eye of Mrs. Chamberlain, who has hardly left the House for two days: she is a loyal, good woman . . . She looked infinitely sad as she peered down into the mad arena where the lions were out for her husband's blood."

And still the question hung in the air: What will Churchill do?

"Would Winston be loyal?" Channon asked himself. "He finally rose and one saw at once that he was in a bellicose mood, alive and enjoying himself, relishing the ironical position in which he found himself: i.e., that of defending his enemies, and a cause in which he did not believe. He made a slashing, vigorous speech, a magnificent piece of oratory . . . How much the fire was real, how much ersatz, we shall never know, but he amused and dazzled everyone with his virtuosity."

But it was not enough. At last the vote was called and the Members rose, those who supported the government going into the Aye Division Lobby, those against into the Nay. Channon shuddered. The numbers in the Aye Lobby seemed ominously thin, considering that the Tories were supposed to be obeying a three-line whip. "We watched the insurgents file out of the Opposition [Nay] lobby . . . 'Quislings,' we shouted at them, and 'Rats.' 'Yes-men,' they replied."

When the figures were finally called, the government had its majority but had, nonetheless, suffered a grievous defeat. Normally, in response to a three-line whip, the government could expect a majority of 213 votes over the Labour Opposition. But when the Speaker announced the figures, the majority had dropped to 81 (281 for, 200 against). Forty-five members of the government had deliberately defied their leaders, and sixty-five had either abstained or stayed away from the House. It was a devastating slap in the face for Chamberlain, and when the significance of it sank in, there were immediate shouts of "Resign, resign!"

Channon wrote: "That old ape Josh Wedgwood began to wave his arms about and sing 'Rule Britannia.' Harold Macmillan next to him joined in, but they were howled down. Neville appeared bowled over by the ominous figures, and was the first to rise. He looked grave and thoughtful and sad . . . What can Neville do now? He can reconstruct his Government; he can resign; but there is no doubt that the Government is seriously jarred and all confidence in it is gone . . . Oh, the cruelty of the pack in pursuit . . . shall I too crash when the Chamberlain edifice crumbles?"

Channon survived; he was of the type that always does. But after forty-eight hours of haggling and false hope, Neville Chamberlain resigned. On the evening of May 10 the announcement was made to the public that a National Government, a coalition, of all parties, had been formed, and that Winston Churchill was its Prime Minister. The government was at last facing up to the problems and the perils of war.

It was none too soon. By the time King George had officially confirmed Churchill's appointment, the German armies were well on their way: since dawn on May 10, they had been on the march, and the Luftwaffe was in the air. Nazi troops had crossed the frontiers of neutral Holland and Belgium. BRUSSELS AND LILLE BOMBED, said the newspaper placards in Piccadilly Circus. The phony war had ended not with a whimper but with a bang.

The Buds of May

All over London, diarists were busy scribbling prophecies of doom. "This is the final fight," wrote Harold Nicolson. "I go to bed and shall, I hope, sleep. We shall be attacked from the air tonight in all probability."*

For Channon it was "perhaps the darkest day in English history. . . . Another of Hitler's brilliantly conceived coups, and of course he seized on the psychological moment when England is politically divided, and the ruling caste riddled with dissension and anger." He added: "Will it be our turn next?"

---

* *Diaries and Letters, 1939–1945.*

4

"A Miracle of Deliverance"

Men were afterward to call it the blitzkrieg, or lightning war. In less than a month it was to change the face of Western Europe, alter the political and ideological shape of the world, and place Britain in its direst peril in a thousand years.

As far as the Dutch were concerned, there was little to be done. Some shots were fired, some brave souls died. The locks were opened and their hard-won green fields flooded with salt water in an attempt to block the Nazi tanks rolling in from the Reich. But a division of paratroopers were dropped on Schiphol and other airfields. Within a day or two Queen Wilhelmina fled the country with her government to take refuge in England, and the men who were left behind announced Holland's capitulation. The obvious helplessness of the Dutch people in the face of a ruthless enemy did not prevent Hermann Göring from sending his bomber fleet against the undefended city of Rotterdam, whose hospitals, churches, ancient buildings and citizens were almost totally destroyed. To be sure, the Germans subsequently said that the raid was a mistake and that they had tried to stop it, but it did have the advantage of showing others—Londoners and Parisians, for instance—what could happen to a helpless city and its civilian population. *"Pour encourager les autres,"* they might have said.

Belgium was the next to go. King Leopold sent a plenipotentiary to the German High Command asking for an armistice on May 27, and early the next morning his troops laid down their arms, leaving uncovered the flanks of the British Expeditionary Force which had come north from France to help them. Meanwhile, German panzer columns had not bothered to throw themselves against the French forces sitting solidly behind their armor-plated defenses in the Maginot Line. Instead, spurred on by their commanding officer, General Heinz Guderian, who had learned the technique in Poland, they dashed around the Line and came up behind the entrenched defenders. Always accompanying them were Stuka dive bombers, which hurtled down on the terrified French troops, banshee wails shrieking from the "screamers" attached to their wings and bombs from their bellies. The French army had been regarded as the finest in the world, but in fact it was composed of a mass of unskilled, ill-paid, badly led civilian conscripts, and they and their commanders panicked. The German columns sliced through them and split the bulk of them off from the British troops on their left flank. Guderian then curled his armored divisions around in two directions to attack both forces from the rear. By May 24 the bulk of the French were surrounded in one great pocket in the north, and the British and the First French Army in another in the region of Dunkirk and the English Channel.

It was now that the *Entente Cordiale* between the British and the French began to crack. Faced with a mounting German attack upon their pocket and the inexorable shortening of their perimeter, the British generals were in favor of calling for help from the Royal Navy and evacuating their troops from the trap. But the British Expeditionary Force was under the overall command of the French, and the newly appointed commander in chief, General Maxime Weygand, refused. They must stand and fight where they were, he ordered. The British felt that this was madness; to them the strip of coastal plain on which they were trapped was just another battlefield, and a bad one from which to fight. But to the French it was the soil of France, and must be defended at all costs. Or so they were saying now.

The British continued to plan an evacuation, but now they did it in secret. The French, on the other hand, prepared for a last-ditch battle. They did not believe that any large-scale evacuation was possible. Already 500,000 British and French troops were crammed into the Dunkirk area, "like prawns in a pot," as one French officer put it, "waiting for the Boches to start the fire and boil us all alive." There just weren't enough ships to take them away, and what ships attempted to come would be bombed and sunk by the Luftwaffe.

Though Churchill and his Cabinet considered that evacuation was the only step to take, they were not hopeful of the outcome, either. When Admiral Sir Alexander Ramsay was ordered to muster his ships, he estimated that he might get no more than 45,000 men away.

Rumors began to reach London of the complete collapse of morale of the French government. On May 22 Churchill had decided to go to France himself to see what was happening. At first exhilarated and hopeful, he soon became profoundly disturbed. He realized that the French were seriously tempted to give up the struggle. They had never been enthusiastic about the war in any case, and now that German boots were once more marching over their soil, their resolution had failed. They were in despair, and the situation seemed hopeless.

The feeling must have been catching, for it seems to have had its effect on Winston Churchill. He had always been fond of the French, and their growing antipathy to him and to England influenced him deeply. He knew that if the disasters continued, Britain would be alone and isolated. Was it the moment for England, too, to think of making a deal with Hitler?

On May 27 Churchill cabled the British commander at Dunkirk, General Lord Gort: AT THIS SOLEMN MOMENT I CANNOT HELP SENDING YOU MY GOOD WISHES. NO ONE CAN TELL HOW IT WILL GO. BUT ANYTHING IS BETTER THAN BEING COOPED UP AND STARVED OUT . . . This was sent on the day that the Belgians capitulated, and the new Prime Minister warned the House to prepare for continued bad news.

But the next afternoon, in a meeting with the Cabinet in the Hole in the Ground, a fifteen-acre complex of rooms tunneled one hundred and fifty feet below Whitehall, Churchill told his colleagues: "I have thought carefully in these last few days whether it was part of my duty to consider entering into negotiations with That Man . . . I am convinced that every one of you would rise up and tear me down from my place if I were for one moment to contemplate parlay or surrender. If this long island story of ours is to end at last, let it end when each one of us lies choking in his own blood upon the ground."

In his own mind, that was how Churchill imagined most of the troops would soon be lying on the beachs of Dunkirk. Only a miracle could save them.

Later, the legend was to grow that the people of London could see the smoke from the battle of Dunkirk rising on the horizon. It was too far away for that. In truth, 99 percent of London was ignorant of the Dunkirk evacuation until it was over. All they knew was that things were going from bad to worse in Belgium and France, and a sort of stunned apathy had spread among the people. The great rescue operation had already been under way for two days before the writer, George Orwell, whose wife, Eileen, worked in the Ministry of Information, was even aware that the British Expeditionary Force had fallen back to Dunkirk. "People talk a little more of the war," he wrote on May 28, "but very little. As always hitherto, it is impossible to overhear any comments on it in the pubs, etc. Last night E[ileen] and I went to the pub to hear the 9 o'clock news. The barmaid was not going to have turned it on if we had not asked her, and to all appearances nobody listened."

For days, small-boat owners from all over England had been making for the Channel to join convoys for Dunkirk. Yachts, outboard dinghies, pleasure boats, barges and scows, manned by old salts, middle-aged owners of Thames "gin palaces" and eager young Sunday sailors were on their way downriver to join the Royal Navy in the great rescue operation. As they passed under Blackfriars Bridge and sailed past the Tower of London, through the heart of East London from Limehouse to Greenwich, few who watched them knew where they were going.

Robert Elvins, a sixteen-year-old copyboy, worked in the editorial room of the *News Chronicle*, in Bouverie Street, just off Fleet Street. On the night of May 27 one of the reporters walked up to the news editor's table. He was swearing, and his face was red with anger. "Goddamn that bloody Ministry of Information," he shouted. "It's a first-class story, and they won't let us print it!"

He had just come from Greenwich, where scores of small boats were mustering for the journey to Dunkirk. "Can you imagine?" he said. "They're nothing but a bunch of amateur sailors. It looks like a bloody regatta, old boy. And d'you know where they're going? To bring the British army back from the beaches—and the MOI says we can't use it!"*

The news editor remained calm. "Well, I don't expect they want Jerry to know what a mess we're in," he pointed out. "But we'd better get a picture, anyway."

"They'll never let you print it," the reporter said.

---

* The Ministry of Information had powers of censorship over any military information in wartime Britain, and could stop any stories calculated to injure domestic morale.

"A Miracle of Deliverance"

"For the files," the news editor said, and he picked up the telephone. It was then that Robert Elvins knew what he was going to do. He slipped out of the room and down the back stairs into Bouverie Street. The office car was waiting there, and he climbed into the seat beside the driver just as the cameraman came across the road with his equipment. "News editor says I'm to go along in case there are messages," he said.

As the car started off for Greenwich, Robert Elvins fingered the small square shape in his jacket pocket. It was his membership card for the Lambeth Sea Scouts, and with a bit of luck it would act as his passport to Dunkirk.

Most of the roiling mass of troops strewn across the beaches and sand dunes around Dunkirk were dirty, unshaven, thirsty, exhausted and bewildered. They had seen nothing of the enemy except his planes, they had not fired a shot, and nobody had told them what was happening. All they knew was that they were going back to England—if they were lucky.

For ten miles along every road leading into the town of Dunkirk, trucks, armored cars and guns had been run into the ditches. At first NCOs had ordered their men to set the vehicles afire, but this attracted swarms of strafing Messerschmitts, so sugar was poured into the tanks instead, cylinders split with hammers, and guns spiked or buckled. RAF fighters flying overhead on protective patrols looked down on what seemed the biggest holiday traffic jam of all time. The fruit of the hard years of British rearmament was being left behind on the coastal roads of France.

The sunny skies which had been such a boon to the German armies in their lightning thrusts through Belgium and northern France was hazing over now, but not enough to stop the waves of bombers from concentrating on Dunkirk. By the night of May 27 the inner harbor was choked with sunken and burning ships, and no more Royal Navy destroyers were able to get through. Only 7,669 men were taken off that day, and only 17,804 the next. It looked as if Admiral Ramsay's gloomy forecast would be fulfilled, and less than a tenth of the half million men now crouched in the sand dunes or lying along the water's edge would escape.

From the air, the thousands of figures on the beaches may have given the appearance of Bank Holiday, but down below there was misery and fear. Out at sea the Royal Navy destroyers moved back and forth like pacing animals, waiting for the tide to rise and enable them to come in near enough for the men to wade and then swim toward them. But too often when they ventured in, the bombers would appear; Stukas would scream down upon the ships, forcing them to sheer away to open, more maneuverable water, leaving the struggling soldiers to make their way back to the shore again or drown.

What was needed were small boats to form a ferry service between the shore and deeper waters. But it was not until the night of May 28 that the first of them came.

At first light of dawn on May 30, Robert Elvins looked over the side of the motor launch *Lucy* and gasped. All night long, as he shivered in the well of the boat trying to sleep, he had smelled the smoke, glimpsed the flicker of fires in the darkness, and heard a strange mixture of sounds: the thud of guns, the revving of motor engines, and sometimes the faintest snatch of human voices singing. Now he could see why he was here. Just to the south was Dunkirk itself, great pillars of thick black smoke rising high into the sky from what looked like gas tanks on the edge of the port, and on either side the lighter, bluer smoke of blazing buildings. But what caught his breath was not smoke but men: men everywhere, hunched in a great line under the wall of a long jetty leading out to sea; men crowded on the beaches or wading through the water toward the little ships that were now moving inshore; men crawling like ants over the sand hills beyond.

"Gawd, there's thousands of the buggers," said Mr. Crabtree, the owner of the *Lucy*. "Come on, boy, let's go in and get some of them."

The *Lucy* was a fifteen-foot launch which normally ran supplies for ship chandlers in the Pool of London, and Mr. Crabtree had welcomed Robert aboard with no questions about age or parental permission, as all the others had done. His own brother, who had volunteered to come with him, had slipped on the dock at Greenwich and broken his ankle, and Robert's appearance had made the difference between staying and going. There were a few questions to test his seamanship, and then they were off downriver and out to sea on what seemed to be the longest and slowest voyage of Robert Elvins' life. From three in the morning until the evening of May 29 it had taken them, and everything that could float seemed to be making better speed: cabin cruisers, destroyers, patrol boats, Channel packets and pleasure steamers, all making in the same direction and all overtaking them. Robert did not know it then, but over a thousand boats were on their way that day, and more would be coming.

"A Miracle of Deliverance"

"We had been told by a loudspeaker from one of the destroyers that they would be looking after the men waiting on the mole, and that we were to concentrate on the men on the beaches," Robert recalled later. "Our orders were to load up as many as we could manage, then ferry them out to the three big Channel passenger steamers waiting out at sea. It seemed simple enough when we set off, but we didn't know what we were getting into. We put a small ladder over the side and just went in there among all those soldiers waiting in the water. We only took two foot six inches draught, and we could go quite close on it, and when they saw us coming, every soldier in the British army seemed to decide that he wanted to come aboard. Some used the ladder, but most scrambled up the sides of the boat, rocking it just like we were in a storm, and then flopping in great wet piles all around me. There must have been about thirty aboard already and more were coming, and you could feel the boat going down under their weight. 'That's enough,' I heard Mr. Crabtree shouting. 'I can't take any more. Keep clear, I'm leaving.' "

But so many men were clinging to the boat or struggling to climb aboard that though he revved up the engine the old boat refused to move. Mr. Crabtree shouted to Robert to take over the wheel, and scrambled toward the side with a spanner in his hands.

"He was good and mad, I remember," Robert continued. "He waved the spanner at the men, who were all shouting and pushing, and he called out, 'Now stop being bloody fools, or none of us will get away. Act like Englishmen, can't you, and wait your turn! Or do I have to take this to you?' It worked, too. The men dropped back into the sea. I even heard one man say, 'How can I act like an Englishman when I'm a bloody Welshman?' It was the strangest thing. They all started laughing and choking in the water. Then I heard Mr. Crabtree shout to me to get cracking, and I revved up the engines. That's when they stopped— and that's when the Jerries came."

The formation of Stukas were, in fact, making for the mole, along which a mile-long line of soldiers was patiently waiting. But some of their bombs came close enough to send great waves rolling over the *Lucy*'s side, so that the well was suddenly awash with water as well as bodies.

"Bail!" cried Mr. Crabtree, and every soldier grabbed his forage cap and frantically began spilling water over the side.

"But it wasn't any good," Robert recalled. "There were too many bodies in the boat. I could feel her going down under my feet, and then

I was in the sea and swimming to shore. I'd wanted to go to Dunkirk, and there I was, right in the middle of it."

It didn't take long for the troops to drag the *Lucy* ashore, for she was in shallow water, and while a couple of army drivers helped Mr. Crabtree take the engine apart and dry it out, Robert Elvins wandered over the sand dunes, his young senses drinking in the devastating sight, sound, smell and taste of defeat. The mood of the men varied from fatalistic to ugly. Most of them seemed too stunned to do anything but stand in line and wait their turn, but there were others who cursed and shook their fists at the sky, especially when German planes came over to bomb or strafe them. "Where's the RAF?" they would shout.

That afternoon, as the German ring tightened around Dunkirk, the rear guard started to arrive at the beaches, black-faced, red-eyed, swearing at the chaos and confusion. But the mere fact that they had been able to fire their guns at someone seemed to have purged them of their bitterness, and they did not whine like those already waiting. They marched and queued in formation, and fired their guns in unison at the attacking planes. But they too raged against the absence of the RAF.

Among the rear-guard troops were many Frenchmen, most of them as eager as their allies to get aboard the boats for England. But when they joined the lines, they found themselves jostled aside; orders had gone out that "British only" were to be taken aboard. Robert spoke to a wounded French sergeant sitting dismally in the sand dunes, weeping quietly. "He and three comrades had waited for four hours on the mole under continual air attack, and finally got aboard one of the boats and were on their way, when someone shouted out, 'I thought we weren't taking any Frogs with us.' An NCO had made them jump over the side, and they had only just made it to the shore.* 'So much for the Entente Cordiale,' he kept saying."

Robert said later, "Personally, we didn't care who we took, as long as we filled up the boat. Once we got the *Lucy* working again, we loaded twenty at a time and ferried them out to the *Princess Maud* and the *Royal Daffodil*. It was one hell of a picnic, but we were lucky. On the first day we got dive-bombed twice, but they missed. Next day they strafed us three times. We had a queue of the boys waiting in the water to board us, and each time the planes came over we would duck below deck and the boys would duck under water, and when the planes were past we would shake ourselves and see what had happened. Somehow

---

* It was not until May 31 that Winston Churchill's order was received by the beach commanders to evacuate British and French troops on an equal basis.

only the woodwork got chipped, but over the side there would be bodies floating around and the sea would be dark red, and we were all covered with blood when we hauled the men aboard."

In the early hours of May 31, while they were anchored out in deep water, Robert and Mr. Crabtree awoke to find water lapping around them. They tried bailing, but it was no good. The engine wouldn't start, so they couldn't beach her.

"One of the bullets or bomb splinters must have opened us up below the water line," Robert said. "We went over the side and tried to tow her in by swimming with the rope wrapped around us, but she sank before we'd made more than fifty yards. We just made the beach and lay there until first light; then we went over to the mole and joined the queue of troops."

It was there that a sergeant major from the Royal Ulster Rifles found out from Robert how he had got there, and took him to the naval beach commander in charge of the boarding parties. An hour later he was aboard a destroyer and on his way back to Dover.

Late that night, weary, face still black from smoke, his ears still ringing with the blast of bombs, Robert Elvins walked into his home in Lambeth. His mother was sitting at the kitchen table, her face gray with worry and strain.

"And just where might you have been?" she cried out when she saw him. "What on earth have you been up to?"

All he could manage was, "I've been to Dunkirk," and then he stumbled up to his room and fell asleep. When he woke up, it was daylight, his clothes were gone and he was covered with a blanket. His mother was sitting on the end of the bed, looking at him. She had a newspaper in her hand, and he could see the name DUNKIRK spread across the front page.

"Hello, Mum," he said.

"I'll give you Dunkirk, you little monkey!" she said, laughing and crying at the same time.

On June 4 Winston Churchill announced in the House of Commons the end of the Dunkirk evacuation. He called it "a miracle of deliverance," and described it as having been achieved "by valour, by perseverance, by perfect discipline, by faultless service, by resource, by skill, by unconquerable fidelity . . ." Robert Elvins and most of the others who had been there would have added, "And by sheer bloody good luck."

Nearly a thousand vessels had been used in the operation, and

338,000 British and French troops had been brought back to England. True, they had left their guns, rifles and armor in France, but they were safe.*

"We must be very careful not to assign to this deliverance the attributes of a victory," Churchill told the Commons. "Wars are not won by evacuations." But even he seemed to be inspired by it, and there was no more talk of "parlaying with That Man."

A few nights later, after Parliament had adjourned, Churchill went across Whitehall to the Hole in the Ground for a meeting with the Imperial General Staff. The Prime Minister and his generals moved into the Emergency Cabinet Room, and for a moment they all stood in a silence broken only by the humming of the fans. The news was bad and would get worse. Italy was readying to collect some of the spoils of German victory and declare war on Britain and France. The French government was preparing to flee the capital for Bordeaux and seemed to be on the verge of accepting defeat. The German armies were nearing Paris. The isolation of England was almost complete.

One of the men at the meeting, Colonel Leslie Hollis, reflected that "at this moment this bare unlikely room underneath London was the most important room in the free world. Cut into the living earth, beneath the roots of the world's greatest city, it was the heart and core of all resistance."

Churchill took the cigar out of his mouth and pointed it at the simple wooden chair at the head of the conference table. "This is the room from which I'll direct the war," he said. "And if the invasion takes place, that's where I'll sit—in that chair." He put the cigar back in his mouth, took a puff and added, "And I'll sit there until either the Germans are driven back or they carry me out dead."†

On June 17 one of France's greatest military heroes of World War I, Marshal Philippe Pétain, came out of retirement and announced that he was taking over the reins of the French government. "I bestow on France the gift of my person to alleviate its misfortune," he told the French people.

---

* It is estimated that between 30,000 and 40,000 French troops were left behind. Some authorities declare that "all" British troops were rescued, but they were not. A rear guard (including men of the 1st Royal Scots) was captured or killed by the Germans.

† Leslie Hollis and James Leasor, *War at the Top.*

"A Miracle of Deliverance"

Pétain was then eighty-one years old. His first act was to order the French army to lay down its arms. Since he had made no arrangement beforehand with the German High Command, the Nazis continued their advance into France and their bombing raids on towns and roads, now jammed with refugees. Nor had Pétain warned his allies that he was capitulating, and British and Polish troops still in France were trapped.

That night Winston Churchill addressed the British people and the world over the BBC: "The news from France is very bad, and I grieve for the gallant French people who have fallen into this terrible misfortune. Nothing will alter our feelings towards them, nor our faith that the genius of France will rise again. What has happened in France makes no difference to our actions and purpose. We have become the sole champions now in arms to defend the world cause. We shall do our best to be worthy of that high honour. We shall defend our island home, and with the British Empire, we shall fight on unconquerable until the curse of Hitler is lifted from the brows of mankind. We are sure that in the end all will come right."

The rest of the world thought that he was being hopelessly optimistic. But not the British people. Reporting the reactions to the French surrender, George Orwell wrote in his diary: "People everywhere are to be heard discussing it. Usual line: 'Thank God we've got a navy.' A Scottish private, with medals of the last war, partly drunk, making a patriotic speech in a carriage in the Underground, which the other passengers seemed rather to like. Such a rush on the evening papers that I had to make four attempts before getting one."

There was not only news of the French collapse in that night's papers. An item prominently displayed on the front page read:

EVACUATION

In view of the present situation, all parents whose children are still in London, and all those who sent them away last September but subsequently brought them back, are urged to evacuate them without delay. Parents should apply to the nearest town hall or Citizens' Advice Bureau for further information. Don't delay! Don't say it may never happen! Air raids could begin at any moment.

George Hardiman read the item on his way home from work but didn't mention it to Ellen. It was on his insistence that they had brought their two children, John and Sheila, back to West Ham from Suffolk three months before.

In Battersea, where she had moved with her three children, Mrs.

Jenny Martin didn't see the item at all. She had brought them back to London after only six weeks in the Midlands, and had received a furious letter from her husband, Corporal Jimmy Martin, beginning: "Dear Jen, What on earth got into you? Are you mad?" She hadn't written to him since. It was no use trying to explain; he wouldn't have understood. In any case, she didn't have the courage to tell him about the real reason for her return to London. It hadn't been just a whim. There had been a man, and an irate landlady, involved in her precipitate departure from the Midlands. But Jimmy mustn't know about that.

So widespread were the rumors of RAF "inactivity" during the evacuation of Dunkirk that furious pilots who had logged hour after hour over the battle area, trying to ward off German raids on the beaches, angrily urged their commanding officers to protest to the Air Ministry.*

One pilot who was particularly aggrieved was a young New Zealander named Al Deere of 54 Fighter Squadron. After two weeks of continuous operations over Belgium and northern France, his Spitfire had been shot down near Dunkirk. He had a head wound and was near exhaustion, but when he arrived at the Dunkirk jetty in search of a place aboard a boat for England some of the troops had hooted at him, and most of the army and navy officers aboard the destroyer taking him to Dover refused to talk to him. "For two weeks I had flown my guts out, and this is all the thanks I got for it," he wrote later.

As early as June 4 Winston Churchill had tried to give the RAF the praise they deserved. He told Parliament: "There was a victory inside [the Dunkirk] deliverance which should be noted. It was gained by the Air Force. Many of our soldiers coming back have not seen the Air Force at work; they saw only the bombers which escaped its protective attack. They underrate its achievements. I have heard much talk of this. . . ."

He went on to give the main credit for the escape of the BEF from France to the gallant flying of the RAF in the skies above Dunkirk. But that June few people believed him. The RAF was unpopular with everyone.

Just how unpopular was something Pilot Officer Geoffrey Page discovered on an afternoon in June as he traveled back to London. His leave was over, and that night he was due to report back to 56 Fighter

---

* In fact, the RAF was in constant action against German planes over the Dunkirk area, but sight of the planes was blotted out by low clouds and smoke.

"A Miracle of Deliverance"

Squadron at North Weald RAF Station just north of the capital. He was blond, brown-eyed and just nineteen years old, and he considered the Royal Air Force the greatest service in the world.

It was unusual at the time, but there was only one other passenger in the car when he climbed aboard the train at Oxford. His fellow traveler was young, pretty and in the uniform of the Wrens, the Women's Royal Naval Service. The Wrens were considered the loveliest and brightest girls in the armed services, and Page looked forward to ninety minutes of friendly flirtation.

What he got instead was the freeze. The smile he directed at the girl evoked no response whatsoever. He offered his morning paper; it was refused. Digging into his briefcase, he pulled out a copy of a magazine and passed it across; the Wren gave a curt shake of her head and said not a word.

For the next twenty minutes they rode in silence. Watching the Wren covertly, Page wondered how he could penetrate the unnatural wall of silence. Finally he rose to his feet, stood on the carriage seat, and reached up his hand to the chain that worked the emergency alarm.

That did it. A startled look came on the girl's face. "What on earth are you doing?" she asked.

"I'm going to stop the train," Geoffrey Page said. "It's obvious that you think you're sharing your carriage with a disease-carrying leper. I wouldn't want your pretty nose to drop off, so I'm going to leave you."

Suddenly her tight face relaxed and she began to laugh. "Get down, you fool!" she said.

"Only if you'll tell me why you're being so damn unfriendly."

It was then that she told him what the Royal Navy thought about the RAF, and it wasn't pretty. "Where were you at Dunkirk?" she asked accusingly. "My brother in the Navy was there for four days, until his ship was bombed and sunk, and he says he didn't see a RAF plane the whole time he was there. The Germans had it all their own way. It was terrible. What were you doing—that's what we'd all like to know?"

"Me?" said Page lightly. "As a matter of fact, I was having a little joy ride—"

She did not let him finish. "It isn't funny," she interrupted bitterly. Getting up, she grabbed her bag off the rack, and looking down at him, said angrily, "The girls at the depot decided we wouldn't talk to any of you RAF boys until you stopped strutting around like peacocks and realized there's a war on. I see now we were quite right."

Then she was gone, leaving Pilot Officer Page miserable with anger and frustration. Because what he had been about to say to her was: "As a matter of fact, I was having a little joy ride over Dunkirk myself, try-ing to shoot down Germans."

Only, it hadn't been a joy ride, as several of his friends, now dead or captured, had discovered.

5

The Lull

Early on the morning of June 19, 1940, two young Frenchmen walked across Hyde Park in the direction of Stanhope Gate. One of them, Pierre Maillaud, was the acting chief of the London bureau of Havas, the semiofficial French news agency. Until two days before, the other had been an attaché at the French embassy in Albert Gate, but he had resigned the moment he heard Marshal Pétain announce the capitulation of France to the Germans. His name was Robert Mengin. Both young men were appalled at what had happened to their country over the past few weeks, but Mengin was sickened as well as heartbroken. In the embassy he had been living in a France in microcosm, and there he had seen the extent to which the rot had set in among his countrymen; they had been defeatists from the start, and most of them were antipathetic toward the British. What had particularly nauseated him was the remark of one senior official when the news reached the embassy that France had accepted defeat. "Now the British are on their own," the man had said. "Good! They'll get what they deserve. They have it coming to them."

It was in a mood amounting to despair that Mengin spent the day after his resignation. What would he do? His wife was frantic about their small baby, who had been left behind in France with relatives while she had made a trip to America. Now back in England, she found herself cut off from her child. Mengin made it plain to his colleagues that he would have nothing to do with the Pétain regime in France, which was already beginning to kowtow to the German conquerors, and this frankness would mean danger for him if he returned to France. But what was there for him in England? How could he serve without betraying his own country?

Before the day was over, however, all Mengin's doubts vanished. He turned on the radio to listen to an address by Charles de Gaulle. He had known it was coming, but just hearing the radio appeal galvanized him. Mengin had seen De Gaulle at the embassy a couple of weeks earlier, when the general had flown to England on a mission for Paul Reynaud, at the time still Premier of France. He had asked his colleagues about this tall officer in khaki and kepi, who stared through you when you saluted him, and was told that De Gaulle was one of the few officers on the front who had fought with success against the invading Germans.* He had been promoted in the field from colonel to brigadier, and was then called to Paris to advise the government. The purpose of his trip to London had been to ask Churchill for troops to back up the French army, and fighter planes to operate with the French troops fighting south of the Loire. Mengin had watched him drive away from Albert Gate with the ambassador, Charles Corbin, for his rendezvous with Churchill at 10 Downing Street; later he heard that the Prime Minister, impressed by De Gaulle's sincerity, had promised to send troops but reluctantly denied him the planes. De Gaulle flew back to France and that, Mengin thought, was the last he would ever see of him.

But on June 17 De Gaulle was back in London, this time with a different mission: to promote himself as the incarnation of a still-resistant France. He had talked with Churchill again, but this time his mission was not to persuade the British leader to send troops or planes, nor to give any further support to the politicians in France, for whom De Gaulle exhibited such contempt when he talked of them that his long nose wrinkled as if from a bad smell. No, this time he asked to be accepted henceforth as the voice of France—the voice of a nation still at war with Germany—and he requested air time on the BBC to announce to Frenchmen everywhere that he was their leader. Churchill had told him that he was being premature, that the French really hadn't capitulated yet, that there was still hope that the government would leave the country to carry on elsewhere.

At this De Gaulle shook his head in imperious disagreement. "They

---

* On May 19 he had driven a four-mile bridgehead into the German advance at Abbeville and captured several hundred prisoners.

will never go," he said. "They will stay in France and they will truckle to the Germans. They are no longer Frenchmen."

Churchill was impressed. De Gaulle was his complete antithesis, totally lacking in humor, never for a moment relaxed, and never once did a smile crack the grave face atop that eucalyptus tree of a body. But he exuded integrity and patriotism. "The destiny of France oozes from his pores," someone said, and that was certainly an asset at this black moment in France's history. So Churchill had given De Gaulle his backing, and time on the BBC as well. However, he insisted that De Gaulle must do nothing to widen the gulf between Britain and France at a moment when the French government might still decide to fly to North Africa to continue the fight, or order its great fleet to sail to British ports. His time would come, he told the Frenchman, but he must be patient.

The time had come that evening, De Gaulle decided; when Marshal Pétain instructed the French troops to throw down their arms. He dictated a radio speech, and the next day, June 18, he sent it to Downing Street for Winston Churchill's approval.

Did Churchill read it before he gave his consent to its broadcast? Apparently not. That day he was immersed in domestic matters and had an important speech to make to the House on the war situation. Had he considered the matter more, he might have hesitated. He still wanted the French fleet on Britain's side; he still wanted the political and military leaders of France, especially in its empire, to fight on. But would they do so if a French officer of whom few had heard, who was considerably their junior in rank, chose to come forward and claim to be speaking for them? But circumstances were working in De Gaulle's favor, and permission for the broadcast was granted.

"We must listen tonight at six o'clock," Mengin's wife had told Robert.

At six o'clock they turned on the radio and heard the announcer say, "*Ici Londres.*" Then the voice that was to become so familiar the world over filled the room and—for a time, at least—Robert Mengin's heart:

Men of France, women of France. The leaders who, for many years past, have been at the head of the French armed forces have set up a government.

Alleging the defeat of our armies, this government has entered into negotiations with the enemy with a view to bringing about a cessation of hostilities.

It is quite true that we were, and still are, overwhelmed by enemy mechanical forces, both on the ground and in the air. It was the tanks, the planes, and the tactics of the Germans, far more than the fact that we were outnumbered, that forced our armies to retreat. It was the German tanks, planes and tactics that provided the element of surprise which brought our leaders to their present plight.

But has the last word been said? Must we abandon all hope? Is our defeat final and irremediable? To these questions I answer—No!

Speaking in full knowledge of the facts, I ask you to believe me when I say that the cause of France is not lost. The very factors that brought about our defeat may one day lead us to victory.

For, remember this, France does not stand alone. She is not isolated. Behind her is a vast Empire, and she can make common cause with the British Empire, which commands the sea and is continuing the struggle. Like England, she can draw unreservedly on the immense industrial resources of the United States.

This war is not limited to our unfortunate country. The outcome of the struggle has not been decided by the Battle of France. This is a world war. Mistakes have been made, there have been delays and untold suffering, but the fact remains that there still exists in the world everything we need to crush our enemies some day. Today we are crushed by the sheer weight of mechanized force hurled against us, but we can look to a future in which even greater mechanized force will bring us victory. The destiny of the world is at stake.

I, General de Gaulle, now in London, call on all French officers and men who are at present on British soil, or may be in the future, with or without their arms; I call on all engineers and skilled workmen from the armament factories who are at present on British soil, or may be in the future, to get in touch with me.

Whatever happens, the flame of French resistance must not and shall not die.

It was an appeal to the heart of every Frenchman, and Robert Mengin was ashamed to find so few of the young men in the French embassy affected by it. They talked loftily of their duty to their government, and when Mengin questioned them it turned out that they meant Marshal Pétain's government. As for the senior officers, they sneered that De Gaulle was an upstart. How could they respond to a call from one so newly risen in rank? In any case, to do so they would have to resign their positions, "and in wartime a man can't resign. It's equivalent to desertion."

The Lull

Mengin knew what he had to do. Since he had De Gaulle's telephone number and address, he called the general's aide-de-camp and asked for an appointment. Later he called again. His friend Pierre Maillaud had heard the speech and had been equally carried away. Yes, said the A.D.C., General de Gaulle would be glad to see them in the morning.

So here they were in Hyde Park walking toward Seamore Place and a meeting with the man who refused to admit that France had lost the war. It was a lovely day in early summer and the memory of it remained in Mengin's mind years later. "The sky was of the purest blue," he recalled, "and the lawns were so green." The great capital seemed strangely silent that morning, and it had a purity and a freshness that overwhelmed him with a sense of transience and fragility.

But suddenly he was assailed by doubts and fears; he was aware, as these Londoners around him did not seem to be, that a world was coming to an end. As he and Maillaud entered Mayfair and walked toward 6 Seamore Place, he felt frightened. Was De Gaulle really the man for France? Could France in fact still be saved?

The meeting with the self-appointed savior of France a few minutes later did nothing to assuage Mengin's anxieties. The apartment where De Gaulle had set up his headquarters in London had been lent to him by a rich French supporter, and it was expansive and opulently furnished. The two young men were shown into a vast room bathed in June sunlight. The general sat upright, remote and statuesque, his back to the window, and stared coldly at them. A silence followed the introductions. Finally it was broken by Maillaud, who explained that they had both heard and been much moved by the general's appeal, and that they had come to offer their services. How could they help?

De Gaulle asked him his profession, and he replied that he worked for the French news agency.

"*Eh bien*," said De Gaulle, "tell me the news."

Maillaud reeled off the events of the past twenty-four hours, most of them depressing, in as much detail as he could remember, and then, assuming his duty as a newspaperman, he in turn began asking for news. What did the general have in mind? What were his plans?

"I will be speaking again tonight over the BBC," De Gaulle said coolly, "this time to Frenchmen everywhere, in the Empire, in North Africa especially. I will tell them where their duty lies." He paused and then uttered a sentence which Mengin found disturbing: "I am conscious of the fact that I shall be speaking in the name of France."

The words jarred uncomfortably on Mengin's ear. They were said

6 5

with such confident detachment, with such lack of humility, that it became evident that the man who was speaking had no conception of their enormous arrogance. But Maillaud did not seem to be taken aback, for he hung on the general's words. Mengin, on the other hand, was watching the man rather than listening to him.

"I could only see three quarters of his face," he recalled; "the one eye visible to me somehow suggested the eye of an elephant, quite round when the heavy lid was raised . . . He had very little chin, so little that I found myself wondering whether it wasn't the result of a war wound. Yet it gave no impression of weakness, but rather of smugness, of self-sufficiency, as did the mouth under the little brush of a moustache." He was suddenly reminded of a very tall Boy Scout.

On the way home Maillaud asked Mengin his impressions, and he answered that he thought De Gaulle was blown-up, inflated. Maillaud at once objected to the French word (*gonflé*); it wasn't quite the word.

"But *I* think it is the right word," Mengin said. "You haven't had to do your military service, so you have had no experience of that kind of officer—inflated with the concept they have of themselves. If you stuck a pin into them, you'd hear it—their idea of themselves—come out whistling, like the air from an inner tube."*

Maillaud asked what he actually had against him. Mengin replied that he had been shocked to hear De Gaulle saying that he would be speaking "in the name of France." It seemed the epitome of arrogance to him that this man who had so failed to impress him should so calmly assume the mantle of France.

The two friends walked back across the park in silence, the rapport between them lost. Mengin felt the gulf between them and looked enviously at people going about their business all around them. How lucky they were. Defeat stared them in the face. It was the gravest moment in their history. Yet they had no doubts about themselves and what they had to do. They were united in their resolve, not torn, like the French; there were no divided loyalties. He was suffused by an enormous but affectionate jealousy of the English.

They rarely said what they felt, he thought to himself. They left that to Churchill, who said things so very well. He said them with a passion that sometimes would have embarrassed most Englishmen, even though he did faithfully express what they were thinking inside themselves. It would be easy to think that this quiet determination to fight it out was due to the eloquence of Winston Churchill. As he said himself,

---

* Robert Mengin, *No Laurels for De Gaulle*.

The Lull

Churchill had the privilege to roar; but he did not create the lion—that is to say, the British people. When the lion is determined, then, whether it is Churchill who gives the roar, or Chamberlain who points the way with the umbrella, the lion charges.

But who would roar for him? General de Gaulle? He wanted passionately to go on fighting for France, but could he accept this tall, frigid Boy Scout as his leader? With a premonitory *frisson*, Mengin sensed that there was trouble ahead.

The war was being won too quickly even for Adolf Hitler, and for four weeks after the fall of France an ominous lull fell over Europe while the German armies halted to digest their conquests. Hitler himself undertook a sightseeing tour of Paris and posed for pictures at the Eiffel Tower. Seeing the glint in his eye, his companions wondered whether it was an anticipatory one; did he imagine himself striking a similar pose, in front of Buckingham Palace in London? Certainly there was little doubt in the dictator's mind that he would soon be there; the war was finished, and even the British must realize it by now. He would give them time to start negotiations, and even now he might be lenient with them. But if they continued to be stubborn he would crush them.

Vere Hodgson remembers June 1940 as a time especially sweet and poignant—"People were so nice to each other." She noticed it among her co-workers at the Sanctuary in Holland Park and among those who came for help; no one seemed to grumble or quarrel or shout any more. Even the shopkeepers were being polite to their customers, which was rare since rationing had begun in January; several times she found a couple of eggs or a small bag of sugar shoved into her shopping basket with a smile or a wink from over the counter.

But if there was good will in those days of the lull, there was also a good deal of suspicion, and the activities of the government did much to stir it up. With the end of the campaign in France and the threat of imminent invasion, a whole stream of emergency powers had been presented to Parliament and passed into law, all designed to give the authorities sweeping control over the populace. To judge by what had happened in the Low Countries and France, paratroops might descend upon Britain at any moment and find fifth columnists ready to help them. So steps must be taken to see that the invading forces would not find easy transport awaiting them, and spies and fifth columnists must be prevented from communicating with them. Therefore it was made a serious offense to leave a car unattended without first removing its distributor arm, and those motorists who failed to do so returned to find a summons on their windshield and their tires deflated.* Car radios had to be inactivated so that they could not be tuned to instructions from the enemy, and a number of motorists were heavily fined for transporting a portable radio from one place to another. For a stranger in London, driving became not only hell by night because of the blackout but hell by day because of the elimination of all signposts—and if the bureaucrats had their way, no one would tell him where he was if he asked. Even children had been taught to reply to strangers:

> *If anyone stops me to ask the way,*
> *All I must answer is "I can't say."*

There was an intensification of the government campaign, started at the beginning of the war, to stop rumor-spreading. In 1939 and during the months of the phony war it had been confined to a ban on talk about the sailing of ships or troop movements, and there had been posters plastered over London walls saying: TITTLE-TATTLE LOST THE BATTLE. But now, with Britain a beleaguered island, the public was officially encouraged to regard *any* kind of loose talk as dangerous to the welfare of the state. An emergency regulation passed that June, for instance, made citizens liable to a £100 fine and a term of imprisonment for spreading "any report or statement relating to matters connected with the war which is likely to cause alarm and despondency." As many a watchdog of the people's liberty in Parliament was quick to point out, this was a heaven-sent opportunity for every busybody in the country to telephone the police the moment he heard someone exercising the Englishman's long-cherished right to grumble about the weather, the police or the government. This campaign was backed by a series of newspaper advertisements by the Ministry of Information dedicated to the discouragement of gossip, that British national pastime. Headed THE SILENT COLUMN, it showed a series of drawings of people who should henceforward be regarded as "unpatriotic citizens." They were:

MR. SECRECY HUSH-HUSH: He's always got exclusive news, very private, very confidential. He doesn't want to spread it abroad but he doesn't mind whispering it to you.

---

* Many a London policeman learned to regret taking this action. If a motorist had immobilized his car by another equally effective method, he was apt to insist that the policeman reinflate his tires for him.

MISS LEAKY MOUTH: She simply can't stop talking and since the weather went out as conversation* she goes on like a leaky tap about the war. She doesn't know anything but her chatter can do harm. Tell her to talk about the neighbours.

MR. PRIDE IN PROPHECY: Here is the marvellous fellow who knows how it is all going to turn out. Nobody else but he does. He's a fool and a mountebank.

MR. KNOW ALL: He knows what the Germans are going to do and when they are going to do it. He knows where our ships are and what Bomber Command is going to do. With his large talk he is playing the enemy's game.

MISS TEACUP WHISPER: She is a relative of Mr. Secrecy Hush-Hush and an equal danger.

MR. GLUMPOT: He is the gloom brother who is convinced that everything is going wrong and nothing can go right. He is so worried by the enemy's strength that he never thinks of ours. Tell him to cheer up and shut up.

TELL THESE PEOPLE TO JOIN BRITAIN'S SILENT COLUMN.

This was followed up by an announcement reading: "If you know somebody who makes a habit of causing worry and anxiety by passing on rumour, and who says things persistently that might help the enemy —tell the police, but only do this as a last resort."

Since there were still plenty of active Fascists and Communists opposing the war effort—they were responsible for the anti-Jewish and antiwar posters which were pasted on London walls in June 1940—one would have thought that the bulk of the public's complaints would have concerned these two dissident elements. Instead, innocent drunks or crochety but loyal critics of government policy felt the sting of the new regulations. An Irishman with a skinful was reported by a girl for saying that the British Expeditionary Force in France had run away, and that all England was good for was finding jobs for Irishmen. He got a month in jail. A wine merchant, angered that the tax on alcohol had been raised, shouted to a customer that the government "are a bunch of robbers, and the sooner Hitler teaches them a lesson the better," and was sent to jail for three months. A girl who had spent an adulterous night

---

* Publication of weather forecasts had been banned since the outbreak of the War. With the occupation of France by Germany, Britain was now allowed to read only about "weather conditions in the English Channel." A staple ingredient of English conversation had been stifled by the war.

in a hotel with an air force officer was reported by a shocked chamber-maid who heard her saying, "Who cares if Hitler does come so long as we can have fun like this." She got a month for signing a false name in the hotel register. Even a British soldier was arrested in a famous French pub in Soho and hauled off to Cannon Row Police Station for creating alarm and despondency. A couple of French sailors at the bar had raised their glasses to him and cried, *"Vive la France! Vive l'Angle-terre!"* To which he had raised his own glass in return and shouted, "To hell with Hitler!"

A woman rushed out and brought back a policeman. It took some time for the soldier to convince the law that he had *not* been crying "Heil Hitler!" while giving the Nazi salute, but by the time he did, tempers had become so hot that he was fined the next day anyway for being drunk and disorderly.

Vere Hodgson thought of Londoners at this time as being rather like a quarrelsome family who, faced by a death in the house, are re-united by the misfortune. It was a good analogy. Air-raid wardens on their nightly patrols noted that passers-by no longer sniffed contemptu-ously at them, as if it were beginning to sink in that they might have their uses. Two months earlier they had been called "a bunch of slack-ers." In April a City magistrate, told that a traffic offender was an auxili-ary fireman who had joined up at the outbreak of war, had given him a thumping fine and asked him why he was "skulking in the fire service and wasting the nation's money instead of doing a useful job." But now even firemen were being looked at through fresh and more understand-ing eyes, as people realized that they too might soon be needed.

Every church hall and playing field throughout London resounded with drill sergeants' bawling orders. The call had gone forth for a Home Guard* of civilian volunteers to be ready to repel the German invader, and they had swarmed to the recruiting centers in an embarrassing surge of patriotism. In Kensington and Belgravia every retired colonel rushed out to do his duty, and there were squads recruited in which no one was below the rank of major. One such contained eight generals and only one civilian. The first time they paraded, the generals all came in uniform and medals, jingling martially beside their crestfallen civil-ian comrade, a local shop assistant, clad in jacket and flannel trousers and feeling like a goose among swans.

But it was not just in the ex-officer enclaves of the West End that the Home Guard flourished. Smithfield Market, where the meat porters

---

* They were known at the time as Local Defence Volunteers.

slung great hunks of beef; Billingsgate, where they handled the fish; and the London docks, where they unloaded the nation's food—all formed Home Guards and went on parade, drilling in preparation for the invader.

Not that there were arms for them, even if German paratroops had landed. They drilled with broom handles instead, and the sight of them infuriated Robert Boothby as he walked back from the House of Commons. Six weeks had gone by since he was in Belgium earmarking a big consignment of small arms. If the deal had gone through, they would have arrived just in time to re-equip the troops evacuated from Dunkirk, or to give the Home Guard something more useful than broom handles. He groaned as he thought of those gleaming new Belgian rifles and machine guns, all ready for shipment, being parceled out to soldiers of the German army in Brussels and Antwerp.

At this time Boothby was working at the Ministry of Food, helping his chief, Lord Woolton, to organize an equitable rationing system and build up reserves for the ordeals ahead. It was a job he relished. With Woolton he found little to complain about, for here was a man after his own heart who also despised civil servants and their careful rules and regulations. Until the war began, Lord Woolton had been plain Fred Marquis, managing director of a chain of department stores in the north of England, and to the horror of the bureaucrats of Whitehall he ran his department in the same way that he ran his stores. "Feed the people!" was the motto on the wall in his office, and he didn't care how he went about it so long as he built up his stocks of food. With Boothby as a willing accomplice, and with a shrewd millionaire miller named James Rank to advise him, he had just pulled off a coup in wheat. The wheat world, and particularly Canada, was hoping to unload its storehouses of grain on the British government at inflated wartime prices, and was waiting for the official buyers to come along so that they could make the killing.

But what the market didn't know was that Woolton's own buyers, under a hundred different guises, had already been in and earmarked their stocks at reasonable prices. There was only one hitch; now they had to be paid for.

Woolton picked up his telephone and called Sir Kingsley Wood, the new Chancellor of the Exchequer. He had secretly been buying wheat, he said, but he needed $100,000,000 to complete the deal. Could he please have it?

There was a shocked silence, and then Kingsley Wood spluttered reproaches. How dare he make a deal of this magnitude without consulting the Treasury? He must write a paper and send it through normal channels at once, and after the Cabinet considered it, the Treasury would decide whether he could have his money.

Boothby, who was on the other side of Woolton's desk when the conversation took place, watched the shrewd, amiable businessman's face fall as he absorbed the rebuke. Here we go again, he thought. There would be the same run-around as in the case of his guns—no Cabinet consent, no dollars, no deal—and no wheat, except at prices they could not afford to pay, which could mean bread rationing within six months or a year.

But Woolton, unlike Boothby, was no politician, and he didn't care about his career. He was not overawed by Cabinet consultations and the ponderous prognostications of self-important Treasury officials. He was prepared to fight, and if the government and its advisers couldn't see that he had acted in their best interests, then the hell with the lot of them. He assumed his blandest manner and replied, "Now, look here, Chancellor, I will not write a paper about a commercial transaction of this magnitude. It would be impossible to keep it secret, the prices would go up, and the loss to the Treasury would not be less than twenty million dollars once the market knew what was happening."

Kingsley Wood said, "You've no right to go out and buy like this in the name of the British government."

"I haven't used the government's name," snapped Woolton. "I'm not that big a fool. They'd have piled the price high. Not likely. I've used every name and every nationality in the book to get the wheat I want."

There was a pause and then the Chancellor asked, "My God, Woolton, is this how you usually conduct your affairs?"

Woolton said it was.

Another pause. "I'll call you back," the Chancellor finally said. At two o'clock that afternoon, with an hour to spare before the deadline, he was on the phone to tell Woolton that the $100,000,000 was his.

"Thank you," said Woolton. "You will be glad to know that we now possess enough wheat to last Britain for the next six months, and I have bought it at seventy-two cents a bushel. I think you will find that never again in our lifetime will you be able to buy wheat at that price. And you won't have bread rationing, either."

"I don't care about that," said Kingsley Wood. "Just keep me out of it. And don't ever do something like this again."

Yes, Woolton was a man after Boothby's own heart. If only there were other ministers of Woolton's caliber in the government! But though

The Lull

Churchill was now Prime Minister, too many of the old gang were still around. They were a poor lot, and he had no faith in them.

For a Jew, or for anyone who had been a prominent and vocal opponent of the Nazis, this was an uneasy time in London. They not only shared the menace of invasion; with all other citizens they knew that if it succeeded and Britain capitulated, their fate would be sealed. Already stories were filtering back across the Channel of the ugly punishments to which anti-Nazis were being subjected in France and the Low Countries. There was little chance that things would be better for those in Britain under a German occupation. So unabashed enemies of Hitler, Jews and non-Jews alike, quietly decided to end it all the moment his soldiers began treading the streets of London. Some of them, like the famous anti-Nazi publisher, Victor Gollancz, went around with phials of poison in their pockets, in case they could not get home to the medicine cabinet. But remarkably few panicked and even fewer took steps to get out of the country.

Robert Boothby had a friend, Richard Weininger, who had little to hope for if the Germans took London. He was a Jew who had fled Prague just ahead of the Nazis in 1939. The two men had been associated in various enterprises for a long time, and Boothby had tangible as well as fraternal reasons for valuing Weininger's friendship. Once, in a time of great financial stress when the young Scot needed money quickly, Weininger had lent it to him without interest. It had been paid back, but Boothby would never forget the gesture.

Weininger's beloved younger stepdaughter, who had been living in France, had succeeded in escaping from Paris ahead of the Germans and had reached neutral Lisbon; from there she had cabled Weininger asking him what to do next. He showed his friend the cable when they met for lunch in Boothby's apartment in Belgravia on May 10, and the MP did not hesitate to urge his Czech friend to fly with his elder stepdaughter, who was with him in England, to Lisbon without delay, and then take his reunited family to the United States.

But Weininger said he had no intention of leaving. He had already cabled his stepdaughter in Lisbon and instructed her to come to Britain as soon as possible. He had made up his mind; if Britain was invaded, he would fight; if Britain was defeated, then nothing mattered any more.

Shortly after lunch the two men were discussing the future over a glass of port when the doorbell rang, and in came Boothby's secretary to announce that two officers from Scotland Yard would like to see him.

As they entered, Weininger got up to leave. "Don't go, sir," said one of the men from the Yard. "Am I right in thinking that you are Mr. Richard Weininger?" The Czech nodded. "Then, would you mind getting your hat and coat and coming with us, sir?"

Boothby protested vehemently, but to no avail. The detective would say only that Weininger had been ordered detained under Regulation 18b.* "I'm just following my instructions," he added.

After they were gone, Robert Boothby, still in a fury, called in his secretary. "I want this letter taken down and sent off at once," he said. He paused and then began: "Dear Prime Minister, I want to tell you about a shocking affair which happened today . . ."

It was a letter which was to cost Boothby his political career.

Vere Hodgson was proud of her fluency in languages, and she had found General de Gaulle's appeals over the BBC most exciting. "What a magnificent personality he sounds!" she wrote in her diary after the second broadcast. "His voice is thrilling, and his answer to Pétain made me shiver in my chair, such tragedy there was in his tones." But her aunt, who lived in Kensington, was of another opinion, and so were several of her neighbors. "Auntie Nell is not too enthusiastic about De Gaulle. She thinks we have trusted foreigners too often."

If there was much neighborliness and mutual understanding among Londoners that summer of 1940, it did not always extend to anyone with a foreign accent, foreign name or foreign appearance. Ever since the fall of France the newspapers had been crammed with stories about how the fifth column there and in the Low Countries had helped to undermine the morale of Britain's allies by spying, sabotage and panic-mongering. Most of the refugees who had been made welcome and settled in Britain during the thirties were victims of Fascism in either Spain, Italy or Germany, but the flood of newly arrived Belgians, Dutch and French were greeted with suspicion. Most people were not prepared to evaluate them on an individual basis and thought the whole lot was a potential threat to the safety of the country. Stories began to filter through London of female Nazi spies disguised as nuns fleeing

---

* Regulation 18b was part of the Defence Regulations passed in 1939, and was designed "to provide for the custody on security grounds of persons against whom it is not practicable to bring criminal proceedings." Boothby had protested its passage at the time.

from Liège, and of SS men in ringleted wigs and false beards posing as Orthodox Jews from Amsterdam. Even the Jews themselves were looking with wary eyes at their fellow religious from abroad, and in Whitechapel, London's largest Jewish colony, a tale was told about a spy discovered among a group of Dutch Jews.

But it was not only ordinary people who now suspected the foreigners in their midst; so did the government, and it had the power to do something about it, as it soon demonstrated.

Tothill Mansions was a row of four-story Victorian houses on the fringes of Westminster into which a number of government ministries had moved shortly before the hostilities, and this was where Charles Percy Snow was working that summer of 1940. Until then the physicist had spent his life in academic and scientific circles, living the easy, urbane existence of a don at Cambridge and outlining a series of novels called "Strangers and Brothers," which was to become one of the literary landmarks of our times. But now he was a civil servant—a commissioner, he was officially called—charged with the task of recruiting scientific experts and putting them to work for the war effort. He was a large, untidy, kindly man with a melancholy look that may have been due to his lonely bachelor existence or to the fact that he was worried about the war. Unlike most of his fellow citizens, he was not at all sure that Britain was going to win it.

For the moment Snow was desperately short of scientists, and he was combing the universities of Britain and Ireland to find more of them. If large-scale bombing began soon over Britain—and he was sure it would—and if this was followed by an attempt at invasion by the German armies, there was one device which could well tip the balance in favor of the defenders of Britain—radar. Radar could spot and precisely locate enemy planes as they came in to bomb; radar could sight the invasion barges even if they approached at night or through fog or smoke screens. But it was still suffering from bugs which only technological skill and application could eliminate, and to get an improved system installed both in ground stations and on planes it could guide through the air, Snow must find additional scores of scientists to work with the inventor, Sir Robert Watson-Watt.

"Thank God Adolf Hitler isn't a scientist," Snow was apt to say, "and thank God he never lets a scientist get anywhere near him. Otherwise he would never have driven so many of them out of Germany and handed them over to us."

It was true. The Nazi persecution of the Jews and of German liberals had not simply impelled world-famous physicists—Albert Einstein among them—to leave Germany. There were scores of others from Nazi-dominated countries whose names were unknown to the general public, all men of great scientific skill and vision: Rudolf Peierls, Egon Bretscher, Hans von Halban, Lew Kowarski, Otto Frisch, Joseph Rotblat, Nicholas Kurti, Heinrich Kuhn, Dr. Heitler, Herbert Frölich and Klaus Fuchs, among others. They asked for nothing other than to use their brains and knowledge against the Nazis, and Snow was eager to put them to work.

That was where the trouble began, for though they were eager and he was eager, Security was not. When the order went out from the Home Office to round up all aliens in May and June 1940, no discrimination or selectivity was shown by the police. Only those aged seventy years and over were spared, and the authorities even got around to some of them later on; the rest were taken without warning from their homes. To many of them, still living the nightmare of Nazi domination, it seemed at first as if a new Gestapo, English-speaking this time, had come to persecute them. The knock on the door would come at seven in the evening instead of at four in the morning and the manner was polite instead of brutal, but the end result was the same: they were still wrenched away from their families and not told why, or where they were going.

For days during this period Charles Snow had to storm the bastions of the Home Office in search of information about where his cherished scientists had been incarcerated, and to threaten tightmouthed officials with dire consequences ("If I have to go to the PM he'll have your heads"). Most of them were still in London, in Brixton Prison,* where he went to get them out; his heart bled at the thoughtless cruelty which had put so many sincere anti-Nazis in jail, sometimes in the same cell as jeering Fascists, simply because of a foreign name or a foreign accent. There were distinguished scholars, writers and physicists among them, as well as businessmen and artisans, all of them capable of helping the British war effort. Snow would have released them all if allowed his way, but he had to be content with rescuing his own experts and soothing their hurt pride with the promise that they would soon be at work and all this humiliation forgotten. Or so he thought. But authority had decided otherwise.

The Ministry of Aircraft Production had held a meeting and made a decision: no appeal would be allowed. The release of the foreign

---

* Though some, like Klaus Fuchs, were in detention camps on the Isle of Man.

scientists earmarked by Snow was confirmed, but—and it was a catastrophic but—none of them was to be allowed to work on developing radar. This ban extended not only to recent refugees, but also to naturalized British subjects and anyone else not having native-born British parents. Not only that: whatever work they engaged in henceforth, they must keep in closest touch with the police; they must not possess automobiles, bicycles or maps; they must not move from one area to another without first obtaining official permission (which meant that they might not, for instance, travel between London and the universities); and they must obey a nightly curfew and be in their homes or lodgings by ten each evening.

Snow swore. It was not only humiliating; it was a waste of tremendous scientific talent at a moment when it was desperately needed. But he knew the workings of the Whitehall mind well enough to realize that as long as the invasion scare was in the air, there was no use protesting; he would not change anyone's mind, not even if he went as high as Churchill himself.

But he was determined not to let all that brainpower go to waste. It was an affront to his pride to have the rust gather and despair set in among these men of such brilliance and with such eagerness to serve. He must find a place for them in the war effort. But where?

Then he had it. In his dry voice he dictated a long memorandum to his immediate superior. He followed this up with urgent letters to three close friends of his, a trio of the most distinguished scientists in Britain: Professors P. M. S. Blackett, George P. Thomson and John D. Cockcroft. Could they use his scientists, was the substance of his plea to the professors. Would they let his scientists work for the Maud Committee, was his request to his superior.

He had replies a few days later. The professors were delighted to employ the talents of the refugee scientists, and the sooner the better. As for the Home Ministry, it gave the matter its earnest consideration and decided that since the Maud Committee was engaged in work of no immediate value to the war effort, and since matters of immediate security were not involved, it had no objection to seeing the refugee scientists employed on such nonvital experimental work. Only, the refugees still must obey the regulations: no bikes, no cars, no maps, and no nights out.

Joyfully Snow sent instructions to his scientists. Drs. Bretscher, Halban, Kowarski, Fenning, H. F. Freundlich and N. Kemmer were to report to the Cavendish Laboratory at Cambridge University; Drs. Frisch and Rotblat to Liverpool University; Professor Franz Engen Simon and

Drs. Kuhn, Arms and Kurti to Oxford University; Dr. Peierls to Birmingham University (where he was later joined by Dr. Klaus Fuchs); Drs.
Heitler and Fröhlich were to be available for consultation.

And that was how sixteen refugee scientists who were considered
too much of a security risk for radar development in Britain in 1940
went to work instead for the Maud Committee* on the creation of the
atom bomb.

Polly Wright swallowed the last mouthful of her gin-and-tonic and
took a compact out of her handbag to see how her face looked.
She dabbed some powder on her nose and repaired the lipstick, and then
laughed to herself. Fancy making up your face to walk home in the
blackout. She'd never get used to the fact that the streetlights were
doused for the duration.

"I'm off," she said. "I've got to be at the Labour Exchange first thing
in the morning."

"Aw, just one more," one of the musicians said, but she shook her
head.

"Honestly, no. I really have to look my best in the morning. You
know what they're like at the Labour Exchange." Then she stopped and
said bitterly, "No, you don't know what they're like. You've never had
to ask them for dole or a job. But I can tell you, if you look a bit cheap
or anything like that, they send you off to be a waitress or a charwoman."

It was ten in the evening at the end of a beautiful June day, and
with the blackout blinds and curtains drawn, the pub was stiflingly hot.
It was crowded too, and very noisy. Ever since the end of the war in
France, people in London seemed to be drinking more, as if liquor and
noise and crowded rooms eased their tensions. The pub was called The
George, but most of the regulars referred to it as The Gluepot, probably
because once you entered it for a drink it was difficult to get away.

* Maud Ray was the name of the English governess of the children of Dr. Niels
Bohr, the Danish scientist. Just before Nazi troops overran Denmark, Bohr had
sent a personal message to a scientist friend in England saying he was safe, and
adding: TELL COCKCROFT AND MAUD RAY KENT. Sir John Cockcroft and his colleagues, puzzling over the words, decided that MAUD RAY KENT was an anagram; if
you changed the y to i it could make the words "radium taken," which they presumed
to be Bohr's way of warning them that the Nazis were using radium and working on
the bomb. They decided to adopt the name Maud for their own atomic committee,
and did not discover until Bohr had fled to England that there was a real Maud Ray
who lived in Kent. (See Ronald W. Clark, *The Birth of the Bomb*.)

The Lull

The Gluepot was on Mortimer Street a few yards from Upper Regent Street in the West End. It had long since become the "local" for staff members of the BBC and members of the BBC Symphony Orchestra, for Broadcasting House and the Queen's Hall, where the orchestra played, were just around the corner. It was a drab, brown, nondescript pub smelling of spilled beer and potato chips, but its habitués gave it a sparkling ambience. Conductors like John Barbirolli, composers like Constant Lambert and Alan Rawsthorne, poets and artists like Dylan Thomas and Elizabeth Lutyens, comedians like Tommy Handley, and Fleet Street and U.S. newspapermen were to be found there, elbows on the beery counter, swopping the latest gossip about the war and the BBC.

Polly Wright had known the pub since her husband first took her there in 1937, when she was a bride of twenty and new to London. She had met her husband at a concert in Birmingham, and for both of them it had been, she told herself cynically, sex at first sight. He was a violinist in one of the London symphony orchestras and she was a secretary in an automobile factory, hating her job and her parents, with whom she lived on the outskirts of Birmingham. On her day off, a friend had taken her to a rehearsal of the orchestra, and afterward they'd had lunch with some members of the string section. Halfway through the performance of Sibelius' Seventh that evening she was convinced she was in love, and by four o'clock in the morning so was he. They were married at a registrar's office in Marylebone in the spring of 1938, and everything had gone downhill ever since.

That summer the orchestra left on a tour of Germany and the Low Countries, and it was at a reception after a concert in Cologne that Polly met the young German engineer. He was working, he said, on a big project not far away (he was, she subsequently discovered, in charge of construction on one of the sections of the Siegfried Line). Their meeting came after one of the quarrels with her husband which were now an almost daily part of her life, and if they had stayed longer in Cologne she might have succumbed there and then. Instead she returned to London, and at Christmas the young German flew across to see her. In the spring of 1939 ("I must have been mad; I *was* mad") she went off to Cologne to stay with him.

It was an idyllic spring and an ecstatic summer. "I have never been happier," she admitted later. She never read a newspaper and didn't listen to the radio; when she did have any doubts, her lover laughed and said, "There isn't going to be any war," and she believed him. Toward the end of August, when it looked as if he might be wrong and she talked of going back to England, he assured her that she needn't worry.

Even if there was a war he would protect her; it wasn't as if she was politically minded, he said, so there wouldn't be any trouble. She believed him because she wanted to.

At the end of September 1939, the German police came for her and took her off to an internment camp. She and her lover spent most of the last night weeping in each other's arms. Of course he couldn't protect her. "An engineer on a secret fortification with an English mistress—he must have been mad to have thought he could get away with it," she said later, and then added, "Or in love, and we were in love."

Early in 1940 she was among a group of British citizens released in exchange for German internees in Britain. When the train pulled into the little Dutch frontier station, she disembarked with the others to have her passport checked by the police, her face pale under the tumbled mass of Titian-red hair.*

Polly was sick on the ferry from the Hook of Holland to Harwich, but that didn't stop the police from questioning her for three hours after her arrival. In London there were more questions, this time from some men who said they were from Security, but they proved to be more sympathetic and seemed to believe the innocence—the political innocence, anyway—of her story. She had found a one-roomed apartment just off Marylebone Road and started to look for work. At night she would go to The Gluepot because she liked the company of the musicians and writers she found there. They all knew what had happened to her, but it seemed to draw them closer to her rather than repel them. "Welcome to the kingdom of the lost!" said a drunken Dylan Thomas the first night she came in, folding her in his arms.

Now, walking out of the pub into the warm June night, she glanced again at the man at the end of the counter toying with his glass of beer. He had been watching her all evening, and she felt in her bones that it was not her looks that attracted him.

Once out in the blackened street, she knew that he was following her. But when she turned out of Mortimer Street into Upper Regent Street, she forgot about him, for she was too busy concentrating on getting her eyes accustomed to the dark and watching out for the down-pointed shafts of light from the muted flashlights of the other pedestrians. Once she had crossed Portland Place and picked her way across it into New Cavendish Street she was on home ground; she knew all the obstacles and he didn't, and she could hear him stubbing his shoe against the raised curb on the corner of Harley Street and listened with

---

* It was here that the author first met her.

satisfaction to his grunt of pain when he caught the railing jutting out a few yards farther on.

She was not afraid, as once she might have been; the past few months had changed her considerably, mentally, emotionally and physically. She felt she could handle anything this man might do. In any case, she was convinced that he wasn't going to attack her; he hadn't looked at her in that kind of way.

When she turned into the mews where she lived she saw at once the dark blur of a car parked at the door. The footsteps behind her quickened, and then she heard a door open and a shape emerged from the blur and said, "Mrs. Wright? Mrs. Polly Wright?"

"That's me," she said.

"May we come inside, please, madam? We're from the police."

An hour later the doors had closed behind her in Holloway Prison, and the first thing she was aware of once the policeman had departed was the pulsing noise which seemed to emanate from its heart. It was a continuing wave of sound, like the chatter and chirp of a thousand birds, and it was only later that she realized the noise was human.

"My God, not another one!" she heard one of the female wardens saying as they brought her in. "How many do they think we can cram in here?"

A large heavy woman said, in a not unkindly voice, "All right, dear, take off your clothes. We won't keep you long."

"What, here?" said Polly.

"Yes, here," the woman said. "We're a bit busy tonight. Go on, dear. It won't take but a minute. We just want to see what you're wearing."

She slipped off her clothes and stood naked, feeling cold and lonely, while they went through her garments one by one, then through the overnight bag in which she had brought dressing gown and toothbrush, and finally through her handbag.

"All right, dear, you can get dressed again," the large woman said. "We'll just find a place to put you for the night."

They went through a number of doors and into the main body of the prison, and it was then that the noise hit her. It sounded like an animal house at the zoo. Some women were shrieking, others were singing or shouting in unison, and amid all this was the frightening sound of sobbing.

The matron walked down the row of cells, peering through the opening in each, until finally she halted. "It'll have to be this one," she said.

She unlocked the door, and at once a tall, bony, red-faced woman burst out. "You've got to take me out of here," she cried. "I won't be in the same cell as this scum. They're Jews—dirty, filthy Yids! I won't have it!"

The matron said mildly, "Now, calm down. We'll see about it in the morning. It's too late to do anything now." And then to Polly, "In you go. Take the top bunk."

Polly looked around the cell. Three girls were sitting huddled close together on the bottom bunk, all of them with stains of dried tears on their faces. The tall woman stood glaring down at them, and then swung around to Polly. "Are you English?" she asked.

"I am."

The woman indicated the three girls. "Not foreign pigs like these Yids here. They can't even speak English." Then, "You aren't Jewish, are you?"

"No."

"And they haven't brought you in here because you're a thief or a tart or something, have they?"

Polly said, "I don't know why they've brought me here. If I've committed any crime, then it's something I don't know about. All they said was I was being held under Regulation 18b."

A wide smile broke over the woman's face. "You must be one of us!" she cried. As if for the first time, she seemed to notice that she was looking at a very pretty girl. She came over and put her arm in comradely fashion around Polly's shoulders. "When did you join the Party, my dear?" she asked.

"What party?" Polly asked. "And take your arm off me, you big lunk!"

It was, she decided wryly, going to be quite a war.

The announcement in the newspaper the next day was a brief one. It read:

> For reasons of national security, a number of British subjects have been taken into custody during recent days. They include Captain A. H. M. Ramsay, M.P., and Sir Oswald and Lady Mosley, together with a number of others whose freedom of movement at this time would not be in the public interest. Certain non-British residents are also being temporarily deprived of their liberty of movement.

Captain Ramsay was a well-known anti-Semite, and Sir Oswald Mosley was leader of the British Union of Fascists, whose members wore blackshirts and marched through the East End of London baiting Jews.

The Lull

Polly Wright was damned if she could see what connection there was between them and her. "My God," she had told the policeman, "all I ever did was sleep with a German. What else do you think I gave him— the score of Handel's *Water Music*?"

Yet here she was in jail, and she hadn't done a thing. On the other hand, neither had the three poor frightened German-Jewish girls who shared her cell. Regulation 18b was nondiscriminatory. It applied to Fascist and non-Fascist alike.*

June was a testing time for the young pilots of 56 Squadron, and Pilot Officer Geoffrey Page found it particularly hard to bear. Every day the red warning blinked on in the operation room at North Weald, and soon afterward they could hear the air-raid sirens wailing in the towns along the Essex shores of the Thames and over the river in Kent. But instead of scrambling for their Hurricanes, they were more often on the ground. They sat in their deck chairs outside the dispersal huts and glumly wondered why they weren't up there in the skies searching for Germans. It was not that Page was itching to get into a fight; he had learned enough from those wearying patrols over Dunkirk to know that being a fighter pilot was not quite the fun it had seemed to be in flying school. But the idea that Jerries were up there flying around almost at will was infuriating and frustrating.

These were the days of respite for England. Hitler was pausing for breath while he digested his conquests, and waiting for the British to make peace. Just in case they didn't, the Luftwaffe, while settling into their new bases in northern France, were sending over an occasional bomber and small flights of fighters to keep the pot simmering. Their bombers would nip across the Channel to drop a few incendiaries on fuel tanks along the Medway River in Kent or on an odd ship on the Thames, and then leg it back to France. The fighters were bolder. They would come in as far west as Chichester, on the south coast, turn east and fly along the Downs up to the Thames, and then make for home. The idea was to tempt the RAF into coming up and intercepting them, thus giving the Germans a clue to their locations, numbers and tactics.

Air Chief Marshal Sir Hugh Dowding, who as Commander in Chief, Fighter Command, controlled the fighter groups facing the

---

* Altogether, 65 percent of the aliens and refugees in Britain were taken into custody under Regulation 18b in 1940. At least three quarters of them were victims of Fascist persecution in Germany, Italy or Spain.

Channel, was too wily to be trapped by such a ploy. He desperately needed the pause to build up his defensive strength in Hurricanes and Spitfires, and in the pilots to fly them, and he had no intention of wasting either of them on "penny packets of Huns." So though the squadron was working grimly on tactics and maneuvers, trying to perfect the hard lessons they had learned over Dunkirk, often when the red warning came on they stayed on the ground while the impudent intruders buzzed enticingly in the clouds above.

But toward the end of June the situation began to change. On June 25, German planes came so far up the Thames that air-raid sirens sounded in London for the first time since the previous September. The raiders turned away before reaching the capital and bombed a Kent airfield instead, but they gave Londoners a scare and convinced Fighter Command that the Germans were about to turn the heat on.

The next day, when the red warning came, 56 Squadron scrambled. Although no raiders were encountered and they returned to base forty minutes later, Page felt different when he strolled over to the mess for a beer. He sensed that his life was entering a new phase.

Indeed it was. And so was the war.

6

The Rehearsal

According to official records, the first air raids on London did not happen until several weeks later and what came to be known as the Blitz did not begin until September, but no one in the capital who heard the sirens sounding the warning in the early hours of June 25, 1940, afterward dismissed it as a false alarm. *
Bombs were dropped on a town in Kent and on an airfield some miles from the capital, and though no one was injured, both the authorities and the public took the raid with deadly seriousness and regarded the night spent under the stairs, out in the garden shelter or in the public shelter down the street as being a dress rehearsal.

One of those who recorded her experiences of the June 25 alert was Mrs. Humphries, a housewife who lived in the East End of London. Mrs. Humphries was one of several hundred volunteers who had elected to send reports of their everyday activities to a remarkable organization called Mass-Observation. These correspondents, who came

---

* The Blitz and the Battle of Britain were two different phases of the war. The Battle of Britain, which was fought in the air over the United Kingdom between the Royal Air Force and the Luftwaffe, began officially on July 10, 1940, and ended on October 31 of the same year (pilots who flew over England after that date, even if they shot down enemy planes, are not considered Battle of Britain pilots and do not "belong to the club"). The Blitz, which was the bombing of London, began officially on September 7, 1940, and ended on May 11, 1941.

from all walks of life, had agreed to set down their own thoughts and activities, to "listen in" on their neighbors and record what they said, how they felt and what they liked and hated. In addition, they were encouraged to criticize governments, officialdom, policies, fashions and trends. From their daily or weekly reports Mass-Observation constructed a remarkably accurate picture of how Britons reacted to given situations, and their observations on how Londoners saw and experienced World War II are a treasure trove.*

Mrs. Humphries reported:

Listened to the midnight news on the B.B.C. but as it went off (prob. due to enemy aircraft) I did not re-tune but came up to bed. Next thing I knew, Harry was shaking me and saying the sirens were going. I heard them but had been log-like for the first few seconds. Harry had heard them in the distance before ours began. Lately I've let the dog sleep on my bed at the foot. I leant over, grabbed his collar from the rail and put that on. Into my stockings. Out of nightie and into my other things. Skirt a bother— the old one has hooks, they get jammed. (Note: Although I hate the look of them, I must get slacks if raids continue—one garment to put on instead of knickers and skirt.) Put on glasses. Turned out my light, got behind curtains and opened the windows wide. Sirens now doing a fine concerto. Searchlights sweeping the sky in almost frenzied urgency. A bloody sort of moon showing through the clouds. A good crack of light showing from a house at the back. Funny how much one can take in at a quick glance. Dog was quite good, he'd gone downstairs without being told. I followed. Got into gumboots, unlocked the back door. Collected two gas masks, the pile of rugs I always prepare by the kitchen door each night. Came back for a torch. Remembered to turn off the gas, then turned off fridge's gas jet, remembered what happened in one of last September's warnings (false alarms) when we nearly gassed ourselves afterwards. Turned off kitchen light and went down to shelter and told Wags to go ahead. He did so and was waiting at the door for me. Sirens still going.

Flew back to house, turned on shelter light, got our axe, unlocked tool shed, got my watch from dining room, got dog's milk from fridge, took down the basket with thermos flask and various tins. Told Harry to bring deed box and stirrup pump. Sirens stopped, searchlights went out. All was still. I was trying to sort things out in the shelter. Harry got very angry with me (sure

---

* See Foreword. To preserve the standards of Mass-Observation and the independence of its observers, the identity of some of them has been concealed by pseudonyms, but their reports are exactly as they wrote them.

sign he was bothered and worried). Told me to shut up and settle down, how could he listen for guns? Retorted I must put things up and give Wags his bromide. My training of the last few months proved good. Several times I had taken Wags to the shelter and given him a drink of milk. Suggested it to him now. Harry said he must go on his shelf first. Put him there for me. Dog thrilled and had a good sniff for rats in holes between the posts. We have a shelf in the roof for the dog. Even smells could not prevail against a drink of milk. Lapped up his bromide and got back to work.

Down in the ground as we were we could feel deep thuds going on. Harry surmised bombs. I didn't know. I asked Harry if he had locked the back door, so he went back to do so and brought me down the bottles of water. Rushing about had given me wind; fearful of a heart attack I asked for some magnesia. Harry couldn't seem to understand where it was in the bookcase cupboard so I went in for it. Found he had left the bedroom light on. Turned that off. Got the front door key, my mags, and put a big rug round the bird cage. Not a sound outside, and dark now, more clouds. Made the shelter tidy. Frank came to the edge of the fence and wanted to know if we were there, they'd been so busy they had not heard us. David's crib would not go through the shelter door, they had to take him out and get the crib in sideways, they'd never thought to do it before.

When I made my first trip to the shelter I heard two police whistles and thought, "Ah, W. and his neighbour." Wondered if A.C. had heard and got up; could imagine him trundling round long after the others. On my 2nd trip I heard B. (next neighbour to the young C's) calling out, "Are you there, Win?" They have no shelter and were apparently going into their neighbours' at the bottom of their garden. While dressing I had worried over the parents all by themselves in a large house; would they hear? Would P. come over and give them a hand? Would it start Father wheezing again? How active one's mind is at a time like this.

In the shelter we had settled down now. Half covered the light, which pointed straight at me and was glary. Harry sat in his corner with the old cape rammed behind his head, I at the end seat with the dog's bed at my back and a woolly door mat to sit on. The plywood back rests seemed too sloping for me; could not get comfy. Gave dog 2nd bromide. It seemed to work; he settled down in a few minutes and was soon snoring. Harry said he was going to sleep. We felt some bigger thumps. Harry crawled into the shelter porch. Came back and growled because my Marks and Spencer watch ticked so loudly he could not hear if the guns were firing.

Frank came over for another chat. Said they couldn't feel the bumps in their shelter. Harry told him we would give them a cup of coffee later; I secretly hoped it would be warm enough. We settled down again and Harry went to sleep. I tried to but was not comfy enough. Thought of all kinds of things. Of course I was not frightened because it was so unreal, and so far we had heard no gunfire. . . . Then I remembered I'd not paid a call before coming out. I wanted to go most badly. Woke Harry and told him so. He said, "Go in; you can dash out if you hear guns." Went indoors and tended to myself. Washed my face too and powdered it. Got my identity card. Collected a rug and a small woolly mat. Looked at the time—2:15. Incredible that we had been out there more than an hour. Crawled into shelter and was greeted by dog, who leant down and licked my head. Made Harry move over and let me remake his seat. Found I'd been so uncomfortable because my seat was reversed and slanting outwards. Harry said he was going to sleep again. Wished he had a sling for his head. Had also brought two hot-water bottles last trip, and hugged those, but my behind was cold, and wind seemed to go up my legs. Made a 2nd decision to get slacks. . . .

I dozed but didn't go right off; heard noises as before. Getting light outside now and wind coming in at intervals was refreshing. Waited for the first bird sounds. Dorothy and Frank made several trips to their house. I was so cold that I woke Harry and asked for a cup of coffee. He very stiff, and also chilly. More cheerful now and thought coffee sounded good. Got it out and it was lukewarm. Drank my coffee and the all clear sounded. Dog woke up and at once wanted to be let down. Harry lifted him down and they had a cuddle on the seat. I gathered up the rugs and deed box and paddled indoors. Threw off clothes and was getting into bed as Harry came up. Dog begged to be allowed again on bed; let him and he very determinedly crept into my arms and put his head on my shoulder, lying with his back to me. We do spoil him since the war.

More sirens went off; dog flew off bed. I calling to Harry that they were beginning again, but Harry said it was another all clear. To make sure, I looked out of window. Frank and Dorothy were also hanging out of theirs. Said they too were just in bed and not sure whether it was a warning or an all clear. Back to bed, 4:15 a.m., lovely morning, and suddenly the bird song began.

Only a few confessed the next day that they had slept through the alarm, and Vere Hodgson chided one of her staff at the Sanctuary who had done so. "A very dangerous thing to do," she wrote in her diary that night, and then added: "But how lovely to be killed asleep."

In Maida Vale, Mrs. Rosemary Black looked back on the disturbance with some satisfaction. A young and attractive widow of twenty-eight whose husband had died two years earlier, she was apt to describe herself in Mass-Observation questionnaires as *Upper-middle-class;*

mother of two children (girls aged 3 and 2); of independent means.
She lived in a trim three-story house in a quiet street of the fashionable part of Maida Vale, a short taxi ride from the center of the West End, whose restaurants and theatres she knew well. She was chic and attractive, and lacked very few of the niceties of life: there was Irene, a Hungarian refugee, to look after the children; Helen, a Scottish maid, to look after herself and the house; and a daily cleaning woman to do the major chores.

During the period of the phony war Mrs. Black had little compunction about enjoying herself, but now that the situation was growing serious she thought it was time she found herself a worthwhile job. The raid, and the reactions of her household to it, renewed her determination, because now she was certain that all of them could cope. "The maids seemed as cool as cucumbers," she reported. "It's a great relief to know that they're not liable to faint or become hysterical. I shall not feel afraid to stay away from home for a night in future. Our drill worked well. . . . But we clean forgot to open the front door in case anyone in the street wanted shelter. Also we forgot to dress, which was silly and wouldn't have done in winter. However, we shall know not to make these mistakes next time."

She was glad London had had such a nice, peaceful try-out, and the next day, while dining at The Ivy, she was surprised to find her companion, Mrs. C., so dismal. Her friend wasn't a jitterer, she thought, but she really was *gloomy*. She had two favorite sayings: "My dear, this looks like the end, doesn't it?" and "Let us eat, drink and be merry, for tomorrow we die." On this occasion Mrs. Black decided why not, and ordered caviar. Afterward she confessed that she felt "somewhat guilty over doing so, but after all, if it's still being imported, that is the Government's funeral. Anyway, if, as I imagine, what we are being offered is part of the prewar stock, it might just as well be eaten up."

At dinner they were later joined by a male friend, and he and Mrs. C. urged her to take the children to America now that the raids were obviously coming. "I told them that nothing would induce me to run away from my own country," she wrote that night. "I believed the upheaval would upset the children more than a few air raids, judging by the trouble I had with them when they were evacuees at the beginning of the war. I am sure, anyway, that this would be so if I did not go with them, which I would never do. It is true that my continued presence in England cannot be considered vital to our war effort; in fact, like all civilians who are not doing war work, I suppose I am a liability—one more creature to be defended and fed. On the other hand, I am spending money and employing labour, and I do feel most strongly that although staying does no positive good it does no positive harm. Everyone who runs away does something to lower the general morale. Everyone who stays can do something, however slight, to raise it."

In any case, she decided, her own self-respect would not permit her to run away.

Jenny Martin remembered the air-raid warning on June 25, for it was the day the doctor at the clinic told her she was pregnant. When the sirens went off that night her first feeling was one of relief; thank God the bombs were coming to kill her off before she had to make up her mind what to do. Her three children were still asleep in the bed against the wall, and her instinct was to leave them there and go out into the street and wander about until a bomb hit her. But her landlady had banged on the door and told her to get the kids down to the shelter.

There was a crowd at the street shelter and a lot of shouting because the door was locked and the warden with the key hadn't turned up. By the time he arrived the kids were wide awake, frightened, and beginning to cry. It took them at least an hour to get to sleep again, and even longer before all the other people on the benches stopped talking. Jenny put her arms around Doris, the youngest, who was snuggling on her lap, and suddenly felt sick again.

The doctor at the clinic had been one of those old jokers, and when he came back with the news he tried to be funny about it. "Well, Mrs. Martin," he said, "that must have been a very enjoyable embarkation leave you had with your husband three months ago, and you can write and tell him so. He's in the Western Desert, isn't he? Well, you just let him know that he's going to be a father for the fourth time. That should cheer him up."

The trouble was, how could you tell your husband you were three months gone when it was ten months since he sailed for Egypt?

What was she going to do? She was no nearer to a solution when the all clear sounded.

The Hardimans spent part of the night in a surface shelter built by the West Ham Council on the edge of the Star Road recreation ground in Canning Town. The room smelled of cats and human excrement, and at about two o'clock two youths who had climbed up on its roof to see the searchlights along the Thames suddenly crashed through onto the people crouched on the benches below.

Ellen, who had been too frightened and cold to doze, awakened George and the children, who were sleeping like logs, and told them what had happened. By this time one of the women was having hysterics and all the babies had begun to cry. They decided to go home, as did several others. Neither said anything as they lay in bed later, but each knew what the other was thinking. If the weight of two boys could collapse the roof of a shelter, what would happen when a bomb dropped near?

Early on the morning of July 4 people living on the southeastern fringes of London heard a buzzing, as if from innumerable bees, in the sky above them. It was the sound of squadron after squadron of Spitfires and Hurricanes taking to the air and flying toward the English Channel. From North Weald, Hornchurch, Biggin Hill, Kenley and other RAF stations on the outskirts of the capital, Air Chief Marshal Dowding's fighter squadrons had been ordered to forward stations to meet the Luftwaffe.

Since the end of June, Field Marshal Hermann Göring, supreme commander of the German air force, had been itching to unleash his planes against the RAF. Bases had been established and headquarters set up: in Scandinavia to hit Scotland and the Royal Navy's bases at Scapa Flow and Rosyth, as well as the great shipyards along the Clyde; in Belgium and Holland to pound Birmingham, Coventry and the heart of the industrial Midlands; and behind Calais and Boulogne along the plains of northern France for the onslaught on London. All these massive attacks, by which Göring planned to smash Britain's great cities into rubble, would follow once his fighters had wiped out the defensive screen of Spitfires and Hurricanes across southern England.

Göring was certain that the destruction of RAF Fighter Command would not take long. He had 1,000 Messerschmitt 109s and 110s ready to take on the British fighters in the sky, and 1,200 bombers and dive bombers to destroy their airfields and lines of communication. Most of them were only twenty-two miles and five minutes' flying time away from the English coast, and the RAF could muster only 675 single-engined fighters with which to fight them.*

---

* These were figures presented to Göring in an official report. They were close enough: the RAF actually had 666 front-line fighters by July 10.

It was obvious from German tactics that the first stages of this phase of the war would be fought over the Channel and the cliffs of Dover. To demonstrate his command of both air and sea, General Johannes Fink, the Luftwaffe commander in the Pas de Calais area, had ordered his forces to close the English Channel to British shipping. Any convoys attempting to move past Dover into the Thames Estuary were to be sunk. Though hampered by bad weather, from the beginning of July his bombers attacked any ship heading for the Thames. The raiders—level-flying Heinkels, Dorniers and Junkers, and dive-bombing Stukas—were covered by weaving, watchful banks of Messerschmitt 109s and 110s.

Fink knew this was a sure way to force the RAF's hand to fight, for if his plan succeeded the Thames would be closed, the great port of London strangled, and its population blockaded. It was a battle the RAF could not allow him to win. So every day from July 4 on, planes from each fighter station flew to a forward airfield close to the Channel so that they could scramble in time to meet the raiders the moment radar stations along the coast showed them taking off in France.

The gladiatorial contest that came to be known as the Battle of Britain was about to begin.

56 Squadron had got their orders on the night of July 3, when their flight commander, "Jumbo" Gracie, came into the mess and announced, "At three A.M. tomorrow we're off to Manston to do forward readiness. There's a big convoy coming through the Straits of Dover, and Command reckon Jerry will have a crack at it."

Geoffrey Page asked, "Are we coming back here afterwards?"

"Don't know," Gracie said. "Anything may happen." He added, "Our orders are to maintain strict radiotelephone silence on our way to Manston. Anyone disobeying that order needn't bother about their future in the air force, because they won't have one."

At dawn the next day, Page and five other pilots from B Flight stamped up and down beside their Hurricanes, trying to shake the sleep out of their bodies and warmth into their bones. Four hundred yards across the field A Flight was being refueled from the gray tanks. The *thump-thump-thump* of the delivery pump came clearly through the crisp morning air. The breaking day promised to be clear to start with, but low woolly clouds were beginning to form a few miles away, where sea and land met at the Channel. Suddenly the crack of a Very pistol, followed by the soaring flight of two fiery red balls of light, sent them running for their planes, as the orderly shouted! "Scramble, B Flight! Angels ten."*

Each took the quick nervous pee that relieves every fighter pilot's tension, and then they were in their cockpits and away. Even as they were gaining height, Page could hear the suppressed excitement in the ground controller's voice as he called out to them, "Ninety bandits approaching from Calais, Yorker Blue Leader. Twenty-plus at Angels six, remainder Angels twelve. Over . . ."

The sections lined up in attacking formation behind their leaders, and Geoffrey Page remembers thinking, Six of us against ninety are hardly fair odds.

Then out of the corner of his eye he saw them: twenty Heinkel 111 bombers, which the other section were diving to intercept, and above them the Messerschmitt escort his flight was to engage. There was no mistaking the ugly outlines of some thirty Me 110 twin-engined fighters, and higher still another formation of about forty rakish Me 109s. Page's mouth was very dry.

By this time three of the Hurricanes of B Flight had managed to climb above the Me 110s, but they were still below the single-seater 109s. Jumbo Gracie dived into the attack, and the others followed.

"As my machine gathered speed, I noticed a strange thing," Page recalled later. "The 110s were forming up into a defensive circle to protect themselves from the oncoming attack from our three planes. Being uncertain as to the best way to assail this orbiting group, I decided to spray the area near two of the enemy before diving through the center of the circle. The eight Browning machine guns chattered away happily in the wings when I pressed the firing button, and for a moment I was having the time of my life."

The enjoyment ceased the moment the enemy rear gunners opened up on him. "Fascinated for a second by the appearance of orange-glowing electric light bulbs suspended in the air, I suddenly ducked my head at the frightening realization that the pretty little balls of fire were hundreds of rounds of deadly cannon fire aimed at Geoffrey Page personally."

After that it was a nightmare. Streaking down out of the sun, the forty Me 109s came in to finish off the impertinent British fighters, and all Page remembers of the next few minutes was flashing wings painted with Iron Crosses, and streaks of tracer tearing across the sky. He was

---

* Angels ten = 10,000 feet, the height at which the "angels" should fly.

damn-and-blasting himself every time he fired because he always seemed to press the button just a little too late and never saw his bullets strike home. Once a lone 109 came zooming down on him, and as the distance between them closed he could see lights winking in the 109's wings and realized he was being fired at. He pressed his own button, again too late, and the planes roared past within inches of each other.

"Suddenly I was alone over the Channel," said Page. "The only other human being in sight was swinging down towards the water at the end of a parachute."

He circled him, radioed his position to the launches, and then turned for home.

A fellow pilot, Barry Sutton, was waiting for him on the ground. "How'd you get on? Did you get any?" he asked.

Page shook his head savagely. "I fired at a hell of a lot, but never saw a single one strike."

Barry patted him in a fatherly manner. "Better luck next time. We got five for the loss of one machine—and he's safe." He added, "What's more, the convoy got through."

Suddenly Page remembered that he hadn't seen the convoy at all.

General Johannes Fink had seen it, however. He had watched the battle from start to finish through his binoculars, from the steps of his trailer atop the cliffs at Cap Gris-Nez.

He was not disappointed, even though planes had been lost and the convoy had reached port. That was simply bad flying and bad bombing, which could be rectified. Much more important was that the RAF had been tempted up into the skies and forced to fight.

The battle was on.

From July 10 onward the Battle of Britain raged in the skies above Kent, Essex and the English Channel. Correspondents from all over the world lay in the sunshine on Shakespeare Cliffs above Dover harbor, and watched the fate of the Empire being settled among the white contrails in the blue sky overhead. A handful of young pilots, out on the hunt from dawn to dusk, was engaged in a battle which would open Britain to invasion and her cities to destruction if they lost.

For Londoners it was a battle they could not see. Dover was only fifty miles away, but since the fall of France all travel to the south coast had been forbidden to anyone except residents and permit holders. Each day, however, the newspapers covered the clash in the sky with all the verve they usually reserved for a test match or a world soccer cup final.

The headlines across the front pages carried figures which changed with each edition, like cricket scores. IT'S 65 FOR 12 a typical one would read, informing readers that sixty-five German planes had been knocked down for the loss of twelve British.

On July 14 the Battle of Britain came into Londoners' own living rooms through the loudspeakers of the BBC. A radio correspondent, Charles Gardner, was on Shakespeare Cliff reading from a prepared script when out of the clouds in front of him enemy dive bombers suddenly appeared. They were after a long convoy of ships and their escorting destroyers. But as the Stukas screamed down toward the ships, in came Spitfires and Hurricanes and the battle was on. Gardner took a deep breath, wondered what his stern boss, Lord Reith, would say, threw away his script, and in a moment he was describing the battle in a torrent of breathless prose: "Now the British fighters are coming up . . . you can hear our own guns going like anything now . . . There's one going into the ditch . . . They're being chased home now, and *how* they're being chased home! There are three Spits chasing three Messerschmitts now—and, oh boy, look at him going and look how the Messerschmitt is . . . Oh, oh, that's really grand! And there's a Spit just behind the first two—he'll get them, he'll get them . . . Oh yes, yes, yes. Oh boy!" It all sounded like an exciting game.

"Jolly good!" commented Vere Hodgson in her diary. That night she tuned in to listen to a radio speech by Winston Churchill, and once again she felt inspired. "He sounded as if he had got over the shocks France had given him and was in command of the situation again," she wrote.

It was Churchill, in fact, who had shocked the French. Ten days earlier he had ordered the seizure of all French naval units in British ports, and since by no means all French sailors had rallied to General de Gaulle, some of them did not surrender their ships willingly. There had been scuffles and even one or two shots exchanged. At the same time the Royal Navy's Mediterranean fleet stood off Mers-el-Kébir, the chief French naval base in Algeria, and shelled the French fleet sheltering there, as a result of which several ships were sunk or immobilized and seven hundred French sailors killed. This had to be done, Churchill explained, to make sure the French navy was neither seized by the Nazis nor handed over to them by the Pétain government. It was a bitter blow to all Frenchmen, even the Free French now ranged alongside De Gaulle, for most maintained that the French ships would have scuttled themselves rather than surrender to the Germans. But the Prime Minister had decided to take no chances.

Vere Hodgson was not the only one who agreed with him. "It seems we have seized the French Navy," she wrote. "What a world we live in. I feel that if we come out of this I will never leave England ever again. I have finished with foreigners." And her heart filled with a splendid sense of English pride as she listened to Churchill saying, "This is no war of chieftains or of princes, of dynasties or national ambition; it is a war of peoples and of causes. There are vast numbers not only in this island but in every land who will render faithful service in this war, but whose names will never be known, whose deeds will never be recorded."

Vere Hodgson approved of that. Looking out of her window at the barrage balloons floating in the sky over Notting Hill Gate, she felt resolute. Britain had suffered some blows that week. First there had been the rationing of tea, then the announcement that henceforth the allotment of butter and fats would be only six ounces a week.

Also, there was a shortage of eggs. "That's bad, as I rely upon them. I shall have to switch over to baked beans." Then, buoyed up again by Churchill's words, she wrote: "No invasion yet. I recall the man who said that every Britisher should put up a Union Jack on his chimney pot when the Germans arrived and it should not be hauled down until a Nazi had crawled up and hauled it down over the dead bodies of the household."

Those were her sentiments too.

Robert Boothby had been to Brixton Prison and was appalled by what he saw there. The drab old jail in the even drabber inner-London suburb was crammed with all sorts, sizes and shapes of men who had one thing in common: they were being held without any charge having been made against them. Perhaps twenty, all of them British subjects, knew why they were being detained. There were Sir Oswald Mosley and his followers in the British Union of Fascists; they had publicly proclaimed themselves against the war, which they blamed squarely on the Jews, and they did not conceal their admiration for German National Socialism and Italian Fascism. There were other wild anti-Semites and some even wilder pro-Nazis, most of them retired army and navy officers, who had been put out of harm's way for the duration.

However, the remainder of the prison population consisted either of naturalized subjects or of German, Czech and Italian refugees who hated Britain's enemies even more strongly than the British, and they were in despair.*

Boothby was shocked at the sight of his friend Weininger, for he was a completely broken man. He had been kept in solitary confinement, and he looked at Boothby without hope. "He sits there day and night racking his brains to discover what it is all about," Boothby wrote to Clement Attlee later, "with no allegations made and nothing to answer. One of his stepdaughters, a most charming and intelligent girl whom I have known for years, and who has been working like a slave at a communal kitchen, has similarly been carted off to Holloway [Prison]; the other, who served with the Czech forces in France and subsequently escaped to Portugal, is refused permission to enter this country."

Weininger kept asking, "How can these things be?" and Boothby was asking the question himself. It was something he felt he must fight, and not just for Weininger's sake; all over Britain people were kept in jail without charge and without trial, simply because they had German names, foreign accents, their parents had been foreigners or because they had once been in close proximity to the enemy. It was a battle after his own heart, and his friends encouraged him to go to it. "For God's sake, fight this thing," said a government official, Sir David Waley. "Weininger's case is only one of many. I know of several myself. But we are helpless." And Waley, a high civil servant at the Treasury, was not without influence.

Boothby knew full well that if he espoused this cause, he would be venturing on dangerous ground. It was the Home Office which had ordered the detention of these foreigners, and as rumors spread of the hardships which Regulation 18b was responsible for, there was rising indignation among thoughtful Britons. It was not pleasant to discover that in fighting for freedom against tyranny, Britain herself had resorted to tyrannical methods. "What have they done to our Magna Carta?" asked a speaker at Hyde Park Corner. "Torn it to bloody pieces!"

In the face of such criticism, the Home Office was on the defensive,

---

* The bulk of the internees being held in Britain under Regulation 18b had by now been shipped to the Isle of Man, in the Irish Sea, where they were living in holiday camps and lodgings. Hard-core Nazis and Italian Fascists, and a number of anti-Fascists too, had been sent to camps in Canada. Those shipped aboard the vessel *Arandora Star*, most of them Italian, were, ironically enough, drowned when an enemy submarine torpedoed the ship.

and among its officials none was more sensitive than the Home Secretary himself, Sir John Anderson. A kind-hearted and highly civilized man, he was well aware of the dangers implicit in the blind application of Regulation 18b; it went against all the principles of freedom and justice for which Britain stood. Nevertheless, he was steadfast in his contention that the roundup was necessary for the sake of national security as long as invasion threatened. He genuinely thought it preferable that thirty thousand people should have their lives, families and beliefs shattered than that a single potential spy or saboteur remain free, and he blazed with anger when it was suggested to him that this was not the way to trap spies—who could easily disguise themselves*—and that the blanket application of Regulation 18b was cruel, expensive, time-wasting and the product of panic. Further, Anderson refused to believe that there was any real hardship in the wholesale jailing, and he sturdily maintained that any case of genuine suffering would receive his immediate personal attention.

To some extent, this was true; in fact, it was through Anderson's intervention that C. P. Snow had secured the freedom of his refugee scientists. It was Snow, too, who had given the Home Secretary a further opportunity to demonstrate his liberalism by introducing him to the scientist J. D. Bernal, who had been working on several ideas for the protection of civilians during air raids that might prove invaluable to the Home Office, which also was responsible for Air Raid Precautions. Bernal was a Communist, a real party-line-toeing member, and since during this period Russia was still linked to Germany in the non-aggression pact, he refused to turn his brilliant talents toward helping Britain win the war. But he was not averse to helping to protect civilians, and so Anderson talked to him, was enthusiastic about his ideas and took him into his department.

"But how can you do that?" his colleagues asked him. "Bernal is a rabid Red."

"I don't care if he is as red as the fires of hell; he will go on working for me as long as I find him useful," the Home Secretary replied. This was cited as an example of his broad-mindedness and as proof that there was no vindictiveness or xenophobia in his application of Regulation 18b.

But the fact remained that thirty thousand foreigners, the bulk of

---

* The most successful of them, for instance, was Kim Philby, who worked for Passport Control (MI6), possessed an official pass and free access to the Home Office and several other government departments.

them anti-Nazis, vegetated in jails and camps throughout Britain, and Richard Weininger was one of them. The Home Office was adamant about his case, and nothing that Boothby said or did would move them to let him out of jail; on the contrary, it appeared to invoke at the Home Office an anger all but amounting to vindictiveness—and the vindictiveness was directed against Boothby.

"Why did they react this way?" said Boothby later. "I really don't know, except that they were suffering from a guilty conscience over the refugees and didn't like my campaign."

As mentioned earlier, Weininger had once loaned Boothby money. Also, shortly after the German occupation of Czechoslovakia, Boothby had gone to Prague to get the Germans to release the small fortune which Weininger had left behind when he fled, but they refused to let it go. Subsequently Boothby spoke in a debate in the House of Commons about the assets of the Czech government and Czech civilians which were being held by the Nazis, and he attacked the government (then still eager, under Chamberlain, to appease Adolf Hitler) for not insisting on the release of these funds to their rightful owners. It did not occur to him, since he believed in the principle of what he was saying, that he should have declared a "personal interest" in the subject, in case someone finding out about the loan from Weininger and his trip to Prague would add up the innocent facts and call the total "corruption."

He knew the letters concerning all their dealings were in Weininger's files, but that did not bother him. "It would have, had I known that the Home Office was gunning for me," he said later.

The trouble began shortly after Scotland Yard had removed Weininger's correspondence files from his office, at which time Boothby had just written letters to Winston Churchill and Sir John Anderson protesting Weininger's imprisonment in the strongest possible terms. The letter to Churchill he had handed to Brendan Bracken, the Prime Minister's parliamentary private secretary. He hoped it would get immediate action. He expected as much from Churchill, who was an old friend.

Within a few hours Osbert Peake, Undersecretary of State at the Home Office, called him. "Bob. This is Osbert—Osbert Peake." The voice was smooth and friendly. "The Home Secretary asked me to call you. You mention in your letter to him that you are also writing to Winston about the Weininger case. Dear boy, do you mind if I make a suggestion?"

"Any suggestion you like," said Boothby, "so long as it helps to get Dick Weininger out of jail."

"Well, it won't do that exactly." Peake's voice became a little more crisp. "But it might help you." He paused and then went on, "The Home Secretary asks you not, I repeat *not,* to send your letter on to Winston for the time being. Hold it, dear boy."

"Why on earth should I?"

"I can't go into details on the phone," said Peake. "Shall we just say that we have been through Weininger's papers and that we have found some interesting—some very interesting—letters. They concern you, dear boy. Please, *please* don't send your letter to Winston—not, at least, until you have had a chance to look at the letters and talked to the Home Secretary. He would like to see you. Meantime, you will hold the letter?"

Boothby said, "I'll see what I can do."

He called Bracken, but found that it was too late. Boothby shrugged his shoulders. What did it matter, anyway?

But it did, for Winston Churchill had taken action as soon as he read Boothby's letter. A sharp message went to Sir John Anderson. What was all this about imprisoning Weininger? Boothby said he was a completely innocent man, and he should be released at once.

"I'm damned if I will," muttered Anderson when he read the PM's note. That afternoon certain letters from Weininger's file were sent to 10 Downing Street for Churchill's perusal. With them went a note from the Home Secretary insinuating that Boothby was not exactly unbiased in the Weininger case, because of their business dealings. Worse still, he had entered the debate on Czech financial affairs without revealing that his friend Weininger was closely connected with the matter.*

It was a moment when Winston Churchill was preoccupied with the battles to come, in no mood and with no time to consider other matters, and his anger turned against Boothby for involving him. How dare he deceive him? It was insufferable that he should waste his premier's time over his personal affairs at a moment of such national crisis. In an instant, instead of being Boothby's friend and sponsor, he became an angry and aggrieved antagonist. No pleas could persuade Churchill that this was a trivial offense—or, in fact, no offense at all.

Soon Boothby was summoned to see the Prime Minister and looked forward to this opportunity to explain. But there was no discussion;

---

* It is considered a breach of privilege (and a grave offense) if an MP fails to declare an interest in a House of Commons debate which ends in a vote. In this particular debate there was no vote, and he was not required to declare an interest.

Churchill simply told him that he had decided to refer his case to a Select Committee of the House of Commons.

The men who formed the Select Committee could hardly be described as Boothby's friends. "We were fighting a bitter war with Germany," he said later, "but the MPs in the House of Commons were still the same shoddy lot who had cheered Chamberlain and screamed insults at us because we had been against appeasement."

In due course the Select Committee found that Robert Boothby, MP, had indeed committed a breach of privilege (though it is now generally accepted that he had not), and in parliamentary eyes, he was disgraced. He resigned his post with the Ministry of Food, and since his future prospects for a political career were now nil, he discreetly absented himself from Parliament and joined the RAF. He was not to make his mark in Parliament again until 1942, when he returned to make a remarkable fighting speech. Ironically enough, it was in defense of Winston Churchill, and it helped save the Prime Minister from defeat at the worst moment of his wartime career.

In the meantime, like many another refugee, Richard Weininger stayed in jail.

Neither his French nor his English friends in London could understand Robert Mengin. He insisted that he wanted to fight for France and that he hated the Vichy regime, but when they assumed that he was supporting De Gaulle, he denied it heatedly. Then how could he be on their side, his French friends asked. If he wasn't with them, he was against them.

"It isn't quite like that," Mengin would begin, and then attempt to explain his feelings. It was no good; no one could comprehend that he was pro–Free French but not pro–De Gaulle. How could he persuade them that in his opinion the general, though indubitably a patriotic Frenchman, was also a man of overweening ambition playing a dangerous game of which Mengin was determined to have no part?

All over London in the summer of 1940 there were posters reading:

A TOUS LES FRANÇAIS
LA FRANCE A PERDU UNE BATAILLE!
MAIS LA FRANCE N'A PAS PERDU LA GUERRE!*

---

* To all French men and women:
France has lost a battle!
But France has not lost the war!

The message went on to ask Frenchmen to rally to General de Gaulle and enlist in the Free French forces.

A recruiting center had been set up at Olympia, the great indoor arena in Hammersmith, one of London's inner suburbs, and it was here that Robert Mengin came one afternoon that summer to sign up. He had been working at Free French headquarters in Carlton Gardens for some weeks now, helping a colonel who was a friend and a passionate Gaullist, and it was he who had suggested that the time had come for Mengin to get his position "regularized." "It is about time you started wearing the Cross of Lorraine on your uniform, *mon ami*," the colonel had said. "People are beginning to stare at you."

By "people" the colonel probably meant De Gaulle himself. The general had passed Mengin in one of the corridors a few days before and had returned Mengin's salute by looking pointedly at the bare blue breast of his naval uniform. It must have been the only one which did not flaunt the insignia of the Free French forces.

Mengin was quite willing to join, and said so. "Then get on with it," said his friend curtly.

Olympia had been loaned to De Gaulle as his main military supply depot, and as a Free French barracks and recruiting center. At the gates, where sentries stood guard in front of groups of admiring London urchins, Mengin explained his mission and was directed first to the medical department, and then, after a thorough examination, to a naval recruiting lieutenant seated behind a table.

The officer looked at Mengin scornfully when he revealed that he had been in England for some time. "*Eh bien*," he said, "nobody could say you came here all out of breath to rush to answer the general's appeal! But now that you have finally made it, sign this," and he pushed the Act of Engagement across the table.

Mengin read the document through. With growing concern, he noted that General de Gaulle was cited as chief of the Free French forces, and that anyone signing the document undertook to serve with honor, fidelity and discipline for the duration of the war and three months after it. Thus, he would be swearing to obey the orders of General de Gaulle himself, in peace as well as in war. "I'm not signing," he said finally.

The lieutenant looked at him in astonishment. "But why not?" he asked.

"This is an oath of allegiance to General de Gaulle personally," Mengin said. "I can't sign it."

The lieutenant's face went white with rage. "Then what the hell do you think you're doing here?" he shouted. He pointed to the door. "Get out!"

Mengin leaned over, caught the lieutenant's gesticulating hand and held it tight. "You might try to learn some manners, *mon gros*," he said, and shook the man hard. Then he walked out of the room.

But he was in trouble, and he knew it. As he walked back across London he envied once more the British all around him, who were in no doubt where their allegiances lay. What was going to happen to him when he returned to Carlton Gardens?

Nothing much at first, as it turned out; they were very understanding. Successions of friends and officers were sent to argue with him, but all the discussions ended at the same point: he must sign on the dotted line.

Finally the celebrated jurist Professor Rene Cassin,* who was one of General de Gaulle's most trusted advisers, consented to speak to the recalcitrant young man. Mengin expected to be intimidated by him, but the professor was so amiable and understanding that he plucked up courage enough to ask, "Do you approve of the wording of this enlistment oath, monsieur? Was it you who drafted it?"

Cassin looked hard at him and said, "Look, young man, when your house is on fire, do you look to see whether the firemen are using filtered water to put out the blaze? We found ourselves in a position of some urgency, and we did the best we could. You mustn't attach too much importance to unimportant things."

"Good," said Mengin. "Then I will not sign the paper, since you tell me it is not important."

There was a long silence, and then Cassin said, "The night brings counsel. Go and think things over calmly. You are young. You have let your feelings run away with you. Come back and see me tomorrow. We will work it all out, and you, my boy, will remain in our ranks."

The next day Mengin came to see him. He had thought things out. "I will sign," he told the professor, "if above my signature I can write in the formula employed in the French navy—namely, that I will undertake to obey any order given to me by General de Gaulle 'for the good of the service and the success of the arms of France.' That is restrictive, for if in good conscience a man considers that an order is not 'for the good of the service and the success of the arms of France,' he can most certainly be put in irons, but not for breaking his oath. He can be shot, but not as—"

---

* Professor Cassin was awarded the Nobel Peace Prize in 1968.

He was not allowed to finish; Professor Cassin's demeanor toward him had changed overnight. Icily he said, "You are to sign exactly the same oath as the others. If you add or subtract a single word you must leave us."

Mengin picked up his naval cap and walked out of the room. Yes, he was really in trouble. What would De Gaulle do to him—and to others who did not accept him as the omnipotent arbiter of France's destiny?*

---

* There were other Frenchmen in London at the time who shared Mengin's doubts about General de Gaulle, and at least two of them were his superiors in rank and experience. The French ambassador, Charles Corbin, and his minister and counselor, Roger Cambon, both broke with the Vichy regime and refused to accept France's defeat. But they preferred to wreck their careers rather than join De Gaulle. Roger Cambon kept in close touch with the British government and also worked for the BBC. He made his home in London after the war and gave the author much information and advice on the French sections of this story. He died in London in 1970. For the full story of what happened to Robert Mengin, his *De Gaulle à Londres* (English version: *No Laurels for De Gaulle*) is strongly recommended.

7

The Fatal Error

The battle over the English Channel was growing more intense. On July 11, on his way home from a convoy patrol and too low in fuel to be of any help, Geoffrey Page saw a Spitfire and an Me 109 careering toward each other overhead, their guns blazing. Bullets were thudding into each of them, and through his earphones he could hear a voice he recognized as that of Al Deere, the New Zealander from 54 Squadron, shouting, "Pull out, you bugger!"

Then they sliced into each other in what was just short of a head-on collision. The Me 109 turned over like a cartwheel and went spinning away. The Spitfire gave a sickening lurch and then went into a slow dive toward the shore. As he flew closer, Page could see that the props had stopped; they had been bent back by the collision. Inside the cockpit Al Deere was fighting and clawing at the plastic cover, trying to get out. Forward of him the engines were afire.

By the time Geoffrey Page landed, word had spread through Manston that Al Deere had "bought it." Although these were the early days of the Battle of Britain, already most pilots had lost a comrade. The survivors were learning to take the death of their friends with no outward show of feelings, but the thought that the cheerful, brave New Zealander was gone plunged the station in gloom. Then, when news came that he had made a successful landing in a cornfield and coaxed half a bottle of whisky out of the farmer's wife, joy was unconfined.

Deere's health was liberally drunk in the messes at North Weald, Kenley, Rochford, Biggin Hill and Debden that night.

On July 14 Page shot down a Stuka* and was officially credited with his first kill. That night he went up to London, and in the Berkeley Hotel a beautiful Wren officer made it plain that she was available. Remembering his previous encounter with that branch of the service, he briefly considered snubbing her. But why look a gift horse in the mouth —especially such a beautiful gift horse?

The RAF, he subsequently discovered, was now very popular with the Royal Navy, and by the way ATS officers behaved toward him, the army had changed its mind about the RAF, too.

". . . This is a war of the unknown warriors; but let all strive without failing in faith or in duty, and the dark curse of Hitler will be lifted from our age."

The rotund phrases rolled out and finally stopped. "You have just been listening to the Prime Minister," said the BBC announcer. Winston Churchill reached for his whisky-and-soda and cigar, leaned back in his chair, blew out a cloud of smoke, and said, "Well, now." He reached across his desk and pressed one of the three buttons, marked SECRETARY. When she entered, Colonel Leslie Hollis was with her. When he congratulated the Prime Minister on his speech he got a grunt in return. "Get me the President," said Churchill.

Hollis and the secretary exchanged glances; each knew what the other was thinking. This was the trickiest diplomatic task they faced, and they knew that for the next half-hour they would be playing the protocol game. Neither President Roosevelt nor Churchill liked to be kept waiting, and this meant that each wanted the other to be on the line when he picked up the receiver.

It was from the Hole in the Ground, the vast honeycomb of tunnels beneath Whitehall, that Churchill made his wartime broadcasts. He spoke in a room marked simply PRIME MINISTER, at a wide desk on which were candles and matches in case the electricity failed while he was speaking.

Just down the corridor was another, smaller room which looked like a bathroom; in fact, it had a bathroom-door catch fixed to it with a slot marked VACANT or ENGAGED. It was in here that the telephone with a direct connection to the White House in Washington had been

---

* He already had a "share" in an Me 109.

installed, and Winston Churchill had been using it often in the past few days. With Ambassador Joseph P. Kennedy forecasting in every dispatch that Britain was all but defeated and that her only hope was to sue for peace, Churchill had some earnest talking to do in order to convince Roosevelt that all was not yet lost.*

The calls were made without a warning to anyone. "Churchill would suddenly decide to speak to the President, regardless of what hour it might be in Washington," Hollis recalls. "In his slippers with pompoms, wearing his magnificent mandarin dressing gown embroidered with red and gold dragons, the belt pulled tightly around him, his cigar clamped like some miniature torpedo between his teeth, he would stump along the corridor towards the telephone. Even in the unhealthy light from the electric bulbs that lit the corridor, his complexion seemed cherubic and as pink as if he had just come from eight hours' sleep . . ."

But Roosevelt was determined not to pick up the telephone until he was sure that Churchill was on at the other end, and the Prime Minister, knowing that someone would have to push the President in his wheelchair from wherever he was in the White House, and having no wish to wait in the cramped telephone room while this occurred, was equally adamant. So it became a game of transatlantic oneupmanship to get both parties moving toward the instrument at the same time, the goal—rarely achieved—being a simultaneous lifting of receivers at either end. "The President is just coming, sir," his aide would say. "He is picking up the telephone at this very moment," while Colonel Hollis would be swearing that Churchill was just stubbing out his cigar and reaching for the phone.

On the night of July 14 it was Churchill who had to wait, and the delay infuriated him. Hollis had slipped out of the room once the White House was on the phone, pushing over the catch from VACANT to ENGAGED, and then stood in the corridor. As soon as he saw the blue cigar smoke beginning to curl under the door, he knew that Roosevelt was keeping the Prime Minister waiting. He could guess why. What did Churchill have to tell him that he did not already know from the newspapers? That the RAF had had another triumphant day battling with the Luftwaffe over the Channel? Roosevelt had heard it over his own radio. That the British would fight on, whatever happened, even if London lay in ashes? But that also he knew, because he had read an advance copy of the just-completed broadcast.

---

* Through various channels, Churchill was well aware of the pessimistic nature of Kennedy's reports.

What FDR needed to know was whether Adolf Hitler had decided to invade the British Isles, and if so when. Would the German air fleets dare make war against London's civilian population? Only one or the other of those two events would rouse the American people out of their determined isolation. But at this moment Churchill could not answer those questions, and Roosevelt knew it, so he did not hurry to the telephone.

At the moment Adolf Hitler could not answer those questions himself, for he could not make up his mind. For weeks every neutral capital in Europe had been alive with rumors that the British would like to come to an arrangement with Germany; both the King of Sweden and the Vatican had even offered to act as intermediaries. There had been mysterious talks in Madrid, and since the recently appointed ambassador there, Sir Samuel Hoare, had once been Chamberlain's most fervent supporter, it seemed logical to conclude that he might have been sent to his post by Churchill to made a deal with the Germans.

But the sinking of the French navy at Mers-el-Kébir by the British fleet had jolted Hitler's optimistic view that the British would sue for peace. In another regard, however, he was pleased that a large part of the French fleet had been immobilized, because he had been afraid that it would go over to the British and all but double her strength at sea. In Munich on June 18 he had said, "With regard to the French fleet . . . the best thing would be to have the French sink it. The worst thing would be to have the fleet unite with the British, because in view of the large number of light French ships, the united British-French fleets could organize extensive convoys."

The British had at least relieved him of the latter possibility, but in breaking their last ties with Vichy France, they had also demonstrated their determination to carry on the war. This meant that all the sly talks in neutral capitals, all the oblique indications that they were ready to parley, had not been meant seriously, but were only a ploy to gain time.

On July 16 the Führer sent for General Wilhelm Keitel, chief of the Supreme Command of the Armed Forces, and handed him Directive No. 16, with orders that he circulate it among the military chiefs. "Since, despite its desperate military situation, Great Britain shows no sign of good will," the directive began, "I have decided that a plan of invasion will be prepared, and, if necessary, carried out."

The Fatal Error

But the emphasis was on the words "if necessary," and Field Marshal Göring simultaneously reminded the commanders of his three air fleets that his previous order still prevailed: under no circumstances was London to be bombed without written permission from him and the Führer.

First it was necessary to destroy the Royal Air Force.

On July 19, speaking to his party members in the Reichstag in Berlin, Adolf Hitler made what he called his "final appeal" to the British people to start negotiations for peace:

"At this hour I feel it is my duty to appeal, in good faith, for reason and wise counsel on the part of Great Britain, as of all other countries. I consider that my position allows me to make this appeal, since I do not speak as a defeated man begging favors but as the victor speaking in the name of reason. I really see no reason why this war should continue."

The only obstacle standing in the way of peace, he charged, was a drunken, cigar-smoking boor named Winston Churchill. The megalomaniac Churchill and the ignorant fools who surrounded him were duping the British people and concealing from them the terrors which might soon be raining down upon their heads.

"Mr. Churchill ought for once [he cried at one point] to believe me when I say that a great empire will be destroyed, an empire which it was never my intention to destroy or harm. It gives me pain when I realize that I am the man who has been picked by destiny to deliver the final blow to the edifice that these men have already shaken . . ."

Full reports of this speech were printed in the British papers; extracts in the original German, together with translations, were even rebroadcast over the BBC. Thus, the British people were fully aware of what Hitler had offered and threatened. The Führer did not seem to know this, however, for a few nights later German bombers ranged over Britain scattering leaflets containing the speech in full. "Now you can read the truth your government is trying to conceal from you," the leaflets said.

Winston Churchill pondered whether to issue a reply to Hitler's threats, and then decided against it. Why tell the Germans anything? Let them stew in ignorance. Britain still needed time—time to bring coastal defenses to readiness in preparation for the invasion; time to get tanks, guns, transport and rifles to the army to replace those they had lost at Dunkirk; time to build planes and train pilots to back up the squadrons fighting the battle along the south coast. The longer the Germans were left in doubt the better; every day counted.

One man who knew how much each day counted was Air Chief Marshal Sir Hugh Caswell Tremenheere Dowding, commander in chief of Fighter Command and the mastermind in charge of the Battle of Britain. At his headquarters at Bentley Priory, Stanmore, on the northern outskirts of London, Dowding kept a marked diary on his desk. Each twenty-four hours ticked off meant that four new aircraft had been built and delivered to the RAF. No one knew better than he how urgently they were needed.

Dowding was a strange, remote character to be guiding the destinies of the ebullient young men fighting the Battle of Britain. An introvert, a vegetarian, a spiritualist and a teetotaler, he often gave the impression that he did not like people. Stanmore was at the end of a branch of the Underground leading into the center of London, yet Dowding never went anywhere near it unless ordered to a conference or Cabinet meeting. Nor did he consort much with his fellow brass hats in the RAF, and behind his back they had nicknamed him "Stuffy." Yet his young pilots knew that he loved them all, and most of them worshiped him in return.

As the battles raged over the Channel and the Kent coast that July, Dowding fretted over his charges' ordeals. If London's citizens still slept peacefully in their beds, undisturbed by any more air raids, and if the invasion was still held at bay, the credit was due to his young men. But they were losing their planes and their lives, and they were outnumbered and exhausted. What would happen when Göring committed his full resources against them?

On August 6 Göring summoned his fleet commanders to a meeting in Berlin and told them that the invasion of Britain was definitely scheduled; it would be launched in the second week of September. But first the Luftwaffe must blast the way open for the invaders by annihilating Dowding's fighter defenses once and for all.

Despite the fierceness of the battles raging over the Channel, the Reich Marshal did not seem to think that the task would be too difficult. "I expect to see them destroyed in fantastic numbers," he said. "Our Messerschmitts are much superior to the English Hurricanes, and with skillful pilots—and our pilots are the greatest the world has ever known—they can outfly the Spitfires. There will be casualties, but that is what our boys are flying for—to fight and die. And in the end, our numbers will tell."

Simultaneous to the strike against the RAF, there would be saturation bombing of the string of radar stations which had been built along England's south coast to warn of the approach of Nazi planes and ships. In concert with these operations, there was also to be a series of heavy attacks upon the RAF's airfields, so that those British fighters which survived the battles in the sky would have no place to land.

Göring gave the name *Adlertag* (Eagle Day) to the attack. He ordered it to begin on August 10,* and he instructed his commanders to ground the planes for a few days before and let their pilots and crews relax in preparation for the onslaught. So while Luftwaffe pilots went off to Deauville and Le Touquet to enjoy good company, good food and good wine, a lull fell over the Channel and southern England.

Dowding sensed that it was the lull before the storm. On August 8 he issued an order of the day to the RAF:

> The Battle of Britain is about to begin.†
> Members of the RAF: The fate of generations lies in your hands.

On August 13 the Luftwaffe swarmed across the Channel toward England in force. To begin with, their targets were radar stations and airfields.

One of the things they had always emphasized in flying training was to keep your gloves and goggles on to protect you in case of fire.

That was all very well, but Geoffrey Page had found that in the battles over the Channel it was a matter of the quick or the dead. Gloves slowed you down when you needed instinctive command over the gun button and the controls, and goggles prevented you from seeing enemy fighters out of the corner of your eye. Like many another pilot, he had discarded both accessories, and it was a great relief, like bathing naked after swimming in one's clothes. He gave credit to his new freedom when he did a tight turn and a flip that saved him from two Messerschmitts that had come at him out of the sun, and for the quickness

---

* In fact, owing to bad weather it did not start until August 13.

† Dowding's message was ignored by the RAF historians, and the official date for the beginning of the Battle of Britain has been put as July 10, 1940.

with which he pulled up under one of them and riddled him from stem to stern.

August 13 is a date that is riveted in Geoffrey Page's mind because he remembers it as the day when it all started. But what he recalls thereafter is a confused jumble: moments of fear, triumph, relief and utter exhaustion, culminating in a climax of panic, pain and despair.

That first day, 56 Squadron was standing by at Rochford, on the northern shores of the Thames Estuary, their task being to protect the approaches to London and the coastal towns of Essex and Kent. It was unseasonably cool, a cloudy day with some bright patches. Page and his fellow pilots played cards or read in the dispersal hut. They were not called that morning, but everyone was nervous; they knew that the Luftwaffe was swarming across in force, and that things were happening at their forward field at Manston.

Late in the afternoon the telephone shrilled, and you could feel the tension as every pilot stopped talking. Then, "North Weald squadron scramble!," and they were racing for their Hurricanes. A heavy force of thirty-plus German bombers had apparently failed to find their target in the clouds and were making back for France. When the squadron caught up with them over Canterbury and Ramsgate, they found the enemy without fighter protection, and so they had a field day, shooting down or damaging at least half a dozen. But when Page flew over Manston on his way home to Rochford, what he saw made him feel less cheerful. Clouds of smoke hung over the airfield. The hangars were wrecked, burning aircraft littered the dispersal areas, and white dust covered everything.

The Germans flew 1,485 sorties against England that day, and in Berlin they were claiming the first of many victories. Seventy Spitfires and Hurricanes and eighteen Blenheims had been destroyed, they announced. In fact, as records subsequently showed, they were exaggerating by 700 percent; the RAF had destroyed forty-five German planes at the expense of thirteen of their own.

In the days that followed, 56 Squadron moved its forward field to an emergency landing ground outside Ramsgate while volunteers, coated with dust, struggled to get Manston operational. Now they were scrambling as many as four or five times a day, and the skies were filled with the tortuous contrails marking the paths of the great battle. Some days it was as easy as mowing down skittles, as when the Stuka dive bombers came over in clouds and the Hurricanes were waiting for them. But some days were frightful as when three friends in your own flight screamed for help over the intercom and you were too late to help and had to watch them go down.

One August afternoon, after a day of Stuka hunting over the Channel, Page suddenly felt sick as he put down on the Ramsgate field. Not from fear or reaction, but with a sudden self-revulsion at a memory of how he had shouted with glee as his bullets tore into a German dive bomber.

On the ground Jumbo Gracie was saying, "Six enemy aircraft destroyed without loss calls for a party! Is everybody on?"

It was impossible to opt out, and the race began back to North Weald and then by road to London. For their good behavior in the air, 56 Squadron was released earlier than usual.

"With the single-mindedness of our kind," Page said, "we headed up to the 'Big Smoke' for the pubs and nightclubs to spend our meager pennies. What was there to save for?"

But in a maudlin frame of mind in the early hours the next morning, he sat down in the dispersal hut and wrote to one of his old university professors at Cranwell:

It is difficult to know where to take up the threads again after so long, I sometimes wonder if our time together ever happened, and if this whole war isn't a ghastly nightmare from which we'll wake up soon. I know all this sounds nonsense, but I'm slightly tight and it's only an hour to dawn. Dawn— it's a lovely-sounding word, isn't it? It personifies a new hope, a second chance—at least that's what it should mean. To me it means nothing but another day of butchery. Oscar Wilde said it of fox-hunting and it applies to us: "The pursuit of the uneatable by the unspeakable." I know what you'd say in your kind, understanding way: you'd say that it's all a terrible mess and that I mustn't blame myself personally for the chaos of the world. Maybe I am a bit sorry for myself at this moment, but, and it's a big but, I enjoy killing. It fascinates me beyond belief to see my bullets striking home and then to see the Hun blow up before me. It also makes me feel sick. Where are we going and how will it end? I feel as if I'm selling my soul to the devil. I need someone to talk to who isn't tied up in this game of legalised murder.

Page read the letter later, put it away and never mailed it.

The next day, high in the sky over Ramsgate, Page and his Hurricane got on the wrong side of a formation of German bombers.

"One moment the sky between myself and the thirty Dornier 215s was clear," he said later, "and the next it was criss-crossed by streams of white tracer from cannon shells, all converging on our Hurricanes. Jumbo's machine peeled away from the attack. The distance between the German leaders and my solitary Hurri was down to three hundred yards. Strikes from my machine gun began to flash around the port engine of one of the Dorniers. It was a desperate race to destroy before being destroyed oneself."

When the first cannon shell hit his plane, he felt a shock of disbelief. Two more great thuds shook his aircraft, and as if by magic a gaping hole suddenly appeared in the starboard wing. "With that the tank behind the engine and just in front of me blew up in a violent explosion, and the cockpit became an inferno of smoke and flames. Fear changed to blind terror as I looked down at the flames sweeping upwards from the bottom of the cockpit. Horror joined terror as the bare skin on my hands, gripping the throttle and control column, shriveled up like burned parchment. I started screaming at the top of my voice, all the time trying to throw back my head out of the way of the fire. At the same time I was instinctively groping for the release pin of the restraining Sutton harness. Then I was tumbling, tumbling, tumbling in the clear cool sky."

It was some seconds before he found the ring and pulled the ripcord of his parachute. As he floated gently down, he noticed a peculiar odor. "The smell was my own burnt flesh, and it was so loathsome that I wanted to vomit. However, there was too much to attend to even to allow this small luxury of relief. Self-preservation being a basic animal instinct, I took stock of the situation to assess the chances of survival— and they looked slim. Away in the distance, six to ten miles, was the coastline. (The flesh around my eyes was beginning to swell now and hinder my vision.) Below me, ten thousand feet away, lay the deserted sea. Not a ship crossed its blank face. Still looking, I began to laugh. The force of the exploding tank had blown every vestige of clothing off me from my thighs downwards, including one shoe. Carefully, I eased off the remaining shoe with the toes of the other foot and watched it tumble. Then I began to shiver as the cold air hit against my damaged skin."

It seemed ages before he hit the water, and the shock was devastating. "Kicking madly, I came to the surface to find my arms entangled with the multiple shrouds holding me in a grip like an octopus. The battle with the metal disc of the harness had to be won now, or else the water-logged parachute would eventually drag me down. Spluttering with mouthfuls of salt water, I struggled with the release mechanism. Pieces of flesh flaked off me, and blood poured from the raw tissues.

But I got the harness off, and started off on the next phases, that of inflating my Mae West."

He was still struggling when a small motorboat came into view. In it sat two men, and as the boat circled around him one of them called out roughly, "Who are you—a Jerry or one of ours?"

Anger flooded through Page. With a great effort he pulled himself up, expelling the salt water from his mouth, and shouted, "You stupid pair of fucking bastards, pull me out!"

The boat altered course and drew alongside. Strong arms leaned down and dragged him over the side. "The minute you swore, mate," one of the men said, "we knew you was from the RAF."

As the boat turned for shore, pain bit into every part of his body, and Geoffrey Page began to scream.

The great battle to destroy the Royal Air Force should have been over in a couple of weeks. But the Germans had underestimated the RAF and overestimated the capacity of their own air force.

Furious that his promises to the Führer were not being fullfilled, Hermann Göring raged against his pilots. On August 21 his special train pulled into a station on the Pas de Calais and he set off on a tour of the Luftwaffe fighter and bomber bases strung along the flat coastal fields of northern France. He found his pilots dispirited. They had been flying 1,500 sorties a day against the RAF, and their losses had been catastrophic.

In Berlin, Göring had believed the figures his ministry had been issuing about the number of RAF planes shot down, and had decided that the British no longer possessed an air force worth worrying about.* Therefore he had called off the concentrated attacks on the British radar stations, for he thought not only that it was a waste of planes but that the British radar system could not be destroyed. It was a truly stupid decision. In fact, one station had already been put out of action, and a hole blown in Britain's defenses. With another week of concentrated attack, the RAF would have been "blinded" by the loss of radar's all-seeing eyes.

Göring arrived at Pas de Calais prepared to celebrate with his pilots as they gave the RAF the *coup de grâce*. Instead, he found that the RAF was not only still in existence but fighting well and making the Luftwaffe

---

* The Luftwaffe figures of RAF losses were grossly exaggerated.

bleed. Angrily he accused his men of cowardice. "You have the best aircraft in the world," he cried. "What more do you want?"

"A squadron of Spitfires," replied Adolf Galland, one of Germany's fighter aces.*

Though the RAF pilots were still hitting back, they were hurting even more than the Germans, for they had fewer planes to spare. If something were not done soon, they would bleed to death. Though British aircraft factories were now working at full speed turning out planes, they could not keep up with the losses; nor could men be trained fast enough to replace those pilots who were killed or maimed.

After Göring's angry criticisms, the Luftwaffe redoubled its efforts to destroy the RAF. "The enemy is to be forced to use his fighters by means of ceaseless attacks. In addition, the aircraft industry and the ground organization of the air force are to be attacked . . . by night and day," he had ordered. His pilots responded with determination, intrepidity and cunning. German commanders were growing more wily; they were learning how to evade or trick the chain of radar stations watching the coasts. Formations of planes would go up in France throughout the day and fly back and forth just within range of the radar screens thirty miles away on the other side of the Channel. The plotters at RAF stations would guess from the blobs on their screens that a raid was coming and order their fighters to scramble, only to discover, once the RAF was airborne, that it was a bluff. When the British began to run out of fuel, the Germans would send other squadrons straight for the targets. Around the clock the Luftwaffe was striking everywhere now where they were likely to do most harm to Britain's defenses: airfields, aircraft factories, oil and gas depots. They were getting badly hurt, but so was the RAF, which could less afford the pain and suffering.

Only one place stayed remote from the battle: London. The Germans had drawn a line around the outer perimeter of the metropolitan area, and there was an embargo on all targets inside it. There were raids on the huge oil tanks at Thameshaven, there were lightning attacks on the RAF airfields nearest London, at Biggin Hill, Hornchurch and Croydon, but the city itself was off limits. Göring and Hitler were well aware of the propaganda effect the bombing of London would have on millions in the neutral world, particularly in the United States. They might even have heard the story that every night Winston Churchill was purported

---

* Adolf Galland, *The First and the Last.*

to shout up at the black sky, "Why don't you come? Bomb us, bomb us!"

He knew, and so did Göring and Hitler, that only a London laid waste, its monuments destroyed, its citizens burned, its children wiped out, would arouse America to throw its weight wholeheartedly on Britain's side.

Hitler was not going to fall into that trap. He told Göring that the Luftwaffe must at all costs stay away from London. So the people of the capital slept peacefully in their beds while the German air force continued to pulverize their defenders and defenses.

Then, on August 24, 1940, a pilot's panic changed everything.

It was on one of the nightly raids which the Luftwaffe was now making against the fuel dumps along the river at Thameshaven, some ten miles downstream from London. The bombers swept over after darkness on August 24, flew through the flak and dropped their bombs, then swung around as the flames erupted, and raced back to the safety of their bases in France.

All except two planes. Their identity will never be known, for they were expunged from the records of the Luftwaffe. As well they might be, for in a way they cost Germany the Battle of Britain.

The planes had lost their flight leaders by the time they reached the Thames and already they must have been jittery. The flak was heavy, and they could see little of what lay below them. At the time when they were scheduled to turn for home, they still had not seen their target. What to do? They knew there would be trouble if they came back with their bombs, and so they unloaded them.

Down below them, as air-raid sirens wailed, the first bombs of the war fell with a crunch on inner London. One smashed down onto St. Giles' Church in Cripplegate, in the heart of the financial district; the blast ripped Milton's statue off its pedestal in a square nearby. Other bombs scattered death and destruction over Islington, Tottenham, Finchley, Stepney and Bethnal Green, killing customers just turned out of the pubs at closing time, and theatregoers on their way home from the West End.

Death came quickly and as quickly stole away, but not only bodies and wrecked buildings were left behind. The error gave the British government the excuse it needed to change its tactics.

The next day, after a meeting of the Chiefs of Staff Committee in London at which Winston Churchill presided, an order was passed on to the RAF Bomber Command. That afternoon the order filtered down through the chains of command until it reached a wing of Hampden twin-engined bombers in Norfolk commanded by Squadron Leader John Oxley. For the past weeks the unit had been principally engaged in dropping leaflets over Germany. Now they were told to load their planes with bombs instead, and that evening they were given their target: Berlin.

It was to be a reprisal raid.

While this decision was made, and while his fellow fighter pilots fought on against the Luftwaffe over the Kent and Sussex cornfields, Geoffrey Page lay in the Royal Masonic Hospital in London in a drugged haze of pain.

The RAF launch which picked him up had taken him straight to a first-aid station at Margate, in Essex, where the doctor and nurses examined his raw, blackened face, lacerated back and dreadfully burned hands and followed the prescribed routine for such cases. As his teeth chattered and he moaned with pain, they coated his bleeding flesh with a thick application of orange-brown tannic acid. It was supposed to make the blood coagulate, and thus provide a protective covering which would ease the pain and prevent Page from dying of shock. But far from being a substitute skin, it was a horrid encasement, for tannic acid hardens on contact with open flesh, and by the time the ambulance arrived at the Royal Masonic Hospital a thick, unyielding hide had formed over his face and body.

The RAF's bombers were on their way across the North Sea to Berlin when, in the early hours of the morning, Page awoke to find a pretty nurse bending over him. She was looking down at him as if hypnotized. "Following the direction of her stare," he recalls, "I glanced down with watery eyes at my arms. From the elbows to the wrists the bare forearms were one seething mass of pus-filled boils. Then for the first time I noticed my hands: from the wrist joints to the fingertips they were black. Not only that; they were so *small*, smaller than I remembered them to be. I shared the nurse's horror until a sister, standing behind her, said, 'That black stuff's only tannic acid. It's not the color of your skin.'"

Page saw his face in a mirror a few days later. His face had swollen to three times its normal size, and it too was black. "I'm a monster," he told himself and burst into tears, out of exhaustion and despair.

He was not the only one. In hospitals all over London and the south coast, there were at least a hundred young RAF pilots suffering from third-degree burns sustained in battle. They too had had their hands, faces and bodies coated with tannic acid, and they too believed

The Fatal Error

that they would never care to show themselves to the civilized world again.

Göring had sworn that Berlin would never be bombed. He was so sure that the German capital was safe from the RAF that he was reputed to have boasted to his officers, "If a bomb drops within the confines of our capital, you can call me Meier."

On August 26 that is what Berliners were calling him, because British bombs had hit the city in the early hours of that morning. True, not much damage was done, but many people had panicked and it was a severe blow to Göring's prestige.

In London, Winston Churchill and his Chiefs of Staff waited for the inevitable reprisals. But Hitler was not going to be drawn; he decided to regard the Hampden raid as a gnat bite and to ignore it. The bombers continued their raids against all other areas of Britain, but there were no more attacks on London.

The RAF, however, continued to raid Berlin. The targets were always military ones, but they were in Berlin and its environs just the same.

It was too much. On September 4 Adolf Hitler addressed a meeting in the Sportpalast in Berlin in his most rancorous and sardonic mood. He attacked Churchill and his supporters with heavy sarcasm, and soon his audience was roaring with laughter at his sallies and fervently applauding shrill threats.

"In England they are filled with curiosity and keep asking, 'Why doesn't he come?'" Hitler raised his voice to shout. "Be calm. Be calm. He's coming, he's coming!"

He went on to the air raids on Berlin: "Mr. Churchill is demonstrating his new brain child, the night air raid. Mr. Churchill is carrying out these raids not because they promise to be highly effective, but because his air force cannot fly over German soil in daylight."

Then the Führer's tone changed as he explained to his audience why there had been a pause in the operations of the German armies and why the invasion had been postponed: "For three months I did not answer because I believed that such madness [as this war] would be stopped. Mr. Churchill took this for a sign of weakness. We are now answering night for night. When the British air force drops three or four thousand kilograms of bombs, then we will in one night drop three hundred thousand or four hundred thousand kilograms."

Now his voice rose to a shriek. "When they declare that they will increase their attacks on our cities, then we will *raze* their cities to the ground. We will stop the handiwork of these night pirates, so help us God. . . . The hour will come when one of us will break, and it will not be National Socialist Germany!"

The next day Reich Marshal Hermann Göring's special train set out once more for France. Hitler had given his consent: London was to be bombed. As a prelude to Operation Sea Lion, the capital of the British Empire was to be destroyed, its people panicked, its factories paralyzed, thus opening the path for the invading armies of the German Reich.

Göring wanted to be with his bomber squadrons when the great operation began. Two days later, on September 7, 1940, he stood with his aides on the cliffs at Cap Gris-Nez and looked at England twenty-two miles away across the Channel. Overhead roared wave after wave of bombers on their way to London.

Part Two

THE BATTLE OF LONDON

8

The Blitz: Openers

Police Constable David Meade glanced at his watch and then hurriedly drank off the dregs of his mug of tea. Two o'clock: he was due back on the beat again.

"I'll be off, then," he said to no one in particular, and waved his hand at the old girl behind the canteen bar. Then he walked quickly out of Limehouse Police Station into the sunshine of West India Dock Road. Saturday, September 7, was a day of hazy sunshine over London, and the streets of Limehouse had never looked drabber. A year of war had peeled the paint off the doorways and caked dust and cobwebs onto the blacked-out windows of the squalid tenements. Yet somehow the sight of it cheered Meade and made him glad to be back on the beat again. He passed Charlie Brown's, the famous pub by West India Dock, just as some of the lunchtime crowd emerged, and half a dozen customers called a greeting as he passed.

" 'Ow are you, then, love," said one of them, an aging Chinese crone, in a strong Cockney accent.

"Nicely, Mum, and I hope you are too," he replied and chuckled to himself. Less than a year ago, when he had first been posted to Limehouse as a new policeman, every Oriental he met looked sinister and threatening, and every house into which they disappeared he suspected of being an opium den or a center of the white-slave traffic. He had been brought up on a diet of Fu Manchu and "Limehouse Nights" and to him Chinese were both inscrutable and wily. He had soon discovered that whether they kept laundries or restaurants or worked as clerks and shop assistants, they were Cockneys like all the others, and this was true as well of West Indians, Poles and Indians who were sprinkled around the dock area too. Meade had learned to like and respect most of them.

Saturday was always the busiest day of the week for a policeman in the East End of London. Meade enjoyed it, even though he knew that by closing time he would be busy coaxing drunks home from pubs, peacemaking between husbands and wives, breaking up the pitch-and-toss gambling gangs by the docks, and seeing that the two attractive but naughty sixteen-year-old daughters of Mrs. Lee-Yung and Mrs. Davies were back home and out of mischief before blackout. It was the day when money was flowing and people came out to spend it, and what Meade liked about them was that they were so cheerful about it. Not like the stodgy, respectable citizens of the outer suburbs or the snooty residents of the West End, who seemed to take their pleasures so sadly. The Cockneys of the East End wore their hearts on their sleeves and jingled the money in their pockets; the beer flowed, washing down great quantities of sausage and mash and jellied eels, and at the slightest excuse someone would break into "Doing the Lambeth Walk," "Knees up, Mother Brown" and other Cockney songs as the evening wore on.

Just a year earlier, Constable Meade had helped pile hundreds of weeping mothers and children into evacuation buses, and he could remember their wail as they disappeared down Old Kent Road. He knew what a wrench it must have been for them to leave their homes and friends for the lonely wastes of brickless countryside and the frigid welcome of the hostesses with whom they were billeted. It was official police policy to frown on those who had returned to the East End in the past few months ("I just 'ad to come back, Constable. I couldn't get to sleep for those bleedin' cows bawling all night. It was drivin' me mad"), but he sympathized with them. For an East Ender, trees didn't have the same feeling as bricks and mortar.

Meade's musings were interrupted by the sound of the air-raid siren, and at once he was aware of a sudden hush as the babbling voices all around him stopped in midsentence. Everyone was looking up at the sky; it was bright blue and cloud-flecked, and not even a single vapor trail was scrawled across it. Meade decided that it must be another raid downriver on the Thameshaven tanks, but he dutifully called out to the people crowding the sidewalk, "Now keep moving, please! There's a big warehouse shelter just down there on the dock—enough room for all of you and more. Let's get moving, shall we?"

While he spoke he was aware of the buzzing in his ears, like the faint murmur of summer bees; only, this noise grew louder and louder until it drowned out the renewed chatter of the people around him. Then once more he was conscious of a sudden halt in conversation, and again they were all staring at the sky.

"I see them, I see them!" someone called out.

"Up there! Look, two—no, three of them! By that big cloud!" cried someone else.

Meade said, "Come on, there! Let's get to the shelters, shall we?"

As the crowd started to run across the road, he gazed upward and sucked in his breath. "Shelters, everyone, quick!" he shouted urgently.

"Gawd," said a bystander. "It's not just two or three—there must be hundreds of the buggers! Look at them!"

The sound had become rather like a muffled scream, Meade said afterward. It was joined by others, and then it was as if a hundred trains were roaring toward him at top speed out of a tunnel.

"Down, down, down!" he cried, but now he couldn't even hear the sound of his own voice.

Lieutenant Commander "Dick" Fordham, late of the Royal Navy and now with the London Fire Service, was soaping the last trace of oil off his body and preparing for a long wallow in the tub when there was a knock on the bathroom door. "Can you come at once, sir?" It was the voice of one of his firemen. "You're wanted on the phone."

"Tell them I'm in my bath," Fordham shouted. "*And* remind them that it's my day off."

Saturday, September 7: a whole afternoon and evening free. After what had happened over the past forty-eight hours, he felt he deserved it.

The fireman went away, but presently he was back again. "I'm sorry, sir," he called, "but they still want you urgently. Please, sir—they seem a little upset."

Commander Fordham sighed, slipped down in the bath until the water covered his shock of red hair, and then porpoised to the surface, rose in a gush of water and reached for the towel. What did they want him for? Certainly it couldn't be more spectacular than his experiences of the past two days, he told himself. Or more ridiculous.

On the evening of September 5, just as Fordham was leaving his home for dinner, the telephone rang and F. W. Jackson, chief of the London Fire Service, was on the line.

"Dick, we're in trouble," he said at once. "The Jerries have bombed

Thameshaven again, and there's quite a blaze there. Oil *and* petrol are on fire."

"That's not our affair," said Fordham. "It's out of the London area. We only go there if we're asked for help."

That was the problem, Jackson explained. Thameshaven *had* asked for help earlier in the day, when the first bombs were dropped. A London Fire Service officer had been sent downriver with fifty pumps to help the firefighters on the spot. A 2,000-ton tank of gasoline was ablaze and its flames were threatening seven other tanks close by. But the London officer had been reminded before he left headquarters that by the Fires Act of 1938, under no circumstances was he to try to take charge when operating in another area; he must put himself under the command of the local officer.

"It hasn't worked out very well, I'm afraid," said Jackson. "The local officer wasn't . . . well, experienced, shall we say. A volunteer, you know—good chap, but an amateur. He told our man that the fire was well in hand, that he wouldn't need anything like fifty pumps, and that he should send forty-five of them back to London." Jackson paused. "A mistake, I'm afraid. They not only failed to put out the blaze in the tank, but now it looks as if the others are seriously threatened."

Fordham said, "Then why doesn't he order the pumps back to Thameshaven again?"

"Yes," said Jackson, "that's just what he should do. The unfortunate thing is, he isn't there any more—this local commander, I mean. About an hour ago he pointed out to our chap that he was just a volunteer and couldn't stay up all night fighting a fire because he had to go to work early next morning. So he just left."

"My God," said Fordham, and began to laugh.

"Yes," said Jackson, "it is funny, isn't it?" There was no humor in his own voice, though. "The trouble is, our chap can't do anything without having orders first from a local commander, and they just can't find another. He's in a bit of a bother, you might say, especially with all that oil running round asking to be set alight."

Fordham said, "So you want me to go out and look at the situation, is that it?"

"That's right, old chap. Only for God's sake don't try and take charge, will you? Remember it's out of our area. And please be tactful to whomever they've put in command."

By the time Dick Fordham got to Thameshaven he didn't have to ask directions. The blaze from the burning fuel dumps lit up the last two miles of his way. Another tank was on fire. The protective brick wall enclosing the tanks was feet deep in petrol and water, and the way the two tanks were blazing the flames would soon engulf the remaining ones. The London fire officer was running around, grimy and distracted, unsure of what to do; he was only allowed to take orders and the local man did not know how to give them.

Fordham took one look at the situation and then asked where the nearest telephone was. It was apologetically explained that the administration offices were locked up, but that there was a telephone booth at the gate. He called headquarters and after some delay got through. "We're in a hell of a mess here," he said. "I want fifty pumps and three fireboats at once."

It was the administration officer of the London Fire Service on the other end. "You can't order reinforcements," he said crisply. "That's for the officer in charge, and you aren't in charge."

"Yes, I am," said Fordham aggressively. "There's no one else here who knows anything. I'm taking over."

"No." The administration officer's voice was firm. "That is something you will not do. It is out of our area. The 1938 Act says that when we are called into another area we—"

"—take orders from the officer on the spot," Fordham interrupted. "I know all that. But it so happens that there isn't any officer on the spot, and at any moment this bloody place is likely to blow up and kill us all."

"Keep calm, Commander," said the voice at the other end. "We'll get you a local officer as soon as possible. We are in touch with Sir Will Spens about it at the moment."

"Who the hell is Sir Will Spens?" asked Fordham.

It turned out that Sir Will Spens was a Cambridge don, the Master of Corpus Christi College, who had been made Regional Commissioner for the area, including Thameshaven. The administrator interrupted this explanation to say, "—and we have just had a message that he has nominated an officer to take charge and the man is now on his way. So everything is in hand, you see."

Only it wasn't. When Fordham went back to the fire the situation was grim. The flames were getting higher and the few pumps were failing to keep them under control. How long would it be, Fordham wondered, before they all went up? He wished he'd had time for a bite to eat before being blown to perdition.

At this moment a young man in a tweed suit stepped out of a small car; he had been sent to take over, he said.

"D'you know anything about oil fires?" asked Fordham.

"Not much," said the young man. "You see, I'm from the borough surveyor's department, really—though," he added hurriedly, "I did have a week's fire-fighting course at the ARP school."

"I see," said Fordham. "I suppose you wouldn't mind me giving you advice, would you?"

"No, sir. I'd be delighted."

"Right. Then you just nip down to the phone and order up fifty pumps and three fire vessels immediately. Then come back here, make yourself comfortable and leave it to us."

"At once, sir," said the young man, rushing away.

By the time the pumps had arrived and the fireboats were in position, the glare from the tanks could be seen twenty miles away. The hard fight began. The boats pumped water from the Thames to the shore pumps which sprayed it on the tanks. Fordham ordered his men in for "close-fire" fighting, and led them over the protective wall into the trough of steaming oil and water. From this position, close to the burning tanks roaring away above them, they directed their leaping high-pressure jets. For some of the auxiliaries it was their first fire, and it was a terrifying experience even for the veterans. Not only were they up to their waists in water; at one point, where a bomb had dropped among the tanks, there was a deep crater now filled with water into which men kept dropping and disappearing beneath the murky surface. Their companions would drag them out and then they would go back to fighting the flames.

But by daylight the conflagration had been mastered and five of the gasoline tanks saved. Fordham wiped the oil out of his eyes, emptied his soaked boots and sloshed across to the tweedy young man standing a few yards away. "Fire under control, sir," he said. "It's all yours."

"Thank *you*, sir," the young man said. And he added with a grin, "I don't know what I would have done without you!"

Now Fordham was back at his headquarters in London, getting out of the tub and looking forward to an afternoon of sleep and relaxation, when here they came after him again. More help for Thameshaven?

"No, Commander," said the voice on the telephone, "it isn't Thameshaven—it's us. There's an urgent call out for all pumps. You're to get down to the East End at once. It looks as if Jerry is attacking us in force. May I wish you good luck on our first big test?"

"First big test?" exploded Fordham. "What the bloody hell d'you think we've been doing at Thameshaven for the past forty-eight hours?"

That Saturday afternoon there was a grudge match on at West Ham Stadium. The local soccer team was playing Tottenham, the champions from the neighboring borough. For football fans in the East End of London it was a game not to be missed, and there were ten thousand people in the stands when the whistle blew for play to begin.

George Hardiman was one of them, and so was his son, John. George had been working overtime for the past three months, and this was his first free weekend. Ellen Hardiman had decided to go off and see her sister at Ilford, and Sheila was staying at home to look after Winston, the spaniel puppy her father had given her for her ninth birthday.

John was a West Ham fan, but his father liked the Tottenham club. Their team hadn't lost as many players to the armed services, and it showed; they ran all around the home side. By the middle of the second half, they were leading, 4 to 1—and then the sirens sounded. The referee looked up at the sky and blew his whistle. The players gathered around him, and then began to walk off the field to the sound of boos and catcalls from the fans in the stand.

"Why do they have to stop the game for a silly old siren?" John asked.

"It's government orders," George said. "Come on, we'd better get home."

The crowd dispersed. The two Hardimans were halfway back to Canning Town when they heard the noise of engines in the sky above.

At 4 P.M. in Bentley Priory on September 7, Flight Lieutenant Robert Wright knocked on the door of his boss, Air Chief Marshal Sir Hugh Dowding, and entered. As usual, Fighter Command's commander in chief was bent over his desk, staring at a long list of statistics. He looked grimmer and even more remote than usual, and Wright guessed that he was close to despair. The Luftwaffe pressure on his airfields, planes and pilots was becoming too great to bear; they were simply losing too much and too many. If the pattern of the enemy's attack continued like this for another week, the RAF would crack and the path would be open to the invader.

Over the past four weeks the Luftwaffe had steadily been destroying Dowding's forward airfields and pushing his squadrons inland. His pilots were exhausted. Once, when informed that the Germans had air superiority of five to one, he had told the Air Minister, "Then our young men will have to shoot down their young men at the rate of five to one." For weeks now, that is what they had been doing, but it couldn't go on. The end of their endurance was dangerously near, and the Germans probably knew it; only this morning the Air Ministry had sent him a short message—*Invasion Alert No. 1*—which meant that invasion was imminent.* Enemy barges crammed every port and lock along the French and Belgian coasts, and no amount of bombing seemed to disturb the build-up.

"Yes, Wright?" Dowding said without looking up.

"It looks like a big one, sir. Ops say that several formations of twenty-plus are building up over Calais."

"Let's go down and have a look," said Dowding.

They moved to the operations room of Fighter Command and leaned over the railing. Below them a great map of the English Channel was spread across an enormous table. Above it sat RAF officers taking in the radar reports. Around the table were the girls of the WAAF in their shirt sleeves, rakes of the kind croupiers use in their hands. But the pieces they were pushing across the table were not chips but planes, and the stakes were not money but lives. Each block they moved nearer to the English coast represented an enemy flight, and Dowding saw at once that this raid was indeed a big one—perhaps the biggest of them all. Already the blocks indicated that 100-plus Nazi bombers and 300 Nazi fighters were on their way over.

Dowding looked across the table to see what his group commander, Air Vice-Marshal Keith Park,† had done with his defending Spitfires and Hurricanes. Yes, they were airborne already. Dowding knew the tactics they would follow; they would wait until the big groups of Nazi planes split up, as they always did, some to go for RAF airfields, others for factories, others for the oil tanks on the outskirts of London. Already the defending RAF squadrons were gaining altitude and waiting for the enemy to split up before attacking.

---

* There were three alerts. *Invasion Alert No. 3* meant "An attack is expected in three days"; *Invasion Alert No. 2:* "An attack is expected within forty-eight hours"; and *Invasion Alert No. 1:* "They're coming any moment."

† He commanded 11 Group, Fighter Command, responsible for the defense of London and the south coast.

Suddenly, as he looked down, a thought stabbed Dowding like an icicle. What if this time the Luftwaffe did not split up? What if it just came in en masse? There would be no fighters to stop them; the path to London would be wide open.

"That's funny," said Robert Wright. "They don't seem to be splitting up, do they?"

In the Hole in the Ground in Whitehall the Chiefs of Staff Committee was holding an emergency meeting. It had been called by General Sir John Dill, who had succeeded General Ironside as Chief of the Imperial General Staff, to discuss the invasion Britain might face at any moment. All reports from agents, all reconnaissance photographs, every speech by Nazi leaders seemed to point to this weekend as the moment when Hitler would strike at last.

Dill had called in his defense chiefs to hear how they had disposed their forces. The discussion had just begun when Colonel Leslie Hollis, the committee secretary, came in with a message and laid it before Dill. The general looked at it and then passed it around. "Well, gentlemen," he said, "this may be the opening blow." He turned to Hollis. "I think we should inform the Prime Minister. Will he be awake yet?"*

As he spoke, there was a heavy thud in the distance, followed by another and then another.

"If he wasn't before, he is now," said Hollis. "I'll go and tell him that they're bombing London."

On the cliffs of Cap Gris-Nez, Reich Marshal Hermann Göring was being interviewed by German reporters while more than 300 bombers and their 600 protecting fighters passed overhead toward England.

"I have come to take personal command of the battle," Göring told his audience. The target was London, "a stroke straight to the enemy's heart."

The first wave of German bombers came in from the east and made straight for the Thames Estuary. A few dropped their bombs on Thameshaven once more and started more oil fires, but over a hundred and fifty other Heinkels and Dorniers proceeded upriver toward the

---

* Winston Churchill always took an afternoon nap, no matter what the situation.

East End and the docks. They were flying very high—between 16,000 and 20,000 feet—and Messerschmitt 109s and 110s wheeled in protective screens over and under them, glinting in the rays of the afternoon sun.

Chief Superintendent Reginald Smith of the Metropolitan Police, who was driving from his home in Ilford to his headquarters in East Ham, stopped his car and got out to look. "They're going for us," he said when he saw the planes. He meant London, but a moment or two later he was able to be more specific.

Superintendent Smith had been in command of K Division of the Metropolitan Police since early spring. His bailiwick covered a great stretch of East London: East and West Ham, Silvertown, Barking, Plaistow and the great sprawl of locks and waterways known as the Royal group of docks. Now he could see showers of bombs coming down, flashing as they fell, and could hear the thud as they made their impact.

"It's us, all right," he said, and told his driver to hurry.

All along the river, antiaircraft fire had opened up, and the path of the invading bombers was sign-posted by the puffs of exploding shells. But save for a few dogfights on the fringes, there was no opposition from the air. The Nazi bombers droned in, squadron after squadron, like lines of trucks, and at fixed points they unloaded. What the hell has happened to our fighters? Smith wondered. The bombs fell first on the great arsenal at Woolwich, a veritable powder keg, and on the factories around it. The whole area went up in a great cauliflower of smoke. Then the vast complex of docks strung out along either side of the Thames—the Victoria and Albert, the West India, the Surrey Commercial—were hit. More and more gusts of flame and smoke burst from both banks of the river, and soon it was not just arsenals and docks and warehouses that were being hit but narrow streets and housing clusters and blocks of flats—the homes, from West Ham to Bow, from Bermondsey to Whitechapel, from Limehouse to Poplar, of the East Enders of London.

Fighter Command headquarters was desperately trying to recover from its error. Air Vice-Marshal Keith Park was frantically rerouting his Spitfires and Hurricanes and getting every plane he could muster into the air. Already they were moving into battle, slicing through the Messerschmitt screens to get at the bombers. But for the East End it was too late. The bombers had unloaded and were heading for home. In the meantime, another wave had come in from the west and was dropping a second load of high explosives and incendiaries.

The Blitz: Openers

Now the great fires began. Not in the ramshackle houses on either side of the river, however; there was nothing left of them to burn. In the slum areas of Canning Town, for instance, people lived in row upon row of tenements which had been thrown up in the 1860s to house the influx of workers for the new Thames Iron Works at Silvertown. They were cheap, crammed back to back, jerry-built by grasping Victorian capitalism for their semislave laborers. When the first bombs dropped on September 7, the shacks of Canning Town collapsed and shattered, burying their occupants beneath piles of rubble.

Canning Town was where the Hardimans lived.

George Hardiman and John had almost reached Upton Park Station when the first bombs fell. George's first instinct was to keep going. "All I wanted to do was get home," he said later. "All I could think of was Sheila back there, all on her own, poor kid. I didn't think it was going to be serious, and I knew she'd be frightened out of her wits. But when we got to the station there was a barrier up, and a notice on it saying NEAREST SHELTER RAYMOND ROAD. Just then there was a whistling and a thud that practically blew our heads off, and Johnny flung himself against me and put his arms round my legs. I decided we'd better go and find the shelter."

It was an ordinary street shelter, which didn't look much safer than the one whose roof had caved in on the night of June 25, but once they were inside, the walls seemed to deaden the noise of the bombs. It was crowded, mostly with locals who didn't look friendly when the Hardimans entered, and they made room for them on the benches only when a little man with a band around his arm came over and said, "Come on, there, ladies and gents. Give the small boy and his dad a little room." Soon Johnny recovered his nerve and began tugging George's sleeve and saying, "Couldn't we go out and have a look, Dad?" George was sick with worry. What was happening in Canning Town? The bombs sounded as if they were dropping in that direction. And where was Ellen?

When the all clear sounded they returned to Upton Park Station, but now there was a chalked notice on a board outside saying LINE BLOCKED, so they started to walk. Ahead of them, great clouds of black smoke rose in the sky, and the air was filled with the smell of burning. Soon they came upon their first crater, then their first row of wrecked houses, and then a great pile of rubble where a street had been. There were firemen and fire engines and a great confusion of hose, men running about everywhere, whistles blowing and dust thick in the air.

Suddenly George Hardiman realized that though he was in his own district, he was lost; he didn't recognize any of it any more.

Now he began to be very scared. Even John had fallen silent. Several times ambulances screeched past, their bells jangling. They were going along one half-wrecked street when George saw a body lying half out of a door, and what seemed to be part of a tailor's dummy heaped on top of it; it took him a moment to discover that it was a human trunk.

He was pulling John to the other side of the road when a man in a tin helmet came running toward them. "Hey, you there! Where the bloody hell d'you think you're going?" he shouted. And then, with a cry of alarm, "Look out!"

George jerked to a stop, just short of the side of a house which had suddenly collapsed.

When the man came up, George saw that he was a warden. "I'm looking for Star Road," he said desperately. "Can you tell me where it is?"

"What would you want to go there for?" the warden asked.

"That's where I live. My daughter Sheila is there."

Police Constable Meade put his hand to his head and felt for his cap, but it was gone. Through the singing in his ears he could hear the continual *thud, thud, thud* of bombs, and each one of them shook his body like a convulsion. He climbed unsteadily to his feet and looked around him. Although it was still early evening, it seemed to have gone dark and he could hardly see across the road; it took him some time to realize that the street and the sky above him were thick with dust and smoke. The dust was everywhere. He looked down at his hands; they were black and greasy. He ran a dirty finger over his face and decided that it too must be black.

The first people he saw when he looked around him were a young man and a girl who were slowly rising, on their knees first, and then gingerly upright. He remembered seeing the couple just before the bombs began falling; a nice pair of kids, he had thought, and he had glanced more than once at the girl, a very pretty blonde. Now he saw her back, and was startled because she seemed to be colored; not only that, she was naked to the waist, her long legs and backside distinctly brown. When she straightened up and turned he realized that her hair, though streaked black and mussed, was still blond. She was uttering great heaving sobs as she crossed her hands below her waist to cover herself. As he started to move toward her, her young man suddenly seemed to understand what had happened, and he slipped off his jacket and tied it around the girl's waist by the sleeves.

It was the first freak effect of a bomb blast that David Meade had seen; there would be others in the hours and months to come. The lucky ones were those who only got their clothes whipped off by the shock effect.

The first thing Chief Superintendent Reginald Smith saw when his car rounded a bend in Canning Town was a huge sow spread-eagled at the edge of a bomb crater, its entrails spilled across the road. On the other side of the crater two pigs were running aimlessly around in circles, and their terrified squeals sounded above the crash of bombs. Here, in the center of one of the most populous slum areas in London, a family had been keeping a pig farm. Some of the animals were badly wounded, and his first order on reaching his office was to issue guns and send a squad of men to dispatch the injured pigs. Then he asked the question uppermost in his mind: "What about West Ham Stadium?"

"Two bombs on it, sir," the sergeant said. "But Jerry was too late. Everyone had gone home ten minutes earlier."

"Where have we been hit the worst?"

The sergeant went over to the map on the wall. "There's two slum areas that won't need clearing after this," he said. "Jerry's done it for us." He was pointing at Silvertown and Canning Town.

"And what about casualties?" Smith asked.

"They're bad, sir," the sergeant said. "Lots of people buried, too. You know those tenements, sir. Just fell down on top of people. The rescue teams are digging them out now."

Where the Hardiman house had been there was a mound of brick and plaster rubble sprinkled with bits of floorboard, furniture and torn rolls of linoleum, all piled in a heap. When George Hardiman and his son came up with the warden, a stretcher team was scrambling down the last slope; the warden stopped them and then gestured to George to take a look at what they were carrying. Through the dust that caked her face, George recognized an old woman from the end of the street. He shook his head, and the warden signaled the stretcher-bearers to move on.

The rescue squad was working at the far end of the mound, picking their way through the rubble and filling a number of buckets and baskets and a large, buckled tin bath with debris. "That's our bath, Dad," John said suddenly.

A couple of official-looking men who stood at the bottom of the mound turned and looked at the warden. "Who are these people?" one of them asked. "What are they doing here? This is a prohibited area, you know."

The warden explained about Sheila, and the official turned at once to the men on the pile and shouted, "There's someone here says his daughter was in the house."

A voice from someone they could not see called, "Ask him if he had a dog."

John broke in, "Yes. Winston. We left Winston behind with Sheila!"

One of the men on the top of the pile looked down at them and said, "You'd better come up here."

They scrambled to the top, and when they got there, the man looked down at John and said gently, "What did you say your dog's name was?"

"Winston."

"And what's your name, son?"

"John."

"Then call your dog, John," the man said.

They all waited while John crouched and began shouting down through the wreckage, "Winston! Come on, Winston! Good boy, Winston!"

Suddenly the man motioned him to be quiet, and they all stood there listening in silence. Presently, from somewhere deep down, there was the sound of scrabbling and the broken whine of a dog.

In the evening about six-thirty, when the all clear sounded over Chadwell Heath, Arthur Ketley said to his wife, "Let's go down to the Cooper's Arms. I could do with a drink this evening."

Ever since tea they had been listening to the sounds of planes going over, and their son, Donald, had caught them glancing uneasily at each other each time there was a thud in the distance. But on this occasion Chadwell Heath was not in the target area.

The Cooper's Arms was the Ketleys' local pub. They liked it because it had a small garden with tables and chairs, which meant that they could take the boy with them. They walked down the road in the evening sunlight and when they reached the pub Arthur Ketley went inside for a pint of mild-and-bitter for himself, a shandy for Mrs. Ketley and a ginger beer for Donald.

When he came out again his face was troubled. "I hear they've caught a packet in Silvertown and Bermondsey," he said "It's terrible, they say. People are streaming out of the East End." He glanced at the boy and then back to his wife. "Lots of rumors around, too. They say Jerry may be coming at any moment now."

"In that case, we know what we're going to do, don't we," said Mrs. Ketley firmly. "We're staying put."

For the past few days there had been an advertisement in all the newspapers. It had been issued by the Ministry of Information and printed in space bought and donated by the Brewers' Society, and it said:

WHAT DO I DO

if I hear news
that Germans are trying to land,
or have landed?

I remember that this is the moment to act like a soldier. I do *not* get panicky. I *stay put*. I say to myself: "Our chaps will deal with them." I do *not* say: "I must get out of here." I remember that fighting men must have clear roads. I do *not* go on to the road on bicycle, in car or on foot. Whether I am at home or at work, I just *stay put*.

CUT THIS OUT—AND KEEP IT!

Mrs. Ketley had kept hers and it seemed good advice. She was not going to make the same mistake as those poor souls in France and Belgium. She had seen newsreels of them marching along roads with prams and bundles, and she had seen the human debris in the ditches after German planes had bombed and machine-gunned them. She was determined that this would not be the way she and her family were going to go; if it must be, they would die in their own home.

The Ketleys sipped their drinks in silence. It was growing dark now, and as they looked westward toward the city they noticed the glow in the sky.

"Gosh, Dad, look at that sunset," Donald exclaimed.

"Lovely," Mrs. Ketley agreed.

There was silence, except for the clattering of glasses from inside the pub. Then Arthur Ketley said, "That's no sunset."

He was echoing words that were being said all over London at that moment. At St. Paul's Cathedral the Dean, the Very Reverend Walter Robert Matthews, was walking in the twilight across the floor under the great dome when he lifted his eyes to the stained-glass windows. It was usually from the west that the luminescence came, but this evening it was the eastern windows that glowed with a strange red beauty.* Farther west, in Piccadilly and Leicester Square and in Hyde Park, pedestrians in the streets thought that something had gone wrong with the universe, for the sun seemed to be setting in a great red splash of color to the east.

At around nine o'clock the Ketleys, still sitting silently in the garden of the Cooper's Arms, their glasses long since empty, heard the sirens starting up again. First they wailed faintly in the distance, from the shores of the Thames Estuary in Essex and in Kent, and then, like cocks crowing to one another, those nearer and nearer took up the cry, passed Chadwell Heath and began sounding in the center of London.

"Home, I think," said Arthur Ketley.

Without haste they made their way down the road back to their terrace house in the dead-end street. Just as they were turning off the main road they heard a noise. Into view through the pale September night came an open cart of the kind used by Cockney junkmen. An old nag was pulling it along, spurred on by a man in a cap and muffler, with a woman beside him. The cart was piled high with a table, several chairs and an assortment of carpets and junk. Three children walked beside the vehicle, holding on and allowing themselves to be pulled along.

Behind the first family came two men pushing bicycles with sacks over their crossbars, and then more women and children, some of them pushing baby carriages and wooden trollies, others carrying small cases and handbags stuffed with odd impedimenta. The Ketleys had stopped to watch, and as the caravan passed they noticed that most of the people were black with some sort of stain, and that their eyes looked bloodshot, and that none of them talked. Not even the babies were crying.

"Where have you come from?" Arthur Ketley asked of the man on the cart.

"Silvertown," the man answered brusquely. "It's bloody murder back there, sheer bloody murder! We've 'ad it, mate, we've really 'ad it this time."

Hesitantly, for tea was rationed now, Mrs. Ketley said, "I could give you a cup of—well, maybe some water or something? You look tired."

"Thanks, missus," said one of the women, "but we ain't stopping till we get out of this mess. I wouldn't stay 'ere either if I was you. They're going to blow this place to bloody smithereens."

---

* W. R. Matthews, *St. Paul's Cathedral in Wartime.*

The Blitz: Openers

As she spoke the faint buzz in the air which had been tantalizing their ears for the last few minutes grew into an angry hum, and soon the sound came over them in waves as planes in great numbers roared overhead on their way to London from the east.

Now the children began to cry, as did some of the mothers, and the man on the cart tugged at the reins and urged the old horse into a canter.

The Ketleys walked silently back to their house. They did not attempt to put on the light, but went to the space under the stairs and crammed themselves inside the cubbyhole. Arthur Ketley took down the glasses and reached for the bottle of rum, and they settled in for the long night.

At eight o'clock that Saturday night the British government did a foolish thing. It might even be said that they panicked. Throughout the daylight bombing of the East End, Winston Churchill had been in conference in the Hole in the Ground with his Chiefs of Staff, and the reports that reached them were grim. The RAF had been tricked; they had been in the wrong place when the fleets of bombers came up the Thames, and though they had mauled the Luftwaffe planes on their way home, most of the enemy had succeeded in dropping their bombs just where they wanted. Moreover, antiaircraft defenses along the Thames had proved to be woefully inadequate and had hardly bothered the German aircraft. It had truly been a bad day for Britain. Apart from the East End, the targets hit were vital ones, and the blow to civilian morale was considerable.

But however dire these circumstances, they were no justification for the action taken by the Chiefs of Staff that evening: the code word "Cromwell" was sent out to the Home Forces.

There is still some argument about whether "Cromwell" was supposed to mean that a German invasion was under way, or whether it was a signal that invasion was about to begin.

Whatever it was, there seems no reason why it should have been issued at all, and pending another explanation, Winston Churchill must take his share of the blame, for the action was taken with his consent. There was no reason to believe that an invasion was any nearer that evening than it had been that morning, when a message saying that invasion seemed imminent had been sent out. Certainly the raid on London was heavy and its results catastrophic, and it could have been interpreted as the predictable prelude to a landing. But there was no movement in the North Sea or the Channel to indicate that the massed invasion barges had set out from France and Belgium.

What may have frightened the Prime Minister and his military advisers was the vast number of planes the Germans had used. Might not some of them be paratroop carriers? Was an airborne landing part of the operation against London? In fact it was not, but an unnerved General Staff obviously thought it might be, and Churchill allowed himself to be persuaded. The "Cromwell" signal was meant for army eyes only, but all over the country military units now had Home Guards attached to them, and these in turn worked in close liaison with air-raid wardens, fire services and the police. Within an hour of the issue of the code word, all Britain knew about it. In most places it was interpreted as an alarm indicating that the invasion had actually begun. It was, of course, not meant to indicate anything of the sort. Church bells were rung as a warning to the populace, the Home Guards turned out with their shotguns and staves, wives and children went down to the cellars, and stout civilians prepared to die in the ditches.*

In the East End the chaos caused by the bombing was compounded as fire fighters and ARP wardens were ordered, amid the flames and fumes and the crunch of bombs, to watch out for paratroopers and fifth columnists.

" 'Ow the 'ell d'you tell friend from foe," asked one Cockney fireman, "when we're all covered with the same shit?"

Shortly after eight that night the German bombers returned. At his headquarters in northern France, Hermann Göring was exultant. What did it matter if forty-five planes had been lost? Most of them had dropped their bombs first, as had the two hundred and forty others which had returned.

Every target had been hit, and London was in flames. From now on, his pilots were told, the job would be easy; all they had to do was to drop their bombs wherever they saw fires.

By nine o'clock the rescue squad had managed to get a shaft down into the rubble, and one of the men had been lowered into it. It was too narrow for a spade or a pickax, so he was working with his hands and a

---

* "Cromwell" was called off before too much damage could be done, though roadblocks were set up, some bridges where blown in the Midlands and three army officers were killed by mines planted along a road leading to their encampment. Later on, much more elaborate anti-invasion plans where drawn up.

small coal shovel filling baskets with the debris, which the man above hauled away.

George Hardiman was helping the rescue squad. The men had tried to dissuade him, but after a time they seemed to think that it was a comfort to him, so they let him alone. He was covered from head to foot with fine dust, his face caked like a clown's except where the tears had run down his cheeks. John had fallen asleep and had been taken to a warden's post around the corner. From time to time the man ; the shaft would ask everyone to be quiet, and then, in the silence, would call, "Winston!" They still heard some scrabbling, but there were no whines any more.

Every so often the baskets lifted out of the shaft contained something that George Hardiman recognized: one of the Mickey Mouse mugs they had bought for the children; a saucepan; a wedding picture of himself and Ellen from the mantelpiece, the glass still intact. At half past nine the man in the shaft called out; "Ask him if he recognizes this!"

It was one of Sheila's shoes. The man said, "I think I'm getting close. Everybody quiet for a moment."

They all fell silent again; the only noise to be heard was a faint buzzing in the distance and the sound of the man poking and prodding the debris.

An air-raid siren began to wail again, and then one after another took up the cry all along the Thames.

When they stopped, the man down the shaft called up, "It's her, all right. And the dog." They could tell by the tone of his voice that both of them were dead.

Suddenly, all of them noticed the strong smell of escaping gas, and the men in the rescue squad hastily put out their cigarettes.

For Commander Fordham's crews who had fought the oil fires at Thameshaven on September 5 and 6, the East End raid of September 7 was the same, only worse, but it was the baptism of most of London's firemen. Four fifths of them had no previous experience of actual fire fighting, for they were volunteers who had joined up as auxiliaries (some of them to escape being drafted into the army). At their training lectures they had been taught that a thirty-pump fire was a big one. By midnight on September 7 there were nine fires alone in the East End needing a hundred-plus pumps to fight them, and on the operations map at London Fire Brigade headquarters notices reading FIRE OUT OF HAND were pinned to several places.

The biggest of these was in Quebec Yard, in the Surrey Docks, where acres of warehouses were ablaze. The heat was so fierce that it had set alight the wooden paving blocks in the road some distance away.

A blaze covering such an area is not only worse than a smaller one in direct proportion to its area [the London Fire Brigade's historian wrote later, in *Front Line*], but is harder to fight than its mere extent would suggest. The greater the cumulative heat, the fiercer the draught of cold air dragged in to feed it, and thus the quicker the movement of the fire and the greater the length of its flames. They were so long and their heat so great as to blister the paint on fireboats that tried to slip past under the lee of the opposite river bank 300 yards away. Solid embers a foot long were tossed into streets afar off to start fresh fires. Stocks of timber which the firemen had drenched began at once to steam, then to dry, then themselves to burst into flame in the intense heat radiated from nearby blazes. . . .

At Woolwich Arsenal men fought the flames among boxes of live ammunition and crates of nitro-glycerin, under a hail of bombs directed at London's No. 1 military target. But in the docks themselves strange things were going on.

At one blazing warehouse on Commercial Dock the firemen waded in through a fog of smoke and then staggered back, clutching their eyes; it was as if they had been attacked by a swarm of savage flies, and when they tried to breathe their lungs felt like liquid fire. The warehouse stored pepper and it was afire.

There were rum fires, with torrents of blazing liquid pouring from the warehouse doors and barrels exploding like the bombs themselves [the historian reported]. There was a paint fire, another cascade of white-hot flame, coating the pumps with varnish that could not be cleaned for weeks. A rubber fire gave forth black clouds of smoke so asphyxiating that it could only be fought from a distance, and was always threatening to choke the attackers. Sugar, it seems, burns well in liquid form as it floats on the water in dockland basins. Tea makes a blaze that is "sweet, sickly and very intense." One man found it odd to be pouring cold water on hot tea leaves. A grain warehouse when burning produced great clouds of black flies that settled in banks upon the walls, whence the firemen washed them off with their jets. There were rats in their hundreds. And the residue of burned wheat was "a sticky mess that pulls your boots off."

The German bombers coming over in wave after wave had no trouble at all. Even the Thames itself was alight along part of its length, a highway of flame indicating the target. In addition, the holocausts had ringed off several areas so that they became diminishing islands whose boundaries were defined by the encroaching flames or by the Thames itself. Some of the people trapped within were taken off by boat, but that was not always possible, so hundred of thousands of them waited inside the encroaching rings of fire while firemen outside battled to get through to them before it was too late. Bombs were still coming down and gas mains were going up; the houses had crumbled into dust, the heat was mounting and smoke made it hard to see and breathe. The injured lay in the rubble, with not even water to wash their wounds or quench their thirst. In these circumstances, panic might have been expected, but in fact there was very little of it. The bombing seemed to have stunned everyone.

Mrs. Nancy Spender, an ambulance worker, managed to reach East Ham after a nightmare drive past burning warehouses and over bomb-cratered roads. Eventually she reached a shelter where a bomb had struck. "We went over . . . and put our heads in," she reported. "I suppose there were about forty people there. I said—Anybody hurt?— and not a soul answered. So I said again—Anybody hurt?—and still nobody answered, so I went up to one woman and tapped her and said —Is there anybody hurt here?—and she said—Over there there's a mother and a two-day-old baby, they've both been dug out, and I think further up there's a boy with a very bad knee, he got dug out, he was buried up to his waist, but I don't know about the others. So I went over to the mother, she didn't speak, and I wrapped her in a blanket and put her on [a] stretcher, and I said—Is there a warden here?—and somebody said—No, he was killed half an hour ago. So I got a couple of men, anyway, to help me, and we took her back on the stretcher, put her in the ambulance, then I came back again and collected the boy, with some help, and then we got back to the ambulance with him and after that I just filled the ambulance with as many people as I could cram in, about fifteen or sixteen. Still nobody spoke, it was all the most deadly silence, and I got in beside them, not beside the driver, and drew the curtains to shut out the ghastly glow, and deafen the noise a bit, and we drove off."*

In another ambulance, with the body of Sheila on the bunk beside them, George and John Hardiman arrived shortly before midnight at a first-aid station set up at the London Heart Hospital in Mile End Road. The first bombs of the night raid dropped at the end of Star Road shortly

---

* Constantine FitzGibbon, *The Winter of the Bombs: The Story of the Blitz of London.*

after they had recovered Sheila's body and while an ambulance man was still trying to revive her. She and Winston had died not from blast or the crush of the rubble, but from a pocket of gas escaping from the wrecked kitchen stove. They worked on the body for a long time, but everyone knew it was no good; she must have been dead for hours.

They stopped when the bombs started to fall again and the Hardimans found themselves bundled into the ambulance and driven away. At the hospital Sheila's body was taken to the mortuary, and they were given cups of tea and left in a waiting room. No one seemed to know quite what to do with them. They sat around until the all clear went off at five o'clock, and then George awakened John and they went out, hand in hand, into Mile End Road. Neither buses nor the Underground seemed to be running, so they began walking back toward Canning Town. George wanted to be there when Ellen returned; he didn't want anyone else to tell her that Sheila was dead.

All through the night and morning hours, groups of people from Stepney and Bermondsey and Canning Town trekked by cart or bicycle or on foot to the safety of the woodland glades of their favorite playground, Epping Forest, where they lay down and slept. But many more stayed among the bomb craters in a daze, too exhausted, too frightened, too stunned to talk or move.

But, being Cockneys, they had plenty to say before long. Four hundred and thirty of them had died in the raids; sixteen hundred others were in the hospital. There were hundreds of thousands of survivors, however, and as the hours went by, their tempers rose. Their houses had been destroyed, and most of them had nowhere to go. No one did anything about them; Why not? they asked. Why weren't there shelters, food and evacuation plans? And why was it that the poor people in the East End had been chosen, while the bigwigs in the government and the posh folk up West in Knightsbridge and Mayfair had slept safely in their beds? And why had the German bombers got through so easily?

In official circles there were two views of the great raids of September 7. For Air Chief Marshal Dowding and his staff, the night's attacks were a welcome change in the Luftwaffe's tactics, and though they shared the nation's shock and horror over the bombing of London, they also felt a sense of relief. From a tactical point of view, the raids on London could not have come at a better time, for they had switched the pressure from the RAF's fighter stations just at the moment when they were all but destroyed, and had given a respite to the RAF pilots dogfighting over the Channel just when they were about to collapse from exhaustion.

Winston Churchill shared London's anger and agony, and the RAF's satisfaction as well. It would be false to say that he rejoiced over the night's raids; far too many people had been killed and far too much damage had been done for that. But he was well aware of the propaganda effect the death toll would have upon the neutral world, and President Roosevelt had already been on the private line from the White House to extend his sympathies to the British people.

The statisticians who had been advising the government were, however, somewhat disconcerted; they had expected many more people to be killed. Considering the amount of explosives dropped, the fires started, the houses destroyed, they had calculated that there would be thousands, not hundreds, to be buried. It was somewhat awkward; with so many people still alive and so many houses destroyed, there were far more homeless to take care of than they had told the authorities to expect, and no one had made adequate arrangements for this eventuality.

Even the pigeons in the East End no longer had any roosts to return to; flocks of them were now flying over Bermondsey and Poplar and Bow, looking vainly through the smoke for the back-garden lofts where they used to perch.

One of Mass-Observation's most assiduous correspondents during this period was twenty-eight-year-old James Donald, a writer and conscientious objector who lodged with a Mrs. R. in East London. Besides Mr. R., a post-office employee, there was a daughter, Vi, and a son, who was serving in the RAF. The time of this report is September 1940:

FRIDAY   Vi has gone to the pictures. Mr. R. is on late duty again. Mrs. R. is sitting before me knitting. Quite chatty but about war and what we ought to do to Germany. Every few minutes she looks out of the door ostensibly to "see the stars." I suspect she is waiting for the searchlights to pop up and to listen to the distant drone of planes. The raids now terrify her.

9.20 P.M.:   Wow! Sirens! Mrs. R. is off to the Shelter. Slams door. This time I'm taking her impedimenta down for her. She forgot it last time.

9.30 P.M.:   That's that. She's got all she'll want for the night, I hope. Vi is still out. Mr. J. (the other lodger) is in and gone to bed. Now I'm going to do some writing and study.

10.30 P.M.:   All quiet. Still alone. Conclude Vi returning from the pictures (if she came out) has gone down to the Shelter with her mother.

10.50 P.M.:   Vi returned bringing with her two friends (sisters) aged 19 and 16 (artisan class). They stayed about fifteen minutes. Most of the time they talked about knitting jumpers. After that Vi washed and ate some biscuits and knitted until 11.35 P.M. I'm tired and so is she. Then since her father has not returned and there is no All Clear she decides to make up her bed on the floor of the front parlour. I lay down on my bed.

SATURDAY, 12.57 A.M.:   I can't get to sleep so write the above notes. At the moment of writing there is heavy gunfire. A bomb. Very close. A violent thump. I go down to Vi's room, the front room downstairs. She moans.

4.25 A.M.   I stayed with Vi most of the night. There was gunfire most of the time and an occasional distant bomb. Mr. R. did not come home and Mr. J. stayed in bed. Vi was very amorous but owing to the constant tension of circumstances and the state of nervous excitement present during a raid I found it almost impossible to pay her any attention for more than a few minutes at a time. She seemed to forget the danger we were in and couldn't understand my feelings. At any normal time I expect I should have been eager enough for her but at normal times she is almost prudish. The excitement of a raid causes her to become sexually excited. I can't fathom this at all. Must be due to some psychological or glandular change caused by fear. I don't know. (Note. This matter interests me. I wonder if other observers have met with similar cases of sexual excitement during air raids. Personally I'm just the reverse!)

Later: There was a raid from 9–10 A.M., from 1–2 P.M. and 6–6.40 P.M. Only dogfights overhead and a few bombs. We are getting used to it now. I think I am. Visiting a local baker's I questioned the young lady assistant (aged about 26).

"What do you think of these raids?"

"Oh, they don't bother me much now. I say if you are going to be killed, you are, so what? I say the chances of a direct hit are very small. I guess it's like getting a lead pencil and throwing it on the floor and chucking grains of salt on it to see how many stick on it. I'm pretty calm."

"Do you think this war will last long?"

"No. Matter of weeks. Why, 80 million Germans can't be kept down for ever. They will be free and in fifty years all this will be history."

8.15 P.M.:   Have a bath. 9.05:   Sirens. Mrs. R. to shelter. Mr. R. still at G.P.O. Vi stays at home. Nothing to report.

10.15 P.M.:   Mr. R. returns. Came through raid from G.P.O. Shall now try to get some sleep.

SUNDAY, 2.05 A.M.:   The last hour has been a lifetime! About 1 A.M. I was half asleep, planes overhead. Suddenly came a distant whistling which I knew to be a falling bomb. I leapt out of bed. The whistling probably lasted about two seconds. It seemed a lifetime. I wrenched open the door and dived for the front room where Vi lay. I yelled her name, then with a cracking crunch the bomb fell somewhere close at hand—there was no actual explosion. I grabbed hold of the girl who was asleep. She moaned and somehow I made her realise that bombs were falling. Somehow I shoved her in the cupboard under the stairs. No further explosions occurred but outside the firemen were yelling: "We're coming, coming!" Mr. R. who was asleep in the kitchen stirred and said: "What's all this commotion?" I told him, but he was too sleepy to understand. I heard crackling and leaving the girl, saying "Now you stay there" I ran outside. At first I thought that the big furniture store under which Mrs. R. was sheltering was alight, but it was a photographer's and a tailor's with a block of flats above. Right next door to the depository. I suppose I was outside about two minutes after the bomb fell. I've never seen anything catch alight so rapidly. Within three minutes the roof had collapsed and flames were gushing out. The ARP services were *wonderfully efficient*. (The fire was only 25 yards from their HQ.) About 1/4 mile away, two more fires had broken out—bigger than the ones close at hand. I ran indoors. Mr. R., very white, said: "I'm going down to the shelter." I heard a shout from outside and thought I heard a gas warning. I grabbed my mask and yelled: "Be prepared for gas!" I felt oddly calm, but it proved I was wrong.

Mr. R. said: "Christ! I'm going down to the shelter and Vi is coming with me, no nonsense."

"I'm *not* going down there," said Vi.

"I wouldn't go down there for £100,000," I said. "Why, man, it's the most dangerous place in the neighbourhood. Think what it would be like if all that caught alight."

"Well, I'm going," said Mr. R. and he walked off.

Vi and I and Mr. J. watched the fire in the street until the latter thought we had better clear out in case the walls collapsed. But I didn't think there was any fear of that, it was not close enough.

"The police will turn us out if there is any danger," I said.

"Isn't it awful," said Vi, as we stood watching the flames.

"Now look here," I said. "If you've got to get out of the house, what is it you value most to take with you?"

"My clothes, of course."

We went back home. Presently Mr. R. returned. "No, I didn't go down the shelter." Gives us details of fires and their location. "Now I'm going to see how Mum is in the shelter." He goes off.

Vi says, "I'd like to go and see the fires. Take me." She slips on her coat and we go off too. She holds my arm until we get into the main street, then she drops it and holds my hand. People are running to the fire from all directions. The All Clear sounds. Vi says, "Let's go back, I'm a bit frightened." (The glare from the 6 fires within 300 yards was rather spectacular. Gave me an unreal sensation as if I was seeing it on the screen.)

We came back and Vi practically collapsed on the stairs with exhaustion and reactions following excitement. I lifted her into a comfortable armchair but she would not take any of the sal volatile I offered her. Presently I made her lie down on the front room floor and covered her with rugs etc.

"You won't go out again will you in case the sirens go again?"

"No."

By degrees we calmed down. Mr. R. returned from seeing Mrs. R. in the shelter (who simply refused to come to the surface) and we all fell asleep. 6.50 A.M.: I rose early and surveyed the damage in the neighbourhood. Raining.

MONDAY, 11.10 A.M.: The remainder of yesterday was too strenuous for writing in this diary. Nervous exhaustion today. Don't feel capable of writing of the vast fire I viewed from a point seven miles from the City. Pepys would have given a graphic description. I can't—not now anyway. It is too ghastly, too tragic, too unnerving. I am tired. Only two hours sleep for the past 48 hours. It seems we live for the moment. I am more strongly pacific than ever. Quietly determined as never before to work for peace when this mad war is over. Perhaps tomorrow I shall feel more like writing of personal matters but I have to make this note today to let you know my *mood*. Quiet determination that I shall do my bit to assure that *this* time we will say and *mean* "Never again." It rests with US.

8.05 P.M.: Sirens early tonight. Everyone in this house except myself and Mr. J. is irritable. Several times during the day we were on the verge of rowing.

Vi said, "If there was a raid and I saw *anybody* going by, I should ask them in—even dirty gipsy people."

Said her mother, menacingly, "You try, my lady! Asking people into my house!"

Still don't feel like writing about war. The rumours and news I hear makes me dully antagonistic, a kind of impotent rage against the leaders, especially Chamberlain.* A friend of mine (radio dealer age 50, mid-class) expressed *my* feelings when he said: "And old Neville came to the window and said 'Peace in our time' and within a year he said 'England is now at war with Germany.' The double-crossing old nitwit. Look at his speech when he came back from Munich. 'When I was a lit-tel boy (said with a lisp) my

---

* Neville Chamberlain remained a minister in Churchill's Cabinet until October the following year. He died on November 9, 1941.

muvver said ter me, hif at first you don't succeed, try, try, try a-gain.' How very very very nice, dear friends of dear Mr. Chamberlain."

Another friend (Baker, 42) said to me: "Friend, keep this under your hat. We're going to lose this war. I told my brother that months ago. There's no sense in this war—just slaughter for slaughter's sake. I was in the last war and I know. It's the leaders' war. The people don't count—of course they don't."

Later: Now I'm in a fatalistic mood. What will be will be. Mrs. R. tends to give me the jitters—she's so very panicky. Mr. R. reads at great length the reports of the bombing and tends to get the wind up as a consequence. He spent last night in the shelter with his missus. Vi and I stayed behind. There was much gunfire. The noise and tension made her sexually excited (see previous remarks) and I felt in such a don't-care-what-happens-now mood that I was intimate with her but she got more kick out of it than I did. Felt fed up afterwards.

9

The Big Raids

Chief Superintendent Reginald Smith of the Metropolitan Police picked up the telephone as it rang in his office on the morning of September 12, 1940, and tried to concentrate on what the voice at the other end was saying. He had not been out of his clothes for more than four days and had snatched only catnaps during that time. His body was crying out for sleep and a bath, and his heart was sick.

Ever since the big raid of September 7 the Germans had been concentrating on the East End. He and his policemen had done what they could by clearing the way for firemen and ambulances, working with air-raid wardens and shepherding people from their wrecked and burning homes, helping demolition squads dig for broken beings whimpering underneath the rubble. Five of his men had died in the line of duty during these days: one by flinging himself on top of a baby just as a bomb dropped fifty yards away; one while trying to activate the sprinklers in a burning warehouse; another by drowning in a Thameside lock covered with blazing oil; a fourth underneath the walls of a collapsing factory; and a fifth blown against a building in Canning Town. Those who survived had worked night and day, and in most places they had brought some sort of succor and comfort to the populace.

But not in Silvertown. In Silvertown they had failed, and its inhabitants' nerves had cracked.

Silvertown was one of London's worst slum areas. Most of its people lived three and four to a room in row after row of insalubrious ramshackle houses. The name came from the biggest factory in the district, S. W. Silver and Company, which employed a large force of young women in the manufacture of rubber goods and waterproofing materials. There were fertilizer and soap factories nearby, and the air of the district curdled with a mixture of appalling smells, which the natives had long since ceased to notice. In addition to factory workers, there was also a large population of seamen and dockers, for Silvertown was surrounded on all sides by the docks and wharves of the Pool of London, and these waterways cut the area off from neighboring West Ham, to which it was administratively attached.

When Superintendent Smith had made his first tour of K Division after being posted there in the spring of 1940, his police guide saved Silvertown for the last. As they drove through the neighborhood, the man said, "This is the place you'll have to watch out for, Reg. It's not the people—they're all right. Typical Cockneys, friendly lot. Get a bit drunk on Saturdays. Did you know there are more pubs in Silvertown than in any other equivalent district in London? They use 'em, too, but they don't do any real harm. No, it's the West Ham Council. Real lot of Bolshies, if you ask me. Won't do a thing about the war."

Superintendent Smith was to discover that, though he used the language of a die-hard Tory, his guide had truth on his side. Not that the councilors of West Ham *were* Bolshies; they were simply stubborn, short-sighted old men. Their average age was over sixty, and they refused to listen or to learn. West Ham was a stronghold of the Labour party, and most of the members who filled the safe seats on the council were party hacks who had slavishly followed the party line all through the nineteen-thirties. That line was to express loathing and abhorrence of Hitler, the Nazi party and Fascist Germany, but to do nothing to help rearm Britain so that she could face up to the inevitable enemy. When the government instructed local councils throughout Britain to start building air-raid shelters for their people in 1937, 1938 and 1939, the old men of West Ham refused. They stubbornly insisted that war was not necessary and therefore would not come, so why waste money on protecting people from it? When Whitehall pressed them, they had tried blackmail. They would build shelters, they said, if the government would pay for them—but not unless. That will show those Tories they can't bully us, they told each other gleefully.

Unfortunately, the government didn't try to bully them. If the

The Big Raids

Socialists of West Ham wanted to leave their people unprotected, that was their concern.*

When the enemy planes came over on September 7, Silvertown seemed to get more than its share from the start. Silver and Company was soon on fire, and black smoke from the burning rubber billowed up, acting as a target for the second, third and fourth waves of bombers, and high explosives and incendiaries rained down on the houses surrounding it. The trek of refugees had begun; people fled with what belongings they could gather across the swing bridges to the higher ground on the other side. Police, firemen and air-raid wardens were glad to see them go, because Silvertown was no longer a place for anyone to stay in. Those who remained behind were either the dead, the sick and infirm, the wounded or those stubborn souls who refused to leave their damaged houses and life's possessions.

In the early hours of Sunday morning, September 8, Superintendent Smith had managed to get through to Silvertown from his headquarters to see the situation for himself. Even today he does not like to talk much about the journey. Bombs were dropping almost continuously, roads were barred by bomb craters or collapsed buildings, firemen were battling great fires everywhere, and several times his car had to be helped over great piles of crisscrossing firehoses leading down to the pumps on the Thames. There was too much noise from the fires and the bombs to talk, and in any case, everyone was wearing a face mask against the appalling stench from the wrecked fertilizer factory.

In the center of Silvertown, Smith found a local clergyman trying to control the situation. All air-raid wardens were either dead or had fled with the refugees.† The Reverend Walter Paton had taken over and was trying to round up women and children from the ruins and get them to some sort of shelter. His own church and home had been hit; indeed, there was barely a house standing in three square miles, save for one

---

* For those who wonder why West Ham (and its satellites, Silvertown and Canning Town) did not benefit from the antiair-raid policies, grants and preparations of the London County Council, it should be pointed out that though West Ham was in the social and economic orbit of London, administratively it came under the Essex County Council. It was a semi-independent county borough. On the other hand, its neighbor, East Ham, also a county borough, had a better-organized and much more effective antiair-raid system.

† Like West Ham's councilors, most of the borough's air-raid wardens were over sixty.

semibombed school into which he had crammed nearly seven hundred men, women and children. Their state was pitiful. They sat on their baggage, stunned out of their minds by shock, the continual noise and the bombs, waiting to be rescued from the inferno. "You've got to get them out, you've got to get them out," the reverend kept saying.

Smith had vowed that he would. Somehow he made his way to a police station that was still functioning and went to work on the telephone. Yes, he was told, the situation in Silvertown was known; yes, it was clear that the people were in desperate straits; yes, a convoy of buses had been sent to get the people out of the school; and yes, it was understood that the school was vulnerable not only to bombs but to blast.

Later on Sunday morning Reginald Smith had received confirmation that a convoy of buses was on its way to Silvertown to rescue the homeless. After that, the multiplicity of his other tasks had made him forget those miserable, stunned people sitting on their luggage in that forlorn school, waiting amid the crescendo of bombs to be taken away to safety. That is, he forgot until Monday morning when his secretary said, "Isn't it terrible about Silvertown, sir? They had a direct hit on a school there—four hundred and fifty people killed. A lot of women and kids among them."

Smith cried, "But they shouldn't have been there! They were sending buses for them. What happened to the buses?"

What had happened to the buses was that the drivers had been told to assemble at a pub called The George and then drive in to collect the refugees. But the convoy leader had taken them to a pub of the same name on the other side of the river. By the time they reached the school, the sirens had started again; deciding that Silvertown was no place to stay while bombs were falling, the drivers had retreated back across the river. Some hours later, when they returned, the school was gone along with most of the people in it.

No wonder the few survivors of Silvertown were bitter. As for Superintendent Smith, he was sick at the thought of what he might have done.

Now, as the voice on the telephone had just been reminding him, Smith was faced by another problem of people in shelters, and this time there were thousands, not hundreds, involved. By this time what came to be known as the Blitz had really begun, at least in the East End. There were three or four raids every day and alerts all through the night. Desperate for some place to hide, Cockneys were searching for any place which looked deep and safe. One sanctuary they had found was an unfinished stretch of the London Underground just beyond Stratford Broadway Station.

"You'd better come and have a look," his sergeant said. "You won't believe your eyes, or your nose."

When he got there it was two o'clock in the morning and there was a raid on. He and his companion stumbled over the last stretches of railway lines leading out of Stratford Broadway Station until they came to a black mass ahead which was impossible to see as a shape but easy to identify from the great wafts of hot air and the sounds which came pulsing out of it. "I'd put your hankie over your face if I was you, sir," the sergeant said. Smith, who got queasy on boats, felt the blood draining from his face.

"The first thing I heard," he recalls, "was the great hollow hubbub, a sort of soughing and wailing, as if there were animals down there moaning and crying. And then, as we went on, this terrible stench hit me. It was worse than dead bodies, hot and thick and so fetid that I gagged and then vomited. About fifty yards in I stopped. Ahead of me, I could see faces peering towards me lit by candles and lanterns, and it was like a painting of hell. There were young voices singing and old voices wailing and babies crying. And everywhere these faces staring out of the flickering darkness."

His sergeant said, "There's all sorts in there, I can tell you—white and black and yellow, though most of them are so filthy you can't tell the difference. Some of them haven't been out for days, and they refuse to leave. Some of the old folks are dying, but we won't know how many until they bring the bodies out. You can't tell from the smell. They do everything in there. No sanitation and no shame, I can tell you."

The sergeant started to walk farther in, but Smith was suddenly overwhelmed; four days of sleeplessness, bombing and responsibility had taken their toll at last. He began vomiting again. "I can't go on," he said. "I've got to get out of here. But something's got to be done, it's got to be done." He turned and hurried away to the light at the entrance to the tunnel.*

The first night after George had made contact with Ellen, the Hardiman family moved into the Stratford tunnel and remained there for the next

---

* Stubborn to the last, West Ham Council refused to accept responsibility for the tunnel, despite Smith's pleas. Finally the whole borough was taken over by the government, and the tunnel, among other areas, was cleaned up.

three days. They seemed to be in a state of shock and did not notice the filth and stench around them. Ellen stayed huddled up on a blanket, weeping and sleeping and refusing the food that George and Johnny brought her. But she had to attend Sheila's funeral, and when she got out into the daylight and looked at herself in her handbag mirror she took a deep breath. "Gawd," she said, "I do look a mess. What must you think of me, George?"

They found a public bath, got themselves cleaned up, and then went to the cemetery. They had been too stunned to say anything when it was suggested that Sheila be buried in a common grave with all the others, and now it was too late. But after the ceremony Ellen wiped away the tears, and with them seemed to wipe away her apathy and hopelessness too.

"We've got to find somewhere to live, George," she said. "We can't go on staying in that stinking hole."

"I've been working on that," George Hardiman said.

For four continuous days after September 7, 1940, while the East End was feeling the full fury of the German bombing campaign, living on the other side of London was like being in another world. In Kensington, Hammersmith, Maida Vale and Ealing one could hear the sirens and many people went to their shelters, but the planes overhead dropped their bombs on Plaistow and Poplar, Mile End Road and Bow.

The Cockneys did not even have the satisfaction of reading about themselves in the newspapers; the Ministry of Information saw to that. Though it was impossible to disguise East London from a reconnaissance plane, and the Germans must have had a clear picture of the damage they were inflicting, all details of buildings hit and localities destroyed were deleted from both local newspapers and the reports of foreign correspondents. The result was that the people of the East End felt isolated in their suffering, and the feeling spread among them that as long as it was just the Cockneys who were taking a beating, the folks up West weren't losing too much sleep. "What d'you think we've got down here—smallpox?" one docker asked a reporter. "We feel as if we've been put in bloody quarantine."

As a result of the mealy-mouthed nature of the official communiqués, rumors spread rapidly across the country about what was happening in the East End, and it was these rumors which were mainly responsible for the legend that riots and demonstrations against government apathy had started in certain dock areas in mid-September. In fact these never happened, though there was more than enough neglect, stupidity and official indifference to individual suffering to justify such protests.

The rumors were so persistent that four or five days after the bombing had reached its peak, commanding officers in army camps all over the country began to report restiveness among their conscript troops, particularly among those from London. An M-O observer with a Cockney regiment reported just how his fellow soldiers were feeling:

Interest in papers and radio immediately quickened after the bombing began, and that was when they began to be delayed, arriving sometimes at lunch sometimes at tea. Our judgment of the gravity of the situation was made more on the speed of the communication than anything else. Radio bulletins vague in their geography, measured in their admission of damage, spread the alarm they were calculated to allay. "A school in the East End of London" means nothing to a German but to an East Ender in search of information it is the school at the corner of his street. Vagueness may confuse the enemy but it diffuses anxiety through a much larger section of the public than precision.

One of the troopers attached to the regiment had gone home to Poplar on a forty-eight-hour leave shortly after the Blitz began.

Brown did not return until Monday lunchtime, over twelve hours overdue. We'd all fantasised his death, his injury, and when he came in there was a cheer. He stood between the cots for a second, his usually pale white slum face flushed and drawn.

"East End," he said, "they've wiped it out."

And then he ran to his cot and lay there, helmet and gas mask still slung, head buried in the pillow, weeping. Some had not been looking, and they called out to him, brushing their boots, getting their equipment on. I thought his wife or daughter had been killed and I shouted: "Shut up!" Then there was silence, the unnatural, uneasy silence of a mass faced with the emotion of an individual. It became intolerable until someone shouted: "For God's sake carry on!" So we carried on talking, sometimes casting a glance at the little man crying on his iron cot. His wife and child were not dead but a time bomb had fallen on his house, he had left his family in an air raid, had had no sleep all the time he had been in London. Emotionally expecting Armageddon, he described later the destruction to fit this picture. Not the the East End only but the docks, Woolwich and God knows what else were wiped out. The flames of fire against the smoke of burning buildings had coloured his whole imagination. Others coming from London filled in the panorama of misery and destruction, and the fear which we had hitherto suppressed during our separation rose again like giants after their sleep.

The invasion scare was still on. In his latest broadcast, shortly after the start of the Blitz, Churchill had warned that the Germans might be landing at any moment, and by now 75 percent of all troops were confined to barracks and kept on alert. The result, this army observer reported, was increased talk of desertion among the soldiers, many of whom slipped away to see how their families were doing.

We queued constantly in our spare time to telephone to London to be told of infinite delay, almost no letters arrived, morale sank very low, we learned that Charing Cross, Waterloo, Vauxhall Bridge had been bombed, no ships floated in the Port of London. We feared that this was true and no news, each day no news, and when news came it was a telegram to say F's mother is dead, C's wife, H's house had been blown to bits, J's wife had been blown on top of her baby by bomb blast. We know the calculation of the enemy was to cause just such disquiet among us, but the absence of any machinery to inform us of communication depressed us. Idle in camp, waiting, we thought of our people, sleepless, huddled in shelters, the horrors we knew had happened to our comrades happened to us. Our commanding officer realised the danger. The regimental secretary was instructed to go to the East End and get news of various people, but this is a clumsy machine to operate.

It was a relief to the government when, on the night of September 13, a German plane strayed off course and dropped a bomb on Buckingham Palace. "Dolts, idiots, stupid fools!" cried the Prime Minister when he heard that the censors at the Ministry of Information had deleted the location from an Associated Press dispatch to New York. "Spread the news at once. Let it be broadcast everywhere. Let the humble people of London know that they are not alone, and that the King and Queen are sharing their perils with them."*

A few days later the Queen was quoted in the newspapers as saying, "Now I feel I can look the East End in the face."

The incident seemed to have a tonic effect upon most Cockneys;

---

* Though it was not revealed at the time, the King had a very narrow escape. Two bombs fell thirty yards away in the courtyard in front of his study. "A very accurate piece of bombing, if I may say so," remarked a Palace constable to the Queen. Buckingham Palace was bombed several times after this, and a dashing RAF sergeant pilot named J. H. "Ginger" Lacey became a national hero when he jumped one bomber in the act and shot him down over Westminster.

The Big Raids

Union Jacks began to appear miraculously on burned houses all over dockland, and the royal family got a warm welcome when they toured the bombed areas.

But by that time everyone in London was sharing the load. After September 13 the Luftwaffe attacks gradually spread across the whole capital, and the East End was no longer alone. Bombs fell on the City, and churches, hospitals and stockbrokers' offices collapsed on one another in the rubble. The fleets of planes moved toward the West End and dropped their loads on Westminster, Chelsea and Kensington. Night after night the enemy returned, and it was all the same whether you were a docker in Bow or a debutante in Park Lane; you ducked for cover as incendiaries, high explosives and land mines crashed down on Mile End Road, Ealing Broadway, Piccadilly, Leicester Square and Hampstead alike.

Soon Mrs. Rosemary Black in her fashionable house in Maida Vale was writing: "The papers now say that London has taken the worst punishment from bombing anywhere, even worse than Rotterdam. We are all delighted to hear this."

Some were more delighted than others. There were some brave and intelligent men and women who knew the odds of survival were in their favor, and yet were terrified the moment the bombs began to fall. There were others who reveled in the noise and the inferno of fires. Winston Churchill was one of these. Colonel Leslie Hollis later recalled that the Prime Minister's servant, a Royal Marine named Ives, was worried because Churchill wanted to leave the Hole in the Ground the moment raids started and wander around St. James's Park in the pitch-black to watch the effects.

Eventually the risk of falling shrapnel was so great [wrote Hollis] that we told him that on no account must he allow Mr. Churchill out after dark on such expeditions. These orders poor Ives did his best to carry out—by hiding Mr. Churchill's boots. Then one night at the height of the Blitz, Mr. Churchill rang for him.

"Ives," he said, sitting on the edge of the bed in his bare feet, "Ives, my boots."

Ives, mindful of his orders, gave him all sorts of excuses; the boots were not there, they were being cleaned, mended, anything. At last Churchill stood up, hand outstretched. Out of excuses, poor Ives had to produce them. Mr. Churchill put them on and then addressed himself to Ives.

"I'll have you know," he said, "that as a child, my nursemaid could never prevent me from taking a walk in the Park when I wanted to do so. And, as a man, Adolf Hitler certainly won't."

Then he was up off into the night.*

The life of London gradually changed that autumn. Dusk became the zero hour, for now that was when the big formations of German bombers came over.

"Everyone knows it, for just before dusk the streets are noisy with the chatter of those who are rushing for the public shelters," reported Robert Nichols to M-O. He was an armaments worker who lived in Eltham, a suburb of southeast London. "They carry their suitcases with spare clothes, others carry blankets and pillows. I am told that some of them get to the shelters shortly after teatime and stake out their claims to a favourite corner by placing their gear on the seats. Then they go away like theatregoing pit-ites,† leaving their gear as evidence of priority. When the alert sounds they just walk into the shelters and claim their places. This causes hot arguments and even fights among the women. A warden of my acquaintance had a finger broken intervening in such a fight."

Nichols preferred to sleep during the raids in the Anderson shelter he had dug in his small back garden. The shelter, named after Sir John Anderson, the Home Minister, in charge of Air Raid Precautions, had steel sides, a steel reinforced roof which was cushioned with soil, and was supposedly safe from all but direct hits. Many a London householder made it snug with electric light, chairs, table and bunks. "I feel as safe in an Anderson as anywhere," Nichols maintained. But in the poorer areas of London not many people agreed with him, though even when the Blitz was at its worst, a surprising number of Londoners never took shelter. A poll taken at the end of September 1940 revealed that during the long night raids 44 percent of Londoners stayed at home, 44 percent went to shelters, and 12 percent made other arrangements. And once people got used to the raids, even more of them decided to risk staying at home.

But the poorer Londoners continued to patronize the shelters—

---

* Hollis and Leasor, *op. cit.*

† Those in line for pit and balcony (unreserved) seats at London theatres could rent a stool and leave it with their name outside the box office, claiming it just before curtain time.

except, of course, in West Ham, where there weren't any—and this was hardly surprising. When one lives in a tiny one-up-and-one-down struc- ture in a slum row, there is no room in your paved backyard for an Anderson shelter, and there is no use reinforcing a nook under the stairs if the house is so frail that it falls down at a near miss. So most people in the East End went off every night to the big public shelters; they could be killed even there, but at least it would be in company.

The Tube or Underground shelters had not, in fact, been included in the government's plans when they began organizing protection for London; it was the East Enders who decided to take them over. Driven from their homes by the intensity of the Luftwaffe attacks, they simply bought tickets at the nearest Underground station and rode down the escalator to the platform far below. There they slung down their bedding, gathered their children around them and refused to budge. Soon it be- came a nightly routine. The moment the sirens began, down they went and down they stayed until the all clear sounded.

It was here, in mid-September 1940, that the sculptor Henry Moore discovered them, and they were to change his life. During the summer Moore had been living through what might be called a fallow period in his artistic development. He had hoped that to a certain extent he could keep aloof and continue his individual life as an artist, working on the new drawings and sculptures he was planning—purely abstract works that would take him further and further away from subjective reality.

But of course it was impossible to ignore the war, even before the Blitz began. No commissions were coming his way, no exhibitions were possible, material for his sculptures were hard to get and hard to trans- port. He paid the rent by continuing to teach at the Arts School in Chel- sea, and he and his wife stayed in the studio they had taken over from Barbara Hepworth in Hampstead.

And then it happened. "We had been to Chelsea for the evening, with some friends, I expect," he recalls, "and we were on our way back to Hampstead. We could no longer use the car because petrol rationing was now strict, and I think it was the first time Irene and I had used the Underground for a long time."

When their train reached Hampstead Station and the doors opened, the Moores found that they could hardly step onto the platform. Sleep- ing bodies were lying everywhere. What they did not know at the time was that Hampstead is one of the deepest Underground stations in Lon- don, and that its reputation for safety had already spread across the capital. From miles away whole families had begun trekking daily to make their nightly abode deep down in the warm womb of the station.

"It so happened that there was a raid going on by the time we reached Hampstead, and they wouldn't let us go up to the surface. It was only then that I began to look around me, and suddenly I was excited by what I saw." He smiled. "You could say that in every direction I looked I could see what have since been called Henry Moore reclining figures. I just stood there, watching them—the chatterers and the withdrawn. When they announced that the all clear had sounded and we could go up to the surface, I went reluctantly. That night and all next day I worked on a sketch. But when the evening came, I stopped; I put some notebooks in my pocket and set off for the Underground. I stayed there for several hours, making myself inconspicuous and drawing figures and groups."

Two or three days later Sir Kenneth Clark telephoned Moore again and asked whether he would enroll as a war artist.

"Now that the situation had changed and we were all in it," Moore recalls, "and now that I knew it wouldn't just be soldiers in uniform and tanks and guns, I said yes. I told him about my Underground sketches and what I wanted to do. So I was made a war artist and they gave me a pass which allowed me to go wherever I wanted and move about during the raids."

Moore's experiences in the Underground shelters changed the whole direction of his artistic drive, away from abstract shapes; the Cockneys sprawled across the platforms of Piccadilly, Hampstead, Bayswater Road and Liverpool Street drew him back to the human shape and the human predicament.

Talking to Moore about his experiences in London in 1940 and 1941 is a curious experience compared with the recollections of most of the other people who went through the horrors of the Blitz. It is as if his artistic compulsion kept him aloof from the battle raging all around him. He was one of those who were never once afraid, and as he talks the impression grows that he was somehow never involved, and that the people he transferred so strikingly from the Underground platforms to his famous series of Blitz drawings were truly, as he says, nothing more to him than Henry Moore reclining figures.

"From September 1940 onwards," he said, "I would spend the evenings going from shelter to shelter. I would go down the moving staircase and tuck myself away in the corner of an exit and survey the people sleeping on the platform from there. It wasn't so easy when the trains were still running, because the place would be full of people stepping over bodies and milling around. But when the trains stopped

The Big Raids

and quietness came I would settle down to serious work. I took care not to let them see me sketching; that would have been much too rude. People were trying to get a little privacy, even down there. They were undressing, snuggling down on to the platform, often two under the same blanket. Children were being put on their little pots. There wasn't any real order down there at that time—people had just come down to escape the raids spontaneously—and in some ways it was a quite extraordinary mess.

"But that was just what I wanted: the unexpected, the unorganized. The impact made by the whole improvised succession of scenes down there in the Underground was quite important for me. It humanized everything I had been doing. I knew at the time that what I was sketching represented an artistic turning point for me, though I didn't realize then that it was a professional turning point too. You see, I wasn't really well known at that time; I certainly wasn't making much money. But when I handed my first book of sketches to Kenneth Clark he showed them to everybody, and then the Ministry of Information started to distribute the others. And once the drawings were seen . . ."

As the weeks went by, the authorities gave up all hope of persuading Londoners to abandon the Underground for the official refuges they had set up in streets and parks. The Cockneys didn't trust them; they preferred to be deep down in the earth where they could not hear bombs or guns, and there would have been a revolt if the government had tried to move them. So having failed to persuade the populace, the officials sent wardens and welfare workers down to them, and the job began of organizing the platforms for the thousands of nightly tenants.

"What I was trying to portray in my groups," Moore says, "was the profound depth of this place where these people were talking and sleeping, the distance they were away from the war that was raging above their heads, but also of the awareness of it in their faces, in their attitudes, in the stale air around them. I was excited and engaged by everything I saw around me—until it got organized and then it was no longer interesting for me."

For the sake of his wife, who liked neither the raids nor the crowds, Moore found half of a farmhouse which was for rent in Perry Green, on the Hertfordshire-Essex border, some twenty-five miles from London. Each afternoon, however, he and a friend pooled their gas coupons and drove into London, where he stayed until dawn, wandering from shelter to shelter. Discovering the unfinished Underground railway tunnel beyond Stratford Broadway, in East London, whose noisome conditions had so nauseated Superintendent Reginald Smith, he spent hours there, sketching in the gloom, unaware of the stench and only conscious of the sights and sounds all around him.

"Then there was a great old warehouse of a shelter at Tilbury," he recalls. "It can't have been safe at all, and thousands would have been killed if it had been hit. It was full of great bales and tins and packing cases. It was quite theatrical. I loved being there and watching the people.* It was a fascinating time. You could come up into the streets and see the fires and gaps in the buildings, and the patterns of the twisted tramlines and tangled overhead wires. I found it continuously exciting, and I worked like a glutton. I particularly loved the fires."

That autumn Moore felt that his mother would be safer staying with his sister in Manchester, and when he was saying good-bye to her at St. Pancras Station, decided on impulse to go with her. "It was just as well that I did; when we got to Manchester there was absolute chaos. The city had been bombed, there was a milling crowd at the station, and in the blackout you couldn't see or find anything or anyone.

"The next afternoon I set off for the station in Manchester to catch the evening train back to London, and just as I reached Piccadilly [Manchester has a Piccadilly too] the air raid started, a heavy one. I just stood there watching it. I got so fascinated that I missed the train. I just stood there all night watching the bombs crashing down and the buildings crumbling. It was marvelous."

From these experiences came the series of drawings that made the name of Henry Moore known all over the world. And like Churchill, he enjoyed every moment of it.

rs. Rosemary Black was enjoying it too, though she felt guilty about admitting it, even to herself. As the bombs dropped nearer and nearer to her house in Maida Vale that autumn of 1940, she found life in London had suddenly taken on a new flavor. She wrote in her diary:

Thinking it over, though, I've come to the conclusion that I am enjoying *all this* in so far as it has yet affected me personally. Doubtless I should sing

---

* Moore seems to have been unaware that this shelter was one of the great scandals of the winter of 1940. It was a food warehouse containing rations for half of London. The warehouse had been taken over spontaneously by the local people and was soon swimming in filth, which contaminated the bales of food. It was some time before it could be cleaned up.

a very different tune if a bomb wrecked my house or maimed me and my children, but it's no use worrying about such things. I do get such a kick out of finding myself comparatively fearless and also self-controlled and calm with regard to dealing with others, and remaining immune from their fright. I who have always considered myself the world's most arrant coward—I used to feel physically sick at the thought of being woken in the night by a siren— to pass through an ordeal such as even the comparatively safe civilian must endure these days in London gives me a new self-respect and certainty. I believe I shall feel prouder and stronger all my life for having been so tested.

And of the bombing itself, she added: "It's like mountain air. It seems to make one tireless and wide awake and vital. Boredom, the biggest enemy of modern man's soul, has indefinitely disappeared."

Six months before, she had been a bored rich young widow wondering every morning what to do with her day. Some extracts from her diary illustrate the change in her outlook and attitude, the growing awareness by an upper-middle-class Englishwoman of the people and conditions around her which had previously been beyond her ken; of the poor and the underprivileged who were her neighbors, though she had ignored them before; of the stirring feeling that something ought to be done. In September 1940 she was still looking for a job and had been making the rounds of the service bureaus, but the time had not yet arrived when she would start working to ameliorate the misery around her. Still, war conditions and the bombing were opening her eyes, and she was learning.

Every night from mid-September on the Luftwaffe came over regularly, and seven million Londoners prepared for the ordeal according to their facilities, temperaments and location. The Black household— Rosemary and her two baby daughters, the Hungarian nurse, the Scottish maid and Mrs. C., a volunteer ambulance worker—retired to the reinforced air-raid shelter which the widow had had built into her pantry next to the basement kitchen of her house in Maida Vale. For the moment it was still a class-conscious English household in which the servants were expected to remember their place. On September 16 Mrs. Black wrote:

The Blitz came most uncomfortably close tonight. There was the usual violent barrage after the evening siren. Then about 9:30 just as I was crawling into my bed in the dugout there was a violent bomb explosion which sounded as if it were in the next street. Anyway it was close enough to rock the house on its foundations. It really seemed to me that the beams and walls of the dugout were rocking from side to side like those of a ship in a heavy storm . . .

Mrs. C., who had been standing beside me, turned as white as lard and nearly fell down. I thought she was going to fall against one of the upright supports and cut her head open. Then she caught hold of it. I felt pleased with myself because I never moved a muscle except for my lower jaw which I must admit slowly dropped further and further. Mrs. C. said slowly, "It's not that I'm frightened, it's just that terrible noise." What a fool remark. Of course it's the noise that one's frightened of. There were several more explosions, though not so near, and the planes sounded extremely loud, so I called the maids into the shelter and we sat about rather uncomfortably while the children slept on like the dead. Marvellous. I felt most uncomfortable about sleeping in the shelter myself and leaving the maids always in the kitchen—not that one can't reach the shelter from the kitchen in half a split second, but the shelter's far quieter and one's bound to feel rather more confident in it. I should like to take turns about with them since it would really be hopeless for us to sleep in the shelter together in any comfort, but the trouble is that Mrs. C. refuses to have "a great smelly maid six inches from her. She couldn't sleep a wink." I suppose it wouldn't be very nice for the maids either. It's obviously nicer for them to sleep separately and, so to speak, unchaperoned . . .

In any case, it was Mrs. C. who had to be thought of first: "On account of her hard and dangerous war work, for the sake of us, she is the one who must receive first consideration."

Mrs. C. did not fail to keep Mrs. Black informed of all that was going on during the bombing, and some of it was alarming.

The interesting thing she said is that her ambulance station is a hotbed of fear.

She said they're all working each other up into a state of nerves in which they can think and talk of nothing but how frightened they are. Fear, of course, is very infectious, and the fearful ones spread their fright among the others. They've gone into a state of real jitters, jump at every bang, shriek when there is a loud crash and when the lights go out, start brooding on the terror of the ten-minute walk home through the night barrage almost as soon as they arrive in the afternoon.* Some of the girls prefer to spend the night in deckchairs in the stuffy smoky noisy canteen rather than brave the short walk home. These, of course, haven't had their clothes off for a week on end and are rapidly becoming nervous wrecks. All the more honour to these people for carrying on while they're so mortally afraid, but it seems imbecilic that such a state of affairs should have come about. Surely the shift leaders who at present do nothing but rotas and permits should have been given as their

---

* By this time the antiaircraft barrage in London was so intense that there was often a greater danger of getting killed by shrapnel in the streets than by bombs.

first and foremost function the maintenance of morale and the prevention of fear talk. Games, good example, ask people not to talk about their fears, etc. Then, too, Mrs. C. says all the other business is so badly organised. For example, gasmasks broken through being stuffed up with cigarettes, makeup, etc., nearly everyone ignorant of their own first-aid kits, and the use of the tourniquet apparatus with which they had been supplied, which was different from the one on which they'd learned and practised. Above all, no hurricane lights or torches until lights had been off twice. Now wouldn't one think the veriest village idiot would have had more sense than not to have seen to such a thing from the first? Strangely enough, Mrs. C. says that the men, and more particularly the older men, many of them ex-Service, are far worse about fright and panic than the women. "My dear, whenever there's a detonation anywhere they rush about pell mell and fling themselves flat on the floor. Very odd."

Mrs. Black was very conscious that though Britain's situation was now dire indeed, and that all over the country men, women and children were dying or suffering acutely, there was still a lack of urgency in the way the nation was facing up to the emergency. Everywhere she went she saw the muddling amateur or the soulless bureaucrat at work. She was young, strong and willing; she typed, spoke languages, was an expert driver and had taken a course in first aid. But finding a job even as a chauffeur was proving difficult. On September 17, she wrote:

I need hardly say I got no results from the WVS (Women's Voluntary Service) as regards driving. Fool ever to have imagined it. The branch's head had not turned up, and it was 10:45 A.M. and none of the other members of the branch were capable of dealing with her business. One of them seemed to be spending her whole time tidying up some tea things in a corner. Two women who said they had been asked to come in and help by the head were sitting gloomily on hard chairs awaiting her return, as no one else had any idea of giving them anything to do. After explaining myself to a scatty-looking underling who took down my name and address on an odd corner of paper which would obviously lose itself, I said I really must go. She said the head would ring me up as soon as she had a spare moment to do so. Quite certain she will never do any such thing. What a fight it is even to find out how to apply as a volunteer for anything, no matter how badly the need for help is proclaimed.

She went on to the local town hall to sign up for ARP and found the same apathy and indifference there.

Every department seemed to be full to bursting with pathetic people who'd lost their homes and were waiting for emergency food cards, compensation application forms, travel vouchers, instructions. They were standing and sitting everywhere, jammed together like sardines, silent for the most part in dumb, apathetic resignation. Many people wandered unhappily about not knowing where to go or where to get what they wanted. The doorman was in the midst of an endless flow of enquirers. I gather that hundreds had come here by mistake thinking to find the food office, which is in Praed Street. Others had gone to the food office only to be sent here for emergency cards . . . Some seemed to have spent the whole morning being shunted from pillar to post . . . A black-haired slum woman with only one tooth was very angry. She made the doorman a scene and he was rude and harsh. Oh God, the inefficiency and muddle everywhere. Why not clear and definite directions in clear letters as to what to do in an emergency and where to go to do it placarded at street corners, in post-offices and phone boxes and in every ARP and WVS? This after a year of war! Oh, the utterly futile, maddening chaos in this *something* country with its wholly damnable local governments and the filthy rudeness with which they treat their tragic, homeless poor. Came out hopelessly depressed and disgusted, and feeling that if we ever do win this war it will be entirely due to good luck and in no smallest degree to good management, and that we damn well deserve to be thoroughly beaten. Muddle and inefficiency are quite bad enough but the cruelty of petty officials to the wretched victims of war is something quite else.

In the next three weeks the people of London heard the air-raid siren between seven and eight times every day, but the experience seemed to stimulate most people. "Decided to buy a winter outfit," wrote a young architect's assistant named Pamela Slater. "If we are all dead it won't matter, if we are all alive there won't be the stuff to buy by the end of the month. It's a most wonderful moonlight night, searchlights going up for miles among the stars. Perfect night for a raid."

Rosemary Black's home had suffered several more near misses but she too seemed cheerful rather than depressed. Early in October she wrote:

Mrs. C. just came in with the exciting news that a policeman who came into their ambulance station says that apart from the East End, which is beyond all comparision, our part of the world has had the worst damage and the heaviest casualties. We feel thrilled. The morale around the tenement [a block of nearby working-class houses bombed the night before] is now quite magnificent. The weaklings had left for the safer places, and those remaining . . . whose houses have been smashed up, are flatly refusing to leave there, so that the London County Council has eventually given in and arranged for reglazing and general repairs to begin at once. Those whose homes have gone, far from wishing to leave the district, are being accommodated with neighbours right on the spot.

And still the bombs edged ever closer to the Black house in Maida Vale. On October 12, amid a giant's hailstorm of bombing and quick-firing antiaircraft guns, there came the noise that the household had dreaded.

About a minute afterwards there was a horrifyingly loud scream and by the time it was halfway through I was thinking that it was about the loudest and longest drawn out one I had ever heard. But it kept getting louder and louder and louder—hateful!—and after the usual horrid pause there was a long drawn out crashing. The house didn't swing slowly and regularly as with a concussion bomb, but shook sharply like a dog coming out of water. The curtains flew inwards. It seemed as though the walls were thinking of doing the same. One really felt as if we might see the nose of a bomb peering into the room. While this was going on Stan and Mrs. C. (Stan is an airman from a nearby barrage-balloon site) both got up or rather slid off their chairs still half crouching. Mrs. C. had her hand around her head somewhere and I, immovable as usual, went on just sitting where I was, and I remembered distinctly thinking while the crashing was thundering to its climax: "How comic their blank faces look." Then as the house shook there was a jingling of broken glass, part of it obviously from the window of the room in which we all were. I, all at once, in a frightful rage, leaped to my feet gesticulating wildly and crying: "Hell and dammit, now they've got my glass. Oh blast, it just would go in this room!" I was thinking of how chilly the autumn mornings were going to be in a room with panes missing from its windows. Stan said: "That's right, you give it to 'em, Mrs. Black!" We all began to laugh.

But the next day, as bombs came down, it was no longer a laughing matter. The first crack in Mrs. Black's egotistic pride in her fearless superiority appeared when Mrs. C. brought an eight-year-old child, Ann, to the house. The little girl was in shock; the previous night a bomb had fallen on the house down the road, and her mother, sister, uncle and cousin were now hopitalized in serious condition. Ann's aunt had died in the ambulance, and no one had yet succeeded in finding her father. The trembling child was taken upstairs to be bathed and put to bed.

The poor wretched child, miraculously unhurt in all this carnage, had been brought into the ambulance station in a hysterical condition. That was hardly surprising. She was crying out that she wanted her Mummy with her, why had they taken her mother away—there had been a terrible crash and then she had screamed and then they had come and taken her away from her Mummy. She wanted to go back to her, why didn't they bring her Mummy? Her Mummy's face had been all covered with beetroot, wasn't it funny? She started crying hysterically again at the prospect of staying on at the ambulance station, and Mrs. C. had taken the law into her own hands and brought her round here.

It had been a bad night, with heavy damage everywhere, and Mrs. C. poured out the story of Maida Vale and Paddington's sufferings in a gush of gory detail. She had been on the run all night long, for Edgware Road and Marble Arch had been hit as well as Paddington and Maida Vale, and incendiary bombs had showered all over Marylebone. Gas mains and water mains were gone, and there had been an endless inflow into the station: blood everywhere, people having hysterics, "particularly two servant girls who shrieked and wept and laughed insanely every time bombs or barrage became noisy, driving everyone nearly as crazy as themselves."

At one moment in the early hours of the morning Mrs. C. had asked permission to go home for some supplies. She had also asked if she could bring Rosemary Black and one of the maids back to serve as casual labor. "We could have helped to deal with lost children, hystericals and so on, or at least done the donkey work of scrubbing away blood, boiling water for sterilisation, making cups of tea for shock cases and so on. But the answer was a lemon, needless to say."

Mrs. C. was informed that she was not permitted to procure either help or supplies from an unofficial source, and even if the rules were waived because of the acute emergency, it would be impossible for her to leave her post without an official permit, which no one had the time to deal with. Rosemary Black was "almost speechless with fury. To be kept away from such an opportunity to be really helpful and useful and valuable at such a critical time, and by what? By nothing but the everlasting barbed-wire entanglements of red tape which frustrate everyone day in and day out."

Mrs. C. sighed and cried, "Oh, if only you knew how I was aching to have you! Oh, to have someone sensible to help!"

She went on with her tale of the all-pervading disorganization and confusion. Her fellow ambulance driver, Lennie, had rushed away from a bomb site with a badly injured girl who died on the way to the hospital. The hospital authorities refused to take in the body.

The Big Raids

"Lennie said it was impossible for her to drive about with a corpse in her ambulance," said Mrs. C. "She needed the four bunks for other casualties. She said if the hospital authorities tried to put the body back in the ambulance she was just going to drive off. 'Throw it in the gutter if that's the best you can do,' she said, and drove away, back to where she was needed."

But they were all feeling the strain, said Mrs. C. So many bombs, so many sleepless nights, so much blood and suffering. The leader of her shift, a middle-aged volunteer, was losing his voice through nerves. "Even Lennie, who is ever calm and philosophical and brave as a lion and the last hysterical person it would be possible to find, who is cool and calm and upon whom even her seniors rely, flew into a passion and cried out that she couldn't stand this sort of thing any longer and that she was going to leave the bloody ambulance station—they were risking their lives every hour of the night, and for what? They were doing hardly any good, everything was red tape and muddle, and she was going to get out of it for good and go into munitions where at least, if one risked one's life, one knew it was for some purpose."

Finally Mrs. C. began to weep from sheer exhaustion, and was taken upstairs in her turn to be bathed and put to bed.

All over London nerves were fraying everywhere, and there were thousands who wondered aloud how they could go on standing bombs and shrapnel—and red tape as well. But it was also a time when many a Cockney realized what ambulance workers, air-raid wardens, policemen and fire watchers were doing for them. On the walls of many a wrecked house graffiti began to appear. No longer did they read DOWN WITH THE JEWS or THIS IS THE BOSSES' WAR or HAIL MOSLEY, as they had been during the phony war; instead they said OUR ARP WORKERS ARE WONDERFUL or OUR THANKS TO THE AFS [Auxiliary Fire Service].

On one of her walks through Maida Vale and Paddington, Mrs. Black saw that "from many broken windows, and in many half-wrecked, abandoned or broken buildings and from sticks planted in bomb-craters, waved Union Jacks. The sight of the national flag flying over the ruins is for me the most moving thing of the whole war. I never felt so humbly and proudly thankful to be English as just then. How fine it is that after watching one's country gradually degenerating slowly but surely into the ranks of the second rate, to see it glorious again and to feel whole-hearted pride and joy in it. I was very nearly undone by the sight of a nine-inch square of faded tattered paper, obviously the smallest and cheapest flag available, fluttering from the gaping, twisted window of a burned-out tenement. For an awful moment I thought I was going to burst out crying in the middle of the public highway—what was left of it, that is."

On the way home she stopped at a wrecked shop which was still open for business, and bought a couple of Union Jacks. "I feel I am entitled to fly a flag now that the house has sustained a slight amount of damage," she wrote.

hen the air-raid sirens first started wailing over London and news reached Holloway Prison that the East End was the principal target, most of the Fascist detainees uttered a cheer and went around with smiles of triumph on their faces. "That's right, blow the dirty Yids out of their rat holes!" they cried, and they would herd an unfortunate refugee into a quiet corner to dance around her, shouting, "The Yids, the Yids, we're going to get rid of the Yids!"

But as the Blitz moved across London and the bombs came down uncomfortably close to Holloway's high brick walls, the vindictive cries were heard less and less. Polly Wright, whose love affair with a Nazi had brought her to Holloway as a detainee under 18b, was terrified whenever a raid was in progress, but she took comfort from the fact that she was not half as frightened as some of the pro-Hitler bully girls who were sharing her incarceration. Sometimes, in the hush between the crump of the bombs, she could hear the muffled sobs from neighboring cells where the wives of the Fascist leaders had now been collected together. "Don't worry, dear," she heard one of them say. "He knows where we are. He'll see we don't come to any harm. He'll be needing us soon." It slowly dawned on her that "he" was Adolf Hitler.

By this time no one in Holloway really knew what to do about Polly Wright. She had made it clear to the female Fascists that she resented their approaches, both political and amatory. On the other hand, she couldn't put up with the whining and sniveling of the refugees.

"It isn't fair," they kept saying. "Don't they know that we've been persecuted? Must they make us suffer more?"

All right, it wasn't fair. It wasn't fair for her, either, but what was the use of nattering about it night and day? What did it get you but a bawling out from the matrons and a furtive, painful kick from the real old lags, who were exasperated by the noise and overcrowding which the influx of all these "bloody traitors" had caused.

Two weeks after her arrival in prison she had been told that her appeal was to come before the tribunal, but a fat lot of good that did her. The three members of the appeals board listened like a trio of nervous hens to her story, and she knew from the look in the eyes of the woman member that she didn't have a chance. When she told them of her love affair, the look on that face plainly said: "This woman is nothing but a common adulteress. And preferring to give her body to an enemy when she's already married to an Englishman! Lock her up and throw the key away!"

They didn't say that, of course; in fact the chairman of the tribunal, a kind-looking lawyer whose face she had seen more than once in the newspapers, treated her quite gently. But he pointed out mildly that her—ahem—lover was now quite an important man in the Nazi party, and as long as there was a danger of invasion it might not be wise, et cetera, et cetera. But he did assure her that her case would be kept under constant consideration; in the meantime she must realize the difficult circumstances and thank her lucky stars that she wasn't a German girl in Berlin facing a Nazi tribunal. Why, they would have shot her over there.

"I'm not sure I wouldn't prefer it," Polly said, whereupon the woman member looked at her as if she ought to have her head shaved.

When Polly was returned to Holloway she found that she had been moved out of her cell with the German refugee girls (the big Fascist lunk had already joined her ideological sisters). She was glad of that, for their constant weeping got on her nerves. Instead, though it was supposed to be against regulations, she was put in a cell with a couple of "ordinary" prisoners. After a worrying week in which they pushed her around and jeered at her for "getting soppy over a Jerry," they seemed to accept her. One was a thief in her mid-thirties who made a speciality of walking out of stores with fur coats under her clothes. The other was a Junoesque Negro tart from Soho who was in for knifing a sailor when he tried to cheat her. The two of them knew the facts of prison life, and they had learned how to make it bearable. They took Polly to the baths and rid her of the bugs she had picked up in the other cell. Somehow they had procured extra blankets for their beds. They were allowed out at special times to empty their slops, so that their pots never overflowed, as in the other cell. They gave her cigarettes, of which they seemed to have plenty.

One night during a week of extremely heavy raids, when it seemed almost certain that the prison would be hit, Polly lost her nerve. She felt so lonely, and as she told herself, she had made a real mess of her life. What hope was there for her? She began to sob.

Presently there was a movement from the black girl's bed. She slipped in beside Polly, rocked her in her arms and stroked the misery away. It got her through the night, and finally she slept. But, oh dear, she told herself the next morning, it certainly wasn't like being comforted by a man.

There was a new craftsman in London now, and he worked with his nose. Some called him "the body sniffer." He could smell blood, and he could tell you whether the person was alive or dead.

He would wander among the rubble of a wrecked house snuffling like a dog as he picked his way among the split beams, broken furniture, piles of brick and the sad domestic debris of someone's home. All around him wardens and rescue workers would await his signal. They knew that underneath the pile somewhere a human being was trapped. For hours they had been digging their way down, stopping now and then to listen in the silence between bombs for some sort of sound.

But if no sounds came, the body sniffer would take over. How he did it no one knew. Certainly there was enough smell—a raw mixture of powdered brick dust, gas, sewers and smoke—around a bomb incident to make it seem impossible to detect a specific odor. But the body sniffer would snuffle his way through the rubble and then whisper, "Blood down here."

He would press his head closer into the detritus, and then would either shake his head and say, "Stale—it's a stiff," or else would shout excitedly, "Fresh blood down here, and still flowing."

The rescue men would move in and start the tricky work of digging downward until a leg, a hand or a head would reveal the trapped soul for whom they were searching.

All over London now the rescue squads were hard at work digging for trapped citizens. Though they got used to the bombing as the weeks went by, one fear that never left Londoners as they crouched under the stairs or lay in their shelters was that of being buried in the rubble and left there to die slowly, unheard through the noise of the battle above. To most Cockneys the men of the rescue squads became superbeings, their ears always cocked for the moan beneath the rubble, never willing to give up the search as long as there was the remotest chance that the body lying deep down in the cratered earth was still breathing.

In fact, they were mere men doing a difficult and dangerous task, and once they got used to the Blitz, and to what it could do to a house and the people buried beneath it, it was a job like any other for which they would knock off work at the end of their shifts, and expect overtime if they were told to carry on. It was hardly surprising that they soon became hardened and, on the surface, unfeeling about the people they were trying to rescue. "Shut up, you old bitch!" they would cry out in exasperation at a wretched woman whining continuously underneath the rubble. "All right, boys, everyone knock off. Nothing but stiffs down here!" a foreman would cry within earshot of relatives huddled dumbly together, still hoping that a mother, son or husband would be brought up alive.

John Strachey, who was an air-raid warden in Chelsea, has described one incident where the rescue squads had labored for hours to get at some victims trapped under the wreckage of a house. But the beams were too heavy and jacks failed to move them. Each time the floor they were trying to lift would rise an inch or so, only to fall again. "The rescue men began to feel baffled," writes Strachey. "The soaking rain was turning the rubble into a disgusting gritty paste which covered them from head to foot. The droning overhead never ceased. One of the rescue men said, 'Can't do nothing here—let's go.'

"Another said, 'Shut up, you bastard, they'll hear you.'"

In this case they carried on, but in some cases, when it really seemed hopeless, or when the bombs began coming too close, the rescue squads moved away. However, one thing would keep them at work no matter how long or the conditions overhead, and that was when they knew a child was trapped. Then they would work desperately and continuously, and if at the end of their labors the child was brought out dead, their anguish was very real.

Sometimes the digging beneath the soil of London was not for bodies but for bombs. In one of the great mid-September raids a high-explosive bomb fell very close to the southwest tower of St. Paul's. It missed the tower by a few feet, plunged through the soft subsoil into the road outside and ended up in the clay beside the foundations of the cathedral.

A rumor spread through the capital (for the news was censored from the newspapers) that London's most beloved church, the jewel in her crown, the great Christopher Wren dome towering over the Thames and the City, was threatened. Beneath her ticked a bomb powerful enough to blow her to perdition and change London's face and skyline.

Until that moment St. Paul's had stayed open all through the Blitz so that people could worship, and night and day there had been no lack of citizens praying beneath the dome as the bombers droned overhead. No lights could be lit inside, save for a small night light placed on the ground exactly under the dome, and from which those who walked through its great aisles got their bearings. Overhead a relay of vergers and choirsingers and church officials walked the famous "Whispering Gallery" or patrolled the dizzying heights of the dome itself, ready with stirrup pumps and sand buckets to douse the incendiary bombs now raining down on London. Up there the view of the Blitz was an awe-inspiring sight, the sky fretworked with searchlight beams, the river reflecting the fires, the earth palpitating as bombs burst and guns fired. Since the dome acted as an echo chamber, the noise there was like the crack of doom.

Now, save for the Dean and a number of volunteers, St. Paul's was closed to all visitors. (Later the Dean, the Very Reverend W. R. Matthews, said, "It has always been my great regret that we had to break our record, and that, unlike a certain famous theatre* with its naked ladies, we could not claim: 'We never closed.' ")

The bomb-disposal squad, commanded by a mild-looking lieutenant of the Royal Engineers named James Davies, arrived at St. Paul's less than an hour after the near miss. Police had cordoned off all approaches and were slowing down traffic for half a mile in the streets around Ludgate Circus so that vibrations would not set off the bomb. Twenty minutes later Davies lost the services of three of his men; digging into the crater they had hit a jet of gas from a broken main and were knocked out instantly. Gas experts, called in to plug the leak, found a creeping gas fire coming along the pipe toward the bomb, and "for perhaps a minute or two, but not more than that, a complete evacuation was contemplated, with the cathedral thus left to its fate." Then Dr. Matthews stoutly insisted that he would, if necessary, go up with the great edifice, at which point the experts went back to work with extinguishers and put out the flames, so that the dark hole in the ground was open once more to Lieutenant Davies and his helpers.

They found the bomb almost twenty-eight feet beneath the surface, but even then their task had only begun. The clay soil into which the missile had plunged had made it so slippery that neither human hands nor metal clamps could get a sure grip on it. It took twenty hours to put steel hawsers around one end of it; these were then passed up to the surface and run through pulleys to two trucks working in tandem. Between them they delicately hauled the bomb from its bed, though twice watchers all but fell on their knees and prayed because the hawsers

---

* The Windmill Theatre. Matthews, *op. cit.*

ASSOCIATED PRESS

In September 1939 the great exodus of children from London began. Altogether about 250,000 of them left the city in the next few months.

Balloons ringed London to protect them from low-level raids by German planes. The great hydrogen-filled monsters strained at the trucks to which they were anchored, sometimes breaking loose in high winds or ignited by lightning, but they kept the enemy from dive-bombing the city's streets.

FOX PHOTOS LTD.

Propaganda posters, many of them by Fougasse, were everywhere. The public reacted with some sarcasm to them; one retaliatory cartoon showed two Cabinet ministers eavesdropping to overhear the war gossip of two middle-aged housewives in the Underground.

IMPERIAL WAR MUSEUM

you never know who's listening!

CARELESS TALK COSTS LIVES

MAGNUM PHOTOS — GEORGE RODGER

During one of the first daylight raids, people at the entrance to a shelter watch German bombers overhead.

facing page: A Heinkel 111 over Surrey Docks, Bermondsey, on September 7, 1940, the first day of the Blitz.

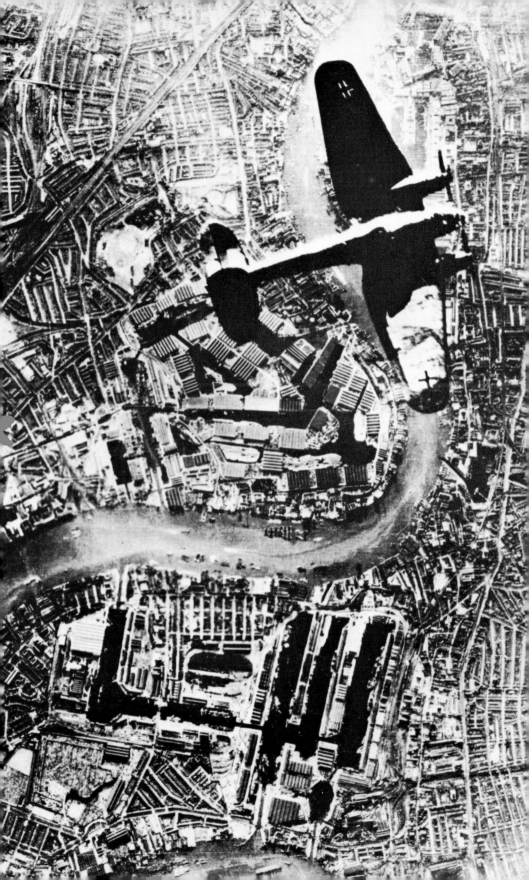

The London docks from the ground on the same day. Tower Bridge is on the right.

A casualty of the Blitz in a London hospital.

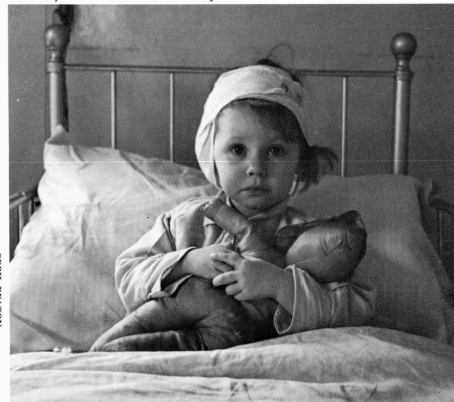

CECIL BEATON

IMPERIAL WAR MUSEUM

WILLIAM VANDIVERT — © TIME, INC.

Tower Bridge again, on September 30, 1940, silhouetted against East End fires.

WILLIAM VANDIVERT—
© TIME, INC.

IMPERIAL WAR MUSEUM

UNITED PRESS
INTERNATIONAL PHOTO

above: A typical scene in an Underground shelter during the height of the Blitz. Later, conditions improved, but some people did not go above ground for weeks at a time.

upper left: October 1940: A flower vendor in Trafalgar Square warms her hands over the remains of an incendiary bomb.

lower left: The High Altar at St. Paul's, damaged in a raid on the night of October 10, 1940.

THE TATE GALLERY, LONDON

Two of Henry Moore's sketches of sleepers in the Underground.

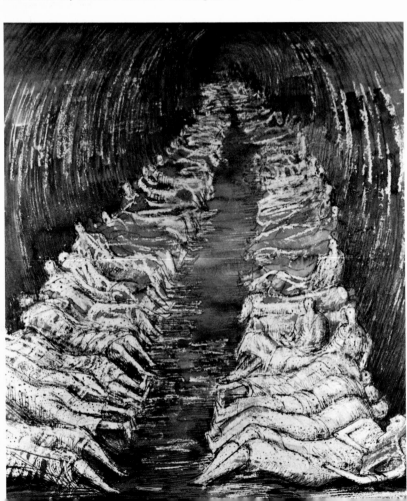

snapped and the bomb slipped back. At the third attempt it came out. It was eight feet long, it weighed a ton and it was very much alive. There was enough explosive in it to raise St. Paul's and quite a few buildings all around.

Lieutenant Davies was asked if he planned to defuse it there and then. "I've a feeling it isn't that kind of a bomb," he replied. "All the time I've been touching it, I've sort of sensed a voice inside it shrieking to get out. I don't think we're going to stop it from going off sometime, no matter what we try."

So it was decided to get the bomb away from St. Paul's as quickly as possible. A route was quickly mapped from Ludgate Circus down Mile End Road and through the East End to Ilford and Hackney Marshes. A call was made to Superintendent Reginald Smith of K Division to clear a route through his bailiwick and evacuate every house a hundred yards on each side along every foot of the way. Davies and his men carefully loaded the bomb aboard one of the trucks and packed its sides with cushions, cloths and wooden blocks to prevent its rolling. Then, with a police car half a mile ahead, and a trail of other cars well behind, Davies drove—alone; he refused to take any of his men—at top speed through the streets of the East End to Barking Marshes. There the bomb was exploded a few hours later. It made a crater a hundred feet across.*

There was another kind of bomb that was even more terrifying than the penetrating high explosive. It was a land mine, and it came swinging down from the skies in uncanny silence, dangling from the end of a huge parachute. When it hit, an entire area for half a mile around was devastated, and windows were shattered up to ten minutes' walk away.

It was, in fact, a magnetic mine invented by the Germans as the first "secret weapon" of World War II, for sowing in waterways used by Allied ships. But now that the Royal Navy had found ways of degaussing vessels against the mine's magnetic pull, it had been adapted by the Luftwaffe for land bombing. It was eight feet long, two feet in diameter, two and a half tons in weight and packed with explosives. On

---

* It formed a convenient hollow, three and a half years later, for the erection of part of the "Mulberry" harbors which were assembled at Barking Marshes and used in Normandy after D-Day in 1944.

moonlight nights—which the Germans preferred—these strange messengers of death would slowly descend, and the problem for people who saw them was which way to run to escape destruction.

In the BBC archives is a transcript of a recording describing what it was like to be on the spot when a land mine fell. This particular one destroyed the Langham Hotel and most of the area around Broadcasting House, at the top of Regent Street, on December 8, 1940. The narrator, who prefers to remain anonymous, had just biked to work at the BBC when he heard a swishing noise in the sky which abruptly stopped, as if in midair. There was an air raid on at the time, but the man looked up, expecting incendiaries. No fires showed, however, and finally he walked through the blackout to the entrance of Broadcasting House and stood talking to the two policemen on duty there.

A saloon car [sedan] was parked alongside the curb . . . and I could see to the left of the car the lamppost in the middle of the road opposite the Langham Hotel. The policemen had their backs to this, so did not observe what followed. Whilst we were conversing I noticed a large, dark, shiny object approach the lamppost and then recede. I concluded that it was a taxi parking. It made no noise. The night was clear, with a few small clouds. There was moonlight from a westerly direction, but Portland Place was mainly shadow. All three of us were wearing our steel helmets; my chinstrap was round the back of my head . . .

Though he didn't know it, the shiny object he had taken for a taxi was actually a huge land mine swinging by the end of its parachute from the lamppost over the middle of the road. A few seconds later the parachute slipped and lowered the canister to the ground.

At that moment there was a very loud swishing noise, as if a plane were diving with engine cut off—or like a gigantic fuse burning. . . . Even at that moment I did not imagine that there was any danger in the road, and thought that it was coming from above, up Portland Place. My head was up watching, and before I could . . . lie down flat the thing in the road exploded. I had a momentary glimpse of a large ball of blinding, wild, white light and two concentric rings of colour, the inner one lavender and the outer one violet, as I ducked my head. The ball seemed to be ten to twenty feet high, and was near the lamppost.

Several things happened simultaneously. His head was jerked back and his helmet blown away, and something hit him hard on the forehead and nose.

The Big Raids

The explosion made an indescribable noise—something like a colossal growl—and was accompanied by a veritable tornado of air blast. I felt an excruciating pain in my ears, and all sounds were replaced by a very loud singing noise, which I was told later was when I lost my hearing and my eardrums perforated. I felt that consciousness was slipping from me . . .

He rallied and forced himself into a crouching position, feet against the curb, hands covering his face.

I remember having to move them over my ears because of the pain in them . . . This seemed to ease the pain. Then I received another hit on the forehead and felt weaker. The blast seemed to come in successive waves, accompanied by vibrations from the ground . . . Later, in our first-aid post, they removed what they described as a piece of bomb from that wound. Whilst in the gutter I clung on to the curb with both hands and with my feet against it. I was again hit in the right chest, and later found that my doubled-breasted overcoat, my coat, leather comb case and papers had been cut through, and the watch in the top right-hand pocket of my waistcoat had the back dented in and its works broken.

The noise, pressure and blast seemed endless and intolerable, but just as he felt he could bear it no longer and would go mad, the torment seemed to slacken.

. . . a shower of dust, dirt and rubble swept past me. Pieces penetrated my face, some skin was blown off, and something pierced my left thumbnail and my knuckles were cut, causing me involuntarily to let go my hold on the curb. Instantly, although the blast was dying down, I felt myself being slowly blown across the pavement towards the wall of the building.

Eventually he staggered to his feet to find on every side a scene from Dante's *Inferno*. The front of the building was lit by a reddish-yellow light; to the left of him the sedan was on fire and its flames were stretching out horizontally toward the building, not upward.

. . . a few dark huddled bodies were round about, and right in front of me were two soldiers; one, some feet from a breach in the wall of the building where a fire seemed to be raging, was propped up against the wall with his arms dangling by him, like a rag doll.

The other was nearer, about twelve feet from the burning car; he was sitting up with his knees drawn up and supporting himself by his arms—his trousers had been blown off him. I could see that his legs were bare and that he was wearing short grey underpants. He was alive and conscious.

I told him to hang on to an upright at the entrance and to shout like hell for assistance should he see or hear anyone approaching. I went back to look at the other soldier. He was still in the same posture and I fear that he was dead. I looked around. There was a long, dark body lying prone, face downwards . . . There appeared to be one or two dark, huddled bodies by the wall of the building. I had not the strength to lift any of them. I wondered where the water was coming from which I felt dripping down my face, and soon discovered that it was blood from my head wounds. . . .

He was one of the few survivors of a land mine which had exploded so close by. He had his wounds dressed and went to work as usual at the BBC. A bomb had already dropped on Broadcasting House earlier in the evening, and its explosion was heard by listeners of the nine o'clock news, though the announcer, Bruce Belfrage, paused only briefly in his recital of the day's happenings.

About three out of every ten of the land mines which dropped on London did not explode. They hung from trees and overhead electric wires, swinging ominously just above the ground. Sometimes they came down and still failed to go off, though in theory they were supposed to do so fifteen seconds after impact. One family in Ealing heard a clattering in their backyard, and thinking that incendiary bombs were raining down, rushed to the kitchen door with shovels and spades. But when they pushed the door, it would not open. They saw why when they entered the yard from the front: a land mine was propped up against the door.

The swinging menaces and the duds had to be disposed of quickly. As long as they were untreated, as many as three thousand people had to be moved out of a district and sheltered elsewhere. Ordinary high-explosive bombs were dealt with by army engineers like Lieutenant Davies, who had dug out the bomb at St. Paul's, but magnetic mines were much more complicated, and only the navy knew how to handle them. Naturally, however, the navy was used to magnetic mines dropping in the sea, and their experts were stationed in naval ports and bases. When the monsters silently descended on London, there was no one to deactivate them. And that was how a Cambridge undergraduate enrolled in the navy, Sub-lieutenant Peter Danckwerts, found himself having a number of intimate affairs with a series of magnetic mines.

Danckwerts had already seen one of the mines and had had its mechanism explained to him by an expert from the Admiralty. When a magnetic mine fell on land the fuse inside it buzzed for fifteen seconds, then went off. But sometimes the fuse buzzed for only a few seconds and then stuck—but would start buzzing again if moved.

"The important thing when dealing with these mines," said Danck-werts, "if you had to move them at all before you took the fuse out, was to listen very carefully all the time, and if you heard it buzzing to run like hell, because you might have up to fifteen seconds to get away."*

But there were other complications. The monster was full of gad-gets. It had an electric detonator at the bottom of a hole in the side of the mine which it was a ticklish job to get at. Opposite this was an-other hole, and when the cover was unscrewed there was a *whoof* and out shot a spring, a yard long—a scary experience the first time it happened. Then there was the top of the huge cylinder which had to be screwed off, and underneath was a plastic cover through which the time clock and all the connecting wires could be seen. These had to be cut: the right ones, and in the right order.

At the time all this was explained to him, it was Danckwerts' job to worry about magnetic mines, but he was interested enough to take one of the fuses back to his headquarters in the Port of London Author-ity, down on the docks. He and his torpedo officer and the third mem-ber of his team, a petty officer in the regular navy, studied the fuse, took it apart and put it together again.

It was just as well they did. At the height of the big raids on south London, Danckwerts' telephone rang. ARP headquarters reported that three parachute mines had dropped in their area and that the army bomb-disposal officer had refused to touch them. They were mines, all mines were the navy's affair, and the ARP controller asked him to come over at once.

Danckwerts explained that mines were not his speciality, and that experts would have to be found.

"Oh, my God, who does deal with mines?" asked the controller.

"I'm afraid the nearest people are down in Portsmouth," Danck-werts said.

"That's all very well," replied the controller, "but I've got several thousand people evacuated around these mines. I can't wait for the people to come up from Portsmouth."

Danckwerts promised to do what he could to speed matters up. What he did, in fact, was call Portsmouth and get permission to tackle the mines himself. He told the mine experts there that he thought he could handle the job, and was reluctantly given permission.

Danckwerts woke the other two members of his team and they agreed at once to go with him. He thought they were both very good

---

* Danckwerts' account is in the archives of the BBC.

with gadgets and "getting difficult things unscrewed and so on. Of course we didn't have any of the proper tools for this job. One was supposed to have nonmagnetic tools, quite apart from which most of the things were very hard to unscrew unless you had tools of the right shape. But we got a lot of screwdrivers and, most important of all, we took a ball of string, that is the essential thing for bomb disposal."

It was a bad night, and south London was a nightmare of roads blocked with bomb craters, wrecked trams and buses, blazing gas mains, exploding bombs and crashing antiaircraft guns. It took them a long time to find the first land mine. Finally they saw a man walking along the street in pajamas and dressing gown, carrying a suitcase, and decided that he might be fleeing from a mine. He was, and he took them to the back garden of a house near his. There it was, lying among the bushes, the parachute draped over the next-door wall.

"We went up and had a look at it with our torch," said Danckwerts, "and we found unfortunately that the all-important fuse was underneath, so we'd have to roll it round before we could get it out. My Chief Petty Officer and I rolled it over very, very cautiously indeed while the third member of the party kept his ear as close to it as he could and listened to see if it buzzed."

It didn't, so next they unscrewed the fuse. But they didn't take it out—not yet. The Germans had started to set booby traps for bomb-disposal experts, placing a trigger fuse under the first one, so that when it was removed the other one would go off.

Having loosened the top fuse, Danckwerts looped some of his ball of string around it and then motioned his companions to follow him over the wall into the next-door garden, and then around the back of the house and into the street beyond. Only after they had unreeled almost a hundred yards of string, keeping it just short of taut, did he yank the string. Nothing happened, except that the twine seemed to pull back and forth like elastic, without coming away; it was caught on a rose bush. He crawled back and freed it, then took up his old position, and this time the string came loose. When they went back to the bomb, the fuse was lying on the ground. Danckwerts picked it up gingerly, walked a few yards and then threw it on the ground. There was a sharp crack; the fuse had still been sensitive.

Danckwerts had a smoke to calm his nerves, took a deep breath and went back to the job of taking the mine's mechanism apart. After which—covered in soot by this time, for mines were blackened by the Germans so that they wouldn't glint if a searchlight caught them hanging under a plane—they set off in search of the two other mines.

The Big Raids

This took some time in a blacked-out London lit only by bomb fires over routes pitted with craters. Eventually they found the second mine standing upright in the middle of a recreation ground. They edged up to it, put down their tools while they examined it—and then, to their mortification, couldn't find them again. After scrambling around fumbling vainly in the grass, they found a bus depot and broke into the emergency tool kit there; the mine was rendered harmless with spanners normally used to mend a London bus.

The final land mine was in a field just beside a gasworks. "The sun was up by then," said Danckwerts, "it was a sunny morning and we had a large, interested crowd which had to be held back by volunteers while we dealt with it. So by this time we'd done three mines and we had a parachute each as a souvenir, which we were very happy about, and a lot of miscellaneous explosives . . . We went home very pleased with ourselves. . . ."

After that, Danckwerts* and his team were made official "mine disposal officers," and dealt with a dozen others before being called off (a dozen was considered the limit a team should risk their lives on). Their worst moments came when mines were buried in roofs or the upper stories of houses, from where they wouldn't have a chance to run if the fuse started buzzing.

But Danckwerts' worst moment came when he once attached his beloved ball of string to a mine fuse and then spun it out from the house where the monster was embedded to the protection of another building across the road. But before he could pull the string it was yanked out of his hand. "God, it's going off!" cried one of his team, and they flung themselves flat.

Instead there was a silence, broken by a clanking sound from the road. An air-raid warden had walked past, kicked the string, pulled out the fuse, and was dragging it along behind him.

All over London, men tinkered with land mines and high-explosive bombs which had failed to explode, but might go off at any moment. Royal Engineers were grubbing in the mud beneath Waterloo Bridge and in the noisome sewers of Stratford-atte-Bow. Naval experts had five terrifying hours standing on top of a half-filled gasometer over the lip of which a landmine hung by the fraying lines of a torn parachute. Two days later the War Office in Whitehall and several other government offices had to be evacuated because a land mine settled on Hunger-

---

* Sub-lieutenant Danckwerts was awarded a George Cross for his work.

ford Bridge, which runs across the Thames from Charing Cross Station. Rendering it harmless was made agonizingly difficult because the heat of an electrified line had welded the mine to the rails. Half of official London held its breath while Lieutenant Giddon from the Admiralty embarked on the long, tedious, perilous job of cutting it free.

By mid-September 1940, even Reich Marshal Hermann Göring had accepted the fact that his Luftwaffe had failed to sweep the RAF out of the skies. Since the destruction of Britain's air defenses was a prerequisite for the invasion of the United Kingdom, Adolf Hitler angrily told his generals to postpone Operation Sea Lion.

There was, however, no halt to the bombing, which continued relentlessly. The first heavy daylight raids had proved so costly to the German air force that they were abandoned, but night attacks increased in intensity. Every part of London wore the scars of bombs: Leicester Square, Piccadilly and Shaftesbury Avenue, Buckingham Palace, the Houses of Parliament, 10 Downing Street, the great department stores in Oxford Street, all the main-line stations, the docks, Marble Arch and Trafalgar Square—where, though Nelson still stood atop his column, one of the lions on guard at his feet had lost a nose.

Londoners who stood in line at the entrances to the Underground each evening were beginning to discover why city officials had tried— albeit in vain—to stop their using the station as shelters. It was not just that they were unsanitary because of the lack of lavatories; that many of them were soon flea-ridden and crawling with lice; that some of the deeper stations had a mosquito problem because the insects were attracted by the fetid air. Many of them were also downright dangerous. Those which were only a short distance beneath the surface provided mere psychological protection, and even that comfort was no longer available at the end of October. By then Trafalgar Square, Bounds Green, Praed Street and Balham stations had all received direct hits. Some lines ran under the Thames and were vulnerable to tunnel falls and flooding. Six-ton floodgates, operated electrically, had been installed to isolate sections of tunneling in case of breach by water, but when bombs knocked out the electrical system the gates would not close, and then there was disaster.

The worst was Balham. The shelterers did not know it, but this station was one of the most vulnerable spots in London. It was only some twelve yards below the street, and above it was a vast cobweb of gas and water pipes, main sewers, and electric and telephone cables. On the night of October 14 a bomb dropped just short of the station, where six hundred people were sheltering. The explosion smashed the water, sewer and gas pipes; first a trickle, then a flood of water and sewage poured in. The lights went out. The smell of gas was everywhere, and women and children began to scream. Soon water was welling up the emergency stairs, and the panic in the swirling, stinking blackness was on.

In an official report written for the London Passenger Transport Board, a motorman on duty at the time stated: "When the station went into darkness panic started; it was a bad panic. I said to them: 'It will be all right; we will have a light in a few minutes' . . . I didn't realise the tunnel had collapsed. Then there was the smell of gas and the children were shouting out for their gasmasks. I got my torch and flashed it up and saw water pouring down in torrents . . . I went back and opened the emergency hatch. I got the people more disciplined and they filed through the escape hatch in single file . . . about seventy or eighty of them. I told them to come up the escalator, to wait in the booking hall, and the rescue squad came along and took my torch and I had to manage without one. All this time water was pouring in and I was up to my knees in water. Soon it was like a waterfall. In about five minutes the anti-suicide pits (which broke the fall of anyone throwing himself down from the Tube entrance upstairs) were full."*

Rescue squads tore their way into the blackness, grabbing at the screaming people scrabbling to get out before the waters engulfed them. Like the motorman, their hands and arms were soon bleeding from the fingers clawing at them in the darkness. They rescued another three hundred, but the rest were already dead, or drowned in the rising flood.

But Londoners continued to believe in the Underground shelters, and as long as they did so, it was up to the authorities to make them safe and sanitary. So the deepest of them were reinforced and strengthened and floodgates made foolproof against bombs and power failures. Lavatory systems were installed and canteens moved in. At one of the most efficiently run, Aldwych, just off the Strand, there was even nightly entertainment by actors from adjacent theatres.

One man who narrowly missed being involved in the Balham Station incident was William Hutchins, a bus driver for the London Passenger Transport Board. These days he often remembered his wife's remark

---

* In Charles Graves, *London Transport Carried On.*

of the year before, when he told her that driving a tank was better than taking a double-decker bus out in the blackout. "At least they won't be shooting at you while you're in a bus," Amy had said.

But for the past month that was just what they had been doing. The Vauxhall route was murder, because it was always blocked by craters or collapsing buildings. You couldn't see a thing by the slits of light from the headlights, and there was every kind of obstacle in the way, from beds blown out of bombed houses to potential passengers stepping out into the road at the last moment and expecting you to see them. And practically every night was bomb night, with raids all the way to Vauxhall and shrapnel rattling on the roof like hailstones.

On the night of October 14 Hutchins was taking it easy along Balham High Road when his new conductor, Marlene, rang the bell. He pulled up to the curb. Ahead of them the sky had suddenly gone almost as bright as day; a plane overhead had dropped a cluster of flares which hung in the sky, bathing the black buildings in a dazzling glare.

Marlene came through the dimmed-out bus and spoke through the communicating window. "What shall we do?" she asked. Everybody was experienced enough about bombing by now to know that flares in the sky meant that bombs would be coming down at any moment. But Marlene had been on the job for only a few days, and this was her first trip after dark.

"We go on," William said. "We're late already."

It was a matter of pride these days to try to stick to the time schedules, despite the detours through back streets.

"Okay," the girl said brightly. At least, William decided, she didn't sound scared. She rang the bell and they continued down High Road.

A quarter of a mile ahead, in the glare of the flares, Hutchins could see the red shine of another bus ahead of him; suddenly it began to dance up and down as if somebody were manipulating it with a piece of string. The crunch of an exploding bomb sounded ahead, and then there was an uprush of smoke and earth, and he could see the bus ahead literally leaping. He stamped on the brakes and sat there for a moment wondering what to do. No further bomb fell, so he released the brake and began to edge forward down the road.

Suddenly it was very silent. The bus ahead of him had come to rest in the middle of the road, and now before his eyes it suddenly began to sink. In fact, it sank to its rooftop in the main shaft of Balham Underground Station.

Later that night, as he recounted this to his wife, telling her how they had helped in the rescue, and what "a plucky little kid" his new conductor, Marlene, had turned out to be, he noticed that Amy was silent and unresponsive.

"I don't think it's right," she said finally.

"What's not right?"

"Having girls on the buses," Amy said. "They can't be half as good as the men."

"But the men have been called up, love," he said. "Besides, it isn't true. The girls do the job fine, and they've lots of guts—all the drivers say so."

Amy shook her head. "They'll cause trouble," she said. "You just see if they don't."

"Nonsense," said William cheerfully. "They don't make any difference at all. We treat them like mates—just as if they were men."*

One of those for whom a bomb on an Underground station solved an insuperable problem was Mrs. Jenny Martin. On September 17, 1940, she was walking past Lyons Corner House at Marble Arch when an antiaircraft barrage started in Hyde Park and policemen began herding passers-by into the Tube station. Jenny tried to elbow her way through and walk on, but the crowd swept her down the stairs and onto the station platform below.

She was slightly the worse for drink and didn't particularly care what happened. That afternoon she had been in the adoption society in Marylebone Road, where she got decent treatment from the woman official who saw her until it came to filling in the papers.

"Of course," the woman had said, "you will have to have these papers countersigned by your husband." Seeing the expression on Jenny's face, she went on, "You just can't have your child-to-be adopted, you know, unless the father consents."

There was a pause, and the woman's manner changed. "I see," she said. "Your husband isn't the father." She sighed heavily. "I'm afraid his consent is necessary, just the same, and until we get it there is nothing we can do."

Jenny rose and walked to the door.

"You've forgotten the papers," the woman called after her. "Don't you think he ought to know what you've been doing?"

---

* Mates, perhaps, but not quite like men. Mrs. Amy Hutchins was killed in the great raid on London on April 16, 1941. William Hutchins married Marlene the following summer.

Jenny spent the rest of the week's allowance in a George Street pub on gin-and-tonics and then accepted a couple of rum-and-gingers from a man at the bar; it would have been more if he hadn't suddenly caught sight of her stomach and abruptly departed. When she left she could walk quite steadily, but was no longer worrying either about the kids back home in Pimlico (where she now stayed) or the one burgeoning inside her. Everything seemed suddenly full of hope.

All right, she'd send Jimmy the papers, she told herself. If he loved her, he'd understand. It was only one night, she'd been lonely and needed a drink and had no money, and then this fellow . . .

" 'Ere, ducks," said a woman on the Marble Arch station platform, seeing her condition, "come and sit beside me on this cushion and make yourself comfortable."

That was the moment when the bomb hit.

The bomb on Marble Arch Station that day was one of the unluckiest tragedies of the Blitz. It was only a small bomb, and Marble Arch Station, heavily reinforced against the enormous weight of traffic overhead, was considered one of the safest in London. But the nose cap of the bomb found a tiny hole between two girders and exploded. The force ripped along the corridor of the station with an extraordinary impact; eighteen people were killed by blast alone. There wasn't a mark on them when rescuers found them, but they were all naked and all dead. Others were killed and injured by the tiles which the force of the explosion tore off the walls and turned into projectiles that ripped into flesh and bone.

"There were forty known casualties, of whom over twenty were dead," wrote William Sansom in *Westminster in War*. "The shocked amounted to many more. It was a bewildering, dreadful time; and it is remembered at the Report Centre that when one rescue leader, a strong man and a good worker, telephoned his message—through his words he was sobbing."

Jenny Martin was among the ones who survived the blast but were wounded by flying tiles. When she woke up in St. George's Hospital the following evening she discovered that she wouldn't have to worry about adoption papers any more.

It would be untrue to say that anyone ever got used to the air raids, but, as C. P. Snow put it, "it began to seem quite minor if there were bombs in your actual neighborhood but not on your actual house." Nevertheless, within two months of the start of the Blitz only 22 percent of London's population was still sleeping regularly in public shelters, and Cockneys were learning to believe and be proud of the slogan now chalked on the walls: LONDON CAN TAKE IT. What was remarkable was the small amount of absenteeism in workshops, offices, docks and warehouses, especially since hardly a night passed without a warning and a raid, and from late evening until dawn, antiaircraft guns were banging away with teeth-chattering persistence.

The antiaircraft barrage in 1940 can hardly be said to have been effective in bringing down enemy planes; it probably knocked out more civilians from falling shrapnel. It didn't improve as the weeks went by, either, for so many shells were being fired that the barrels of the guns were wearing out. But Londoners found comfort in the noise, and Churchill told General Sir Frederick Pile, in command of this defense, to "keep on shooting away, regardless." People became worried when the guns stopped to give night fighters a chance to cut into Luftwaffe formations. They preferred the noisy ineffectiveness of the guns to the fumbling operations of the RAF's night fliers,* and most of them refused to blot out the reassuring thunder of the barrage with earplugs now being issued free by the government.

As a result, Londoners didn't get much sleep at night. A poll taken at the beginning of October which asked citizens how much sleep they'd had the night before got these answers:

None	31%
Less than 4 hours	32%
4–6 hours	22%
More than 6 hours	15%

Yet the next morning almost all of them were back at bench or typewriter, some with the marks of the bombing still on them. "Ivy Crouch burst in with bag and baggage," wrote Vere Hodgson, "having been bombed out of the Three Arts Clubs at Marble Arch. She spent the night in a public shelter." The big stores along Oxford Street hit on a Friday night were back in business on Monday morning, lacking only those members of their staff who had been killed or wounded.

Though all London was now under the rain of bombs and officials could accurately say, "We're all in it together, rich and poor alike," it was still the Cockneys in the East End who were suffering the most, and it was here that there was resentment and widespread rumblings of discontent. They were the same bombs, they contained the same amount

* Whose planes had not yet been fitted with radar for night interception.

of explosives, they came down with the same terrifying swish, and they were aimed with the same lack of discrimination. But the fact remained that it still was better to be bombed in the West End than in the East End. The chance of survival was better—and those who did survive were looked after better.

At a moment when London was getting its worst drubbing, Chips Channon wrote in his diary November 5: "Harold [Balfour, Undersecretary of State for Air] fetched me and drove me to the Dorchester, where we dined with the Elvedens, a large party with Peggy Dunne, sweet Nell Stavordale and others. Half London seemed to be there. The [Duff and Lady Diana] Coopers were next to us, entertaining the Walter Elliots . . . Oliver Lyttleton, our new President of the Board of Trade, was throwing his weight and his wit about. He and his wife were dining with the Lloyd Georges, the Gwylyms . . . It was exhilarating. I gave Bob Boothby a champagne cocktail in the private bar, which now looks, seems and smells like the Ritz bar in Paris. . . . Our bill must have been immense, for we had four magnums of champagne. London lives well; I've never seen more lavishness, more money spent, or more food consumed than tonight, and the dance floor was packed. There must have been a thousand people. Leaving, Harold and I wore our tin hats, and the cloakroom attendant said to me, without a trace of a smile, 'You have a screw loose, sir, in your hat—if you can wait I'll send for the engineer.' We left the modern wartime Babylon and got quickly into Harold's Air Force car. The contrast between the light and gaiety within, and the blackout and the roaring guns outside was terrific: but I was more than a little drunk."

This was life under the bombs for the aristocracy. It was dangerous and people got killed, but it was a little different from what the mass of the people were experiencing.

In the West End the stores, restaurants and cafés were back in action within a few hours of the raids. Gas and water mains were reconnected and essential services resumed, the milkman made his rounds, the newspapers arrived.

But that didn't happen in the East End, and people there were slowly coming to the conclusion that nobody "up West" cared a damn as long as the Cockneys stayed quiet. Districts like Stepney had become devastated areas. What houses were still standing had no gas, light or water. Reception shelters for the homeless were hopelessly inadequate. Cafés were shut and pubs boarded up. Schools had either been bombed out or closed. Deep shelters were nonexistent. True, the tunnel whose squalor had so nauseated Superintendent Reginald Smith had been cleaned up and installed with latrines and canteens, but it could only cope with a fraction of the local population. Those who arrived too late trekked every night with their belongings to the West End to queue for tickets to Leicester Square, Holborn and Piccadilly stations, and as they waited in the train were stared at by passing office workers with what they took to be amused contempt.

"More and more people around here are crying for peace," wrote Robert Nichols, the armaments worker who reported from southeast London. "They don't care what ensues so long as the bombing ceases. They've been too mollycoddled and flattered these last few years and they have no reserve of self-reliance. The limit of endurance of some women has already been reached by having to spend a night in a cold shelter."

This was both harsh and inaccurate. To describe the average Poplar, Bow or Whitechapel slum dweller, often out of a job, trying to bring up childen in a noisome rat-ridden house, as "mollycoddled" was sheer fantasy. Certainly there was no more than an isolated urge to give in to the Germans just because of the bombs. The Cockneys of East London were reacting with the same pride and defiance, and showing the same guts, as anyone "up West," but they were fed up with what was being done about them. The jagged ruins whose appearance so galvanized the artistic instincts of Henry Moore were their homes, and if their condition had been miserable before it was appalling now.

Under the circumstances it is amazing how few of them actually rose up in protest. In fact, there was only one demonstration of any size during the whole of the Blitz in London, and it happened in September 1940 in Stepney.

Stepney had two Communist activists among its more prominent citizens. One was their representative in Parliament, Phil Piratin, a thin, burningly intense man; the other was chairman of the Stepney Tenants' Defence League, "Tubby" Rosen, fat and jolly except when he was goading capitalists. For both Piratin and Rosen this was not their war at all—not for the moment, anyway. Russia still relied on its pact with Germany and was not yet in the war, and the party line in Britain was the same as Moscow's: the bosses, rather than Germany, were the enemy.

The two Communists stressed at their streetcorner meetings that they were being treated as second-class citizens during the Blitz. "Our people are dying like rats here in Stepney," shouted Tubby Rosen at a meeting in Commercial Road. "And why? Because the Tory bosses refused us the money that was needed to build deep shelters for our protection. So while we crawl into the surplus hen houses they call street shelters, which wouldn't even protect a rooster from the rain, up West the government's rich friends and their girl friends sleep cozy in double beds, two to a compartment, in their own private deep shelters. Comrades, it's about time we took them over!"

It so happened that most of the big hotels in the West End had made arrangements to turn their basements into air-raid shelters for their customers, and none had done it more efficiently than the Savoy Hotel. Several stories of the hotel had been dug into the ground when it was built, and these were reinforced. One portion of the River Room was kept as a restaurant and cabaret, and had quickly become one of the gayest spots in wartime London; the other was divided by curtains into dormitories for singles, cubicles for couples, and a separate section for snorers. Down below there were more rooms, once reserved for private parties and now turned into guest shelters. For example, the Abraham Lincoln Room was reserved for the Duke and Duchess of Kent, when he came down on leave from the RAF.

The Savoy was therefore an obvious target for a demonstration, especially since it was the nearest big and fashionable hotel to the East End. Piratin and Rosen also knew that most U.S. newspapers now made the Savoy their headquarters, that half the editors in Fleet Street called there at least once a day, that it was a favorite eating place for members of the Cabinet, and that the two biggest gossips in London, Lady Asquith and Lady Diana Cooper, were always to be seen there. So a hundred rebels were recruited and told that the Stepney Tenants' Defence League was about to march on the Savoy. "We'll be in all the papers tomorrow," said Tubby happily.

Unfortunately, they timed their protest march badly. It was not until six o'clock in the evening that the orchestra began to play in the restaurant, not until eight that the cabaret began, not until ten that U.S. and Fleet Street correspondents gathered in the bar, and usually still later that guests descended to the cubicles below for jigsaw puzzles, crosswords, and other fun and games. But for some reason the Stepney protesters arrived shortly after noon.

The Savoy Hotel's historian, whose attitude to the demonstration is not exactly sympathetic, describes what followed:*

"Wendell Willkie, who had come over to observe British morale and report to his government on Lease Lend, was almost due to arrive for luncheon with Sir Harry McGowan and other business leaders when

---

* Stanley Jackson, *The Savoy*.

a crowd of angry women, yelling Communist slogans, marched from the forecourt into the lobby and made determinedly for the restaurant. Some opened their fur coats to reveal incongruous banners proclaiming 'Our Children Are Starving' and 'Ration the Rich,' and a number had even arrived in taxis to storm the barricades."

It seems hardly likely that Piratin and Rosen, both good window dressers if not masters of timing, would have dressed their women in fur coats or transported them in taxis. Even the comfortably-off middle classes possessed few fur coats in Britain in 1940. Perhaps Mr. Jackson was misled by the bulky appearance of the young women who led the demonstrators; several of them were pregnant, and had been told to flaunt the fact, for hotel employees were less likely to be rough with them.

Jackson continues: "A warning from Hansen, the head porter, led to prompt action by 'Willy' Hifflin, the newly appointed general manager, who deployed porters to repel the invaders. Hugh Wontner [the managing director] was also quickly on the scene and ordered that the doors leading to the restaurant should be closed. Half the women were thus cut off from those who had in the meantime sat themselves down at the tables with arms folded, screaming abuse or demanding to be served with food. Others wrapped themselves round pillars, tied their scarves to chairs and clawed at waiters who asked them to leave."

The affair went off rather more calmly and with more English phlegm than this. True, a hotel employee did panic and send for the police, demanding that the protesters be thrown out. "I'm afraid I can't see my way to doing that, sir," said the police sergeant. "You're an hotel, you see, sir. You come under the Innkeepers' Act. If a bona-fide traveler comes in and asks for a meal, and these people look like bona fide travelers to me, then they've a right to be served. Now, if they're making a row, or breaking things, or doing a mischief, that kind of thing, then we'll be willing to escort them off the premises, but otherwise, so far as we are concerned, they're clients of the hotel and have a right to be treated as such."

Piratin and Rosen had gambled on the fact that an air raid would still be in progress when they arrived at the Savoy; they had begun their march up the Strand the moment the sirens sounded. Once inside, they then had every right to be taken down to the shelters with all the debs, Cabinet ministers and millionaires who usually used them. Unfortunately, they didn't know that no one ever used the shelters during daylight alerts, which were no longer serious. Furthermore, as luck would have it, this day's raid was uncommonly short and the all clear sounded while they were still milling around in the foyer. Now they could stay on legitimately if they ordered drinks in the bar or food in the restaurant. But one glance at the menu quickly told them that the prices were beyond their means, and neither Piratin nor Rosen were willing to use party funds to feed their followers. So they filed quietly out into the Strand again and the demonstration fizzled out. It had been badly timed; a night march and occupation of the Savoy's dormitories at the height of a big raid would have made all the difference.

Once they learned that the protest was Communist-inspired, British newspapers buried the story. Most American journalists missed it and filed second-hand reports. Only the German press picked it up from agency dispatches and exaggerated it into a wild workers' riot against the government.

The demonstrators marched back to the bleak acres of Stepney and the world of boarded-up cafés, beerless pubs, broken sewers and the stench of ruptured gas mains. It was not until several weeks later that people "up West" began to take notice, and mobile canteens and squads of dedicated women moved in and gradually turned the East End back into a civilized place again.

10

A Noisy Winter

For C. P. Snow, 1940 was an agonizing year. Somewhat to his surprise and discomfiture, he was one of those who found themselves frightened by the bombing. In one of his books he has written: "As long as I lived, I also knew a different fear, one of which I was more ashamed, a fear of being killed. When the bombs began to fall on London, I discovered that I was less brave than the average man. I was humiliated to find it so. I could just put some sort of face on it, but I dreaded the evening coming, could not sleep, was glad of an excuse to spend a night out of town. It was not always easy to accept one's nature. Somehow one expected the elementary human qualities. It was unpleasant to find them lacking."*

Snow sympathized with those who shared his fears and did not join in the word-of-mouth condemnation then going around London of a famous beknighted actor who had walked off the stage in panic in the middle of an air raid. He knew exactly what the man had been feeling. He envied his fellow citizens who were so much less affected. "My landlady in Pimlico, for instance," he says. "She was a slattern with few qualities, but she was as brave as a lion. So were the clerks in the office, those I met in the pubs in Pimlico, and most of my friends. It made me feel worse."

---

* *The Light and the Dark.*

195

The daylight bombing did not bother Snow as much, and he soon stopped going to the cellar shelter in his office in Tothill Street. "It was no good at all, really. I remember an old civil servant telling me that there was a plan to evacuate certain departments if the bombing got too fierce or invasion came, but, he added, 'Your department can't be evacuated, and anyway, the PM is determined that we are all to die in the last ditch, and no one can say him nay.'" But night bombing terrified Snow, and his friend Professor P. M. S. Blackett, who was an expert on all sorts of things, calculated that the safest place for Snow was the fourth floor of a block of steel and concrete buildings in Pimlico called Dolphin Square. Blackett even found him an apartment there, and though Dolphin Square was solidly bombed a few nights after Snow moved in and got another direct hit later, the scientist-turned-civil-servant stayed where he was because he didn't want to hurt Blackett's feelings.

However, the fear of being killed was something Snow could learn to live with. What agonized him much more was a less personal terror: he was simply afraid that Britain was going to lose the war. He envied the ordinary British citizen who could say proudly and confidently, "Now that France is out and we're alone, we can get on with winning the war." At the same time he resented this cheerful, thoughtless optimism because he himself believed that the betting was at least 5 to 1 against Britain.

Snow would come back late at night from his office, fumble his way into his dark apartment in Dolphin Square and watch the searchlights along the Thames vainly probing the sky for Nazi bombers droning overhead. Somewhere up there, night fighters of the RAF were searching too, and the result was almost always as futile. The invaders were having it almost all their own way, and the defenders were still flying blind. But Snow knew that the balance would soon be changing; soon it would be the bomber crews who would be on the defensive when they entered British air space. The radar system which had guided the RAF to their targets in the summer of 1940 and helped so much to win the Battle of Britain was still being perfected, but already the first prototypes were being fitted into night fighters. Soon their pilots would really be able to "see" enemy planes in the dark.* Soon there would be radar

---

* For over a year after the radar in night fighters was in operation, the British public (and the enemy) were told that the RAF had trained "cat's-eyed" pilots who could see in the dark as a result of special exercises and a diet of carrots.

sets for every searchlight and battery, and then the day of enemy invulnerability would be over.

But radar would not win the war for Britain; it would only make it more difficult and more costly for the enemy to win it. What was needed was a miracle—the United States entering the war, for example, or something even more unlikely, like a German attack on Soviet Russia. But Snow could not believe that Adolf Hitler would be stupid enough to provoke either of these. In the meantime he put what faith he had in Britain's ability to absorb the punishment she was taking while science and the new weapons it was developing came to her aid. But this was an enormous problem. Which weapons should be given priority? Snow is not a man given to toying with the if's of history, but there is one alternative which has always tantalized him: If Winston Churchill had come to power in 1939, at the beginning of the war with Germany, instead of in 1940 after the debacle in France, would the Battle of Britain have been lost instead of won?

It seems a ridiculous possibility, but the facts behind it are not. In 1939 the radar system which eventually saved England was not ready; indeed, despite intensive effort, it did not become operational until just before the Battle of Britain began in July 1940. Any delay in its development during the first crucial nine months of war would have meant that the RAF would have lacked the means to tell them when the Nazi bomber fleets were leaving France, which direction they were heading, and where they were hiding up in the clouds. Radar enabled the RAF to substitute brains for brawn, to be guided into battle, to strike at just the right moment; it more than made up for Britain's RAF's numerical inferiority.

But if Churchill had been in power, would radar have been available? In the years leading up to the war, the development of radar had been strongly attacked as useless and ineffective by one man, Frederick M. Lindemann.

Snow suspected and most of his scientist friends (including Watson-Watt, the inventor of radar) believed that Lindemann's dogged opposition to the development of the system right up to the eve of war stemmed not from his objections to its feasibility but from his hatred of one of its principal sponsors, Sir Henry Tizard, rector of the Imperial College of Science and Technology in London. For a variety of reasons, Lindemann not only was jealous of Tizard's scientific eminence but was also dedicated to bringing about his downfall. In his eyes, Tizard could never do anything right, so it followed that since Tizard was enthusiastic about the development of this invention, it must be unworkable and not worth the money being spent on it.*

In the years before the war began, Lindemann's opposition to radar had reached such vehemence that two professors resigned from the scientific committee of which the Air Ministry had appointed Tizard chairman and of which Lindemann was a member. The reason they gave was that they could no longer countenance Lindemann's savage abuse of their chairman. Fortunately these two professors, Blackett and A. V. Hill, were so valuable that the committee was immediately re-constituted, with Lindemann replaced by another scientist.

But if Churchill had been in power when that quarrel took place, everyone knew that Tizard, not Lindemann, would have been replaced, for Lindemann and Churchill were very close. It was an extraordinary friendship. Lindemann was an ascetic of Teutonic extraction who neither drank nor smoked and existed on a diet of cheese and watercress, and made it plain that he strongly disapproved of anyone who lived otherwise. How he and the cigar-smoking, brandy-swilling, gourmandizing Winston Churchill could be so close, and why Churchill had such faith in him as a friend and as a scientific adviser is a complicated story, though its consequences are not: as far as the Prime Minister was concerned, Lindemann could do no wrong.

Every man of liberal opinions and a belief in a firm stand against the bestialities of Nazism would like to have seen Winston Churchill in power in 1938 or 1939. "We should, without any question, have been morally better prepared for war when it came," Charles Snow was to say later.† "We should have been better prepared in the amount of war material. But . . . I find it hard to resist the possibility that, in some essential technical respects, we might have been worse prepared. If Churchill had come into office, Lindemann would have come with him . . . Without getting the radar in time, we should not have stood a good chance in the war that finally arrived. With Lindemann instead of Tizard, it seems at least likely that different technical choices would have been made. If that had been so, I still cannot for the life of me see how the radar system would have been ready in time."

Now Churchill had come into office at last, and Lindemann had

---

* Lindemann's own pet method for stopping enemy bombers, which he put forward perfectly seriously, was a screen of hydrogen-filled balloons floating thousands of feet high from which wires, hung with bombs, would dangle in the path of incoming planes.

† In his famous 1960 Harvard lectures, *Science and Government*.

risen with him. Within weeks Tizard was forced off his committees and out of his job. Lindemann was quite ruthless. He made it plain that henceforth any new scientific development would have to be cleared through him first, and that he would decide whether to recommend it to the PM. Tizard was dispatched on a mission to the United States, the Prof (as Lindemann was called) took over, and the relationship between science and government changed utterly.

"This is no time for false modesty," Lindemann had said.* "I happen to believe that I have more brains than all these other people"—this with a gesture toward Whitehall that was meant to include politicians, soldiers, civil servants and his fellow scientists. He went on to tell Harrod that because he had more brains he could render a unique service to Britain. For this purpose what he required was power, and power was to be acquired by knowing more about what was going on than anybody else. Therefore, everything must go through him, and with the power that this knowledge gave him he would be in a better position to serve his country and Prime Minister.

Thereafter, as Snow's friends soon discovered, the only way to Churchill was through Lindemann. He was not receptive to many outside suggestions, particularly scientific ones, and did not pass them on because he felt that he knew better. "He was a dedicated gadgeteer," says Snow "and beware the scientist who is a gadgeteer. He was always thinking up wild schemes for confounding the Germans which he passed on to Churchill, who naturally lapped them up—he liked gadgets too. There was Habakkuk, a plan for putting floating ice fields off the German coast and flying bombers off them. There was a crazy scheme for a Commando raid on the Baltic. And others."

Worst of all, this gimmickery wasted valuable time at 10 Downing Street while decisions of scientific importance were pigeon-holed by the contemptuous Prof. It was no wonder that C. P. Snow was a frightened man, and nothing that Professor Lindemann was pouring into Winston Churchill's receptive ear helped him sleep nights.

n October, Italy launched its troops across the Albanian frontier toward Epirus, and Greece became Britain's newest ally. For days the newspapers played the story across their front pages and hailed the Greeks as gallant comrades in the fight against tyranny. Ordinary Londoners, however, suspected that Greece might prove more of a liability

---

* In a conversation with his assistant, Roy F. Harrod. See Harrod's *The Prof*.

than an asset and were muted in their welcome. They had grown disenchanted with foreigners and resigned to more and more enemy victories; in any case, they were immersed in their own affairs, for bombing was intensive at the time. Many people shared the feelings of Pamela Slater, the young architect's assistant, who wrote: "Now it's Greece! If Athens and the Acropolis are bombed and the treasures of the Greek islands, I'll admit that this generation of fools and madmen is not worth saving. What chance have they? What on earth is the point of the radio announcer talking about the courage and fighting spirit of the Greeks when everyone knows that only air power counts?"

Most Londoners, however, hardly reacted at all. The young pacifist James Donald from south London, whose ear for his neighbors' talk was uncanny, reported three conversations with his landlady and her children on the day that Italy invaded Greece.

I came home to lunch and announced to Mrs. R. that Italy and Greece were at war. She said:

"Oh, now that will settle them." I did not answer and she went on: "Are *we* at war with Italy?"

"Yes," I replied, heavily. [Britain had been at war with Italy for five months.]

She said: "That's Mussolini's country, isn't it?"

"Yes, that's right."

"And Greece is Marina's country, isn't it?" *

"Yes."

"That will please old 'Itler," she said.

"Why do you think so?" I asked.

"Well, it will," she said. "I know that. And that will finish him."

"Who?"

"Why, Mussolini," she said.

"What do you think will happen now?" I asked.

"We shall smash them," she said.

"Smash who?"

"All of them," she said.

"*All* of them?"

---

* It should be explained that one of the most popular couples in Britain in 1940 was the Duke and Duchess of Kent. The Duke, a brother of King George VI, was serving in the RAF. The Duchess, beautiful, gay, worldly, was Greek-born and a great favorite of the British, and most of them referred to her as "Marina."

"Yes," she said. And then: "They'll use up some petrol getting to Shropshire."

"Shropshire?"

"Yes, they're going there this morning."

"What," I said, "Mussolini going to Shropshire!"

"Naow. I'm talking about Mr. and Mrs. Blodwick across the way. They're going to Shropshire today."

"Oh," I replied weakly. "I thought we were talking about the war."

"So I was. That's why Mr. and Mrs. Blodwick are going to Shropshire."

At that moment the siren sounded and Mrs. R. dashed off to the shelter.

Presently her daughter, Vi, a pretty girl of twenty who worked in a shop, came in.

I said: "Heard any war news this morning?"

"No, nothing at all," she said.

"Nothing at all?"

"No," she said. "What's happened, is it over or something?"

"No. Italy's declared war on Greece."

"Oh," she said. "That won't make any difference to us, will it?"

"It might," I said.

She thought and then said: "Why, we've had people in our shop all morning and no one's mentioned it."

"Well," I said, "see how long you can go this afternoon before you mention it, and tell me what the first person says."

"Okay," she said.

Later, at tea, Vi said: "I waited three hours and no one mentioned Italy and Greece, so I mentioned it to the manager, and he said: 'Oh that! I know. Greece is the country where Marina comes from, isn't it?' "

Mrs. R.'s son, Tony, twenty-one and a gunner in the RAF, was home on leave.

I said to Tony:

"Italy's declared war on Greece. What do you think of it?"

"Oh, bugger the war!" he said. "You will keep talking about it, won't you," he said. "I'm fed up! Can't you see I'm on leave, man? War, war, war, bombs, bombs, bombs, that's all anyone at home bloody well talks about!"

"Sorry," I said.

fter Flying Officer Geoffrey Page had been in the Royal Masonic Hospital for about three weeks, sleeping fitfully on drugs and in constant pain, he was visited by "a man with horn-rimmed spectacles, broad shoulders and a friendly grin who looked like Harold Lloyd, the old-time film comedian."

The man was Archibald McIndoe, a plastic surgeon. He had been the most famous reshaper of noses and lifter of faces in Harley Street until the outbreak of war, but now he had established a unit at East Grinstead hospital, south of London, to mend the burned bodies of the young pilots shot down in the Battle of Britain. He had plenty of patients; a whole ward was full of them.

"McIndoe didn't stay long on that first visit," Geoffrey Page recalls. "His conversation was light-hearted and inconsequential. Was I wearing gloves and goggles when the plane caught fire, how long had I been in the sea, and how soon afterwards had I been coated with tannic acid? Then he rose, waved a ham-fisted hand, and said, 'Good-bye, young fellow, see you again.' Little did I realize how often this was to be."

In fact, McIndoe left seething with rage. Page was one more example of the damage tannic acid could do to a man badly burned about the hands and face. He knew exactly what was going to happen to the boy's hands, and the knowledge of the torture which awaited this nineteen-year-old in the days to come was hard to bear.

Almost at once the Burns Unit in the London hospital began the long job of picking away the armor plating of tannic acid which had formed on Page's hands, and covering the raw places with saline dressings. But it was too late. "Day by day my strength increased," Page says, "and with it the condition of my hands deteriorated. Fraction by fraction the tendons contracted, bending the fingers downwards until finally the tips were in contact with the palms. Not only this, the delicate skin slowly toughened until it had the texture of rhinoceros hide, at the same time webbing my fingers together until they were indistinguishable as separate units."

The attending physician would come and watch the increasing contraction. Finally he said, "If your hands continue to form this thick scar tissue, I'm afraid it will mean a series of skin-grafting operations. Are you prepared to try and prevent this?"

"What's the alternative?"

"We may be able to keep the skin soft by the use of molten-wax baths, followed by massage."

The hot baths commenced the same afternoon. They were a nightmare, and the massage was worse. But still the fingers curled inward. It went on until the doctor confessed that it was no use.

"Your hands will have to be grafted," he said. "I will arrange for you to be sent to East Grinstead. It is now for Mr. McIndoe to see what he can do."

The Guinea Pigs ward (as it came to be known)* at Queen Victoria Hospital in East Grinstead was in the middle of a crisis just at the time Geoffrey Page arrived. The Welfare Committee of local ladies had been hearing rumors of strange goings-on at the hospital, and had called a meeting at which the urgent attendance of Mr. A. H. McIndoe, the chief plastic surgeon, was requested.

According to their lights, the committee members had a point. Strange things were indeed happening, and the ladies were neither young enough nor pliable enough to accept them easily. The hospital had been built for a small, exurbanite London community, but now it seemed to have been invaded by young madmen. The formal relationship between doctors, nurses and staff had gone; pretty VAD (Voluntary Aid Detachment) auxiliaries swarmed about the wards chatting and flirting with patients. When committee members came to pay their duty visits to the wards, they expected to be greeted by quiet, long-suffering smiles of patients bravely bearing their cross; instead they were often hailed with ribald comments from mouths smelling distinctly of alcohol. The idea that liquor was actually consumed in the wards horrified them, and they were determined to put a stop to it.

The meeting was called in November, a time when McIndoe was sorely harassed and troubled. In the medical canon it isn't considered wise for a doctor to be deeply involved with his patients, but the young men in Ward Three (all Guinea Pigs) were different, and their fate preyed on him. In his charge were over a hundred young men, most of them twenty and under, who were the pick of Britain's youth. In one minute's inferno of flame their faces had burned away and their hands frizzled.

"Imagine how they feel," he said to a friend at about this time. "On Friday night they're dancing in a night club with a beautiful girl and by Saturday afternoon they're a burned cinder. A fighter pilot can't help being vain because he has something to be vain about, and all the girls swarm around him like a honey pot. Think what it must be like

---

* So called after one of the most exclusive organizations in the world, founded by Geoffrey Page. The Guinea Pigs Club membership was confined to airmen shot down during the Battle of Britain whose burns were treated at East Grinstead. Besides native-born members, twenty-one non-British pilots, including four Americans, qualified for membership.

for that young man to go back into the same circle with his face burned away. One minute has changed him from a Don Juan into an object of pity—and it's too much to bear."

Hence, McIndoe found himself concerned not only with the surgical side of his work, but in the rehabilitation of his cases. He had to find a way of preparing them, mentally and psychologically, for re-entry into the world. In the meantime, however, he was determined that no outside influence was going to be allowed to make his problem boys unhappier than they need be. As a result, at that November meeting he listened to the good dowagers complaining about his burned pilots' manners, language and drinking habits, and then he rose.

"I have several things I'm going to say, some of which you are not going to like," he began. "The war has been going on for over a year now, yet your group obviously wish things to continue as they did in peacetime. You had better realize this: your hospital no longer simply serves the local community. Its primary job is to be used for the physical and mental rebuilding of airmen injured flying for their country."*

His jaw jutted. "Some of you object to pilots and aircrew having alcohol in their wards. Normally I might perhaps agree with you, but in this case you overlook two points. Firstly, these men are not sick. Their bodies may be broken temporarily but their youthful spirits are still with them. Secondly, ordinary hospital discipline is all very well for a patient who is admitted for a few days or a few weeks, but it has to be relaxed when they are young and fit and have to be here for months—some for years."

There was a silence after he had finished, and afterward McIndoe said that he could "hear their prejudices turning over."

Then one of the most vociferous of his female critics rose to her feet. "I expect we deserved that rebuke," she said. "Perhaps we did not think it out too well. But now perhaps you would take us into your confidence and tell us how we can help instead of hinder."

"Thank you," said McIndoe. "I suggest that the next time you go visiting in the wards, forget that these are cases. Think of these boys as the fighter pilots they are." He paused, and then added, "Just one more point. You will probably have noticed I am allowing a certain number of my patients to go into East Grinstead. Soon they will be going into London itself. Some of them are not very pretty to look at, because I'm still working on them. A man who has lost a nose and is in

---

* From McIndoe's papers, in the possession of the author. See also *Faces from the Fire*, by the author (McIndoe's biography).

process of getting a new one doesn't exactly resemble a film star. I want you ladies to spread the word around that these men are not to be made to feel uncomfortable. No feeling sorry for them; they don't want sympathy. I want everyone—shopkeepers, pub keepers, girls—to be normal with them. Tell everyone you know that these are normal young men in a temporary difficulty. Buy them drinks, invite them to your homes, and for God's sake don't pity them." To himself he added that once they discovered what sort of boys were under those temporary skin flaps, there was no danger that the daughters of the good ladies would feel any such pity.

In the meanwhile, the long, tricky job of mending Flying Officer Geoffrey Page's face and hands was beginning. In the weeks to come, only one thing made the agony bearable. He looked down at his tortured hands and said to himself over and over, "You're going to fly an airplane again! You're going to fly an airplane again!"

On the door of Ward Three, where Page so often lay sleepless at night, one of his fellow patients had hung up a notice. It read: BEWARE OF THE WOUNDED ANIMALS.

I t was a noisy winter for London, and a killing and miserable one too. Everywhere the capital was ripped and scarred, and every night the bombers came over. Not only the East End now, but the other suburbs too, locked themselves in for the night. There was nowhere to go but the shelters.

Yet in the West End a new sort of night life flourished. The Savoy Hotel in the Strand and the Dorchester and Grosvenor House hotels in Park Lane had in effect become clubs for politicians, the press and café society. Hard drinking went on in all of them while the bombs rained down, and some of the correspondents who "covered" the Blitz rarely moved more than a mile from the Savoy during the height of the raids. They were quite right; they would have been running away had they done so, for the Savoy was in the center of the action. It was possible for a correspondent to cover the battle and interview the general at the same time, for the Savoy was a favorite resort of Churchill and members of his Cabinet.

There was other entertainment. In a back street behind Piccadilly Circus the indefatigable chorus girls of the Windmill Theatre were still prancing doggedly through their high-kicking routines, and behind them the tall show girls were still posing with their breasts uncovered—except for the dust which filtered down all over them whenever a bomb dropped nearby. Once the Windmill had been the mecca of the middle-aged voyeur who paid for a close-up view of a motionless nude, but by now these girls had become a kind of a symbol of imperturbability under fire. Their pictures had gone out all over the world to messes and barracks, posing with tin hats and shovels as their only adornment. The faces changed often because they were drafted, but somehow they always seemed the same: fresh and young and earnest as they tried to keep up with the music against the crashing of the bombs. They were execrable dancers, but nobody really cared; the public, particularly the troops, loved them because they were there.

Most of the other West End theatres closed for a time at the height of the bombing, and then began to open again. Most plays continued in spite of the raids; the management would simply put up a placard saying AN AIR RAID IS IN PROGRESS and then carry on with the performance. Those who wanted to could leave the theatre for a shelter, but few of them did.

"I remember one night," says Harold Conway, who was a show-business writer in those days, "when I went with my wife Eileen to the Apollo in Shaftesbury Avenue. The play was *Margin for Error* with Margaretta Scott. There was a big raid on all through the performance, and at the end it was still going on. It was no use the audience trying to get home, so they all stayed on. Michael Redgrave was playing next door at the Globe in *Thunder Rock*, and he and his company joined us. Between them, the two companies gave us an extraordinary evening of entertainment until four in the morning. They sang, they told jokes, they danced, they got the audience to join them in charades. It was marvelous fun. The audience responded wonderfully, of course. Most of those who were sporting enough to go to the theatre in these days were bright people, of course, and they responded. On this particular occasion the all clear sounded about three-thirty A.M. and the audience was so involved that it elected to stay on, until it became clear that we were being discourteous to the cast, who needed to get some sleep before the performance next day."

 night out in the West End that winter finally changed Rosemary Black from a frustrated young widow into a fighter.

There had been a lull in the bombing for almost twenty-four hours, and after a succession of claustrophobic nights in the shelter she decided that she would go crackers if she didn't get out. Her friend, Mrs. C., had been coming home day after day from the ambulance station with her

hair and clothes covered in blood and with her horrifying experiences
with bomb victims so much on her mind that she had felt compelled to
unburden herself for hour after hour.

Now Rosemary Black cut her short. "We've got to get out of here,"
she said. "You'll drive me mad, and yourself too."

She forced her companion to put on a smart black suit, saw the
children and the maids safely into the basement shelter, and they set
out for the West End. Somehow they managed to procure a taxi, and
they instructed him to cruise around the streets. Mrs. C. thought it
ghoulish to go around "picking at London's sores," as she described it,
but Rosemary Black said firmly, "I have to know."

But when she saw what the Nazis had done to her beloved London,
gloom and misery began to steal over her. In Berkeley Square she nearly
burst into tears at what had happened to its north side. The spot was a
sentimental symbol of her girlhood, as redolent with memories as an old
dance card, where she had wandered hand in hand with her beaus after
an all-night party at the Berkeley or the Ritz or Quaglino's, to sit in the
gardens and dreamily watch the dawn come up over London. Now it
was destroyed.

The taxi driver took them to Grosvenor Square and pulled up by a
pile of wreckage. "You'll 'ave to walk from 'ere, ladies," he said. "They've
plowed up the rest."

They walked along a sidewalk littered with broken glass and came
into Oxford Street, opposite John Lewis' store. In her diary that night
Rosemary Black wrote:

It was the most ghastly sight imaginable. I had no notion that the empty,
charred skeleton with its blackened walls and gaping windows and rust-orange
girders and its wax models lying like corpses on the pavement could look so
terrible and forbidding. The pictures in the papers had given no idea of the
appalling reality. It was so horrifying a spectacle of tragedy and waste that it
reduced Mrs. C. and myself to silence (which takes some doing). We stood
dumbly staring at it in a sort of sick despair. I noticed that the few other
"trippers" like ourselves who had come to see it were affected in the same way.
They too fell silent, or if they spoke at all it would be in a hushed whisper, as
though in church; on their faces too was a look of awe and fear.

They picked their way through the glass and rubble toward Oxford
Circus, where they stood at the edge of an enormous bomb crater and
stared at the wreckage everywhere.

"Empty pavements and an empty silence through which the few pedestrians seemed to hurry furtively. Empty grey air, yet full of an oppressive

feeling of desolation and despair. When we left we agreed as one that it had been quite enough for us and we didn't want to see any more horrors, and picking up our driver we told him to take us quickly to the Café Royal, and sat silently in the taxi in dumb despondency. But we couldn't get away from it all. The western curve of Regent Street was charred and pitted as high as the rooftops; and when we got to the Café we found it shut. We knew it had been temporarily closed some days ago but had supposed it had surely re-opened by this date. It was a problem, now, to know where to go. Many of the restaurants must have closed for lack of customers, for the streets were empty and dead. The Cumberland, which is always full and which we'd thought a certain last resort to fall back on, has been evacuated today owing to time bombs. Prunier's is too far from bus and Tube for us. The Apéritif, where we next turned, proved to be now open for lunch only. Eventually we landed up at the Ecu de France [in Jermyn Street], which actually turned out to be open and to have a few people in it. We sank dejectedly into chairs in the bar and ordered ourselves double champagne cocktails. It wasn't until I was three-quarters of the way through mine that the haunting picture of John Lewis' was erased from my mind.

It was the last winter that Britain was to know for many years when one could still enter a restaurant and gorge oneself on good food. Rationing had not yet begun to pinch. Restaurants were still free to serve a four-course meal, provided you could afford to pay for it, and there were still stocks of wines and liqueurs.

It was as if Rosemary Black sensed that it was the end of an epoch, and that things would never be the same again.

And *did* we do ourselves well! I've never had such a disgusting gorge in my life. 1½ dozen oysters each; hot lobster; grouse, beautifully high [well hung] and raw, and orange-lettuce salad; wood-strawberries and cream; a "pichet" of white wine, masses of coffee and a strange, sun-smelling liqueur from the Pyrenees.

The waiters were tremendously pleased to have such a gay, free-spending twosome at their table and entertained them with a constant flow of chat.

We never heard the usual nightly warning, and never even thought about it being due, in our enjoyment of our little "treat," until a bomb fell close enough to shake the restaurant and rattle the windows. Our perky little white-coated waiter, in whose hands a plate of coffee cups had jarred and slopped, cocked his head. "That's the nearest Jerry's been to us 'ere so far!"

But they found it less amusing when they came out into Piccadilly Circus afterward. Guns were booming, searchlights were threading the sky overhead, and there was "an all too clear sound of bomber engines" in the sky. They had been hoping to catch a bus home, but while the raiders were overhead the buses were drawn up "in a ghostly rank—policemen and wardens everywhere—a sense of haste and urgency and fear in the shuffle of many feet on the darkened pavements . . ."

Halfway across Piccadilly Circus, Rosemary Black turned on her flashlight for a moment to see the way. "Put that light out!" came a sudden deep shout, and up loomed the shape of a large policeman. She tried to put the light out; instead, it stuck. Frenziedly she stuck it in her pocket, but the glow showed through.

Meanwhile the policeman had reached them and grabbed them both by the shoulders. "Don't you know there's a war on!" he cried. With rough hands he bundled them to the head of the stairs leading to the Underground and pushed them down. Rosemary Black lost her balance and fell flat. She was still in a semidaze when her companion helped her off the escalator onto the platform of Piccadilly Station. And there she saw them.

Horrified by ghastly sights in Tubes. I'd gathered from the papers that people were sleeping there, but I thought from what was given out that they did so only in badly bombed areas—East End, Holborn, City. Also the pictures I'd seen of Tube sleepers showed only an odd half-dozen people or so lying in a vast expanse—it looked as if they had far more space and air than they'd have got elsewhere. Now, seeing every corridor and platform in every station all along the line crowded with people huddled together three-deep, I was too appalled for words. The misery of that vast wretched mass of humanity sleeping like worms in a packed tin—the heat and smell, the dirt, the endless crying of the poor bloody babies, the haggard white-faced women nursing their children against them, the children cramped and twitching in their airless, noisy sleep. Even a disused escalator was crowded with dumb, resigned humanity—why, if I wanted to torture my worst enemy, I could think of no better form of Procrustean bed for the purpose. And I saw a woman sleeping with her head on the bare platform, her face about an inch away from a great gob of spit. I was nearly crying. I felt so ashamed and disgusted to have eaten that huge, expensive meal, while here . . .

Like a latter-day Mary Antoinette, Rosemary Black rushed around the clustered platform handing out money from her handbag to the women and children—and then felt ashamed of herself. When she reached home she went to bed miserable, thinking of all the suffering around her and of her own "wholly undeserved" good luck.

I sometimes feel I'd really be happier in a way—though, of course, miserable and raging too—if I were bombed out of house and home instead of always being "one of the lucky ones" in this, as in every other way. Even so, though, I should never reach the depth of suffering in which thousands of my fellow citizens are now engulfed, because I'd still be well off. To lose my home and my possessions would still not be, for me, to lose everything. God must surely have it in for me in my future life, that I, worthless that I am, am granted all this undeserved good fortune here and now.

Rosemary woke in a black mood the next day, for she could not erase the images of Oxford Street and of the women in the Underground. She began to curse aloud the Women's Voluntary Service, from whom she'd had no reply to all her requests.

This being useless and unwanted is miserably disheartening, especially in view of the horrors realised last night. One feels so hopelessly and ashamedly superfluous and ineffective. Yet at the same time the endless muddle and inefficiency has made me feel browned-off about the whole business of getting war work. Much as I wish I could find some way to be of real use, it seems to me that my help can't be needed in the least, since the offer of it is so scornfully treated.

That morning she pleaded again at the ambulance station to be taken on as a helper or a driver, but was firmly told that only qualified persons were being accepted. She was offered a job as chauffeur to a high-ranking member of one of the fire services, but turned it down "because he can well afford to drive himself or take taxis." In frustration she altered the date on the back of her blood card (she had given blood two days before) and donated an extra transfusion. At least she was providing something for London's urgent needs.

It was while she was recovering at home from this gesture with an extra strong cup of tea—it would punch a hole in her tea ration, but she didn't care—that Mrs. C. returned home in a rage.

One of the men ambulance drivers at their station had died in very unpleasant and tragic circumstances as a delayed result of exposure on duty, and Mrs. C. was trying to arrange for his widow to get out of London for a week or so, to escape both the reminders of her loss and the Blitz. She had phoned a woman she knew who was an obvious choice for a provider of refuge for the widow: plenty of money and servants, a peaceful district, a huge house which Mrs. C. happened to know (on good authority from a neighbour) contained not one single "refugee," though every other house in the neighbourhood was just about crowded out.

But this woman always was a bitch—at least such is my opinion. She declared that it would be *most* difficult and inconvenient to take the widow in, as the house was already fully to bursting with refugee friends. She *might* be able to think out some way of managing it—would have to think it over and see—the woman would go in the servants' hall, of course? Before she thought out things any further, could she have some details about the woman. What *class* was she, exactly?

Rosemary Black had never heard Mrs. C. swear before, but she did so now. "My dear, I'm *bursting*," she cried. "Can you imagine that at a time like this anyone could be so perfectly *bloody*. Servants' hall! Class! What does it matter? Damn her, damn her, damn her, I'll never speak to her again! Full house! All lies, she'd never do a thing to help a single soul and she won't do it now! A heart like a stone!" She walked around the room shaking her fist above her head. "I'd like to hurt her. Bitch—yes, bitch!"

She swung around on Rosemary Black. "Bitch!" she said again, and then, "Isn't there something worse I can call her? What's the worst name I can possibly use?"

Rosemary Black suggested the well-known "short and unattractive word."

Mrs. C. said, "Oh!" and looked shocked. But when she disappeared upstairs she could be heard muttering the word over and over under her breath.

The next day Rosemary Black set the alarm at six-fifteen, had a hurried breakfast and started to make the rounds of various offices in London. Late that afternoon she returned to the house in Maida Vale, kicked off her shoes and collapsed in a chair before the fire. She was exhausted—but she had a job. Two days later she reported for duty at an office in the Strand. Henceforward she would be a tea-and-sandwich dispenser on a YMCA mobile canteen. On her service-route card were only two words: BOMB SITES.

O n December 3, 1940, the authorities finally caught up with James Donald, the young pacifist, in his lodgings in East London. He had deliberately failed to register for National Service in May, when his age group was called up. Now Mrs. R., his landlady, handed him an envelope, but he purposely did not tell her what was in it, despite the eager expression on her face. Later, at breakfast, her daughter, Vi, said, "It's the police, isn't it? They're on to you. Now you'll have to register as a conshie."

The letter contained a form asking him to state formally, in not more than 250 words, why he wished to register as a conscientious objector, and that afternoon he settled down to it. He wrote his objections in longhand, and after reading them through was rather proud of his effort. It read:

You will agree that war destroys life and property. You will agree that war mutilates men, women and children and animals alike. You will agree that war causes blindness, disease and insanity, and that during war immorality increases.

You will agree that war takes millions of the youngest and strongest men from the world, leaving weaklings, the infirm and the maimed to produce the next generation. You will agree that war causes men to kill and wound or to assist in killing and wounding each other when there is no hatred between them. It is obvious that they are only roused emotionally by speeches, stories, songs, parades, flags, etc, and above all by press, film and radio propaganda. Could each man speak the language of his so-called enemy, he would find that they had mutual interests, including the desire to abolish all war.

You will agree that those who demand men to fight and to support war escape the horrors and death that they have imposed upon millions. It is because I too believe as you do that war creates these evils that I am a pacifist, for pacifism requires no lying, no distortion, no slaughter, no threats, and no economic loss, whereas war causes at least eight of the Ten Commandments to be broken and contributes nothing to the happiness of mankind.

I refuse to recognise any law supporting war. I maintain that the state has no moral right to order men to fight. I cannot conscientiously support war, either directly by actual physical combat or indirectly by making armaments or performing any work which is essential for the continuity of this war or any future war. I have been a member of the P.P.U. (Peace Pledge Union) since the year of its foundation and have designed antiwar posters for the League of Nations Union and the No More War Movement. I support the abolition of the death penalty and am an anti-vivisectionist.

He signed the statement, put it in an envelope and biked to a mailbox with it. When he got back his landlady and Vi were having tea in the kitchen. "Now let them do their worst!" he said.

Vi said nothing. Mrs. R. said, "The war will be over by this spring."

"What makes you think that?" he asked.

"Well, it will be. We are going to take the offensive."

"How?"

"With all the men we've got, of course!" she said sarcastically. "How else do you think?"

"Yes, yes," he said impatiently, "but what will they *do?*"

"Do? Why, drive the Germans out, of course!"

"Out of where?"

"Why, out of France and all the other places."

He said, "But to do that, France must be invaded."

"Well, that's what we're going to do," she said. "Then there's the other way."

"What other way?"

Vi, who had been listening in silence, chimed in, "Yes, what other way? Go on, say!"

"With our navy," said Mrs. R. "We'll take the offensive."

"Where?"

"Heavens, how do I know?" said Mrs. R. "Nobody knows nothing. They don't tell us nothing—no more than they do the Germans themselves. Yet you go on asking me as if I knew."

"Well, now, are you sure they tell us nothing?"

"Of course. Nothing. No one knows!"

"Well, then, if *nobody* knows, how do *you* know that we are going to invade France?"

Mrs. R. hesitated and then said, "It's in the papers."

"Then they must know, surely—otherwise how did the information get there—and it indicates that someone knows something."

Mrs. R. considered this and then said, "Well, *they* know, of course. I suppose Churchill must know. He's at the top."

"But Mr. Churchill says the war is going to last until 1942 or 1943, and you said it would be over next spring."

"Oh, that's what he *says,*" retorted Mrs. R. "But of course it will be over by the spring. It can't go on all the time—it would cost too much. Besides, the Germans have run out of ammunition. And we've smashed up all their planes, and they can't have many more left."

Just then the sirens sounded, and Mrs. R. departed hastily for the shelter.

James and Vi were left alone in the house, but the girl's behavior was strange, even for her. Though the raid was heavy, she stayed under her blankets on the floor, miserable but remote.

The next day James Donald wrote in his M-O report:

I will now touch upon another subject which you will find references to in other instalments of this diary. There you will see that I wrote that Vi R. (aged 20) seemed to become very amorous whenever an air raid was in progress. Some complex functioning of the nervous physio-psycho systems, I conclude, and don't know enough about the matter to be definite.

Well, this condition has now ceased. Just in the same way that people have become accustomed to air raids and lost their fear, so she, having become hardened to the Blitz has lost this state of what I might term artificial or perverted sexual excitement.

On the night of Donald Ketley's ninth birthday a large piece of shrapnel from an antiaircraft gun came through the roof of his parents' house at Chadwell Heath, in East London. A heavy raid was on at the time but Donald followed his father, who ran upstairs to see if it was an incendiary bomb, and he retrieved the slice of torn metal lying beside his parents' bed. It was still warm. Donald decided that it was a wonderful birthday present and added it to his collection of war souvenirs, which included a melted blob of metal from an incendiary bomb they had doused in their backyard in September, a strip of fuselage from a downed German bomber, and an autographed picture of "Ginger" Lacey, the RAF fighter ace who had destroyed the plane that bombed Buckingham Palace.

Donald was enjoying the war, though he did not say as much. He knew his parents were not, and he knew that there was much terror and suffering around him. Sometimes in the air-raid shelter under the stairs he could hear his father and mother talking in whispers about the poor people who had been bombed out of their homes. He remembered the morning his father had come home unexpectedly from work. His face was white and his lips were trembling. He was working as a clerk in a customs warehouse at Wapping, and on that morning he had found the whole place ablaze from the bombing of the night before. The firemen were desperately trying to get to one of their comrades buried under a wall which had suddenly collapsed on top of him. His father had returned to the gutted warehouse a few days later to see if he could find any papers and office records, but all he had retrieved were a pair of pliers, a drill and some wirecutters. The heat of the fire had made them too brittle for use, so Donald added them to his collection.

By this time Donald had learned to distinguish bombs from guns, even in his sleep. The bombs always woke him up, but he didn't mind the guns at all. Not so his parents. One night he heard his father grumbling about the noise, for there was an antiaircraft unit in a park a few blocks away. Finally, when the din was at its worst, his father muttered "Oh, for God's sake, shut up and let them bomb us in peace!"

The Ketley family had slept under the stairs for the first couple of months, but one morning they almost didn't wake up after the night's raid. The near misses had broken a gas pipe and the escaping gas had all but asphyxiated them. Thereafter they joined their neighbors, a middle-aged couple with a teen-age daughter, in their shelter in the back garden. In Chadwell Heath few people slept in public shelters— they were just far enough out of the East End to have small gardens with Anderson shelters in them. Some people were stubborn, of course, and used neither public shelters nor Andersons but stayed in their beds. A neighbor of the Ketleys' was killed when the bed in which he was sleeping was blown through the roof of a house on the opposite side of the street by blast.

Blast did very strange things, Donald was discovering. He heard his mother talking one night about a relative killed in East Ham. "And then the firemen got through the hole and there they found her," she was whispering to his father. "You remember her. Really pretty, she was. There wasn't a mark on her, but the blast had ripped every stitch of clothing off the poor soul, and she was dead."

Six in an Anderson shelter was pretty crowded, but apart from being awakened by the racket from time to time, the Ketleys and their neighbors managed to sleep. Afterward his father claimed that he had never felt better; it was rather like camping out. Certainly, being in an Anderson was preferable to the public shelters. The Ketleys were forced to go to one on the night when they were evacuated because of an un-exploded land mine. During a lull in the raid, a voice from the alley behind awakened them by crying out, "You in there! All out, all out! There's a bomb!"

It was the air-raid warden. A land mine had floated down at the end of the street, and the parachute had caught in a tree, so that the bomb never quite hit the ground. It was swinging just above it, and Donald stared at it in pop-eyed wonder as he heard the warden say, "Another six inches and this whole street would be flat by now."

Since there was no certainty that the bomb would continue to hang there, like some fearful sword of Damocles, they were hurried off to the public shelter in the park. It was the most uncomfortable night Donald Ketley can remember of the war. The shelter, a long concrete tunnel, was very cold and had nothing but wooden benches along its sides. Two inches of freezing water covered the floor. The Ketleys just sat there, feet tucked under them, and when morning came they went over to a friend's house and were given some breakfast and thawed out.

The friend's wife was still simmering with indignation over the events of the night's raid. She and her husband were devoted gardeners and very proud of a small but lovingly cared-for greenhouse just behind their house. In the middle of the night they had been awakened by a crashing of glass, and looking out of their Anderson, they saw that a magnesium bomb had landed in the greenhouse. Bombs were still dropping, but this was too much for the wife; grabbing a sandbag outside the shelter, she raced for the greenhouse, where she effectively doused the flare with sand. "It's bad enough them bombing us," she said, "but how dare they try to wreck our greenhouse!"

The Ketleys were allowed to return to their house the following afternoon, after the land mine had been defused by a naval engineer. It was the closest miss so far; they had lost windows and bits of roof from time to time, but that was all. Once Donald went into his parents' bedroom after the window had been shattered, and seeing hundreds of splinters of glass embedded in the wall opposite, he felt momentarily sick at the thought of what would have happened to his father and mother had they been in bed at the time.

But mostly he had no qualms. When the war was spectacular and noisy it was never ever dull. Another good thing: quite early in the Blitz, his school had been totally destroyed by a bomb. Since Donald was shy, a poor student and unpopular with his teacher, he was overjoyed when he heard that the place was gone. Thereafter he went each day to his teacher's home to pick up lessons, which he brought back next day for marking. In the following months he changed from a poor student to an excellent one, and though he was aware that his teacher rather resented it, he didn't care. He was very happy, and he didn't mind if the Blitz went on and on and on.

On Sunday night, December 29, 1940, Winston Churchill was waiting to speak to President Roosevelt on the direct line to the White House when a servant entered. He whispered a message to Colonel Leslie Hollis, who looked across at the Prime Minister and was about to speak, but Churchill waved his hand irritably. Hollis knew that he did not like to be distracted just before he talked with the President, and particularly not this evening. Roosevelt was due to address the American people later in one of his "fireside chats," and the British leader was pinning great hopes on what he would say.

Britain needed from America much more than the sentimental support which they'd had so far from the President and his people. The country needed money to buy food and ships and arms, for it was broke. Churchill hoped to persuade Roosevelt, newly elected to a four-year term of office, to offer specific promises of material aid and concrete support for the British war effort. Such news would help the Prime Minister at home with the increasing number of critics, in Parliament and the press, of the government's purely defensive activities, and would give a needed boost to a citizenry growing tired of being saturated by German bombs night after night.*

But the news which Hollis had received forced him to speak. "It's the bombing of the City," he said.

"I know all about that," said Churchill curtly. He had been informed shortly after seven o'clock that large formations of German bombers were attacking the area between Liverpool Street and Ludgate Circus, where the City of London's financial headquarters and the Bank of England are situated.

"The message says that St. Paul's Cathedral is on fire," Hollis went on.

Churchill's whole manner changed. "No," he said, "that mustn't happen. Get on to the Guildhall at once and tell them that St. Paul's must be saved at all costs. Tell them *at all costs!*"

The Guildhall is the headquarters of local government in London's inner city, and Hollis rushed away to deliver the message.

The December 29 raid was one of the most destructive of the Blitz, not so much in loss of life but in the annihilation of some of the capital's most beautiful architectural treasures. Not the least tragic aspect of it was that it need not have been so destructive had London been prepared. Once again the Luftwaffe had caught London's defenders off guard. It was as if someone who knew London well had suggested to Göring that he bomb the City of London—the financial heart of the Empire—on a Sunday night, when all the stockbrokers were still in the country for the weekend.

The timing could hardly have been better from the German point of view. Not only was it a Sunday night, and one between Christmas and New Year, when some of the auxiliary services were taking a holiday; it was also a period of extremely low tides, so that the water in the Thames nearby was abnormally low. Enemy planes swept over about seven

---

* Roosevelt promised nothing specific on this occasion, though he did state that from now on America would be "the arsenal of democracy."

o'clock and dropped basket after basket of incendiary bombs, with a smaller proportion of high explosives. They spattered like hailstones on the roofs of the ancient Guildhall and a score of old City churches, full of old beams and highly inflammable. Within an hour the City was ablaze. The glow from the raging inferno could be seen from thirty miles away, and wave after wave of bombers droned in to stoke it up.

The irony was that for more than four months every householder in London had been dealing with incendiary bombs and had lost his fear of them. Whenever Miss Vere Hodgson had heard one clattering down from the roof of her house she was out of the door as fast as her legs would carry her, spade in one hand to scoop it up, bucket in the other to douse it and sand to smother it. Everyone knew how to put them out quickly and efficiently. Unfortunately, in the City on a weekend there was no one there to deal with the incendiaries, and up on the roofs the blaze started, leaped across the narrow twisting streets and ran through the area like any forest fire.

Even so, some of the worst conflagrations might have been got under control had not the water run out. The fire services were on the scene within minutes and were soon controlling the main blazes, though not the small fires eating their way in from the roofs at the back of buildings. But as more fires started and more incendiaries were dropped, the supply of water diminished. The pumps were being fed from the Thames, and the river ran dry. Soon there were only gushes of muddy water coming through the pipes, and then they went flaccid.

The firemen stood by, forced to watch old buildings burn to the ground, steeples crash, stained-glass windows melt, and a series of fires that five or six hundred janitors could have doused in a few minutes with a spade and stirrup pump soon engulfed the whole of the City. Four months of Blitz had not yet taught Londoners that no building must ever be left unguarded, and now the nation was paying for its lack of vigilance with some of its greatest treasures.

But not St. Paul's. From the start of the war, a regular watch had been established there. The message had gone out to the world that St. Paul's Cathedral was burning, and the news reached Dean Matthews as he approached the precincts of the great church shortly after the raid began. But he discovered that it wasn't alight yet, though it might soon be. The great dome itself was threatened; a bomb, striking it perpendicular to its surface, had failed to penetrate but was lodged halfway through the outer shell. There was no fire yet, but the lead of the shell was beginning to melt. "It can't be long," they told the Dean.

"We knew that once a fire got hold of the Dome timbers it would, at that high altitude, quickly be fanned into a roaring furnace," wrote the Dean later. "Unless it could be stamped out at the very start the chances of the Dome were very slender indeed."

Practically every fireman in London was standing by ready to help, but what could they do? There is no more heartbreaking sight at a fire than a limp water hose, and there were miles of them, mud oozing from their nozzles.

"All we can do now is pray," said one of the vergers.

"Then do it standing up, and keep your stirrup pump handy!" replied the Dean crisply.

By now incendiaries had begun to fall upon the lower roofs, and these were quickly seized upon by watching choirboys, ushers and vergers. All the buildings surrounding St. Paul's were in flames. The high wind carried sparks and blazing pieces of wood into the cathedral, and they whirled about the great expanse under the dome like fireflies. It was an eerie scene, with the baleful fires licking at the stained-glass windows like hungry hounds. Crouched in one corner of the nave were about fifty people who had been driven by fire out of a nearby shelter and had come to the cathedral for sanctuary. At one moment Dean Matthews wondered whether to mobilize them for fire duty, but they seemed too stunned. Later he noticed that some of them were playing cards in the light from the flames and wondered whether to stop them doing such a thing in church. "What absurd thoughts one has in times of strain!" he wrote.

Up in the dome the lead continued to melt. In the street below, Ed Murrow was preparing a radio broadcast to the United States which would begin with the words: "Tonight the bomber planes of the German Reich hit London where it hurts most, in her heart. And the church that meant most to Londoners is gone. St. Paul's Cathedral, built by Sir Christopher Wren, her great dome towering over the capital of the Empire, is burning to the ground as I talk to you now."

Only it was not. Because whether they were praying on their knees or standing up, stirrup pumps to hand, the silent pleas of the vergers of St. Paul's seem to have been heard that night. "Suddenly," wrote the dean, "the crisis passed. The bomb fell outwards into the Stone Gallery and was easily put out. How difficult it is to write history! I have to confess that it is uncertain how the bomb came to fall. Was it by some artificial means or was it dislodged by its own weight? I incline to the latter opinion because, so far as I know, no member of the Watch claims to have had any part in producing the result. At any rate, the Cathedral was saved from one of its most perilous predicaments, whether by human means or by what we call 'accident.' In either case we thank God that our great Church was spared at a moment when it looked almost hopeless."

But the rest of the City of London was in ruins. A list of the churches and ancient buildings destroyed reads like a tourist's guidebook. From Fleet Street to the Tower of London, whole areas had disappeared forever, and piles of smoking rubble covered miles of winding City streets. It was the Great Fire of London that need not have been, and at an angry Cabinet meeting on Monday, December 30, Winston Churchill ordered that it should never happen again.

That day an Order in Council was issued. Henceforward it would be an offense to leave any building in London unoccupied by night or day. Fire spotters must always be on duty. Mr. Herbert Morrison, who had been made Minister of Home Security in October, told his department to draw up a regulation making a weekly round of fire watching part of the duty of every adult citizen henceforth.

No one grumbled, for most people felt guilty, as if it were their neglect which had brought havoc to the City. On New Year's Day, Rosemary Black took a van from YMCA headquarters in the Strand to the City, to bring hot cups of tea and pies to the firemen still dynamiting buildings and fighting the last fires. It was an icy-cold day, and the men were gray-blue with cold and fatigue. Old buildings rocked in the wind, and outside the ruin of Barking Church someone had underlined in soot a Christmas message, so that it now read as it flapped in the wind: "God rest ye merry, gentlemen, let *nothing* you dismay."

At the end of five hours of picking her way through the rubble, Rosemary Black suddenly felt "black with rage" at how unnecessary the whole business was. Later she wrote:

It is so terrible, that because of sheer wanton neglect of the obvious precautions, millions of pounds' worth of damage should have been done, and hundreds of brave men's lives risked and lost: the loss of beautiful old buildings, tragic as it is, is of minor importance to a people who can look after them no better than this. Are they lunatics, these merchants and wharfingers and landlords, who abandon their invaluable property, unguarded, to the mercies of the night-raider? Are they criminals, these vicars of historic churches, who are so quick to bewail irreparable damage after the event and pass round the hat for restoration funds—clamouring against the atrocities perpetrated by the ruthless Hun and yet caring so little to preserve their charges from going up in smoke?

But of course we ordinary citizens—nearly every one of us—are almost as much to blame. Ours is the guilt for the irresponsible apathy and heedless-ness which made possible this lunatic negligence on the part of our elected rulers. How many of us ever troubled to think out clearly the position in regard to the danger of fires created by the existing set of fire regulations—their limitations, I mean? How many of us, if we had ever troubled to understand the position clearly in the first place, would have been public-spirited enough to agitate about it, and arouse general opinion in the matter? I know I shouldn't. Are we a nation of utter imbeciles? Really, it seems as though the answer must be Yes, Yes, a thousand times Yes!

On her first free day after the raid, Miss Vere Hodgson took a bus as far as Ludgate Circus and then walked past St. Paul's Cathedral into the blackened forest of the City. By the time she had gone a few hundred yards she was crying. "I will never bother with Germans, or any other foreigners (except Greeks) ever again," she wrote in her diary that night. "Oh dear, what a way to celebrate the New Year!"

11

A Queer Life

Vere Hodgson sent a copy of her diary each week to all her relatives abroad, to keep them up to date with her life in wartime London. In a covering letter to one of them in the spring of 1941, she wrote: "I hope you will not find it [the diary] too pessimistic and gloomy. Last night's experience was rather unnerving and quite frankly, my dear, I do not expect to survive the blitzkrieg. I'm not a bit brave, really. The only thing that can be said in my favour is that I've not run away. I'm the only representative of my family left in London. But it's a queer life."

In fact, the bombing of London was no longer so intensive. There were days when there were no air raid warnings at all, and somehow these were difficult to bear. People found themselves getting irritable with one another, and one civil servant reported that his father interrupted his conversation with a friend at dinner to say, "For heaven's sake stop talking so loud, we'll never be able to hear the sirens!"

It was during this period, when the raids slackened off but the war, with all its restrictions and regimentation, went on, that some of the more percipient Londoners began to suspect the difficulties that lay ahead. The danger from the skies had kept people together, united against the enemy, and there were not only no squabbles while bombs were falling, but no worries about the future. But after two or three days of quiet, citizens began to notice the inconveniences, the growing shortages of food, the discouraging news from abroad. As if aware of this, Winston Churchill gave a radio talk in February in which he stressed that the danger of invasion by Germany was not yet over. Actually, it was; the Germans knew it, and Adolf Hitler had accepted the fact and long since dispersed the invasion barges which had once concentrated on the Channel coast. Churchill himself knew it; already his intelligence services were telling him of Hitler's plans to attack Russia. But he considered the threat of invasion a spur to rally his people, and he was reluctant to give it up, especially when the raids showed signs of slackening.

Not that they disappeared for more than a day or so at a time from the life of the average Londoner. In the spring of 1941 the city was still one of the most dangerous in the world, and newly arrived American correspondents taking their first stroll from the Savoy Hotel soon stopped smiling when they saw in the shattered window of Gieves, the military outfitters, bowler hats with the legend underneath: ANTI-SHRAPNEL BOWLERS, SPECIALLY REINFORCED. They were necessary. People went on dying from shrapnel and shells all that winter and spring, and sometimes horribly.

"Today we hear from the Lambeth people that the raid was down their way," Vere Hodgson had written in January. "A bomb fell on some workmen's flats near Lambeth station. The bomb that fell on the Bank subway the other night was a terrible affair. The blast threw many people onto the live rails and they were electrocuted immediately. This was from an eyewitness who came into our place this morning. He also saw two children blown under an approaching train, and a Jew crawled under the train and rescued them, at the peril of his life."

A month later she was writing: "Last night's raid is described as having done 'considerable damage,' but one gathers that it was only one bomb. But today I heard from an eyewitness that it was a new type of bomb and it dropped on Hendon. It had a flare attached to it and it fell into the High Street before the warning sounded. There were lots of people about in the streets and so did not stand a chance. It destroyed five streets and left devastation for three miles. Large numbers of people killed and many injured, and hundreds are homeless."

But later that day she walked from her rooms near Holland Park to Hyde Park, nearby, and wrote: "Tins of sand all around and many army lorries, but the Round Pond is still round and the ducks and sea-gulls were basking in the first sun we've had this year. I haven't found any snowdrops yet, but I have heard they are out near the Peter Pan statue."

Then she wrote of a growing need that was becoming an obsession to Londoners that spring: "I'm just longing for some fruit but could not get any. I went out with the firm determination to spend a shilling per pound if necessary for apples, but to my horror there was not one in any shop in Notting Hill at any price whatsoever. The window seems to be full of turnips. Mrs. Gray was so sorry later when she heard I was looking for an apple that she sent me up a Bramley, and although it was a cooking apple I ate it with great relish."

One of her fellow workers, Mr. Booker, had hated onions all his life, "but now he says that when once more we can get them he will eat one and enjoy it. I think we will all go in for onion binges when the war is over."

For virtually the first time since war began, the rationing system instituted by Lord Woolton, the Food Minister, was beginning to hurt, and citizens were thinking with their stomachs. Rosemary Black came home from a day driving her mobile canteen around the bomb sites to find a note from her maid about the result of that day's shopping:

> Madam: there is
> no honey,
> no sultanas, currants or raisins,
> no mixed fruits,
> no saccharine at present,
> no spaghetti,
> no sage,
> no herrings, kippers or sprats (smoked or plain),
> no matches at present,
> no kindling wood,
> no fat or dripping,
> no tins of celery, tomato soup or salmon.
>
> I have bought three pounds of parsnips.

Mrs. C. was extremely despondent about the home-front situation. To their chagrin, she and Rosemary Black became aware that their conversations were increasingly devoted to various shortages of food, a subject to which they unerringly returned from any other topic like a homing pigeon. One morning that spring, seeking inspiration for the week's catering which she invariably arranged for her household in Maida Vale, Mrs. Black took down for the first time in many months a booklet which had been published just after rationing began in 1939. Entitled *A Kitchen Goes to War,* it had been issued by the Ministry of Food to help housewives cope with wartime shortages. She described her reaction in her diary:

> I remembered this vaguely as being a selection of poverty-stricken sort of dishes of uninspiring drabness. But very much to the contrary. I was bewildered by a rich lavishness and variety mostly quite unobtainable, and, in fact, by present day standards quite beyond one's wildest gastronomic dreams. Can one ever have sighed over the limitations of a diet in which could still be included stuffed onions, stuffed tomatoes, onion soup, ragout of rabbit, or kedgeree of kidneys, fish and leek pudding, prune roll, and such heights of luxury as cream cheese and pineapple salad, cheese soufflé, rabbit pudding with bacon and onion, topped with mousse made with twopenny bars of chocolate, Cornish leekie pie, eggs baked in potato cases with cream and cheese, sugarless water ice cream made with two tablespoons of sweet condensed milk to each gill of cream? Can this ever have been condemned to the category of economic wartime fare? Can one ever have seen even the shadow of privation in a world containing such marvels?

One week in March when Vere Hodgson went to the grocery store in Notting Hill Gate for her bacon ration,* she mentioned to the man behind the counter the rumor that cheese would soon be rationed and that then they would only get a square inch a week. She was very partial to cheese.

> He got rid of all the other customers and then said "Wait a mo'." I waited and found being thrust into my bag with great secrecy and speed half a pound of cheese. When I went for my butter ration at the dairy I found I could get a quarter of a pound of cheese. I had no compunction on taking it. I went straight away and gave it to the Mercury Café (near her office in Notting Hill), where I knew they could not open tomorrow because they had no meat and only a morsel of cheese. I thought I was very lucky. My own

---

* Neither she nor other Londoners ever knew how lucky they were to get it that week. The previous Friday afternoon Lord Woolton had received five separate signals from the Admiralty reporting that food ships sailing in convoy across the Atlantic had been sunk by German submarines. By an extraordinary coincidence, these five ships were largely stocked with bacon. Woolton, determined to keep his pledge that the ration would always be honored, ordered all existing stocks taken out of warehouses and distributed at once. Two days later one bacon ship limped into Liverpool and was immediately unloaded and its cargo distributed. The ration was met, but only just.

piece was very good and I could not resist, as I got in, cutting a hunk and eating it then and there. I sympathise with Ben Gunn when he always dreams of toasted cheese in *Treasure Island*.

London was growing used to the sight of foreign soldiers in the streets, and all over the West End little clubs had mushroomed to cater to them. The bulk of the Polish army in exile was stationed in Scotland, where its dashing troopers were bowling over the girls in Edinburgh like ninepins, and the Dutch, Belgians, Scandinavians and French were in encampments spread around the country. All of them, however, had headquarters in London, ample staffs, and apparently abundant funds for entertaining.

The chieftains of these and of other groups liked to forgather in such fashionable restaurants and hotels as the Mirabelle, Le Coq d'Or, the Ritz and the Connaught, and it was not unusual to see lunching simultaneously at Claridge's Moshe Shertok (later Moshe Sharrett), head of the Jewish Agency; General Wladyslaw Sikorsky, leader of the Poles; Admiral Emile-Henri Muselier of the Free French navy; King Haakon of Norway; Colonel Passy (a *nom de guerre*—his real name was André Dewavrin), of Free French intelligence; and Colonel Maurice Buckmaster of SOE (Special Operations Executive, the British secret-service operation for Europe). They were almost always at separate tables and eyed each other with cold suspicion, not always without reason.

Their subordinates preferred the back-street clubs which had sprung up in the Soho. There you could drink after hours and, unlike the pubs in those days, the liquor never seemed to run out, though it was expensive and sometimes tasted vaguely of surgical spirits. Almost invariably behind the bar would be stationed a tall redhead or plump blonde, with a man hovering in the background; he usually turned out to be a Polish, Belgian or Dutch sergeant, some of whom later became powerful in London's night-club world. The jostling customers would be a motley collection of foreign soldiers, some up from camps, others back from mysterious missions in Europe, all of them accompanied by one or two girl friends—who were nearly always English. Foreign soldiers were very popular with London girls.

The favorite haunt of the Free French was Le Petit Club Français, which was tucked away in a mews behind St. James's Street and numbered among its clientele some of the bravest men and prettiest girls in London. It was presided over by an owlish blond Welshwoman named

Olwen Vaughn, who could sweet-talk an obstreperous drunk and knew at a glance the exact moment when a quarrel between two patriotic Frenchmen, one pro- and the other anti-De Gaulle, needed to be broken up before a duel was challenged. Olwen probably knew more about French undercover operations than anyone outside Colonel Passy, its commander, for most operators who returned safely from a parachute mission into Occupied France made Le Petit Club their first port of call after handing in their reports, and often brought back a bottle of *pastis* or a *boudin* sausage so that Olwen could "smell France again." (Not that she needed to; the club was always redolent with the unmistakable scent of Caporal cigarettes.) Since there was little the proprietress didn't know about Free French activities, early in January 1941 she sensed that a feud which had been simmering at General de Gaulle's headquarters was coming to a head. During the past few nights a certain estrangement had developed between members of the Free French army and navy; they stood at different ends of the bar and bowed with formal politeness to those who only a week or two ago had been bosom friends.

When young Robert Mengin, who was still resolutely anti-De Gaulle and belonged to neither side, entered the club on New Year's Day and tried to bring a navy lieutenant and an army captain together over a celebration drink, he got only muttered refusals from each of them.

"What's happening here?" he asked Olwen Vaughn. "Everyone's acting as if the navy's gone over to Vichy."

"That," she replied, "is probably the most unfortunate remark of the war."

Indeed it was.

At that very moment, Scotland Yard Special Branch officers were drawing up a warrant for the arrest of the commander in chief of the Free French navy on a charge of conspiring to commit treason with agents of the Vichy government.

In 1940 Admiral Emile-Henri Muselier had been one of the first opponents of Pétain's decision to capitulate to the Germans, and he had been against the Vichy government from the beginning. At the moment when the aged marshal appealed to all Frenchmen to accept defeat, Muselier was in Gibraltar with a squadron of his ships. He could have sailed them back to their base at Toulon or taken them to North Africa; instead, he talked to his officers and men, then announced that they were unanimously resolved to keep fighting, and that his ships would rally to the side of the British.

Muselier had many friends in the British navy, and they roundly cheered him on his way when later he came to London to discuss the future of his forces. By that time General de Gaulle had arrived in London and had issued his appeal for Frenchmen everywhere to join him. Nevertheless, most of Muselier's British friends presumed that once in London, he would take over as leader of the Free French, for he was De Gaulle's senior both in rank and experience; in fact, in all three services he was the most senior officer of those who had elected to carry on the war.

The admiration which Muselier had won from British and French alike increased when he met De Gaulle in his headquarters at 4 Carlton Gardens and immediately made it clear that he was not seeking the leadership. He told the touchy and suspicious general that he would willingly serve under him, and he became the first officer among the Free French to pin the Cross of Lorraine to his service jacket as a sign of his loyalty to the cause of Free France.

However, Olwen Vaughn and Robert Mengin were not the only ones to notice in the ensuing weeks that some members of De Gaulle's immediate entourage did not take kindly to the arrival of Admiral Muselier in their midst. Members of the general's intelligence service, which was then in the process of an intensive build-up, seemed particularly resentful. It was a period when General de Gaulle was making strenuous efforts to persuade Frenchmen abroad that he was the incarnation of their country's resistance, and Robert Mengin was not the only one to find this attitude arrogant and presumptuous. Though thousands had rallied to the general's call, a surprisingly large number had not. They resented De Gaulle's use of the royal "we" to emphasize his superior status ("In the name of the French people and Empire, We, General de Gaulle, leader of the Free French . . ."), and they strenuously denied his claim that if they were not for him they must be for Vichy. It was of such men that the general's cohorts at Carlton Gardens were most afraid, for their antagonism might undermine De Gaulle's claim to represent all Frenchmen still fighting, and they were dangerous as long as they had an alternative to turn to—Admiral Muselier, for instance. He was strongly admired by members of his own branch of service, the only arm of the Free French forces which was seeing any action at that moment, and if things went wrong for the general, they might begin to agitate for his replacement by the admiral.

So though Admiral Muselier gave no hint of disloyalty to his chosen leader and obeyed his every order to the letter, the inner ring of fanatic Gaullists continued to view him as a potential rival who must be removed. After an operation by General de Gaulle's forces in September 1940 against the Vichy-held colony of Dakar, they redoubled their efforts. The attempted occupation of the city was a disaster in which everything went wrong.

Dakar, with a splendidly equipped naval port on the West African coast, had treasures that General de Gaulle vitally needed to finance and fuel his government-in-exile. It was the base for the great French battleship *Richelieu,* and inland the gold-bullion stores of the French, Polish and Belgian governments were hidden after their flight into exile. Here was a port which the British could use as an antisubmarine base for the war against the German U-boats that were annihilating their convoys in the South Atlantic. Also, it was a base from which the British could halt any German attempt to push south into Africa from the French colonies and possessions in the north. The capture of Dakar would make De Gaulle a rich man, able to sit at the bargaining table with Churchill and make demands instead of asking for favors.

But it hadn't worked out that way. Though strenuously anti-German, the governor of Dakar had proved to be as equally anti-De Gaulle, and would not surrender his city. When an Anglo-French force moved in, he opened fire. Three days later, the Allied forces retired and Dakar stayed in Vichy hands.

De Gaulle's position seemed more threatened than ever to his supporters, and now more than ever did they deem it necessary to remove from power a man who might replace him.

The chief of General de Gaulle's security, or "action," squad (Bureau Central de Renseignements et d'Action) at this time was a tough and uncompromising loyalist known as Major Howard. Nominally he was a subordinate of the two directors of French intelligence in London, Colonel Passy and Colonel Antoine Fontaine, but General de Gaulle trusted him implicitly and allowed him great latitude. Howard, who had gathered around him a group of fervent Gaullist supporters who were prepared to give their lives for their leader, was no friend of Admiral Muselier's. In fact, in December 1940 relations between the admiral and the major were so hostile that Muselier asked De Gaulle to dismiss Howard from his post for "harrying and spying on my staff." De Gaulle consented to do so, and announced that Howard was being posted to Africa. But the major fell ill with conjunctivitis, so that his transfer had to be delayed, and on December 27 he told General de

Gaulle that Muselier was trying to get rid of him because he had uncovered evidence of the admiral's treachery.

On New Year's Day, 1941, Foreign Secretary Anthony Eden telephoned General de Gaulle at his cottage in Shropshire, where he had gone to spend the holiday with his family, and asked if he could return to London immediately. It was an open line, so Eden did not state the reason, but he did stress that it was urgent and that it concerned a Free French officer of distinguished rank. However, it was not until the following day, January 2, that General de Gaulle decided to leave for London, and by then Admiral Muselier was under arrest.* He had returned to London on the morning of January 2 after taking part in a Red Cross rally at Windsor to find two Special Branch officers waiting on the doorstep of his home in Hallam Street, Knightsbridge. They told him that he was under arrest but either would not or could not specify the charges.

Muselier entered the house to change into mufti; then, wearing his naval greatcoat against the cold, he accompanied the officers to Scotland Yard. He was given a cup of tea, followed by lunch, with relays of officers watching him closely, and there he remained until the afternoon, still with no idea why he was being held.

At this time General de Gaulle arrived in London from Shropshire and was driven at once to see Eden at the Foreign Office. It was a difficult moment for the British Foreign Secretary, and his distress was visible. He was a great friend of France, he knew and admired Muselier, and yet he had to tell General de Gaulle that Scotland Yard possessed evidence showing the admiral to be a traitor.

He had an appalling revelation to make to the general, Eden said. The British had proof that Admiral Muselier was secretly in communication with the Vichy government, that he had tried to transmit to Darlan† the plan for the Dakar landing while it was being prepared, and that he was planning to send the *Surcouf*‡ over to him. The Prime Minister, having been told the facts, had given the order for the admiral to be arrested, and it had been approved by the Cabinet. He needn't conceal

---

* In his book, *De Gaulle contre le Gaullisme,* Admiral Muselier maintains that British intelligence had warned De Gaulle's second-in-command, Lieutenant Colonel Angenot, of the impending arrest and that Angenot must have warned his chief. This De Gaulle denied.

† Admiral Jean Darlan, commander in chief of the Vichy-controlled French navy and one of Marshal Pétain's closest advisers.

‡ A Free French submarine.

what kind of an impression this terrible business would have, but it had been impossible not to act without delay.

Eden then produced notes which appeared to have been written by General Rozoy on the notepaper of the French consulate in London. General Rozoy had acted in London as chief French air force liaison officer with the RAF until the armistice, when he had elected to return to France and join the Vichy government. The French consulate in London was still controlled by Vichy nominees. The notes, which purported to give details of Rozoy's dealings with Muselier, and which also mentioned that the admiral had been paid £2,000, were, according to Eden, on their way to Vichy in the diplomatic pouch of a South American courier when they had been intercepted by British intelligence.

As it subsequently turned out, anyone who studied the notes with a suspicious eye could have seen at once that they were forgeries. But General de Gaulle himself quotes Eden as saying, "After a thorough inquiry, the British authorities were, alas, forced to believe in their authenticity."*

In fact, so far the inquiries had by no means been meticulous, and it is surprising that De Gaulle himself did not see at once that the notes were forgeries, for there were several mistakes in the general usage of General Staff communications with which he might have been expected to be familiar. One must presume that he was still suffering from the effects of his rebuff at Dakar, for instead of the haughty choler he usually displayed toward the British when one of his staff was attacked, he merely said that he must go away and think.

The general's departure from the Foreign Office without demanding Admiral Muselier's immediate release—and without threatening to sever relations between Free France and Britain, which is what Eden had feared—was taken as a signal by the Special Branch to take the next step. On the afternoon of January 2 Admiral Muselier was driven to Pentonville Prison and told to strip by the prison doctor, whose examination, the admiral was afterward to say, was so meticulous that it reactivated a painful wound from World War I. When he protested that he was an admiral of France and should not be treated in such a way, the doctor curtly replied, "If you were an admiral, you would not be here!"

Muselier was still not told what charges had been leveled against him, other than that he had been arrested under a wartime regulation and that he could look forward to an indefinite period of imprisonment.

---

* The War Memoirs of General de Gaulle, Vol. I, The Call to Honour.

But by this time he was sure that he was the victim of an intrigue by his enemies among the Free French at Carlton Gardens.

While he sat and brooded in his cell, guests were assembling in the West End for a luncheon being given at Lancaster House by the new Secretary of State for War, David Margesson, for the commanders of the Allied armed forces. The milling crowd of Belgian, Dutch, Czech, Polish, Norwegian, Greek and Yugoslav generals and admirals buzzed with speculation as the rumor swept through their ranks that "the French have a scandal on their hands." But General de Gaulle gave no sign of being disturbed when he marched toward his place at the table, aloof from the lesser fry around him. A few minutes later he was followed by Admiral Muselier's chief of staff, Captain Moullec. No one had yet told Moullec what had happened to his chief, and as he stopped before the admiral's place at the table and saw that a card had been placed over the holder containing Muselier's name, he looked bewildered. A British officer hastened over to him and led him quietly away, explaining as he went, but everyone in the room had seen the incident. All heads were now turned toward De Gaulle, who stared grimly into space and seemed to take no notice.

That night in Le Petit Club Français there was a fight between a Free French major and a naval lieutenant that might have developed into an ugly brawl had not someone intervened in time. The jeers were going around that the Free French navy's leader was a spy.

It was not until forty-eight hours later that General de Gaulle at length made up his mind that the charges against Admiral Muselier must be false. He went to see Anthony Eden at the Foreign Office and tardily expressed his displeasure over the fact that his second-in-command had unceremoniously been thrown in jail. "The documents are ultra-suspect," he said, "both in their context and their supposed source. In any case, they are not proofs. Nothing justifies the shocking arrest of a French vice-admiral. Besides, he has not even been heard. I myself am not allowed to see him. All this is unjustifiable. For the moment, at the very least, Admiral Muselier must come out of prison and be treated honourably until this dark business has been cleared up."*

Eden promised to do his best but maintained that the charge was such a serious one that for the moment Muselier must remain in jail.

It might have been expected that since De Gaulle was now convinced of the spuriousness of the charges against his second-in-com-

---

* *Ibid.*

mand, he would have threatened a rupture with the British government if the admiral was not taken to more comfortable quarters. He must have been well aware that at this moment the British wanted to avoid an open quarrel with the Free French at all costs. Instead, it was the British themselves who came to Muselier's aid. One of his many friends in the Royal Navy, Admiral Dickens, went to see him on January 3 at Pentonville and was shocked by the conditions* and his state of health. He promised to do something for his friend immediately, and being a man of his word, that afternoon he saw both the First Lord of the Admiralty, Mr. Albert V. Alexander, and the First Sea Lord, Admiral Sir Dudley Pound.

The following day Muselier was taken to guarded quarters at the Royal Naval College at Greenwich, and there he remained until January 6, when he was driven to Scotland Yard. There, for the first time, he was shown the documents which were supposed to be so incriminating.

The admiral took one look at them and said, "But these are fakes. Bring in one of your French experts and he will agree with me."

A French expert was already there. It did not take him more than a moment's examination to dub the five pages of notes "forgeries, and clumsy ones at that."

In the afternoon General de Gaulle called in Major General Sir Edward Spears, who had been liaison officer to the French government, and delivered an ultimatum to him. "I told him that I gave the British government twenty-four hours in which to set the admiral free and make suitable reparation to him, failing which all relations between Free France and Great Britain would be broken off, whatever might be the consequences."

In the opinion of most people concerned with the affair, the ultimatum had been a long time coming.

General Spears went with De Gaulle to Scotland Yard where, in fact, Muselier was being released at that moment, with fulsome apologies. But when the general rushed up to him and embraced him, the admiral did not respond. His attitude was cold.

The next day there was a letter to Muselier from Eden apologizing to him for his ordeal and saying that "His Majesty's Government have satisfied themselves that the documents, which first appeared to cast suspicion on you, are spurious."† This was followed by an invitation

---

* Afterward Muselier claimed that he was badly treated by his guards.

† Muselier, *op. cit.*

to dine with the Prime Minister and Mrs. Churchill at 10 Downing Street, at which more apologies were voiced. Then came a further invitation, to lunch with King George at Buckingham Palace.

General de Gaulle watched with ill humor these clumsy attempts by the British to make amends. "Indeed, the reciprocal change of attitude on the part of the British and of the admiral was so complete that it soon turned out to be excessive," he wrote in his memoirs. He blamed the British for having manufactured the charges against Muselier, and accused their intelligence services of having recruited Frenchmen who had "cooked up" the plot against Muselier. The admiral, on the other hand, remained convinced until his death in 1965 that the plot against him was hatched in Carlton Gardens among the Free French themselves. The truth will probably never be known, though one Free French officer who might have thrown some light on the mysterious affair was quietly arrested by the French a few days after the admiral's release and sent to a Free French colony in Africa, where he died in prison.

Relations between De Gaulle and Muselier remained cool from then on, and they were to grow worse in the months to come.

The only people to draw dividends from the sordid incident were De Gaulle's security forces at Carlton Gardens. On January 15, taking advantage of British embarrassment over the whole affair, General de Gaulle signed an accord with Anthony Eden giving the Free French on British territory jurisdiction over their own forces and the right to conduct their own military courts. Henceforth, in such matters General de Gaulle's investigators and tribunals would be left to handle matters themselves, without any interference from their hosts.

In the spring of 1941 everything seemed to go wrong for Britain. As someone remarked, in the occasional quiet moments of the night you could hear the collective weary sighs of the citizens of London.

On April 6 the Germans had intervened to help Italy in her campaign against Greece, and by the end of the month Nazis were tramping through Athens. Yugoslavia had been bombed into surrender. In the Western Desert the Eighth Army was being driven back into Egypt by a crack German army, especially trained and equipped for desert warfare, under a dynamic commander, General Erwin Rommel. Everywhere Britain was on the defensive, and after more than a year and a half of war, a victory against Germany did not look remotely possible.

Added to this, the bombing of London was continuing, and restrictions in freedom of movement and shortages of food and materials seemed to increase every day.

One day in April, Vere Hodgson was overjoyed to find two oranges in a shop in Kensington. She felt impelled to give one away to a fellow worker, but took herself off to her room to savor and consume the other.

On April 9 Winston Churchill broadcast to the nation to announce that Greece had surrendered, and to hint that Crete would soon follow. Vere Hodgson listened to his words and thought that the Prime Minister "sounded unutterably weary . . . He does love to give us good news," she wrote in her diary that night, "but there was nothing he could say but that there was worse to come . . . He sketched the fearful possibilities of Hitler extending into the Mediterranean, etc. He did not think we could do much about it. He did not explain lots of things we should like to know, but I suppose we shall know some day. First of all, if, as he said, it was inevitable that Yugoslavia should be defeated, why was he so elated the other day when he announced that they had declared for us? Then he never attempted to explain how the Germans got to Libya. Why did we not know they were coming?"

The reader of her journal can almost hear her sigh as she paused before writing the next sentence: "But he did not seem to mind his responsibilities and faced the future with equanimity. So we must do the same. If he cannot win through, then no one can. It must be something within ourselves that is working against us."

Nowadays London wore a gaunt and neglected look that was only partly relieved by the wild flowers beginning to sprout on bomb sites. Newcomers noticed that Londoners walked past bombed buildings in the West End, Westminster and the City with an almost self-conscious refusal to look at them, rather in the way that English people don't stare at beggars or cripples in order not to embarrass them—or themselves. It was as if they did not wish to hurt the feelings of the Houses of Parliament or the Guildhall or St. James's Church in Piccadilly by noticing their misery.

One of the results of the war and the bombing was the restrictive effect it had had on travel, so that citizens of one London borough had little knowledge of what had happened in another just across the river or the park. When they were forced to make a crosstown journey, they were often surprised and shocked. "I knew *we'd* had a rotten time," they would say to a friend in another borough, "but I didn't know it had happened to you too!"

A Queer Life

That spring one voluntary worker drove through the City to the docks and found it difficult to put the cumulative shocks into words:

The further we penetrated into the City, down Mark Lane and past Crutched Friars, the more appalled we were by the perfectly tremendous extent, and degree, too, of the damage. Fire has razed this part of London. For every building that would have been wrecked by high explosive bombs there were twenty completely gutted, and there were acres of entire streets all done for together—barricaded and cut off from the outside world in their charred and smouldering death.

He drove on to the docks, where it was a relief to be among ships and cranes and sea gulls on a sunny morning, with the sun coming through the mist over London Bridge. But more shocking sights greeted him there as well:

Whole rows of three and four warehouses or factories along the waterfront all burnt out, or wrecked and silhouetted in a jagged, gaping unevenness against the milky sky. And of course the worst places of all were those where the casual eye perceived no damage at all, just emptiness; places where whole groups of huge tall buildings should have stood which had all been burned down to the waterline. There is, of course, nothing emotionally horrifying in the spectacle of ruined and gutted warehouses and wharves, as there is in dwelling houses in a like condition; but this first sight of the destruction among the docks gave me an awful shock, none the less. It really opened my eyes to the immense extent of the material damage that has been done.

Somehow, Londoners seemed to have lost the almost gay defiance with which they had faced the concentrated and brutal bombing of the previous autumn. Although the raids were not so frequent now, the bruises they left on everyone's spirit somehow seemed more profound. "I found myself sinking deeper and deeper into a trough of depression," Rosemary Black wrote toward the end of April, "until at teatime I was positively maudlin. Perhaps fatigue has something to do with it, although I didn't feel tired in the least."

The West End as Evelyn Waugh, Cecil Beaton, Oliver Messel and Noel Coward had known it in the thirties was now no more. That fashionable night club, the Café de Paris, had disappeared in a shower of blood and champagne in March, and in April its sister, the Café Anglais, was bombed into rubble. Quaglino's and the Apéritif had suffered heavily in the bombing of Jermyn Street, along with Dunhill's and Fortnum and Mason's. People looking for entertainment now went early, even to lunchtime concerts at the National Gallery (from which most of the pictures had been evacuated) and the crypt of St. Martin's-in-the-Fields.

Also, the appalling losses and dislocation caused by the bombing contributed heavily numbing misery, especially as the casualty lists grew longer. Almost everyone knew a friend or a relative who had been maimed or killed or made homeless by the raids. That vapid cliché, "It's always the best that goes, too, isn't it," was heard increasingly.

A taxi driver described how the garage where he kept his cab had been heavily bombed. " 'E [meaning Hitler] did my old cab in. But what upset us all was that 'e got the old chap 'oo was our washer. Been our washer there for years. Lovely old feller 'e was, too. Seems queer it 'ad to be someone like that to go."

To the visitor from abroad, the West End of London that spring may have looked like a wasteland of smashed buildings and shabby shops, but to the eye of an East Ender it was a world of gaiety full of tempting things.

In their first outing since Sheila's death in the bombing, George and Ellen Hardiman and their son, John, came up from Aldgate one Sunday in March and went to the Empire Cinema in Leicester Square to see *Gone with the Wind*. The fact that the film dealt with the agonies and separations of war seemed to release pent-up emotions in all of them, and after a while Ellen was sobbing so much that people began turning around and they had to leave.

They wandered around the West End ogling the cans of turtle soup in Jackson's, the fur coats in the shops in Bond Street, the colorful uniforms of foreign soldiers in the streets. They had a tea of boiled beef, carrots and dumplings at Lyons Corner House in Piccadilly and marveled at the plenitude around them.

There were still two worlds in London, Ellen Hardiman decided, and she had no doubt which was the privileged one. The small flat which George had procured for them at the back of the factory in Aldgate was cleaner and airier than the old house in Canning Town, and the little Jewish children with whom John now went to school seemed to be cleaner than the ones in Elm Road; at any rate, he no longer came home with nits in his hair. But all around them were dreary expanses of bomb wreckage and damaged shops that never seemed to have enough food. Ellen stood in line for hours every day to get the skimpy rations to which they were entitled, and there was nothing in the shops to supplement them—and no cafés or restaurants to go to for a meal when your weekly quota was used up. She passed most of her own rations over to George and John, but still they were always hungry, so each morning she would set off on a tour of all the surrounding districts, tramping the streets for hours in the hope of picking up an odd apple, orange or some canned goods. It was bad enough to return exhausted from this endless searching, but even worse to have to face George's heavy sighs and John's reproachful, "But, Mum, I'm hungry!"

Ellen looked in the West End shopwindows and decided that here no one ever went hungry. There was always something to give variety to a meal. They went into Jackson's and bought curry powder, and some canned fruit and fish (pilchards), none of which she had seen since before the war. And in the pub they went to off the Haymarket, the Bosun's Locker, they were actually asked what they wanted to drink instead of getting the refrain they heard at The Dragon in Aldgate: "Only mild-and-bitter today, and the limit's a pint."

As they were riding home in the Tube, John said, "Dad, wouldn't it be wonderful if we lived in the West End?"

George patted his son's shoulder and didn't answer. At Aldgate Station he said good-bye to them and hurried off to his weekly drill with the Home Guard, into whose ranks he had now been compulsorily enrolled.

Ellen and John walked back through the gashed and empty streets. The following day she was being registered for National Service, which meant that she would soon be working in a factory. She had a sad feeling that the family was being split up.

ll through the winter and spring of 1941 Rosemary Black drove a YMCA van through the shattered streets of London delivering tea and pies to the workers on the bomb sites, and her keen eye missed nothing. By this time the capital was full of battalions of middle- and upper-middle-class women rallying to their country's aid. They were driving cars for generals, serving tea to soldiers, manning food carts for the homeless in the Underground, solving problems for the sick and poor and helpless. They were brave and indefatigable, and their hearts were warm, but their outward appearance and manner were formidable, and rarely have angels of mercy come in less attractive guise.

From the beginning Rosemary Black had been told that she must regard herself only as a "temporary" until she had "won her wings, so to speak," and she meekly accepted the conditions, hours and the arduous routine. Her companions frankly daunted her; most of the "full-timers," as she called them, were youngish and conformed to a definite type:

Their class is right up to the county family level. Nearly everyone is tall above the average and remarkably hefty, even definitely large, not necessarily fat but broad and brawny. Perhaps this is something to do with the survival of the fittest. They are all heavily uniformed, of course, they all tend to drive their vans rather too fast and dashingly and make a great business of being clever with short cuts which in my opinion are often more swank than useful. Owing to their seniority and experience and owing to the fact that they all know each other, they're inclined to treat the temporaries with casual scorn and throw their weight about.

The older members of the heavyweight group fall into a sub-group of old trouts who are also heavily uniformed and are distinguished for their bossiness, though this is not, in fact, justified by their efficiency. They are obsessed—can this be something to do with their age?—by the regulations as to the exact amount of sugar and milk to each mug of tea, the exact number of pieces to be got out of a slab of cut cake, and so on, to which no one else pays more than casual attention. I was with one of these horrors on the first day of my trials, and she did nothing but nag me for being over-generous with both milk and sugar . . . [Then come] the betwixt and between group made up of drivers like myself, mostly youngish, who are ineligible for the county family heavyweight elite both on account of their inferior social standing and for their junior position, but who are more or less *debrouillard* in contrast to the dead-beats.

It was the latter type who pushed their way through the rubble to get tea to firemen and rescue squads at the height of the raids, and who were up at dawn to serve the demolition squads. For their bravery and persistence they got an occasional pat on the back from their aristocratic leader, Lady Dash, for whom Rosemary Black had nothing but praise; her fey manner concealed her bravery and a sense of purpose.

One morning at the end of an all-night raid the drivers gathered in their canteen in the Strand for breakfast and were listening to news of the latest British defeats in the Mediterranean when Lady Dash joined them. "Oh dear, oh dear, what is one to do with oneself when the news is always so desperate?" she cried in her booming voice. Then she

MAGNUM PHOTOS—GEORGE RODGER

A rescue squad digs into the wreckage of a house for survivors.

MAGNUM PHOTOS—GEORGE RODGER

In the midst of the Blitz, morale was surprisingly high, and Londoners retained their sense of humor.

December 1940: In a city street a movie truck shows crowds a film about the RAF. Hundreds of bombers and fighter planes were built from the donations raised by such efforts.

GEORGE RODGER—© TIME, INC.

St. Paul's Cathedral and the City in the aftermath of one of the great raids.

The King and Queen
visiting a bombed
neighborhood in the
East End.

KEYSTONE PRESS AGENCY LTD.

Smoldering ruins.

HANS WILD—© TIME, INC.

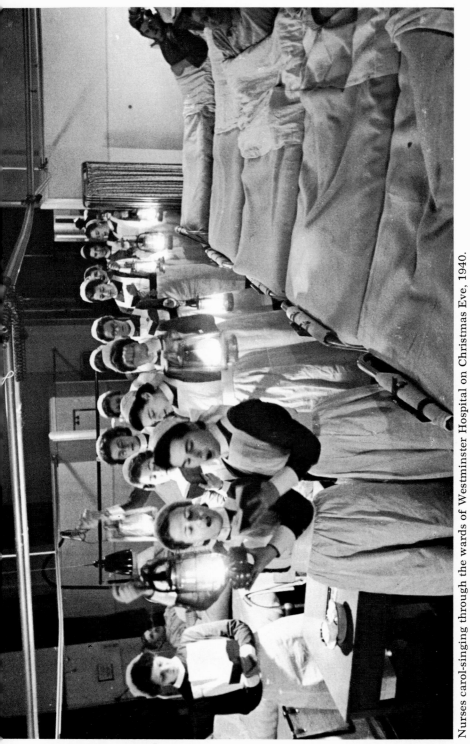

Nurses carol-singing through the wards of Westminster Hospital on Christmas Eve, 1940.

SYNDICATION INTERNATIONAL

ASSOCIATED NEWSPAPERS LTD.

One of the most famous photographs of the war: St. Paul's Cathedral on the night of December 29, 1940.

facing page: May 11, 1941: Churchill and Brendan Bracken in the ruins of the House of Commons.

TOPIX

IMPERIAL WAR MUSEUM

Holborn Circus during a 1941 raid.

looked around at her flock and added, "Though I never have the slightest doubt but that we shall win in the end, so I suppose it is just a waste of time to worry."

Rosemary Black reached out for another piece of toast, and then hesitated. "Should I?" she asked no one in particular. "I've had three already. I'll get as fat as a pig."

"Oh yes, do have it, dear," said Lady Dash. "With things so depressing you must take whatever enjoyment you can. I'm just going out to enjoy myself. Eat too much, sleep too much, drink too much . . ."

As the others laughed, Rosemary Black looked across at the gray-haired old woman. She had been out all night serving tea in the shelters, but not a hair was out of place, not a line on her face revealed the exhaustion and misery she must be feeling.

They all knew the depression and deflation their kind of work could induce, and it wasn't just because of the constant death and destruction. They saw too much hate and intolerance as well. Most of the gangs now cleaning up the bombed buildings were comprised of an odd assortment of refugees, army rejects, ex-prisoners and other types who for one reason or another were not considered suitable for the fighting forces. Lumped together into units called Pioneers, they were given the dirtiest and some of the most dangerous jobs amid the wreckage. With no justification whatsoever, most of the Pioneers were looked down upon by both civilians and military as the lower depths of the war effort. Their uniforms gave them no status with the armed forces and lost them the privileges of civilians. The contempt with which they were regarded was particularly strong toward those Pioneers who were registered conscientious objectors and had volunteered for the work. "How can you bear to serve them?" a soldier's wife shouted at Rosemary Black one day. "If I were in your place, I'd throw the tea in their faces."

In fact, she found that the "conshies" were usually her most amiable and thoughtful customers. At least they never crowded around like some of their craven refugee companions, who seemed to be treated like animals by the British NCOs in charge of them, and in consequence behaved like animals.

One gang had the most frightful bawling British NCO in charge of them, a real last-war sergeant type with a coiffe, a stentorian voice and a real bully mentality. Every minute he was bawling at his men to hurry up. "Hurry up there, don't take all day about it!" he would shout. "Come on, get on with it, can't you, get on with it!" We were nearly demented as well as deaf from this incessant bawling. It made things more difficult for us, for it made the men more pushing and more whining than ever in their desperate haste, while we were nearly frantic at having to serve at such a fevered pace to keep up with this incessant nagging . . . I was reminded of prisons, of snarling bullying warders endlessly nagging at their surly, stupefied convict gangs, driving them almost insane with their perpetual bawling. It was all beastly somehow, the pushing, whining, crouching refugee Pioneers shoving and shuffling like a herd of driven beasts in the pouring, chilly rain and the bawling bully boy metaphorically cracking his whip over them. There was an atmosphere at once of the cattle market and the concentration camp about it . . . His petty bullying seemed more suitable for a Prussian official at Dachau than to the British Army. The whole thing depressed and disheartened us and made the work, hard, anyhow, seem twice as tiring.

By now one of the shortages hardest to bear was sugar, and the ration doled out by the mobile canteens was barely enough to flavor the cups of tea. But Rosemary Black had found a way. Early in May she wrote:

Pouring with rain. We had a pleasant and uneventful day's work serving City fire sites, the General Post Office, demolition workers and Home Guard stations, etc. We were complimented at least half a dozen times on the quality of our tea. One North Country Pioneer said, "It's the best cup of tea I've set eyes on since I left home," and another said, "Why don't you come round here more often, miss? We could do with some more of your tea." I think the provision of saccharine for the tea urns to compensate for the mean sugar allowance is my most successful piece of war work. *What did you do in the Great War, Mummy? Sneaked pills into the tea urns, darling.*

Britain had never forgotten that some of its most distinguished men had gone to prison as conscientious objectors during World War I and that they had been treated with contumely by the public and with cruelty by their guards. It was a measure of the changed attitude that the Rt. Honourable Herbert Morrison, MP, now Home Secretary and Minister of Home Security, was in charge of the department responsible for conscientious objectors; he had once been one himself. No one in the government, and only a small minority of the public, was anxious to persecute conscientious objectors now, and provided they showed willingness to work on bomb sites, in hospitals or on the land, they could be reasonably sure of exemption from military service.

Those who refused to co-operate with the authorities could still be sent to jail, but the state moved reluctantly even toward them and seemed anxious not to make a martyr of any young man just because he was a pacifist.

But James Donald found the dilatoriness of the law in getting around to his case infuriating. He had failed to register for military service with his age group, and the law had not caught up with him until seven months later, when they sent him a registration form and asked for a statement. It had taken them another two months to digest this and summon him to an appeals tribunal in southeast London. Instead of appearing, Donald was determined to force them to take action against him. In March 1941 he had written them:

I have decided not to attend my tribunal on the 31st inst. I am enclosing a letter from my father and a copy of a letter from a friend. These letters will, I am sure, help you in your decision.

I am not convinced that it is any more possible for a tribunal to judge a conscience than it was for Brother Juniper in Thornton Wilder's book *Bridge of San Luis Rey* ["I'll bet they've never heard of this book," he wrote in his diary] to reduce religion to an exact science. To my mind it is as impossible to measure a conscience as it is to calculate a degree of love, hate or faith. Because of this belief I refused last year to register as a C.O. The Ministry of Labour required seven months to "go to it" before they discovered my omission! The Ministry have described me as a Commercial Artist and an Industrial Designer. I am not at present engaged in either of these professions. I am an author. I claim that literature is essential for the culture and diversion of the community and for international goodwill and understanding . . . I have stated on the form [of registration] that I claim unconditional exemption. I will modify this by saying that the only condition I can accept is that I continue my present work. Should the tribunal not grant me either unconditional exemption or exemption under the condition I have named, I should be glad if your clerk would enter my name as one wishing to appeal. Looking forward to hearing of your decision, I remain, etc.

As he left to mail the letter, Donald said to his landlady, "I should like to see the faces of the worthy gentlemen when they read that over!"

"Hm!" said Mrs. R.

"Now we must sit tight and wait. Such a lot of bloody rot—just because a man refuses to fight!"

"Hm," said Mrs. R. again.

"See you in quod [jail]," said her daughter, Vi.

But that had been months earlier, and nothing had happened since.

"Still waiting!" he wrote in his diary in May 1941. "Twelve months have passed—all entangled with red tape!"

When James Donald said good-bye to people and biked away from them these days, he was in the habit of lifting his arm and giving the Nazi salute. They would look startled, but no one commented on it, except once a policeman shouted after him, " 'Ere, you! What d'you think you're doing, riding around one-handed? You watch it. You'll be breaking your neck!"

After he returned to his office in the Auswärtiges Amt in Berlin on May 10, 1941, Joachim von Ribbentrop, Foreign Minister of the Greater German Reich, summoned one of his assistants, Dr. Erich Kordt. He told Kordt that he had just seen the Führer, and ordered him to prepare a briefing for German embassies abroad explaining why it was necessary to turn their "attention to the East."*

Kordt drew in his breath. So Hitler was going through with it! For weeks it had been rumored around the corridors of the Reich Chancellery that the Führer, thwarted in his attempts to crush Britain or invade her was instead looking eastward to the broad, fertile acres of Soviet Russia. What did it matter that he had signed a treaty with Stalin binding the two nations to a pact of friendship and co-operation? For Hitler, this had only been a stratagem to keep Russia from joining the Allies in the war. Now that Europe was conquered and the British were penned up in their island, he could afford to treat the Communists as they deserved.

"So it is on!" said Kordt.

"Yes, Kordt, it is on," repeated Ribbentrop heavily.

The Foreign Minister's yellow face had a gray tinge this morning, and he looked tired and ill. Kordt could guess why. The Russo-German pact had been Ribbentrop's pet project, and he had labored and schemed to bring Hitler and Stalin together in 1939. In addition, he himself had signed the pact in Moscow, and he had persuaded the Führer to strengthen and consolidate the treaty in 1940. It was this pact, which had made her eastern frontiers secure, that allowed Germany to go to

---

* Recounted by Kordt to the author. See also Kordt's *Wahn und Wirklichkeit*.

war in the West. It had enabled the Reich to conquer France and beleaguer the British, and so long as the British were still fighting, Ribbentrop believed that the pact must be observed.

The Foreign Minister hated the British. They had humiliated him when he served as German ambassador at the Court of St. James's, and ever since, he had been possessed of one overweening ambition: to ride beside Adolf Hitler behind a victorious German army along the Mall to Buckingham Palace, where a groveling King and populace would be waiting to greet them. He dreamed of that day, but he also had a nightmare: that in spite of their defeats and the punishment they were taking, the British would survive and somehow strike back. As long as that fear lurked in his mind, he wanted to cling to the insurance of the Russo-German pact, and he had pleaded with the Führer not to drive Russia into Britain's arms.

Now Ribbentrop sighed and straightened his shoulders as he instructed Kordt what to say in order to justify Hitler's decision to turn on Russia. He was to mention provocations, frontier violations, bad faith, the persecution of German minorities in the Ukraine, Bolshevik terrorism, Mongolian bestiality, "that sort of thing." At least this time they wouldn't have to invent it, he added dryly; it was all in the record.*

Kordt asked, "Is this urgent, Herr Minister?"

"Yes, Kordt, it is urgent," Ribbentrop said. "We attack in June. Troop dispositions and the relocation of the Luftwaffe to the East are to begin immediately."

Kordt carefully controlled the feeling of joy flooding through him. He could have asked for no better news. It meant that the pressure was being taken off England, whose defeat he feared much more than Germany's own.† It meant there would be no more bombing of his beloved London.

As if Ribbentrop could read his thoughts, a savage look crossed his face. At least the Führer had granted him one favor, he told Kordt. Before the Luftwaffe was posted to the East, there would be one last bombardment. It would be the heaviest of the war, and the only target the pilots would be given was London, "just London, London, London!"

"When?" asked Kordt.

---

* Based on Kordt's conversations with the author.

† With his brother, Theo, former chargé d'affaires at the German embassy in London, Dr. Erich Kordt was an active member of the conspiracy against Hitler. He escaped the purge by being posted to the Far East in 1944.

"Tonight," said Ribbentrop, and added, "I hope we do not spare a man, woman or child."

This last mass bomber raid on the night of May 10, 1941, consisted of 505 planes of the German air force. They dropped 498 tons of high-explosive and incendiary bombs and land mines. The RAF's night fighters, now equipped with their own radar sets, shot down fourteen enemy bombers for the loss of one of their own. However, 2,200 fires were started, including 9 officially classed as "conflagrations," 20 as major fires, 37 as serious and the rest as medium. At one time seven hundred acres of London were burning, nearly twice the area covered by the Great Fire at the time of Pepys. Westminster Abbey was hit; so were Scotland Yard, St. Paul's Cathedral, the City, East and West Ham and Silvertown. Cannon Street, Paddington, Waterloo, St. Pancras, Euston, Liverpool Street, Blackfriars, and Victoria stations were all out of action; in fact, all main-line railway terminals were, except one. All bridges across the Thames were either cratered or blocked, and the main telephone exchange was destroyed, so that no telephone lines were working.

As to Londoners themselves, 1,436 of them were killed that night —more than died in the San Francisco earthquake of 1906—and 1,800 were seriously injured.

But the raid did more than just cripple the city and kill its people; it all but broke their spirit. When the bombing finally came to an end shortly after dawn on the morning of May 11 and the sirens wailed over a blazing, smoking, crumbling capital, some people in the streets openly wept, not from pain, weariness or fear, but from sheer despair.

Vere Hodgson was one of these. "Just heard the terrible news that Westminster Hall was hit last night, also the Abbey and the Houses of Parliament," she wrote. "They saved the roof to a large extent but some of it is gone. In the Abbey it is the lantern. They thought at first that Big Ben had crashed to the ground. I cannot comment on such disasters. I just feel grievously limp. I feel we must have sinned grievously to have such sacrifices demanded of us . . . There's bound to be further destruction, and there's not much satisfaction to hear of the treasures of our enemies being laid to waste in a similar manner. I don't wish it, but it is grievous not to be able to protect our own. I can see all our ancestors looking down at us reproachfully and saying: 'We gave it to you. You have not guarded it and handed it on as you received it. You have failed in your trust, even those of you who loved it best.' "

But Rosemary Black, who was out in the middle of the raid in her mobile canteen, saw it in a different way: "The shine of headlights on water, gleaming oilskins and tin hats, a contrast of yellow highlights and deep shadows, and the grimy, haggard faces emerging out of the blackness at the counter. The apricot-glowing beauty of light from a fire in Fetter Lane from which streams of sparks poured up into the peacock blueness of the evening. Evil pink and blue flickering tongues of flame from the hell-fire cellar of burning coke in the Temple. The shifting yet solid mass of humanity filling Fleet Street from side to side as a river in full flow fills its banks. Yet the really vivid impression of the night left on my mind after a lapse of some hours was the startlingly casual, unemotional, almost uncaring acceptance which struck me as the general reaction to this terrific smashing . . . a shoulder-shrugging indifference compared with the grief and indignation aroused by last autumn's big blitzes and by the large City fires at the close of the year."

This was partly just case-hardening, she thought. "But also it is said that people who have lost their homes and possessions in the raids seem to experience a curious indifference, almost a feeling of relief and release through fulfilment of their worst fears and worries. I remember Mary [a friend] telling me that after she had been bombed out of her flat with the loss of all her clothes and belongings, she had simply not cared about personal things ever since . . . Then too there is the human inability to take in more than a certain degree of calamity, which is God's merciful tempering of the wind to the shorn lamb."

For the next few days citizens walked through their capital as if in a daze. Foreign observers noticed that though the weather was fine, a circumstance which can make London in spring the most delightful place in the world, no one seemed to smile; faces looked dead. Larry Rue, an American correspondent, saw two separate "City gents" walking to work one morning in their regulation black coat and striped trousers, bowler hat on head, briefcases under arm—but with stubble on their chins. There had been no raid to keep them up during the night, but suddenly people didn't seem to care.

"I began to really worry for the first time," Rue said, "and to realize to what deep depths of their being the May 10 raid had shocked and shaken the people of London. It was just one raid too much."

All through May this mood persisted. "Oh, what's the use," people everywhere seemed to be saying. If the sergeants in charge had bawled and nagged at their men working on the bomb sites before, they now were screaming at them in frenetic rage, for the heart seemed to have gone out of those doing demolition work. They picked at the scarred buildings like small boys picking at scabs. Most Cockneys sympathized with this apathy. What was the use of trying to clean up when everyone knew that the Jerries would be back again at any moment to wreck the city all over again?

And then, as two weeks, three weeks, a month went by without a serious raid, and night after night passed without even the wail of a siren, the zombie attitude began to change to one of uneasy speculation.

"Something's up," said a fellow Bobby to Police Constable David Meade. They were having a farewell drink in Charley Brown's pub in Limehouse, for the next day Meade was to report to the RAF.* "You're well out of it, lad. Jerry's planning something, and you can bet your life it'll be bloody painful."

By the middle of June the absence of bombing still seemed too good to be true, and though everyone luxuriated in the whole nights that could actually be spent sleeping, few of them yet were going upstairs to bed. Every evening the Underground platforms were still littered with the bodies of thousands of shelterers from the East End.

Then, on June 22, 1941, the German army invaded Russia. The war had gone East and the pressure was off. BLITZ OVER, said a headline in the London *Evening News*. MOSCOW'S TURN NOW. Old women and invalids came out of the tunnels and the Underground for the first time in months and blinked in the unexpected sunshine. The creak of marital beds was almost audible throughout the city—though often they were the wrong husbands and wives who were creaking them. What joy it was to live in London and be safe again!

And then a strange thing happened. It was as if something had gone out of the lives of London's people. Was it possible that by July, citizens were actually beginning to *miss* the bombing—or rather, the camaraderie and excitement it had brought to their existence? Pharmacies all over the capital reported a run on sleeping tablets. "It's so quiet at night now that people get restless," one druggist said. Bus conductors and shopkeepers reported that customers were growing increasingly bad-tempered. An air-raid warden, a hero to his neighbors in April, ruefully reported that one of them called him "a bloody nosey parker" in July.

The government also noticed the change. Now that their lives were no longer in nightly danger, Londoners once more were becoming

---

* He left that month for Canada to train as a pilot, but later returned to fly over Europe as rear gunner in a bomber.

aware of the inconveniences, growing shortages and discomforts of war.

"Now I know the Blitz is over," said Arthur Ketley to his wife. "People are beginning to grumble again."

"What are we going to do about Donald's clothes now we've got rationing?" asked Mrs. Ketley. "He either grows out of them or wears them out in weeks. We'll never manage on the coupons we're entitled to."

"See what I mean?" said Mr. Ketley, winking at Donald.

From Vere Hodgson's diary:

SUNDAY, JUNE 22: There is great news. It seems that Germany has invaded Russia, and now we will see what *they* will do about it. They have not been too nice to us in the past, but now we have to be friends and help one another . . . Tonight I heard Mr. Churchill talking about it on the radio. He says we have now reached the fourth climacteric of the war. The first was a year ago when France fell prostrate under the German hammer and we had to face the storm alone. The second was when the Royal Air Force beat the Hun raiders out of the daylight sky, and thus warded off the Nazi invasion of our island. The third turning point was when the President and Congress of the United States passed the Lease-Lend enactment, devoting nearly 2,000 millions sterling of the wealth of America to help us defend our liberties and their own. The fourth was the entry of Russia into the war. He called Hitler a blood-thirsty guttersnipe and said we should support Russia as much as they wanted us to.

JULY 2: I cannot weep for the Russians as I did for the Greeks because they have had plenty of time to prepare for this fight, and if they are not ready it is nobody's fault but their own. Also they have been so secretive and have only looked after themselves. They have not shown any vision about what might happen to them, and I can watch this duel with a kind of detachment. Though I know that if the Russians are overcome, our day will be on us with a vengeance. But somehow I think that Stalin is more of a match for Hitler than any of us. He looks such an unpleasant kind of individual.

JULY 15: Churchill told us to expect a resumption of the air raids in the autumn but said we would be better prepared, and that the shelters would be heated, etc. I listened with amazement to the indictment of P. G. Wodehouse by Cassandra of the *Daily Mirror* on the wireless tonight. I knew everyone was disgusted with him, especially his fellow writers, but I never expected such an attack would be launched. It seems that the only thing for him to

do is jump from the roof of the Adlon Hotel in Berlin and finish. It's amazing
how our popular idols have failed to stand up to the test—Gracie Fields and
now P. G. Wodehouse.* England is disappointed in them.

JULY 18:   I forgot to mention that I was heavily told off by the Kensington
Salvage Council for throwing away a crust of mouldy bread, and therefore
wasting food. Mrs. Gray, my landlady, has no arrangement for storing old
food for the salvage collectors [for use as pig food, etc.] and the charwoman
put it in the tub, where someone poking around found it. It seems rather
hard that I should be the one singled out, since I have several times nearly
poisoned my friends Barishnikov and Miss Hillyard in using up my stores
of ancient food. I am one of the most economical people, but having been
far from well lately, I was afraid to eat the food . . . But anyway, I hope they
drop on the real offenders.

The mood of Londoners in the second six months of 1941 could be
well summed up by a verse which appeared in *Punch* on September 6.
It was by Virginia Graham and entitled "Switch It Off!"

> Any news on the wireless today?
> Nothing to speak of, Madam.
> Only a few bombs here and there,
> They didn't, of course, say exactly where.
> Oh, we've lost some planes in a raid off Crete
> And ten small ships of the merchant fleet.
> They say there's a billion men in Russia
> Fighting a billion men from Prussia.
> And hundreds are dying like flies in the sand
> In Libya and in the Holy Land.
> Thank you, May, so there isn't much news.
> Nothing to speak of, Madam.

It was as if Londoners were living in a state of suspended animation, remote from the rest of the world. Thousands of them had relatives in the forces in Egypt and the Middle East, or in the convoys sailing the Atlantic, but letters home from husbands, brothers and sons

---

* Miss Hodgson was a victim of wartime propaganda. Wodehouse had been
caught by the Germans in France when that country collapsed and had broadcast
from Berlin merely that he was alive and being well treated. The well-known singer-
comedienne Gracie Fields had gone to America shortly after Italy entered the war.
Her husband was an Italian.

were heavily censored and, in any case, took weeks and sometimes months to reach England.* Rations were shrinking, what clothes were in the shops could now only be bought on coupons (and the quota of those was parsimonious), and all the accepted amenities of a great city in peacetime were beginning to disappear or run down. Worst of all, there was no Blitz to take one's mind off them. So there was grumbling and selfishness.

"What a mess the world is in," wrote Malcolm Morley, an actor, to friends in the United States. "It's no good commenting on affairs. I came to London for the production of *Under One Roof* at the St. Martin's. A bad blitz put an end to the run and the play went on tour. I was with it as manager. We visited places like Cardiff, Hull, Bath, Norwich— interesting but wretchedly uncomfortable under war conditions. However, it was a job, and jobs are scarce. I have tried in vain to get something that might make me feel of small service these days—but have been snubbed everywhere. It is still, as ever, a matter of influence. If you have the right relations, you are allowed to do anything in England. I am now in charge at the Apollo [theatre] in London."

Vere Hodgson, of course, kept cheerful, and saw the bright side of things.

"There are magnificent apples in the shops at ninepence a pound," she wrote in her diary on September 14. "I bought a whole pound and felt like wolfing the lot, but instead Auntie Nell and I made blackberry and apple jam with the sugar I had saved out of my ration. The shops are cheering up a bit. There are tomatoes—not hidden behind the counters or anywhere, but on view. Plums too. Lord Woolton [the Food Minister] says if we are bombed again he will increase our rations to keep us going."

On November 14 it was announced that the aircraft carrier *Ark Royal* had been sunk by a German submarine, but the news aroused hardly any comment—possibly because its destruction had so often been falsely announced over the German radio programs in English during the past year. One M-O correspondent reported it thus in her daily bulletin:

"*Ark Royal* sunk. Lunch with vegetarian friend at La Vega restaurant, Leicester Square, good food, mint tea, etc. This is the first day that all parcels are forbidden, owing to the paper shortage. A good plan now is to take the morning paper with one to wrap items in. I walked down Sloane Street and saw a smartly dressed woman carrying

---

* Though a microfilm letter service was about to begin.

a large zinc bucket, unwrapped. I wonder where she bought the bucket. Had tea in a café in Sloane Street. A very attractive young ATS girl was having tea with an older woman, also in ATS uniform. The girl was telling the thrilling story of how she had just got engaged a few days ago, apparently to a young airman she had only met once before. 'Too attractive, and a marvellous voice, and he farms in Dorset. I always wanted to marry a farmer.' They had been to a party and stayed on 'and you know, until 7:30 in the morning,' and now they were getting married."

As she walked back, she noticed a large notice in Piccadilly Circus saying HITLER WILL GIVE NO WARNING. ALWAYS CARRY YOUR GASMASK. Underneath, someone had scribbled: INVADE GERMANY NOW. TAKE THE RISK.

On November 16, Vere Hodgson voiced one of her few complaints: "We shall soon need suitcases to carry around our ration books. Milk is now the big problem. We are to have two pints a week for each adult."

But apathy and shoulder-shrugging symbolized the prevailing mood. In the last week of November and the first week of December, two by-elections were held (in Hampstead and in Harrow) to replace the MPs who had died. Both were Tory seats, and under the terms of an electoral truce for the duration of the war, none of the other official parties (Labor, Liberal or Communist) put up candidates. But at Harrow a woman (calling herself an independent democrat) and at Hampstead three men (a national independent, an independent democrat and a plain independent) opposed the official candidate. At Harrow the Tory campaigned on the standing of his leader, Winston Churchill, while his female opponent called for 1) the opening of a Second Front Now, 2) the dismissal of the Men of Munich, and 3) a square deal for servicemen and their families. There were 61,846 male and 68,870 female voters on the register, but only 18,000 of them turned out to vote. The Tory candidate won with an 11,000-plus majority. In Hampstead there were 24,548 male and 41,027 female electors on the register, but only 12,000 voted. The independent democrat, who like his female counterpart in Harrow campaigned for a second front, the sacking of the Municheers and a square deal for servicemen and their wives, received only 636 votes. The Tory candidate had nearly a 5,000 majority over his nearest opponent, whose main plank was the fact that he supported Churchill and had been born in Hampstead.

At this moment voters didn't seem to care about anything except the nagging petty difficulties of their own daily wartime lives.

A Queer Life

On November 28, Vere Hodgson wrote: "My first egg for a fort-night turned out to be bad. How annoying. Just as milk rationing came in. It is the one thing we have felt most, other than the shortage of fruit. It rather dishes any attempt at hospitality. Tea scarce, no milk to put into it. The cat is being introduced to a milk-and-water diet. He takes it very hard and looks at us as if we were crazed and feeble-minded. Fish is very difficult to get. Mrs. McKay managed to get me a bit of cod, and I made a kedgeree from a tin of salmon I managed to get on points; it was very good. I need a lot of points to get a tin of salmon and I can't get another for at least a fortnight. Sardines are seven points and baked beans four points."*

And a week later: "Powdered milk has appeared in the shops to-day. I bought nine pennyworth with great avidity. It does not sound very nice but it is a standby in case you have a friend, for you can mix two teaspoons with your tea. They only allow us one tin a month. I shall be glad when the cows are working full time again. I am all in favor of cows, more than I ever was. Pears have been seen in some shops, I hear, but at three shillings each."

And then it happened. Here at last was something that would stir Londoners from their gloomy self-absorption. Pearl Harbor was bombed. When the news came over the radio, people bought each other drinks in pubs, talked to one another in the streets, and gathered in Grosvenor Square to cheer the U.S. flag waving over the embassy. Suddenly there was a feeling of animation in the air, and everyone was smiling. It was not America's discomfiture at which the people were smiling, but because, after so long standing up to the Axis alone, Britain had an ally again.

Vere Hodgson wrote on December 9: "AMERICA IS IN THE WAR!!! And we are at war with Japan. And the whole world is in it. There have been air-raid warnings in San Francisco, and though I do not wish anyone to be bombed, a little wholesome shaking up is good for people who contemplated with equanimity the sufferings of others, just as we did the Czechs, and only woke up when we came within the orbit of the enemy . . . We looked at our map of the Pacific for Hawaii and Pearl Harbor. Poor dear people, in those islands of bliss and sun-

---

* A points system for canned goods had been inaugurated by the Ministry of Food in 1941 to prevent supplies being bought up when they became scarce by those who could afford it. Henceforth it was points rather than money which decided whether one could buy salmon, bully beef, beans or canned fruit.

shine—and fruit drinks. They must have had an unpleasant Sunday afternoon, and I expect now that there will be a slump in jazz all over America. It's amazing how serious even the most frivolous become after an air raid. Will the year approaching now see the end in sight?"

Part Three

A PAIN IN THE HEART

12

A Bleak Year

Charles Snow came back to London from a trip to Dublin,* in neutral Ireland, feeling that the worst moments of the war were about to confront his fellow countrymen. It was February, 1942. The U.S. Pacific Fleet was out of action as a result of the attack on Pearl Harbor, and Singapore had fallen to the Japanese. The Russian government had moved to Kuibyshev in October and its armies were battling desperately to stay the German advance toward Moscow.

It was true that the mass air raids on London were over, and no one could be more relieved than Snow. For a couple of weeks he had been savoring the bliss of peacetime existence: of being able to walk through Dublin's lighted streets instead of stumbling through the London blackout; of eating as much meat and butter and drinking as much whiskey and wine as his stomach could take—which in fact was very little, English rationing having severely shrunk his capacity. It was a

---

* Snow made regular visits to Ireland during the war to recruit scientists for work on military projects in England. "It was one of the oddities of the situation," he recalls. "The southern Irish, whose government was determinedly neutral, took a much more active part on Britain's side than did the Northern Irish, who were in the war with us. We had thousands of southern Irish soldiers fighting for us, of course, but we had scores of scientists too. There were many quite good ones at Trinity College, Dublin, for instance, who were passionately eager to work for us. I was dining in Trinity the night Singapore fell, and there were as many drawn faces that evening among the Irish as there would have been in London."

great joy to know that not even a siren would sound, let alone a bomb drop, during the night.

But in London, people still slept uneasily through the dark hours, as if the rumblings of disaster beyond their shores were nagging at them. There was a general feeling of disquiet and dissatisfaction, Snow found, as time went by; life at home had become drab and restricted, and the gloom and boredom were not helped by a desperate shortage of coal and coke for heating during a wickedly cold winter and spring.

The capital was a city of strange contrasts that spring. Parts of it had now been deserted by their inhabitants, and whole streets of gaping, crumbling houses were left to stray cats, rats and sparrows. Silvertown had been so badly damaged by bombs that all attempts to repair it had been abandoned. The last few stubborn old people had been forcibly relocated, the army moved in with guns and bazookas, and Silvertown had now become a battleground for training troops in street warfare. But even those inner and outer suburbs of the capital which had been less damaged by the Blitz became places of the dead after darkness fell. People retired to their beds early because of the cold and the frequent cuts in electricity and stayed there until morning, when another harassing day would begin. Observers began to report an increasing drop in morale among the middle-aged, for whom the zest seemed to have gone out of life. In contrast, younger people were surging into the West End of London in search of variety in food, drink and amusement which they could no longer get in their own boroughs, and every place of entertainment was full. There was no lack of spice to the fun to be had, for Piccadilly and its surrounding streets had suffered an influx of females in the past few weeks; scores of young girls, escaping compulsory work in factories or conscription into the women's services, had swarmed into the West End in search of male company and the money that went with it.

Most Londoners were only half aware of the change in their city, but it struck newcomers like a pain in the heart. One woman who came to London from Dorset to seek a war job early in 1942 recorded her poignant impressions in a diary:

FEBRUARY 22: Very cold. But many people go out at night and the West End on a Saturday night is packed to overflowing. Hotels, restaurants and amusement parks, pubs, snack bars and the streets around Piccadilly, in spite of icy winds. Queues for cinemas, long queues for cheap dine-and-dance places, etc.

A Bleak Year

FEBRUARY 25: Long queues for tinned fruits, which have just come on the market on points. I got the best, most expensive kinds. News is as abominably bad as ever. Churchill admits big shipping losses. Went home by Tube, Piccadilly to Swiss Cottage. What a lot of drunks! On the whole more women than men, and more servicemen than civilians. Not many people sleeping in the Tubes now.

MARCH 1: Cold weather persists. People seem depressed, bad news, bad weather, the usual outbreak of colds and flu. Notice in the cloakroom of a smart restaurant:

> VISITORS ARE REQUESTED NOT TO TAKE
> SOAP OR TOILET ROLLS AS IN THAT
> CASE WE MAY HAVE TO DISCONTINUE
> SUPPLIES *

Another notice near the stove of an office:

> DON'T STEAL THE MATCHES—
> THEY'RE TOO HARD TO GET

Outbreak of stealing everywhere. The rich steal now and are hard to keep up with. For a long time restaurant owners and shopkeepers associated good clothes with honesty. Now that things rather than money are short, their problems increase, and the ban on wrapping paper of course makes things harder on the shops.

MARCH 7: Snowing. Longest cold spell for centuries. Propaganda from the Government urging women into war jobs is having its effect, and many, especially young ones, are beginning to look harassed and worried if they don't happen to be doing strenuous jobs. What a different London from last year, when people were keyed up by raids and threats, and filled with recklessness, very gay and smart. Now they're bored, very concerned with food and what they can get in the way of food, very many drunk late in the evening, especially young boys and girls in the Services. Civilian women not so smart, a distinct feeling of depression, disillusionment, and above all boredom in the air. Curious how little emotional response there is to our desperate position overseas—the Japanese successes, the Hong Kong atrocities published today, the Indian situation—these things are just mentioned and passed over.

MARCH 21: Shopped for bacon. There were two men at the counter and a queue at one as the other had only just appeared. I asked him for my bacon and he served me. A woman in the queue said didn't I know that this was

---

* Soap rationing had recently been instituted.

the bacon queue. The man tried to soothe her as much as he could. People now have a queue mentality and don't believe anything can be had without queuing for it.

MARCH 25: Had a meal at which we were served chicken (very rare), and fruit (tinned). My companion said: "This would cost hundreds of points." Points are the new measure of wealth, not money.

MARCH 29: Sun out. Bright clothes come out and city no longer looks like a city at war. Bright red fashionable colour for women. *But people rarely smile.* No soap in men's West End rest rooms now. Thousands of young women around West End picking up soldiers.

APRIL 5: Fortnum and Mason's serves tea out of unmatched cups. We ordered tea and the waiter took the order and then said: "And now I'll *try* and find you some cups." Eventually came back with unmatching ones.

APRIL 6: You can't leave anything hanging about. Particularly milk outside the door, or flowers in your window box.

Along Piccadilly the ladies come out about 5:30 and there is a great deal of jockeying for position. Some of them really *are* lovely—real *poules de luxe,* and what strikes one is not only quality but quantity. There's hardly room in Old Burlington Street and Cork Street and Burlington Gardens for everyone to get places. Typical uniform: two-piece costume, black kid gloves and very sheer silk stockings. They must have saved up many pairs before they became unobtainable, or do their sailor friends bring them in from USA?

In March 1942, Mass-Observation asked its reporters to give their opinion of Winston Churchill as a leader. The results were startling; the man who was still regarded throughout the world as the savior of Britain and the undisputed, sacrosanct director of the war effort seemed to have a somewhat tarnished reputation. His ringing exhortations which had rallied the people during the Battle of Britain and the Blitz now sounded hollow in the ears of many of his people. Of 200 replies received (from a cross section of M-O observers) more than 100 were more or less critical of some aspect of Churchill's leadership, and a quarter of the remaining 100 praised with faint damns either his personality or the Tory party.

A forty-year-old married accountant wrote:

I think Winston Churchill is over-rated. Probably he has appealed to the public in England and America by his vigorous oratory, but that, though impressive, is not everything. Certainly he is not the man to build up a lasting peace.

A Bleak Year

A solicitor judged the PM a little less harshly:

My own opinion seems to be shared by most of the middle classes, and it is that Winston Churchill is a capable leader and certainly the best man in the country for the job. Some doubts seem to be felt by the working classes, who seem to feel that they have not got his sympathy and that there is something autocratic in his attitude. Although I think this criticism is to some extent justified, this is less important in wartime than qualities of leadership. As a leader he is outstanding.

But a far more common opinion was that expressed by a Londoner who wrote:

I feel that it is time he went. After all, the only connection in which one thinks of Churchill now is with regard to high strategy, whatever that may be. High strategy stinks to high heaven. If Churchill is responsible he should get out. This view I have confirmed by quite a few people. His speeches are no longer listened to. Cripps' * speeches put me off for ever listening to Churchill's in the future. As for the remark that he is the only possible Prime Minister, I say what about Cripps? Churchill made his largest mistake in becoming chairman of the Conservative Party: he thus identified himself to my mind with everything rotten in the country. His refusal to state war aims shows his fear of the future, and a declaration of war aims is the only thing that will bring the country up to 100% production.

Two other comments are worth quoting. A woman wrote:

I know very little about Churchill, not enough to form an adequate judgment. His speeches do not impress me very much. In his pictures he always gives me the impression that he is enjoying the war and the power it gives him.

And a mechanic in Dalston, East London, stated:

I feel that Winston Churchill, though a fine man, is not doing enough to make people believe in him. His speeches hold promise of action which never comes and people are beginning to notice this. Of people I asked, they said: "Not so good as he was" and "Should be replaced by a younger man" and "I don't know what he's up to."

These cross sections of public opinion were sent to 10 Downing Street, and they cannot have improved Churchill's temper. It was a

---

* Sir Stafford Cripps, a socialist, vegetarian and ascetic. Former British ambassador to Moscow, he was now back in London and a member of the War Cabinet.

period of the war when those who saw him most frequently, even those who were his greatest admirers, felt that he was at his worst: short-sighted, selfish, dictatorial and stubborn. They were also surprised to discover that he who took praise so well reacted so badly to criticism. He had glowed under the plaudits lavished on him for winning the Battle of Britain, but he glowered when his government was condemned for losing the battles of Greece, Libya and Malaya. The *Daily Mirror,* which dared to suggest that the PM's Cabinet was composed of incompetent yes men, and that his admirals and generals were poor specimens of their kind, was immediately threatened with suppression under a war-time regulation for publishing, "with reckless indifference to the na-tional interest and to the prejudicial effect on the war effort . . . scur-rilous misrepresentations, distorted and exaggerated statements and irresponsible generalizations."

Yet in the corridors of power in Whitehall it was generally ac-cepted that the *Daily Mirror's* criticism was mild compared with what was really going on. The newspaper had blamed only the government for the disasters and setbacks of the past few months, but the habitués of Whitehall and Westminster were much more specific. It was Church-ill himself who was to blame, they felt. It was on his personal decision that British troops had been pulled out of the Western Desert in Egypt to fight in Greece, with the result that Greece was now lost and Cairo and the Suez Canal threatened. It was Churchill who had insisted on dispatching to the Far East, against the strong advice of his best ad-miral, the two great battleships, *Prince of Wales* and *Repulse,* though, of course, it was not his fault that they sailed out of Singapore without the necessary air cover to protect them. Japanese bombers had promptly sent them to the bottom.* It was Churchill who allowed the British navy to be directed through the great crises of 1939–42 by a First Sea Lord who was obviously unfit, was known to his colleagues as "poor old Pound," and went to sleep during vital conferences. In the Lobbies of Parliament and at the Admiralty it was whispered that Admiral Sir Dudley Pound stayed in his job only because he never argued with Churchill and consented to the Prime Minister's habit of exaggerating the number of German U-boats sunk in the Atlantic.†

---

* Ironically enough, the man who so strongly opposed Churchill on this issue commanded the squadron when it was attacked. He was Admiral Tom Phillips, and he went down with his ships.

† Admiral Sir Dudley Pound retired on the grounds of ill health in 1943 and died in October of that year from a brain tumor.

A Bleak Year

No one who watched Churchill stamping through the corridors of the House of Commons, cigar clamped in his mouth, face red and scowling, cutting a swath through the Members like a clipper in full sail, could help but admire his tremendous energy and dogged spirit. But there were many in 1942 who believed that he was relying too much on his own energy and not enough on that of his collaborators in managing the destinies of the nation, and that by waging a one-man war, he was in danger of losing it for Britain.

It is an indication of the PM's fall from grace in the eyes of his fellow Tories that at about this time Chips Channon referred to him in his diary as "His Obese Highness." He also touched on the topic that had become an open item of gossip in the House of Commons and in Whitehall: Churchill's increasing reliance on the advice of his chief scientific adviser, the ruthless and arrogant Professor Lindemann, now ennobled under the title of Lord Cherwell, but because of his German antecedents known to most MPs as "Baron Berlin."* By this time Lindemann's influence on the Prime Minister was so strong and so effective that even a particularly obtuse Tory MP, Sir Waldron Smithers, made a slighting reference to it during Question Time in the House. Later he was in the smoking room of the House when Churchill strode in pugnaciously. "Suddenly," wrote Channon, "the Prime Minister saw Smithers and rose, and bellowing at him like an infuriated bull, roared: 'Why in Hell did you ask that question? Don't you know that he (Lord Cherwell) is one of my oldest and greatest friends?' "

Indeed he was. And for Britain, a dangerous one.

Professor Lindemann was firmly convinced that there was only one way to win the war: to bomb the German people out of house and home and kill so many of them that the survivors would beg for mercy. Because he had spent his formative years in Germany, he believed he knew the Teutonic character through and through. Lindemann was convinced that it was the crack in civilian morale which had brought about the defeat of the German army in World War I, and it would be the ordinary Germans' suffering behind the lines, rather than the German soldiers' defeat on the battlefield, which would lose them World War II.

The early part of 1942 was the moment in the war when the Allies had to decide what strategy to follow in the West which would best help

---

* He was born in Sidmouth, Devon, of a German-Alsatian father and American mother, but went to school in Germany.

the embattled Russian troops to survive and eventually annihilate Germany's ground forces. Much would depend on what Winston Churchill was thinking, for once he was persuaded of a policy, he could quickly bulldoze his Cabinet and his General Staff into agreeing with it. Their recommendation would then be conveyed to President Roosevelt, and he would pass it on to the U.S. Chiefs of Staff as the combined wisdom of the war-experienced British. Thus, half the battle of getting Churchill's ideas accepted by the American military would already have been won.

But what *were* Churchill's ideas in the spring of 1942?

Charles Snow remembers that in every West End club and at every policy meeting he attended in those days the argument was always the same: should there be a second front now against Germany—that is, a landing by the Allies in France—or should a policy of saturation bombing be adopted?

The proponents of an immediate second front were vociferous, and they did not consist only of Communists jumping on the war wagon now that Russia was involved. The British public had fallen in love with the Russian army—not unnaturally, perhaps, since it had the only troops fighting the Germans and actually holding their own. At least, that is how it read in the newspapers.* Ivan Maisky, the Russian ambassador, was cheered and besieged for his autograph wherever he went. Public meetings, though often sponsored by Communist-front organizations, drew tens of thousands of nonpolitical Britons who raised their hands and cheered their heads off when the speakers on the platforms demanded a second front in the West to take the pressure off "our gallant Red comrades."

The public's enthusiasm for immediate aid to Russia had support in high places as well. After a triumphant career as the man who kept the RAF supplied with fighter planes during the Battle of Britain, the energetic and irrepressible Lord Beaverbrook had gone to Russia to talk to Stalin and had returned a fervent admirer of the Russian troops and a convinced advocate of a landing in France. He urged this tactic on his friend Churchill. But the PM was already lending his ear to Lindemann.

"Beaverbrook's advocacy of a second front wasn't as wishy-washy as some of the wild Reds and pro-Reds running around London at the

---

* Of course the Eighth Army was fighting the Afrika Korps in Egypt, but there was no optimism anywhere about the outcome of that struggle.

264

time," Snow says. "He had talked it out with experts. His idea was that all other campaigns except the single-purpose one of invading France and hitting the Germans there should be abandoned. Out with the sideshows like Africa and the Balkans. But of course what he was advocating was a complete change of policy. Instead of building bombers we would have had to change to building landing craft. The big bomber was already taking up a great deal of our industrial resources and those of the United States, but at that time the change might have been made—and certainly there were plenty of people in America who were all for it. General George Marshall, for instance. His sense of strategy was ultimately better than Churchill's and far ahead of General Brooke's [Chief of the Imperial General Staff], whose judgment, particularly about Russia, was abysmal (he repeatedly underestimated them). Beaverbrook found a ready market for his advocacy of a second front in the United States; they wanted to go in quickly too. Unfortunately, they were out-argued by Churchill."*

As usual, the Prime Minister was convinced that his friend Lindemann was right, and that bombing was the way to win the war. Always conscious of the disastrous slaughter at Gallipoli in World War I, a disaster for which he had been blamed, to Churchill a second front meant the expenditure not only of vast numbers of landing craft but of vast numbers of troops as well, and this he was not prepared to contemplate at this point.

On March 30, 1942, Lindemann produced a report for the Cabinet advocating heavy, continuous bombing as the cardinal measure of military policy for 1942–43. Of it Charles Snow wrote: "It described in quantitative terms the effect on Germany of a British bombing offensive in the next eighteen months (approximately March 1942–September 1943). The paper laid down a strategic policy. The bombing must be directed essentially against German working-class houses. Middle-class houses have too much space around them and so are bound to waste bombs; factories and 'military objectives' had long since been forgotten, except in official bulletins, since they were much too difficult to find and hit. The paper claimed that—given a total concentration of effort on the production and use of bombing aircraft—it would

---

* In a note to the author, Lord Snow writes: "It is important to stress that, with the best will in the world, and granted that production had been shifted from bombers to tank landing craft, there could not have been an invasion until the summer of 1943. This might have shortened the war by nine months to a year."

be possible, in all the larger towns of Germany (that is, those with more than 50,000 inhabitants), to destroy 50 percent of all houses."*

On most occasions when Lindemann presented such a paper to the Cabinet members, it was seen and read by them only. There were no scientists in the group capable of arguing effectively against the points he raised. So, like Churchill, everyone accepted his suggestions as gospel.

However, this time there was a slip-up, and instead of being confined to Cabinet eyes only, the paper somehow was put on another list and was seen by some top scientists. These included Sir Henry Tizard, Lindemann's rival, and a number of Tizard's supporters, among them Professors P. M. S. Blackett and J. D. Bernal, both of them experts on air and naval warfare. (Snow was told about it by them.) It is typical of the times in which they were living that none of them voiced their objection to Lindemann's paper because it advocated genocide. ("What will people of the future think of us?" Snow wrote later. "Will they say, as Roger Williams said of some of the Massachusetts Indians, that we were wolves with the minds of men? Will they think that we resigned our humanity? They will have the right."†) They (the opponents of the plan) did not even put forward the argument that the German Blitz of London had already proved the ineffectiveness of strategic bombing. Morale had never been higher than during those nights when the death-dealing rain came tumbling down, and had sunk to a low ebb now that the bombers no longer came over.

"It was not Lindemann's ruthlessness that worried us most," says Snow; "it was his calculations."

Sir Henry Tizard concentrated his keen mind on Lindemann's paper and quickly proceeded to demolish it. He came to the conclusion —and established it with facts and figures beyond doubt—that Lindemann's estimate of the numbers of houses the RAF's night bombing could destroy was five times too high. Meantime, Professor Blackett was also studying the paper, and he too produced a devastating rebuttal—the difference being that Blackett demonstrated that Lindemann's estimate of destruction was *six* times too high.

The combined reports of these two eminent men dropped on Whitehall like a land mine. Air Marshal Sir Charles Portal, Chief of the Air Staff, read them through and protested that if what these two said was true, the bombing offensive wouldn't be worthwhile.

---

* *Science and Government.*
† *Ibid.*

A Bleak Year

The problem was that if strategic bombing wasn't worthwhile, what were they going to do with all those bombers now rolling off assembly lines?*

"We would have had to find a different strategy, both for production and for the use of elite troops," said Snow. And this would play into the hands of those who advocated an immediate second front.

Charles Snow has been moving in the corridors of power since he was a young man, and of the impact of Tizard's report on Whitehall, Lindemann and Churchill, he says, "I do not think that in secret politics I have ever seen a minority view so unpopular. Bombing had become a matter of faith. I sometimes used to wonder whether my administrative colleagues [he was sitting on several important military-scientific planning committees at the time], who were clever and detached and normally the least likely group of men to be swept away by any faith, would have acquiesced in this one, as on the whole they did, if they'd had even an elementary knowledge of statistics."†

Probably it would have made no difference. Lindemann had Churchill's ear, and he was saying what the PM and his air advisers wanted to hear: that the cheap way to win the war was by bombing German cities into rubble and decimating the civilian population.

Lindemann did not forgive Tizard's latest—and, as it turned out, last—attempt to demonstrate the arrogant stupidity of his ideas, and he made it clear to all the service ministries that there was no room for the two of them in the war effort. Inevitably, this meant that Tizard must go, for Lindemann was to Churchill what Sir Horace Wilson had once been to Neville Chamberlain, except that he was even more ruthless.

"The minority view was not only defeated, but squashed," Snow wrote. "The atmosphere was more hysterical than is usual in English official life; it had the faint but just perceptible smell of a witch hunt."‡

To Churchill, Tizard's opposition to bombing made him a defeatist; he never even bothered to read the scientist's reasoned arguments against it. Since Tizard could have no further say in the direction of

---

* "Use them to bomb U-boats and motor torpedo boats and help to keep British supply lines open at sea," suggested Tizard.

† In a note to the author, Lord Snow says: "You should make it clear that my comments were written some years after the events, though I should not wish to alter any of them. They are a reflexion of what was thought at the time."

‡ *Ibid.*

the war effort, even his closest friends advised him to retire from the scene, and he went off to academic life in Oxford.

"It was not easy," wrote Snow, "for a man as tough and brave as men are made, and a good deal prouder than most of us, to be called a defeatist. It was even less easy to be shut out of scientific deliberations, or to be invited to them on condition that he did not volunteer an opinion. It is astonishing in retrospect that he should have been offered such humiliation. I do not think there has been a comparable example in England this century."*

The humiliation was Tizard's but the loss was the Allies'.

"If he had been granted a fair share of the scientific direction between 1940 and 1943, the war might have ended a bit earlier and with less cost," says Snow.

During every night from then on (and every day as well, in the near future, once the U.S. Army Air Force had arrived), bomber fleets roared across England to smash working class neighborhoods in the Reich.

"Raze people's houses! How's that for a statement of postwar aims?" said Tizard bitterly. He had described Lindemann's estimate of the strategic-bombing program's results as five times too high; Blackett had thought it six. The *U.S. Strategic Bombing Survey*, conducted after the war, discovered that the forecasts had only been one-tenth as effective as Lindemann had predicted.

Yet all those experts weren't needed to prove the ineffectuality of strategic bombing. Any Londoner walking among his ruins could have told the Government that it didn't work.

The agitation for a second front continued, and all over London and the rest of Britain slogans were chalked on the walls. But there would be no "SECOND FRONT NOW" in 1942 or 1943.† Meanwhile the Allies were

---

* *Ibid.*

† In April, General Marshall and the President's adviser, Harry Hopkins, came to London to urge on Churchill a small-scale, predominantly British landing in France in 1942 (Operation SLEDGEHAMMER) and a full-scale Anglo-American invasion in 1943. They expected bitter opposition. Marshall remembered Lindemann's remark to him about Churchill's feelings on such matters as large-scale landings: "It's no use. You are arguing against the casualties on the Somme" (*The Prof*, by Roy Harrod). Therefore they were surprised when the British agreed to the American proposals. But their intention of carrying them out was another matter.

boosting the program for building bombers and sending them out every night to Hamburg and Cologne. "It is a sickening business," Vere Hodgson wrote. "But I am glad the Germans know what devil they have let loose upon the world."

By the beginning of 1942, two hundred and fifty burned pilots and aircrew had passed through the Queen Victoria Hospital in East Grinstead, and most of them had come under the care of Archibald McIndoe. Many of them were still there. Sometimes it seemed as if some of them would never be anywhere else, for there was so much new skin to be grown and then attached to their fried and frizzled bodies.

There was no doubt which patient McIndoe found most fascinating: Richard Hillary,* a Battle of Britain pilot who had been shot down over the Thames on the same day as Geoffrey Page. He too had been flying without gloves and goggles and had been scorched about the hands and face. "[Hillary] is obsessed with death and keeps asking me when it's coming to a patient," McIndoe wrote in his minute book. "I tell him I know but they don't. This doesn't seem to comfort him. He is a strange bloke. The boys in the ward don't like him. He has a sharp tongue and an intellectual approach which gets them on the raw. He mixed them up so much recently that they bombarded him with their precious egg ration."*

The only one who seemed to understand Hillary and feel any friendship for him was Flying Officer Geoffrey Page, perhaps because they both cherished a passionate determination to fly again.

McIndoe had warmed to Page, and treated him almost like a son. "The bloody fool wants to fly again," he noted. "He'll never be able to do it, of course. But fancy thinking of it, after all he's been through!"

The surgeon did not reckon with the young man's strength of purpose. 1941 had been what Page subsequently called "The Year of the Wounded Dog." Time and again he had been wheeled into the operating theater to have skin sewn on to his hands and face, half a square inch at a time. His right hand had been the most difficult, and still was. He had acquired a small rubber ball, and he squeezed it for hour after hour until he was wet with sweat and the pain was exquisite. Also, he had persuaded one of the laboratory assistants in the dental unit to make him four metal splints. By this time most of the nurses—the hospital now had some of the prettiest ones in Britain—adored him,

---

* The McIndoe Papers.

for he had a charm all his own. Each night he persuaded one of them to strap the metal splints to his fingers, and when the bandages were reset he would ask the girl to strap them a little tighter. Inexorably, he was forcing his fingers to straighten. The day when he was able to tie his own shoelaces was an occasion for celebration, because it brought an airplane cockpit just that much nearer.

It was in April 1942 that Page confided to Richard Hillary his determination to fly again.

"So am I," said Hillary, "but no more of this day-fighter nonsense. Night fighters are the answer for us. If you get into a dogfight by day, your hands mightn't be able to cope with the speed of the situation, whereas by night you creep up behind your target, take your time and shoot the bastard down."

Page didn't agree; he considered night fighters too heavy to be handled by men with semicrippled hands.* But Hillary would not be convinced, so they decided to tell McIndoe of their ambitions and get his opinion.

The surgeon shattered them with one sentence. "You haven't a hope in hell of getting back into flying," he said.

Page said, "I don't see why the medical board should turn me down. I feel fit, and I'm certain my hands can cope with a plane."

McIndoe replied coldly, "Not only do I not approve of it; the Air Force simply won't let it happen. How can you expect them to let injured persons like yourselves back into a squadron? It might have a bad effect on the other pilots."

"What about old Tin Legs?" protested Page.†

"Not the same thing," said McIndoe. "I'm sorry, it's a cruel thing to say, but I'm pretty certain that's the way the Central Medical Establishment would look at it. And without their okay, you can't fly."

The two young men slunk away to drown their sorrows. But later, when Page told McIndoe's chief medical assistant, Jill Mullins, about the disastrous interview, "She looked at me with those large, sympathetic eyes, and told me that McIndoe felt that Hillary and I had done our fair share and that now the fighting should be done by someone else. His opposition was just an excuse to hide his feelings."

---

* The Beaufighter, used at night, was not as light and agile as other fighter planes, but it had another advantage: it was able to accommodate the heavy radar equipment which enabled the pilots to "see" the enemy in the dark.

† A reference to the legless flier, Douglas Bader, who had been one of the most successful Battle of Britain pilots.

Page rushed to Hillary with this news. "We agreed on our course of action. Although we differed in viewpoint between the merits of day and night fighters, we were of one accord that McIndoe should be badgered until he gave his support to our ambitions."

It took them several weeks of nagging, but McIndoe finally threw up his hands in disgust. "If you're determined to kill yourselves, go ahead. Only don't blame me," and he sat down to write out their medical certificates.

Three weeks later, with notes in their pockets to an old medical friend of McIndoe's, Air Commodore Stanford Cade, the two young men set off for the dingy London hospital where the medical boards were held. Page was called in first. They leafed through his medical history, tested his blood pressure, urine, ears, eyes, and then made him hop around blindfolded on one leg. When it was over, the verdict was announced: he could elect to be invalided out or classified for limited duties in the United Kingdom only.

It was a blow to all his hopes, and Page refused to accept it. "What I'm after, sir," he said, "is a flying category." He saw Dr. Cade frowning. "I managed to do some flying recently with a friend in one of the squadrons."

He was lying, and the doctor knew it. He leaned forward and said, "Grip my hands."

It was the moment of truth, and Page realized it. He grasped the doctor's hands. "Every ounce of physical and nervous energy," he recalls, "I concentrated into my two maimed hands, and I gripped and gripped and gripped. The months of hard work with the rubber ball had not been wasted, and I saw Cade's eyebrows shoot up in surprise."

The air commodore said, "More strength in those than I imagined, Page." He took up his pen. "I'm passing you fit for nonoperational single-engined aircraft"—he paused and grinned at Geoffrey's disappointed face—"and then if you cope all right, we'll give you an operational capacity."

When Hillary came out of the room an hour later, Page, who had been waiting for him, said joyfully, "I'm back, I'm back—they're letting me fly again."

"Congratulations," Hillary replied. "Let's hope they don't kill you off too soon." He was bitter. One of his replaced eyelids was still troubling him and he had not exercised his clawlike hands as Page had, so the doctor had failed him. "They're going to make me an office boy," he said viciously.

* * *

Donald Ketley was bored. "Nothing ever happens," he complained to his mother one day at the beginning of summer vacation. "Has the war stopped, Mum?"

He knew it hadn't, of course. Otherwise there wouldn't be sweet rationing, which had just started, so that he had to take his ration book every time he bought a bar of chocolate or a bag of liquorice all-sorts. But now that they no longer were bombed every night and he and his pals no longer went out hunting for German parachutists, the excitement seemed to have gone out of everything. You couldn't even have fun at school any more. (They were back in the old school, now patched up.) There wasn't enough paper to make darts, pencils were so scarce that they were taken away and locked up after lessons, and often the teacher ran out of chalk. The only highlight of the academic year had been the discovery of a boy with scabies and a girl with nits in her hair.* As a result, they'd all had their hair cropped, and Donald had a fine time pretending to be a German general called Von Votzisname until it grew back.

What he couldn't understand was why his parents still insisted on sleeping in a shelter every night, when it was obvious that the Jerries had given up bombing, and that it was our turn now. They now had what was called a Morrison shelter—named for the Home Secretary— a channel steel framework about seven feet long, two and a half feet high and five feet wide, with an armor-plate top and steel mesh all around the sides. His father had installed it in the living room, and each night they all crawled into it. It was like sleeping in a cage, and Donald loathed it, especially when it wasn't necessary. But when he asked why he couldn't sleep in bed, his mother would only say, "You never know. You can't trust those Nazis."

Lying in the cage, Donald could hear RAF planes roaring overhead on their way to Germany. It gave him a delicious feeling of security and pleasure, but he was not sure that his parents felt the same way.

"It makes me feel sick in my stomach," he heard his mother say one night. "All those bombs falling on people."

"You can't say they haven't asked for it," replied his father. There was a pause and Donald heard him sigh. "All the same, I don't like it," he said at last.

---

* One of the by-products of the Blitz and the evacuation of the East End slums was the spread of these infestations among British schoolchildren.

A Bleak Year

Sometimes Donald would hear his parents talking quietly about the war and how it was affecting them and their neighbors. The daughter of one of these, a dressmaker and designer, had been called up to work in a munitions factory, and hated every moment of it. "What can you expect?" said Mrs. Ketley. "At least what she was doing before was creative. Now all she does all day long is turn out thousands of little brass stampings. It's soul destroying. She doesn't even know what they're for, and no one tells her. No wonder she's bored."

Mr. Ketley said, "She should have done what Millie down the road did." He lowered his voice to a whisper. "Got herself in the pudding club. That's what they're all doing now if they don't want to be called up—register and then go out with their young man and get pregnant."

"Or something worse," said Mrs. Ketley. "It's dreadful the amount of VD going around. I hear it's driving the army doctors frantic. It's terrible, all this immorality."

"What can you expect when there's a war on?" said Mr. Ketley. "All the politicians can talk about is the brave new world we're going to have when it's all over. Of course they're bluffing. They don't want it now any more than they did before the war. They're just talking to keep us all quiet."

Now it was Mrs. Ketley's turn to sigh. "What *am* I going to give you to eat tomorrow?" she said.

That was the trouble, Donald noticed. Most women looked worried these days, he found, and it was always about the same things: food and clothes. "The war must have been particularly hard on women in London," he recalls. "The combined strain of never knowing whether my father was going to come home and the great strain of getting food certainly showed in my mother. She would be gone for hours searching around for some fruit or tidbit to add spice to the monotony, and time and again I remember her apologizing that this was all she had been able to find, feeling guilty for something completely beyond her control. I think food was more difficult to come by in London than in the rest of the country. There was one period when the only thing we seemed to be able to get was sprats, a minute fish about half the size of a sardine. When the U.S. started to send us dried eggs, milk and Spam, it was an unbelievable luxury."

It was a gray period in Donald's life, and for everyone else too; people went about their daily business as best they could because there was nothing else to do. Nor did life seem to get any better as the weeks went by; people remained just as miserable.

One night in June, Mr. Ketley came home and said, "Now it looks as if we're going to lose Egypt too. Tobruk's gone."

"Oh dear," said Mrs. Ketley. "We don't seem to be having much luck this year, do we?" Then she brightened. "Never mind. We've got a treat for supper. Mr. Roberts let me have three oranges that were going bad, and I've managed to save more than half of them. We're having orange-and-apple salad!"

"But I ate the apples, Mum," said Donald.

"Not the cores, you didn't," she said, laughing.

The news that Tobruk, the British bastion in the Western Desert, had been taken by Rommel's troops hit Britain hard. With people's spirits at such a low ebb, it could not have come at a worse time. In London, reactions ranged from sorrow to indignance.

"I and some of my colleagues think that the loss of Tobruk is in some ways a greater disaster than Singapore," wrote one schoolteacher. "We were given to understand that all was well in Libya and we could meet the enemy on equal terms. Tobruk represents the cumulative effect of Norway, Dunkirk, Greece, Crete, Malaya, Singapore, Burma and Cyrenaica, and the general despondency shows itself in the feeling that Egypt will go the way of all the rest—a danger not lessened by the Government's categorical statement that 'there is no danger of losing Egypt or Suez.' "

Vere Hodgson, who had always been one of Winston Churchill's most fervent supporters, was downcast when she heard that he was in the United States for a conference with President Roosevelt and could not defend himself against his attackers in Parliament and the press. "It really is humiliating," she wrote of the news, "and so discouraging to the Russians, who are still holding out at Sevastopol* . . . Mr. Attlee [the deputy Prime Minister] read a statement in the House today from General Auchinleck [commander in chief of Britain's forces in the Middle East] which seemed to consist almost entirely of the word *unfortunately. Unfortunately* the enemy did not seem to understand what was expected of him and failed to fall in with our plans. As Miss Moyes says, it makes you see red, pink and heliotrope. I squirm beneath the bedclothes and grind my teeth with rage. If we can't do better than this, we don't deserve to keep the Empire."

---

* Naval base in the Crimea which was under siege for 250 days; it fell on July 2, 1942.

A Bleak Year

It was June, but the good weather which suddenly bathed London could not alleviate the general gloom. Rosemary Black's mental condition was not helped by a sudden attack of rheumatism which apparently had been brought on by poor diet and bad teeth. As luck would have it, her two children were home from school and in quarantine as a result of an outbreak of measles. She crawled out of bed each day in considerable pain and groaned at the noise of children at play below:

Poor brats, I've simply loathed their noise and chatter and the endless little activities, unnoticed ordinarily, that their presence involves, and I've been avoiding their company like the plague, poor darlings.

At first the news of Rommel's offensive in the desert did not interest or affect her much.

The war seems to be going badly for us now in the Middle East. Odd, as according to all the reports we had been starting the season so well out there and had air superiority. My dentist said that the very fact of holding Rommel up all this time was success for us, but everyone else seems very depressed. I can't care much; I happen not to know anyone in Libya at the moment, so it all seems remote.

She went on to complain that the price of peas had gone up to two shillings and ninepence a pound, that melons were on sale at two pounds ten shillings each, peaches at eight shillings and sixpence, and that strawberries, normally plentiful at this time of the year, had disappeared from the shops.

I hope to heaven the milk shortage won't get too acute again. As for the fish, which always seems to be more or less decayed these days by the time it reaches the shops, I am completely sickened by the everlasting stink of it. I'm sure I shall never again want to touch it myself, nor can I conceive how anybody who has handled and smelt the flabby muck can ever go on cooking and eating it. The other day R. came back from shopping in high feather because she had got half a dozen herrings, but as soon as they'd been in the warmth of the kitchen for fifteen minutes or so they began to smell so appalling that I couldn't face keeping them about even for the cats, and shoved them in the boiler at once, holding my nose. It seems terrible that men should risk their lives in order that disgusting muck like this should be on sale.

But by June 16 her mind was back on what was happening in North Africa, and now her tone reflected the anxiety she heard all around her:

The position in Libya suddenly seems rather bad. Mrs. C. said she thought it a great pity we couldn't hire Rommel for six weeks or so just to get our side going, as otherwise we didn't seem able to do any good. Well, anyhow I suppose (General Neil) Ritchie (commander of the Eighth Army in Libya) and Auchinleck will shortly be kicked out in disgrace in succession to (General Sir Alan) Cunningham. Where will we go for honey then? Who will fall heir to the short period of publicity? Who'd be a general in the British Army?"

A week later, like most of her fellow citizens, she was in full cry against a bungling government and incompetent generals:

JUNE 23: Front page news space halved between lamentations over Tobruk and chit-chat about Churchill, who, it is announced, is at present in the U.S. conferring with Roosevelt all over again.* It really does seem a remarkable coincidence that he should again manage to be out of the country, doing himself well too, no doubt, just at the moment when things take a peculiarly nasty turn. I expect he'll manage yet again to shuffle out of the "explanation" which is already being demanded . . .

A few days later:

The news of Churchill's being in USA seems to have given rise to a fine crop of rumours. B. said one of her "dailies" told her that "everyone was saying he was selling England to America." Several of the trades people supposed that, in this case as before, he'd seen disaster coming and got out in time, hoping to avoid the worst anger of the people. One particularly wild tale I heard via Ruth alleged him to be a 5th columnist, though if he were it's still not clear why he should have gone to Roosevelt. One thing, I think he'll have a big reckoning to face on his return, and that this time he'll really have to face it. The whole tone of articles, letters and editorials is infinitely more determined and demanding than before, and much harder set against Churchill as Minister of Defence and Secret Session King. I should think his stock can never have sunk so low before. I must say I myself felt pretty disgusted with him when I saw a photograph of him enjoying himself at the White House again. If only he'd keep those great gross cigars out of his face once in a while, I'd feel better about him—though he's still far from being the man to talk about tightening one's belt.

*   *   *

---

* They had met at the beginning of the year and taken some vital steps—to form a Combined Chiefs of Staff committee, for one—but like most members of the British public, Mrs. Black either did not know or appreciate the meeting's importance.

A Bleak Year

Rosemary Black was right: a reckoning was facing the Prime Minister on his return. On June 24 a Tory member of the House, Sir John Wardlaw-Milne, offered a motion of censure against the government over its conduct of the war, and made it clear that the chief target of his criticism was its leader. The same day Churchill flew back from the United States to face his accusers.

It was a grim moment for Britain, and everywhere in London, people sensed the rising tension. In the Western Desert the Eighth Army was in full flight before the tanks and armored cars of Rommel's Afrika Korps. In Cairo the generals at Middle East Headquarters were burning their secret papers. Alexandria, Cairo and the Suez Canal were threatened, and not since the Battle of Britain had the Empire been in greater peril.

Wardlaw-Milne met Churchill in the Lobby of the House shortly after his return and offered to withdraw his motion in view of the gravity of the situation.

"Refused!" Churchill barked.

He was determined to fight back against his critics, but he was aware that it would be a brutal battle. Nor would it be a victory for him if he merely won a majority of votes after the debate. The party Whips could always round up enough Members to give him that. Chamberlain had been given a majority of 81 during the crucial debate in 1940, but it had not saved him, and it would not save Churchill now. He needed not only the votes of the House but its hearty support as well. For this he would need every drop of eloquence and persuasiveness he could muster, and he would need friends on both sides of the House to back him up. Could he, for instance, count on Emanuel Shinwell to rally Labour members to his side? Shinwell, an eloquent Scottish Jew, was a warm friend but a poisonous enemy; he had a tongue like a cobra.

Churchill's parliamentary private secretary, Brigadier George Harvie-Watt, went scurrying to see Shinwell, and handled the interview badly. His chief had a lot of worry, he pointed out, and he didn't deserve to be annoyed by attacks in the House. Besides, the Prime Minister had great military gifts; his ancestor had been the Duke of Marlborough.

"If military genius can be handed down like that," Shinwell replied sourly, "then I should be a good critic. My ancestor was Moses."* But he made it clear he would be on Churchill's side, with reservations.

---

* G. M. Thomson, *Vote of Censure.*

Where would the Prime Minister find a powerful and convincing voice on the other side of the House, among the Tories? Who would speak up for him and sound not like an obedient party hack but a resonant and convincing supporter?

The great debate that would settle Winston Churchill's fate was set for July 1. For twenty-four hours prior to it, men and women from all over London took time off from their jobs, or got leave from their Home Guard duties to listen to it. A huge crowd queued up for seats in Westminster Hall, where the House now assembled, and those who could not get in milled around in the streets outside. It was as if all London were listening.

Twenty members from the two main parties in the House had put their names down to speak in the debate. Churchill went over the list on the night of June 30, trying to pick out friend from foe, the dullard from the dangerous. His thick finger stopped when it came to the name: Boothby, Robert. Boothby had once been his private secretary and his friend. But they had parted in anger and had not spoken since 1940, when Boothby had banished himself from the House and joined the RAF. He was a talented speaker whose delivery had force, strength and conviction. How would he speak tomorrow in the debate that could seal Churchill's fate: as the friend he had once been, or as the enemy he may have become?

Flight Lieutenant Robert Boothby, PM, came up to London on the morning of July 1 from his bomber station in Suffolk, as he usually did for important debates.* He had been working since before dawn checking in the exhausted crews of the bomber wings which had been over Germany the previous night, and he still retained a picture of those strained young faces and bloodshot eyes. To walk into the dining room of the House of Commons at lunchtime and see once again the smooth, complacent faces of his fellow MPs was a contrast that filled him with revulsion. Not for the first time Boothby looked around him and thought what a shoddy lot most of these men were who supposedly represented their people in the nation's tribunal. Thanks to an electoral truce for the duration of the war, they were safe. There would be no general election until Germany was defeated, and until then they would remain members of the most exclusive club in the world, with all the perquisites and privileges of such membership.

---

* MPs in the services came to the House when they could. Those within reach would always be granted leave to go to Westminster if they so requested.

A Bleak Year

Yet they were the same bunch of toadies who, with a few notable exceptions, had applauded Neville Chamberlain for appeasing Hitler, who had hissed Churchill for advocating a policy of standing up to Germany, who had only accepted him as their leader during the debacle in France because invasion threatened, because they were afraid, and because he seemed to be the only man capable of rallying the people behind him. The old supporters of Chamberlain hated him because they knew he despised them, and they would not hesitate to kick him the moment they thought he was down. Now their moment seemed to have come. Disasters were piling up and the populace of the country were no longer hailing Winston as their savior. The man who had led them through the Battle of Britain was now the man who was losing the battle for Egypt and the war at sea. What better opportunity could there be to humiliate this arrogant man?

Boothby sipped his drink and considered his own feelings about Churchill. Winston had hurt him badly, and he still felt the pain of the rejection of 1940. The PM could have saved Boothby's parliamentary career by interceding to point out how unjust and trivial the charges against him were. But he had not spoken; worse, he had refused Boothby the personal interview that their friendship deserved, and had sent him no word of sympathy during the years of political exile.

There was no doubt that he had behaved churlishly, and it was hard to forgive him. There was also no doubt that war had turned Churchill into an irascible dictator who was trying to do too much, that he interfered with his generals and admirals, bullied his Cabinet and ruthlessly rode down his ministers. He could be a stubborn and sometimes even a stupid old man, and he had made some glaring errors in directing the war.

But compared with the pygmies by whom Churchill was surrounded, he was a giant. If he went, who could take his place? For Boothby had no illusions about what would happen if the coming debate went badly for the government. The men who had offered the censure motion maintained that all they wished to do was curtail their leader's powers and save him from himself by preventing him from doing too much. They merely wished, they said, to make him give up the post of Minister of Defence and confine himself to the premiership. But that was nonsense. If such a vote succeeded, it would emasculate Churchill, and he was no man to accept the post of political eunuch. If his policy was not supported heartily, he would resign, and Boothby knew what that could mean. The heart would go out of the nation, and Britain might lose the war. So what choice was there but to rally round the old man, damn and blast his stubborn old guts?

Staring across the crowded dining room as he was ruminating in this fashion, Boothby suddenly saw Churchill beckoning to him from a discreet corner table. As he made his way over to the PM, it did not fail to cross his mind that this would be the first occasion that the old man had deigned to talk to him for two years. And only now, he thought, because he's in trouble . . .

Churchill seemed quite unaware that there was any coldness between the two of them. Looking straight into Boothby's eyes, he asked bluntly, "Are you in favor of the government?"

"Of course. There is no alternative."

"Are you in favor of me?"

"Yes," answered Boothby, "although you have done me great harm."

The old man ignored this. Instead, he said, "Will you speak for us this afternoon?"

"Yes."

Churchill nodded, rose to his feet, and together they walked to the Speaker of the House of Commons, Captain Fitzroy, to whom the PM indicated that Boothby would be speaking for the government. Afterward they went into the smoking room, where large brandies were brought to the table. Churchill raised his glass and so did his companions. "To the Pegasus wings of Bob's oratory," he growled.

An extract from Chips Channon's diary of July 1, 1942:

John Wardlaw-Milne moved his much-publicised Vote of Censure in strong and convincing language today, and I watched the front bench squirm with annoyance. Winston looked harassed and everyone was emotional and uneasy. I thought it all rather horrible. Wardlaw-Milne held the House well, he was fair, calm and dignified, and he was listened to with respect.

He was, that is, until he made a ludicrous mistake. Wardlaw-Milne was a man of imposing appearance and impressive voice, but everyone except his best friends considered him something of a pompous ass, and there was some surprise that he had marshaled his attack against Churchill's Administration so ably. Suddenly, however, having roundly condemned the Prime Minister for choosing such inept military commanders, he made the mistake of telling the House who Churchill should have chosen to lead Britain's troops into battle. In ringing tones he proposed the Duke of Gloucester.

A Bleak Year

This is no place to go into the qualifications of King George's younger brother, except to mention that he had never heard a shot fired in anger. The idea that he should be made commander in chief of the British army made the House first catch its breath in embarrassment and then burst into laughter.

"For a full minute the buzz goes round, 'but the man must be an ass,'" Harold Nicolson recorded. "Milne pulls himself together and recaptures the attention of the House, but his idiotic suggestion has shaken the validity of his position and his influence is shattered."

Chips Channon saw "Winston's face light up, as if a lamp had been lit within him, and he smiled genially."

It was not all over as simply as that. There were other more able and wounding attacks to come, but when Boothby rose to speak, Wardlaw-Milne had given him the opportunity he had been waiting for. His great Scots voice poured scorn on the puny critics who dared imply that the government was incompetent in its strategy and choice of military leaders, when all they could suggest as an alternative were impossible goals and incompetent men. It was a speech exactly fitting the mood of the House; it had just the right leavening of criticism of his own (why were so many young British lives being wasted bombing Germany, when they should be pounding the enemy's ports in the Mediterranean?) to make it clear that he was not absolving Churchill of all blame, but was also larded with savagely funny thrusts at the lumbering bulls who were daring to challenge their leader. The old man sat there, glowering at first, then smiling and even laughing out loud at the sallies.

When Boothby sat down, a new opponent rose to the attack, but Churchill did not even stay to listen. He knew that the originator of the censure motion had been destroyed, and he could handle the rest himself.

Which he did the next day, in a jut-jawed speech which angrily brushed aside all criticism and boldly—and unfairly—dared the House to dismiss him. By now he knew that his enemies would no longer have the courage even to challenge his powers. The rebellion was crushed and the dissidents were in full retreat.

When the vote came, it was 476 to 25 in the government's favor, and the announcement of the figures was greeted with an ovation. It was all over; never again would there be such a concerted and potentially dangerous movement to get rid of Churchill until after the war.

Three days later Churchill flew to Egypt, where he sacked all his desert generals and appointed Generals Sir Harold Alexander and

Bernard Montgomery to take their place. The last act of the dismissed commander in chief, General Sir Claude Auchinleck, was to stop Rommel and the Afrika Korps at a desert ridge called El Alamein.

Churchill was well aware of the part Robert Boothby had played in his victory in the House of Commons, and just before departing for North Africa he sent him a telegram of thanks. But that was all. As far as the Prime Minister was concerned, Boothby had simply done his job, and now he could now go back to the political wilderness from which he had temporarily emerged. Winston Churchill did not speak to Boothby again until two years later, and then it was in a fit of blazing anger.

An extract from the diary of Vere Hodgson:

JULY 4, 1942:   Went to an exhibition of physical jerks [exercises] last night at the Health Clinic in Holland Park. A Russian athlete takes them [directs the exercises]. The Russian did not turn up for half an hour. One young man who was waiting proceeded to talk in a loud voice to a lady next to him. He appeared to be an American and his remarks were anything but complimentary to this unfortunate nation. It was not until later that I discovered his name was O'Brien, and then all was perfectly clear to me. It was a breed I had heard about but never met., I sat perfectly still while the young man finished off the British Empire, which was down and out already because we had sold our souls to the Jews. He seemed to hate the Jews as much as Hitler, and said he did not blame Hitler at all. In 1918 when the Allies were marching on Berlin, houses were going for a few cents and the Jews bought up the lot. Apparently, according to this young man, Australia, Canada and New Zealand were already economically and militarily under American protection. India was going fast and soon there would be nothing left but these islands.

All the British women were rotten because the Government had made slaves of us, etc. The American did not like us, never had. At first I thought I should burst through my skin, but I decided with a resigned mind that probably the British Empire would survive this young man. Then the Russian came in and I much enjoyed the display.

From the diary of L. N. Adamson, a factory manager:

SEPTEMBER 2, 1942:   I saw this morning the American troops parade through the City of London. They made a fine show, and the most noticeable thing about this parade was the silence of their marching, due to the rubber-heeled shoes. The American Marines certainly looked all very much like the type they have been made out to be, thanks to the pictures. But I must say that the physical standard was not at all good, at least not as I expected. For height they are not a patch on the Australians or New Zealanders.

From the diary of Rosemary Black:

OCTOBER 9, 1942: John, by no means pro-American in the ordinary way, is the only person I've come across yet with anything but curses for the Americans over here. It is really extraordinary what a passion of dislike everyone seems to feel for them. I suppose their pay, so enormously higher than that of our own fighting men, is at the bottom of it: that and the amount of time off they get and their double rations-plus, and in general the vast superiority of their clothing and feeding allowances and their accommodation. Then stories like B's of the local billeting officer who went from house to house on the very first day of the fuel target scheme* enquiring whether each had central heating, as, of course, Americans could only be billeted in centrally heated houses! Things like K's boy friend saying he by God hated England, he was so goddamned bored in the damn place, he just wished the blitzes would start over again as it would be *some* excitement. Even with John it's not a matter of any liking, but merely the conscientious refusal to give way to dislike because he feels that to do so is playing Hitler's game. As it is, of course—but how can one help resenting the full-fed, candy-pampered, gum-chewing swagger of our invaders?

---

* A government rationing project to cut down the consumption of coal and coke in homes.

13

The Invaders

Scientists and Lend-Lease officials from America had been in England for some time, but it was not until the summer of 1942 that ordinary Londoners became aware of their presence. In August a friend of Vere Hodgson's named Mrs. Turner with whom she had been strolling in Hyde Park, suddenly said "But it's Sunday afternoon! Let's go and see the Americans—this is the day they always play baseball."

Sure enough, three teams of tall young men were going through the ritual of their national game. Miss Hodgson was curious and amused. "We took two chairs and sat down to watch them," she wrote. "It is a sort of glorified rounders, though I expect they would not want us to call it that. Many of the players wear strong rubber gloves. The ball, which though made of rubber seems to be very heavy, gives quite a wonk when it hits the gloves. They were splendid at catching but the bat is the very funniest thing. It is long and round and it seems very difficult to hit anything with it. Only occasionally did they hit the ball. The players kept shouting to each other terms of encouragement in what seemed to be a foreign language. I don't think we play cricket in such a noisy way."

"The Yanks" were still sufficiently a novelty to attract a crowd of curious Londoners, but soon no one would be able to miss them. Already they were established in discreet offices all over the West End of London; and late at night in the smoking room of 10 Downing Street, or down below in the Hole in the Wall, or in a small house merely marked with the name TUBE ALLOYS in Old Queen Street, the resonant sound of transatlantic accents could be heard. The Americans were conferring with the British to concert their war efforts, and there were plans afoot. Unfortunately, the two countries were not by any means agreed on these plans.

"People like General George Marshall came to London at about this time," says Charles Snow, "and made a tremendous impression on most of us. He thought like Beaverbrook and all the others who believed in a second front in northwest Europe. He and his delegation had come over from America eager to wipe out the humiliation of Pearl Harbor and the setbacks in the Pacific. He wanted to do something positive, and do it soon, in northwest Europe that would materially help the Russians fighting in the East. Almost immediately he ran up against, as Beaverbrook had run up against, people like General Sir Alan Brooke, who were anti-Russian to the point of being ridiculous. Brooke was always wondering when the Russians were going to collapse, especially in 1942, and saw no reason for linking Allied operations with what was happening in Russia."

Every kind of pressure was put upon the Americans to curb their impatience and military ambitions, and to dampen their enthusiasm for the Russian army's achievements.

"Many seemed to imagine that Russia had only come into the war for our benefit," Brooke wrote.* And of General Marshall, whom he thought "a very dangerous man while being a very charming one," he expressed the view that he was urging a second front in France only because he wished to keep his troops out of the hands of his two most ambitious rivals in the Pacific, Admiral Ernest J. King and General Douglas MacArthur. "To counter these moves," he wrote, "Marshall has started the European offensive plan and is going one hundred percent all out on it. It is a clever move which fits in with present political opinion and the desire to help Russia. It is popular with all military men who are fretting for an offensive policy. But, and this is a very large 'but,' his plan does not go beyond landing on the far coast [of France]. Whether we are to play baccarat or chemin de fer at Le Touquet is not stipulated."

But when Marshall flew home to the United States with the President's personal representative, Harry Hopkins, after ten days of conferences with Brooke, Lindemann and Churchill, they brought back an agreement that planning should start at once for a "build-up of American

* Sir Arthur Bryant, *Turn of the Tide.*

military and air forces in Britain for a major cross-Channel offensive in 1943 and for a possible emergency landing in 1942." *

The British had no intention of sending their troops into France so soon, however. Sir Arthur Bryant, biographer and confidante of General Sir Alan Brooke, summed up these London conversations in 1942 as follows:

"Nor had [Brooke] and his colleagues committed themselves to a cross-Channel operation in 1942 or even in 1943 but merely to the desirability of launching one if, and only if, conditions at the time made its success seem probable. What, in effect, the British Chiefs of Staff had agreed to do was to start preparing plans, in conjunction with the U.S., for an invasion of Europe whenever it became a practical operation, and to welcome in the meantime the maximum concentration of American military and air strength in England—the place where it would be most valuable, whether Russia held out and made an invasion of the Continent possible or whether she collapsed and left Hitler once more free to attempt an invasion of England."†

So the convoys, bearing troops, ground crews, tanks and planes, had been making their way across the Atlantic ever since. To begin with, their staging post was Northern Ireland, but soon barracks and encampments and airfields all over Britain were flying the Stars and Stripes, and every tot in the vicinity was chewing gum or munching Hershey bars. Before long the first discreet GIs on leave, with strict instructions to "play it quietly," were filtering into London, silk stockings in their pockets, cigarette cartons under their arms. The American invasion of Britain had begun, and the United Kingdom would never be quite the same again. Nor would several hundred thousand GIs.

Perhaps the first to feel the peculiar impact of British life was a certain U.S. general who had flown in during the spring of 1942 on a reconnaissance trip from Washington. He spent the week deep in conferences with the American ambassador, John G. Winant, the American naval representative, Admiral Harold Stark, and his British opposite numbers. But on Sunday there came a break in work, and when the general was asked what he would like to do, he said he had always wanted to have a look at Windsor Castle.

It was arranged that Lord Wigram, the custodian, would show the

---

* *Ibid.*
† *Ibid.*

general and a companion around the royal dwelling. Wigram did not tell the Americans that Sunday was normally the royal family's own day at the castle and that visitors were generally barred. Instead, he asked George VI's permission to make the tour, and the King promised to stay out of the way.

But it was one Sunday in May when the sun was shining and the gardens of the great castle were at their best, and the King and Queen could not resist it. After lunch they came down from their apartments to sit in a favorite corner of the gardens. They were sunning themselves there and reading the Sunday newspapers when they heard the sound of conversation between Lord Wigram and an American voice.

King George looked at Elizabeth, and without words they decided that a meeting might be embarrassing. The general, his companion and their guide came around the corner just in time to see the royal couple, on their hands and knees, scrambling under the hedge.

"Good God," said the general, "who on earth is that?"

"I am afraid I have to confess," replied Lord Wigram, "that those are the rear views of Their Majesties King George the Sixth and Queen Elizabeth of England."

"Well, well," said the general, "if it isn't just like Sundays at home when unexpected visitors turn up."

That night the King said to Wigram, "I'm sorry we were in the garden when you were showing your American around today. We forgot all about it. Didn't want to embarrass them, you know, by being there—but I think we got out just in time."

"You didn't, sir," said Wigram. "The general saw you."

"Did he, now," said the King. "Ah, well, I don't suppose we'll ever have a chance to explain. Who was he?"

"A general from Washington," said Wigram, "named Dwight D. Eisenhower."

One of the first GIs to reach Britain was Robert H. Reynolds, from Maryland. He was one of a group of eleven combat engineers who had been sent to prepare SLEDGEHAMMER, the abortive operation proposed by General Marshall, and they arrived on the Cunard freighter *Empire Johnson* at Liverpool in April 1942. Reynolds couldn't wait to get to London.

"The most important aspect of my being stationed in England was that I was an Anglophile," he writes in a note to the author. "Being born in Annapolis, Maryland, and being interested in Colonial history,

The Invaders

I had a good background. Moreover, Dr. Ford K. Brown, an Oxford scholar and husband of Leslie Ford, the mystery writer, was my Shakespeare prof. His favorite exam was to draw a map of Old London—this I knew by heart. So when I landed the first thing I bragged about to my other ten companions was, 'Get me to the Strand and I'll take you on a walking tour of London.' "

Since they were waiting for Operation SLEDGEHAMMER to begin, the engineers had plenty of time on their hands, and from their headquarters in South Audley Street in Mayfair they started their exploration of the big city. There was still an Elizabethan liveliness and bawdiness about the wartime capital, and it was a period when the Yanks were more than welcome. One night, at the great ballroom which had been opened for servicemen at Covent Garden, one of their group joined the all-girl orchestra and gave a performance of boogie-woogie, then new to Britain. When Reynolds followed with an exhibition of "the Big Apple," they were cheered and found themselves the heroes of the evening.

In those early days there were no special clubs for GIs in Britain, but Reynolds and his friends found themselves welcome guests at the Eagle Club (for Americans serving with the British forces) and the New Zealand Club. People stopped him in the street and invited him to their homes. They were living on British army rations, but they also got a bottle of beer a day and cigarettes.

"We swopped the cigarettes for tinned ham, and crammed our gas-mask cases with beer, ham and biscuits and set off for picnics with WAAFs from Stanmore, who found us more than cute. I couldn't have been happier. I couldn't believe that within six months or so I'd be seeing signs saying DOWN WITH THE YANKS on the walls—although I might have guessed when a girl I was with said: 'I love you as an individual, but soon there'll be so many of you that we'll begin to hate you.' "

At the end of August 1942, Mrs. Jenny Martin appeared before the magistrates at a London police court on a charge of neglecting her three children. After evidence had been given by Jenny's landlady and a representative of the Royal Society for the Prevention of Cruelty to Children, the probation officer was called and asked to give a report.

"I have talked to Jenny at great length," she said, "and I would ask the magistrates to consider very sympathetically all the circum-

stances which have led up to her appearance here today. At the outbreak of war her husband was sent to the Middle East, leaving her
alone to care for three very young children on what, I am sure, the
Bench will agree is the not very generous marriage allowance from
the army. She was evacuated to the Midlands in September, 1939, and
there unfortunately had a liaison with the husband of the woman
upon whom she and her children were billeted. When this was discovered, she was thrown out of the house and returned to London. It was
there that she discovered she was pregnant. Jenny tells me—and I
believe her—that she bitterly regretted having been unfaithful to her
husband, that it was only one isolated lapse when she was feeling
especially lonely, and she was naturally horrified when she discovered
that she was going to have the man's child."

The probation officer paused, and looked up at the two women
and the man on the magistrates' bench. Their faces were stony and
forbidding.

"She did her best to arrange for her unborn child to be adopted,
but it was pointed out to her that even though the child might
not be his, her husband must give his permission. Then (and she
considers this a piece of good fortune) she was involved in the bomb
incident on Marble Arch Station, as a result of which she had a miscarriage. When she recovered, she came back to her children determined not to stray again. Unfortunately, her mother-in-law collected
some of her belongings from the hospital, found the adoption papers
inside and learned what had happened. Very unwisely and perhaps
cruelly, you might think, she informed her son. He has since written
to say that he will have nothing more to do with Jenny and is anxious
for a divorce."

There was another pause. One of the women magistrates said,
"Is there much more of this, Miss Winton?"

"No, your Honors. But Jenny took her husband's rejection very
badly. She was and still is unbalanced from her experiences in the
bombing. She began drinking and frequenting bad company, going to
clubs and mixing with foreign soldiers. She admits she neglected the
children. But she assures me she is eager to turn over a new leaf. If
you will take a lenient view of her lapse, she promises to get a part-
time job and swears that she will not neglect the children again."

She sat down.

"Thank you," said the chairman of the bench. He leaned over and
consulted first with one and then with the other woman magistrate.

The Invaders

Once or twice they looked across at Jenny Martin, a pale, pretty girl in a light summer dress.

Finally the chairman cleared his throat. "This is a very unedifying story," he began, and then proceeded to launch into an attack upon the falling moral standards of the country. Men were dying in foreign lands while their womenfolk at home . . . the West End was becoming a festering sore of immorality . . . too much illegitimacy . . . women betraying their trust . . . it was necessary to think of the welfare of the children first. The upshot was that Mrs. Jenny Martin was put on probation, and ordered to report regularly to the probation officer and the army welfare officer. In the meantime, the children would be sent to a home.

Everybody looked across at Jenny Martin, expecting some sort of an outburst. She said nothing at all, but on her face was a look of utter dejection.

As she came out of court, a young man in a dark blue suit came quickly toward her and took hold of her hand. "Ah, those old bastards!" he said. "What did I tell you?"

He slipped his arm around her waist. "What you need is a drink," he said.

They walked around the corner to where a car was parked and drove away.

In the bar of Le Petit Club Français in the mews behind St. James's Street, the buzz went around that General de Gaulle and Admiral Muselier were feuding again, and that this time it would be a fight to the finish.

When Robert Mengin, who was now writing and broadcasting in French for the BBC, dropped in for an evening drink these days, he noticed that Free French naval and army personnel were once more gathering at opposite ends of the bar, and bosom friends wearing different uniforms were no longer speaking to each other. He knew how they must be feeling. His own wife and brother-in-law were passionate supporters of De Gaulle, and they could not understand Mengin's suspicion of the general's motives and dislike of his methods. It did not make for harmonious family relationships.

Like most Frenchmen in London in 1942, Mengin was well aware that De Gaulle's headquarters at Carlton Gardens was less a center of military operations than a hotbed of intrigue. The acrid smell of suspicion was almost tangible in the nostrils as one walked down its corridors toward the general's offices.

It was the most frustrating period of De Gaulle's London interlude. Nothing was going right for him. Recruitment into the Free French forces had fallen far below expectations—to such an extent that Churchill was said to regret ever having accepted De Gaulle as the incarnation of French resistance.* Too many Frenchmen now suspected that the general was fighting more for personal power than for the liberation of France. For instance, he had told those who had sworn their personal allegiance to him that they would never be asked to fight against their own countrymen; yet so far the only engagements in which the Free French had been involved were against the Vichy French in Dakar and Syria.

Moreover, strange rumors were being whispered among the French in London about the sinister activities of De Gaulle's secret service. Because of Admiral Muselier's arrest, the general had won from the British the right to run his own intelligence organization, his own courts, even his own prisons. They were operated by men whose standards perhaps were not as high as those of Scotland Yard and the Old Bailey. In Duke Street, where one of the more notorious "investigation bureaus" had its headquarters in the heart of Mayfair, brutal beatings were allegedly inflicted on anti-Gaullists, who were then consigned without trial to a camp outside London where conditions were more dire than the worst French prisons.

Mengin was lucky; he had powerful friends and a pro-Gaullist wife. Otherwise, the goons at Carlton Gardens and Duke Street might not have been content just to spit at the mention of his name and call him a *salaud*.

Amid the disappointment and deception felt among the British— and even more among the Americans—over the activities of the Free French, one branch of it continued to be exempt from criticism. De Gaulle knew it, and it did not please him. The Free French navy under Admiral Muselier was at sea and fighting the Germans, pounding the convoy beat across the Atlantic with their British naval comrades, battling U-boats and the Luftwaffe on the Arctic supply routes to Russia, and winning admiration everywhere for their skill, tenacity and bravery.

---

* He was probably strongly influenced in this by Roosevelt's antipathy toward the Free French. Randolph Churchill told the author that his father was surprised to learn how much De Gaulle was disliked in Washington.

The Invaders

General de Gaulle was a great man and he never resented it when he had to listen to praise heaped on one of his subordinates, as it was upon Muselier, but in the tricky times of 1942 he could not be sure that the admiral *was* a subordinate. In fact he needed have had no fear; Muselier, though De Gaulle's superior in rank, had sworn an oath of allegiance and never thought of betraying it. But the intriguers at Carlton Gardens were not convinced; the man was not to be trusted, they whispered. He was too close to the British, and he wanted power for himself.*

Which was one thing De Gaulle was determined he would never cede. If France was to be saved, De Gaulle was the only man capable of achieving it, and he would ruthlessly remove anyone who threatened his position as France's man of destiny. Did Muselier so threaten him? At first he could not be sure, but then . . .

Just before the end of 1941 General de Gaulle, searching for an opportunity to expand the control of Free France, had thought of Saint Pierre and Miquelon. These two tiny islands not far south of Newfoundland had been French for two hundred years, and though their governor was for Vichy, their inhabitants were said to be enthusiastically pro-Free French. Moreover, a radio station on Miquelon regularly broadcast weather reports which might be useful to German U-boats operating against Allied convoys.

General de Gaulle conveyed these facts to Winston Churchill and told him that he proposed to liberate the islands in the name of Free France. Fine, the Prime Minister replied, but first the Canadian and United States governments must be informed and their permission secured, for the islands were in their defensive orbit.

De Gaulle was furious when a terse and negative reply arrived from Washington a few days later. The United States had a tacit agreement with Admiral Georges Robert, who was Vichy's High Commissioner for the Antilles, Guiana and Saint Pierre. Both Robert and his ships still paid allegiance to Vichy, but they had promised the Americans to stay at anchor in Martinique and take no part in the war as long as Robert and Vichy were recognized as the rulers of France's

---

* As De Gaulle reveals in his *Memoirs* (Vol. I, p. 255), his associates appear to have convinced him that Muselier was trying to use his control of the Free French navy to put himself in political charge. It is De Gaulle's word against Muselier's that he did so. Certainly it is completely out of character.

islands in the Western hemisphere. Saint Pierre and Miquelon were part of that pledge, so hands off, ordered the Americans.

Henceforth, versions differ and documentation is missing. Winston Churchill always maintained that, strongly approving of the American embargo as he did, he extracted a promise from De Gaulle that he would immediately cancel the proposed expedition to Saint Pierre and Miquelon. On the other hand, De Gaulle called in Admiral Muselier, who had already been apprised of the operation and had undertaken to lead it, and told him that Winston Churchill had agreed to the liberation of the islands. But, De Gaulle added, because Churchill did not wish the Americans to know that he was ignoring their embargo, the operation must take place in the greatest secrecy and no one must know where Muselier and his ships were going.*

With two Free French corvettes Muselier set sail from Scotland in November 1941, and after a perilous journey reached Newfoundland on December 9. The attack on Pearl Harbor had taken place two days earlier, and America was in the war, and as far as Admiral Muselier was concerned that changed everything. Even General de Gaulle could no longer ignore America's feelings. On December 15, leaving his second-in-command, Captain de Villefosse, at Halifax in charge of the squadron, he went to Ottawa to consult the U.S. representative. On Washington's instructions, Ambassador Jay Pierrepont Moffat told Muselier that it was of vital importance that the Free French should cancel at once any operation against Saint Pierre and Miquelon. There were urgent reasons for this which he said he could not go into. But the U.S. government would be seriously embarrassed by any Free French assault on the islands.†

---

* This is Muselier's version. De Gaulle's version is that Muselier was sailing for Canada anyway and that there was no reason for him not to proceed there. But he was going with two corvettes of 1,000 tons each at the roughest time of the year. One of them, the *Lobelia,* was damaged early and had to put into Oban for repairs. There the Royal Navy warned him of the hazards of a crossing in such small boats and offered the admiral passage in a cruiser, or plane. Muselier refused and the repaired ship joined its sister, the *Renoncule,* and went on with a particularly eventful voyage. The full story of it is told by Louis Héron de Villefosse, Muselier's second-in-command, in his book *Souvenirs d'un marin de la France Libre.*

† The State Department was worrying not only about Admiral Robert and his ships in the Caribbean, but also about the pro-Vichy navy in North Africa. In the event of an Allied landing in French North Africa they did not wish to face a resentful French navy. Appeasing Vichy was very much a part of American policy at this time.

The Invaders

Disappointed, Muselier immediately cabled De Gaulle in London requesting that the operation be postponed pending further negotiations with the Americans. At the same time Anthony Eden, the British Foreign Secretary, called in De Gaulle and after a long conversation apparently believed that he had extracted a definite promise, as Churchill had previously, that the operation would be called off. At least he cabled the Americans that De Gaulle had agreed "that the proposed action should not repeat not now be undertaken."

However, this was not the way General de Gaulle interpreted the conversation. By this time he had heard rumors that the Canadians were about to occupy the two islands, and he was determined to forestall them.* Accordingly, he cabled Muselier:

WE HAVE, AS YOU REQUESTED, CONSULTED THE BRITISH AND AMERICAN GOVERNMENTS. WE ARE INFORMED RELIABLY THAT THE CANADIANS INTEND THEMSELVES TO DESTROY THE WIRELESS STATION OF SAINT PIERRE AND MIQUELON. UNDER THESE CIRCUMSTANCES I COMMAND YOU TO RALLY SAINT PIERRE AND MIQUELON BY YOUR OWN MEANS AND WITHOUT SAYING ANYTHING TO FOREIGNERS. I ASSUME THE ENTIRE RESPONSIBILITY FOR THIS OPERATION, WHICH HAS BECOME INDISPENSABLE IN ORDER FOR FRANCE TO RETAIN HER POSSESSIONS.

This was explicit enough, but it was followed shortly afterward by another cable, this one from Muselier's chief of staff in London, Captain Moullec:

FOREIGN OFFICE INFORMS US THAT THE PRESIDENT OF THE UNITED STATES IS CATEGORICALLY OPPOSED TO THE SCHEDULED OPERATION.

What was the unfortunate admiral to do? If he refused to go through with the operation he would be disobeying his commander in chief, to whom he had sworn allegiance; on the other hand, if he went ahead in secrecy with the liberation, all the confidence and good will he had built up between the Free French navy and the Allies would be shattered.

Muselier tossed and turned like one of his own storm-swept corvettes until he came to the reluctant decision that he could not go back on his word. He would obey the orders of General de Gaulle, but having done so, he would return to London and resign. Admiral Emile-

---

* They did consider the idea, but were dissuaded by the British government from carrying it out.

Henri Muselier was an honorable man, and as it turned out, that was the tragedy.

On Christmas Eve the French force, now accompanied by the Free French submarine *Surcouf,* arrived off Saint Pierre. The first batch of sailors went ashore and met no resistance. The next day a plebiscite was held and Muselier was able to inform De Gaulle that all but 2 percent of the population had rallied to the Free French. De Gaulle cabled back:

PLEASE TELL THE POPULATION OF THE ISLES OF SAINT PIERRE AND MIQUELON, SO DEAR AND SO FAITHFUL TO FRANCE, HOW JOYFUL THE NATION FEELS TO SEE THEM LIBERATED. SAINT PIERRE AND MIQUELON WILL BRAVELY TAKE UP ONCE MORE WITH US AND WITH OUR BRAVE ALLIES THE FIGHT FOR THE LIBERATION OF THE HOMELAND AND THE FREEDOM OF THE WORLD.

TO YOU PERSONALLY I ADDRESS, IN MY NAME AND THAT OF THE NATIONAL COMMITTEE, MY HEARTFELT FELICITATIONS FOR THE WAY IN WHICH YOU HAVE REALIZED THIS WINNING OVER WITH SUCH ORDER AND DIGNITY. VIVE LA FRANCE!

But if De Gaulle was pleased, the British were not. Churchill, who was attending the "Arcadia" conference in Washington at the time, found himself having to apologize personally to Roosevelt, for he had assured FDR that De Gaulle had given him his word that he would not take the islands.

Roosevelt, who had always disliked De Gaulle, only shrugged and pointed out that the deception proved him right. But the State Department was furious. The action of the Free French, it maintained, had upset all its plans for gaining bloodlessly for the Allies the French fleet and French possessions in North Africa.* Cordell Hull, the Secretary of State, was so angry that in a statement condemning the operation, he committed the error of referring to "the so-called Free French," a pejorative description of a brave group of exiles for which even anti-Gaullists found it hard to forgive him.

The scene moves forward to 1942 and back to London. Home again from Washington, Churchill summoned De Gaulle to Downing Street. French Ambassador René Pleven went with the general, and

---

* In fact, it made no difference whatsoever. The Vichy navy under Admiral Darlan made sure that the Allies were going to win before switching to their side.

Eden was also present. Churchill did not tell the general that one melancholy result of the Saint Pierre and Miquelon affair was that President Roosevelt had decided that henceforth the Free French would be told nothing of the Allies' future plans, and that General de Gaulle would no longer be accepted by the U.S. & British governments as the leader of his country until all the French people had indicated their acceptance of him. In this decision Churchill had reluctantly concurred, but he kept it to himself. However, glowering at the tall Frenchman standing so cool and unconcerned before him, the PM proceeded to rebuke him for having gone back on his word, for having upset his own relations with Roosevelt, and for an overall breach of trust.

De Gaulle was unrepentant. He had already cabled his representative in Washington to tell the State Department:

SAINT PIERRE AND MIQUELON HAVE BEEN FRENCH TERRITORIES FOR CENTURIES AND ARE POPULATED EXCLUSIVELY BY FRENCHMEN. TAKING POSSESSION OF THESE ISLANDS IS A MATTER CONCERNING THE FRENCH AND NO ONE ELSE . . .

But as Churchill quickly made clear, the Americans refused to see the matter this way. Only with difficulty had he succeeded in persuading Roosevelt not to send the U.S.S. *Arkansas* and a force of U.S. Marines to throw the Free French off the islands. Instead, he had compromised by agreeing to the stationing of a joint U.S.-Canadian representation on Saint Pierre to direct the island's affairs. At first De Gaulle angrily refused to accept this; then, when told this would be useless, he asked that the arrangement be kept secret. Churchill crisply told him that the United States would not agree to this.

It was an unhappy meeting, and it was an extremely ruffled General de Gaulle who emerged from it. It did not, however, prevent him from cabling to Admiral Muselier a much happier account of the conversation with Churchill than in fact appears to have taken place. At least this seemed to be the case when it was compared with the British version of the conversation. Captain Moullec had good contacts in Whitehall; from one of them he got hold of the British transcript, and he was appalled when he saw how widely it differed from De Gaulle's own. At once he cabled Muselier in a code known only to the two of them:

HAVING HAD OPPORTUNITY TO EXAMINE THE OFFICIAL MINUTES OF THE CHURCHILL–DE GAULLE MEETING ON JANUARY 22 . . . I MUST INFORM YOU THAT THE ATMOSPHERE DURING THE CONVER-

SATIONS WAS HEAVILY CHARGED. IN THIS LIGHT, TELEGRAMS 2821 AND 2849 FROM THE GENERAL REVEAL GRAVE MISREPRESENTA- TIONS ...

Admiral Muselier returned to London on February 28, 1942. He was greeted by General de Gaulle with a warm embrace, and they drove together to the admiral's lodgings at the Hyde Park Hotel. Three days later De Gaulle called a meeting of the Free French National Commit- tee at Carlton Gardens to discuss the Saint Pierre-Miquelon affair.* Since Muselier was a member of the National Committee as well as the leader of the expedition, he had ample reason for being present. No one, least of all De Gaulle, suspected that he had come to the meeting with a hand grenade fizzling in his pocket.

The members of the committee sat around the large table in the Clock Room at Carlton Gardens and listened happily to Muselier's strictly factual account of the landing on the islands, deliberately avoid- ing any reference to the political maneuverings which had preceded and followed it. The general seemed relieved by this, and said, smiling, "This operation was handled perfectly."

But then he made an error. He added, "So you see, messieurs, how right I was in ordering the liberation in spite of the opinion of our Allies."

Admiral Muselier broke in, "I took great pains not to discuss the affair from the point of view of foreign policy," he said. "But since you yourself have raised the subject, I wish to state emphatically that I do not share your opinion."

De Gaulle tried to wave him aside. "Let us talk about that aspect at a later date," he said shortly.

"No, General," said Muselier, "with your permission we will dis- cuss it now. I wish to declare here and now that on two occasions dur- ing the operation Saint Pierre–Miquelon, I was not told the truth. For example, in the matter of the promise made to the Americans that the operation would not take place without their previous agreement, a promise made in your name, General."

De Gaulle made as if to rise to his feet, but the admiral persisted. "On January 22 you had an interview with Churchill and Eden. You did not send me the official minutes of this meeting as prepared by the

---

* In order to manage the ever-expanding Free French activities, De Gaulle had established the committee on September 24, 1941. As head of each department (Justice, War, Air, etc.) he appointed a "national commissioner."

Foreign Office. On the contrary, I received an account over your signature, sir, and it did not agree at all with the Foreign Office version."

Muselier continued for some time after that, in this vein, itemizing the discrepancies in De Gaulle's account. Finally he said, "I no longer find it possible to continue working with this committee. I herewith resign as national commissioner."

By this time General de Gaulle had stubbed out his last cigarette and was regarding the excited and emotional admiral with the cool gaze of a scientist examining a bug. "I ask you to reconsider your decision," he replied at last.

"I refuse to reconsider," replied Muselier.

De Gaulle nodded. "Very well, I ask you to send me your resignation in writing."

"It will be with you this afternoon," said the admiral.*

That afternoon Muselier dispatched a letter to De Gaulle at Carlton Gardens formally resigning from the Free French National Committee. Not only did the general accept it; the next day, March 4, 1942, he also stripped Admiral Muselier of his post as commander in chief of the Free French navy.

"Do you know what's happened?" A. V. Alexander, First Lord of the Admiralty, asked Churchill that night. "De Gaulle has sacked Muselier. He can't do this! Muselier built up the Free French fleet. It wouldn't exist without him, and it won't exist without him. We've got to have him back. De Gaulle must rescind his decision."

Anthony Eden and Alexander were delegated by Churchill to see the general and ask him to retain Muselier as commander in chief of the Free French navy, in view of the fact that he was so highly regarded by his British and American colleagues.

Loftily, De Gaulle refused. The British must not try to tell the French how to handle their internal affairs. They must treat them as allies, with all that meant—equality and independence. He added coldly: if the British did not, then General de Gaulle and his committee "would cease to slave at a task which had become impossible." In other words, he would resign and throw the whole matter before the British public, who he knew regarded him with affection and admiration.

The two Britons departed, swallowing hard. They knew that such a scandal was the last thing Churchill wanted at this moment. Even Muselier wasn't worth it. He must be persuaded to accept his dismissal.

---

* Muselier, *op. cit.*

But there was worse to come.

At six o'clock on March 10, General de Gaulle arrived at Westminster House, the headquarters of the Free French navy in London. He had asked Muselier's friends in the Royal Navy to keep the admiral occupied elsewhere, for he had a delicate task at hand. He proposed to interview every officer of the headquarters staff personally to find out which were dedicated Muselier supporters—and therefore dangerous —and which were prepared to give De Gaulle their personal and unswerving allegiance.

The officers had gathered in the main hall to await the general. Facing them with a grave expression on his face, he said, "Messieurs, I am General de Gaulle. You are officers of the Free French navy. Respect will be paid where it should be paid, and most particularly to Admiral Muselier."*

As he was saying these words there was a commotion at the back of the hall and Admiral Muselier strode forward. "General, you have sent for all the officers of the navy," he said. "I am an officer of the navy, and here I am."

De Gaulle stared at him in silence, then held out his hand. "Welcome," he said. Then, speaking over the admiral's head to the others, he went on, "I wish to see each officer individually, and I will begin with the most junior."

He walked toward one of the offices, but turned in surprise when he discovered that Admiral Muselier was following him. "I wish to see each officer alone," he said coldly.

Muselier answered, "General, in no French military organization is it customary to interrogate officers other than in the presence of their senior officer."

De Gaulle said, "Admiral, you are committing a breach of military discipline."

"No, general," Muselier replied. "But I know that some of my officers are rather excited,† and I would not wish any of them to put themselves in the wrong."

De Gaulle was now frozen and stiff with anger. He kept repeating, "A breach of military discipline," but finally he turned and started for the exit.

"Under the circumstances," he said, "the only thing I can do is

---

* *Ibid.*

† Many of them were threatening to resign.

withdraw. But, messieurs," he went on, addressing the watching offi-cers, "rest assured that what must be done will be done."

Then he was gone.

Anthony Eden was in his office the next morning when his secre-tary entered and laid a note on his desk. "I think you should read this at once," he said.

The Foreign Secretary ran his eyes over the note before him and then read it again, to verify the incredible contents of the message. "Good God," he said. Then, "Get me the Prime Minister at once."

Soon the news was all around Whitehall. "Do you know what De Gaulle has done now?" said the First Lord of the Admiralty to one of his aides. "He's arrested Muselier and sentenced him to thirty days' imprisonment in the Tower of London!"*

Obviously De Gaulle could not be allowed to get away with im-prisoning Admiral Muselier, of that Winston Churchill was determined. De Gaulle was demanding that the British do his dirty work for him in this quarrel. "Insubordination," he had called it in his note to the British government, and had decreed: "A penalty of thirty days' fortress arrest is imposed on Admiral Muselier."

Aside from the fact that this was no way to treat a gallant and dis-tinguished officer, it was out of the question for De Gaulle to de-mand that the British dispatch Muselier to the Tower of London.† The Royal Navy would never forgive the government for taking such action. Muselier was the only admiral in the whole French navy who had vol-unteered to continue fighting after the fall of France, and though senior in rank to the general, had willingly put himself under his command in the interests of French resistance. He had organized the Free French

---

* Actually, in his sentence on Muselier, General de Gaulle had referred to "fortress arrest," but when a distinguished officer is sentenced to a "fortress" in England, he is incarcerated in the Tower of London. The last officer prisoner there was a famous prewar spy named Lieutenant Baille-Stewart, but known to the British public as "the prisoner in the Tower."

† It is interesting to note that in his *Memoirs*, De Gaulle omits mention of "fortress arrest" but instead writes: "I then ordered Admiral Muselier to reside for a month in a place that would keep him away from all contact with the Navy." But the note he sent to the British government bluntly uses the phrase. The reason the British were involved, even though they had already given De Gaulle complete autonomy, was that the action took place on British soil and MPs were asking questions; moreover, De Gaulle had no prison facilities suitable for an admiral.

navy, had served with great bravery at sea, and had already been humiliated once by being hauled off to jail on a false espionage charge. It mustn't be allowed to happen to him again simply because of a shabby family quarrel.

It was pointed out to the Prime Minister, however, that under the terms of the agreement which he had signed with De Gaulle on January 15, 1941, the general had every right to expect the British government to act on his behalf. The agreement had given him full jurisdiction and discretion over the fate of all Free French military personnel, of which Muselier was certainly one. But Winston Churchill decided that agreement or no agreement, he could not stand aloof. When he had given General de Gaulle his powers, it was not for such petty spitefulness as this. He told his liaison officers with the Free French that somehow they must get out of this obligation. He could not save Admiral Muselier from dismissal; that was certain. If he tried, De Gaulle would publicly announce that the British government had broken its pledge, and the public, who were passionate supporters of General de Gaulle, would never stand for that.

Finally, in March, it was arranged that Muselier should retire "on sick leave" to a house in Ealing, a London suburb, and have nothing further to do with the Free French navy.* When De Gaulle protested, he was quietly told that the Prime Minister was adamant, and the general decided not to make a public issue of it.

But it was the beginning of the end of friendly relations between Winston Churchill and Charles de Gaulle. In May, when the British decided to take over the Vichy-controlled island of Madagascar in the Indian Ocean, to prevent its falling into the hands of the Japanese, Churchill did not inform De Gaulle in advance and did not employ Free French troops in the operation. They would only cause unnecessary fratricidal strife if they had to fight the Vichy forces on the island. When the general came back from Syria in September, he had a meeting with Churchill at 10 Downing Street in which their antagonisms came out into the open. According to De Gaulle's *Memoirs,* the meeting went badly:

Mr. Churchill then attacked me in a bitter and highly emotional tone. When I pointed out that the establishment of a British-controlled administration in Madagascar would constitute an interference with the rights of France, he exclaimed furiously: "You claim to be France! You are not France! I do not recognize you as France! . . ."

---

* He remained inactive until the end of the year, when he rejoined the service after the liberation of French North Africa.

The Invaders

De Gaulle interrupted:

"If, in your eyes, I am not the representative of France, why and with what right are you dealing with me concerning her world-wide interests?"

Churchill could only remain furiously silent. It was true; he had recognized De Gaulle and he could not now renege. But in the next few months he tried to, and he was to discover that when it came to political in-fighting, Charles de Gaulle was more than a match for him.

The moment Admiral Muselier vanished into retirement, the purge had begun. All officers in the Free French fleet were summoned for personal interviews with the general, and were reminded of their oath of allegiance to Free France and to General de Gaulle in person. If they wished to go on serving at sea, they had no choice. By the terms of the agreement Churchill had signed, no member of the French armed services could transfer to the forces of any of the Allies, and any officer who refused to accept the new situation faced a court martial. Moreover, De Gaulle made it clear, it was the French who would handle the punishment of recalcitrant officers.

Such threats did not prevent Captain Héron de Villefosse from making his position clear. Muselier's second-in-command on the Saint Pierre–Miquelon operation, he had been left behind there afterward to take command in the islands. When he heard of his chief's humiliation, he sent the following cable from Saint Pierre:

KINDLY TRANSMIT THE FOLLOWING TO ADMIRAL MUSELIER: LEARNING THAT YOU ARE OBLIGED TO TAKE A REST, I WISH TO SEND YOU IN MY NAME PERSONALLY AND IN THAT OF ALL OFFICERS ON SAINT PIERRE OUR MOST AFFECTIONATE GOOD WISHES, IN THE HOPE THAT YOU WILL SOON BE ABLE TO RESUME YOUR POST AT THE HEAD OF THE FREE FRENCH NAVAL FORCES. IN OUR EYES, YOU ARE STILL THE MAN WHO SAVED THE HONOR OF FRANCE IN THE DARKEST PERIOD OF ITS HISTORY. YOUR NAME AND YOUR EXAMPLE ARE INSEPARABLE FROM THE ENSIGN BEARING THE CROSS OF LORRAINE WHICH, BY YOUR ORDERS, WILL CONTINUE TO FLY OVER WARSHIPS OF FREE FRANCE. RESPECTFULLY, VILLEFOSSE.

Muselier never got this message, but Villefosse received a reply:

FOR CAPTAIN DE VILLEFOSSE, TO BE DECODED BY HIM: HAND OVER YOUR COMMAND TO THE NEXT SENIOR OFFICER AND RETURN TO LONDON IMMEDIATELY. INSUBORDINATION. GENERAL DE GAULLE.

The captain returned to London and there refused to renew his pledge of allegiance to De Gaulle. He was neither pressed to do so, nor was he court-martialed. Why is not quite certain. Perhaps his close association with Muselier made the general decide to be cautious. But Villefosse was forced to shed his uniform. He could not go on fighting at sea because the British navy, which would willingly have taken him, could not do so. Instead, he was reduced to doing odd jobs in London as a translator and broadcaster in French for the BBC.

Others were not so lucky. Insubordination was becoming a favorite word in Free French circles.

Pfc. R. H. Reynolds went to the Palladium Theater on the night of July 4 to see a show put on specially for GIs by expatriate Americans in London. The three stars on the bill were Ben Lyon, Bebe Daniels and Vic Oliver.* Just before the intermission, Ben Lyon came to the footlights and announced that a few hours earlier the United States Air Force had made its first bombing raid on Germany, in planes lent to them by the RAF. "It won't be long before we're flying our own," he shouted above the cheers. "Hold on to your tin hat, Adolf!"

By now most of Reynolds' fellow engineers had gone up to Cheltenham to prepare for the beginning of Operation TORCH, the landings in North Africa, but Reynolds had been transferred with his colonel to a supply unit which had its headquarters in Selfridge's store, on Oxford Street.

"When we had arrived in England," he recalls, "the spirits of the natives were good. Things in Africa seemed good, the Blitz was past, and Germany was occupied with Russia. There was a cocky feeling around. But suddenly after the defeat in the Western Desert at Knightsbridge,† spirits sagged. It was very noticeable. With losses at sea as well, the picture was no longer bright, and the people knew it."

Reynolds was having miseries of his own. That summer he was promoted to corporal.

"It was always a battle between us civilian soldiers and the regu-

---

* Vic Oliver, estranged husband of Winston Churchill's daughter, Sarah, was in fact a refugee from Austria with a home in the United States. Ben Lyon and Bebe Daniels were man and wife, and the three of them were stars of a popular BBC radio program.

† Named for one of a series of "defensive boxes," as they were called, set up in Cyrenaica to hinder Rommel's advance into Egypt.

lar army," he says. "You remember that old saying about the three ways
of doing things, the right way, the wrong way and the army way. We
could never see the reason for doing a million silly requirements. With
a military school background, I was often in charge of detachments because so many new non-coms had no basic training. With double-day-
light-saving time, we'd get up for formations in the dark and no one
ever kept any discipline. Half the roll calls were missed and we'd report by shouting down from open windows. We'd have exercises and
drill in Hyde Park, and lots of the boys would drop out of formation and
wait in doorways, smoking, until we returned. It was always cold and
the billets were icy, so most of my group would head for the Mostyn
Club for hot water and warmth."

Then General John C. H. Lee arrived to take over and organize
U.S. Army Services of Supply in London, and Reynolds and his friends
learned about the other side of army life.

"General J. C. H. Lee, otherwise known as Jesus Christ Himself or
Garbage Can Lee, was a tyrant," Reynolds recalls. "We all fought a
personal war against him. Some of his edicts were fantastic. For instance, at the time when Buckingham Palace was announcing that they
were saving water by having only six inches in their baths, Lee was
ordering the washing of every American vehicle entering London. The
crowning indignity was getting us out of bed before reveille, herding
us into the ballroom of our headquarters in overcoats-only, and giving
us 'short-arm' inspection. Those medics had a system. They put us in a
circle with our rear out. We took off one shoe and a doctor walked the
outside of the ring looking at our one foot bent backwards at the knee;
he was looking for athlete's foot. The inside of the circle had two doctors, one going upright looking for chancres in the throat, the other
bending low looking at our genitalia as we opened our coats. Balancing
on one foot, laughing at the remarks of GIs and doctors alike, it was a
scene I'll never forget."

One day Reynolds was walking through Hyde Park with an English girl when they noticed a caterpillar on the ground. They knelt down
to look at it, and did not hear anything until a voice behind them suddenly said, "Soldier, what are you going to do when the Germans come?"

It was General Lee on his daily hunt around the park for GIs im-
properly dressed, failing to salute or otherwise infringing regulations.

"He was soon making some soldiers long for D-Day," says Reynolds.

* * *

For most Londoners the summer and autumn of 1942 was the worst time of the war because it was the dreariest. The heart seemed to have gone out of the great city. There were no victories to cheer people up, and not even bombing to spur them into defiance. No one was starving, but rationing had reduced the national diet to a dull, starchy minimum that sustained life but lowered everyone's spirit and sapped his energy. Most people were pasty-faced and always yawning, increasingly subject to coughs, colds and stomach troubles—and tired, always tired. The buildings looked drab, for they had not been cleaned or painted since before the war, and civilians looked equally shabby, for now everything which had not disappeared completely from the shops was rationed and available only with coupons or points. New clothes, shoes and underwear took too many coupons, and frayed shirts and darned socks were worn until they no longer held together.

The neighborliness born during the Blitz had disappeared, and people seemed to be filled with envy and resentment. In the shops they watched one another to see that no one got a milligram more rationed meat than anyone else, and they bickered in the queues. Civilians envied the military their clothes and food, and grumbled over their apparent idleness. The women's organizations came in for the bitterest criticism, particularly the girls of the Auxiliary Territorial Service. On weekends the West End seemed to be full of girls in this uniform, often the worse for drink, and stories abounded about their filthy language and slipshod habits, about the increasing number of pregnancies among them and the growing amount of venereal disease. People seemed to have forgotten that all through the Blitz it was the ATS which had helped man antiaircraft guns with great bravery; and they ignored the fact that if thousands of girls were now in uniform, it was usually not because of choice. By now Ernest Bevin, Minister of Labour, had made service compulsory for both sexes, and all women were liable either for work in factories or the military. Since the army needed more women than any other service, it inevitably had harvested what the soldiers referred to as "real scrubbers." The other two branches could afford to be more selective, and consequently, the girls of the WAAF (Women's Auxiliary Air Force) and WRENS (Women's Royal Naval Service) were held in higher public esteem.*

---

* Though there were public references to their lack of morals, too. "Up with the lark and to bed with a Wren," was a typical joke.

The Invaders

If civilians resented the army's easy rations, clothes and privileges, the army resented the RAF's easy-going ways, and all of them resented the pay, privileges and sexual success of the increasingly ubiquitous Dominion and U.S. troops.

But it was the civilians who were the worst off in London that autumn of 1942. Going about their jobs in the scarred and grimy city, eying sullenly the uniforms all around them, aware that the capital was now a gay mecca for all troops on leave, they felt like specters at the feast. For most of them there was never a letup and no light ahead; the years of the war stretched into the future, and it seemed that there would never be an end to them.

We enter the fourth year of war today [wrote Vere Hodgson on September 3, 1942]. How well I remember the day when Mr. Hillyard rang up Miss Moyes [her superior at work] three years ago and said that the Germans had invaded Poland and we must get the blackout ready for the night. It does not seem to have gone according to plan except for our rationing, which is exceedingly good. We expected to be bombed and we have been. Today we all bought Union Jacks in the street. At 11 a.m. Miss Moyes assembled us and we listened to the broadcast service from Westminster Abbey.

Then it was back to the daily grind of listening to hard-luck tales from servicemen's wives, helping out the factory girl who had got herself pregnant by the married foreman, shopping not only for herself but for the old and infirm of Holland Park and Notting Hill.

But Vere Hodgson was lucky, and she obviously had a way with people. Rarely did she find the rudeness or trickery in the shops about which so many Londoners were now beginning to complain.

Struggled to get an onion [she wrote that autumn]. I tried the old Pole's shop but he had none so I went across to Mr. Buy Best, where I sometimes shop. The manager had only a few and those were booked. I agreed very humbly that of course other people had a prior claim, as I was not a regular customer. I bought a pound of carrots and wandered around the shop, still thinking of those onions. Then I purchased a stick of celery. I could see an idea was germinating in the man's mind, so I lingered on. Finally I won without saying more. A voice behind me murmured, "If you only want an onion for flavouring, I will let you have one." I poured blessings on his head and walked away. It was a victory indeed.

The next day she added: "Horses are to have ration books. I wonder when they will issue them for cats? They say nothing about donkeys."

A PAIN IN THE HEART

In this same period Rosemary Black indulged herself in an unusual outburst of grumbling about domestic difficulties.

Tea-cloths [for drying dishes] and towels are suddenly put on clothing rations. No extra allowance, needless to say. Hell! I'd just decided last week that I really must get a new stock of tea-cloths—*if only* I'd taken action at once instead of procrastinating in my usual feeble way. I shall simply *have* to get new clothes soon, too, in spite of rationing. The laundry, to which I was reduced to sending them by pressure of work and rheumatism and lack of suitable soap has turned mine into the condition of Doctor Johnson's net.

Present arrangements really are hard on that section of the community whose members happen to be housewives or mothers. Surely there is a good case for giving us some sort of extra coupon allowance? First of all, various household polishes and cleaners are put on "points"—perhaps the muscular effort these goods save is supposed to be equivalent to their value in "points" food! Then a mother will almost inevitably be faced by the inexorable growth of her children into spending most of her own clothes coupons on her family to supplement their own. And now this final blow of the towels and tea-cloths! I had looked forward, now that the brown clothing coupons are valid at last, to getting a few garments, badly needed, for myself: shoes, stockings and winter underwear above all. But now, with L. growing like a beanpole and new tea-cloths an unavoidable necessity, it looks as though I must give up all idea of ever being able to get anything for my own personal use. Luckily I'm one of the few who don't give a damn about clothes, but if I don't crave to be smart I still should like to be warm!

But she continued to feel guilty because she knew she was luckier than most people in wartime London.

I have a chronic feeling of guilt. *Having a hired car* to take the children to school each morning—not having to struggle there with them in crowded Tubes makes the whole difference to my life, and no doubt to the lives of the other two mothers whose children fill up the car, too, but even so I can't help feeling uncomfortably that any arrangement so agreeable must be wickedly wasteful and wrong. *Giving human food to the cat*: though I'm not convinced that any fish sold during the past six months is fit for human consumption, and anyway I'd like to know who doesn't. *The fuel economy*. What with having no living-in maid and making an effort, I've cut the house fuel consumption by over 50%, but still, alas, without approaching the exiguous allowance of my fuel target, which recks nothing of the height and coldness of my rooms, the dampness of the house, or the hopelessly furred-up pipes, to say nothing of my rheumatism!

The Invaders

She really had tried, she told herself, and she would continue to.

But I have a chronically guilty conscience about hot water, on which I admit I find it impossible to cut down. *Spending too much money on my own pleasure.* Of course I'm saving money, by way of the gradual elimination of more and more expenses, wages, clothes, luxury goods of all kinds, but I'm dismally aware none the less that I'm still spending more than I ought—on drinks, expensive fruit etc. when there is any, restaurant meals, books—and nothing at all that I can help on the war effort. *The state of the dustbins.* I simply cannot get K. or Mrs. G. to cooperate in the slightest degree in regard to salvage. Their idea is to stuff anything that will burn into the boiler including perfectly clean paper, rags and all the rest of it . . . I've even gone so far as to stick up a diagram saying which dustbin is for tins, and which for ash or refuse, and where paper and bones are to go, but no good. The same old muddle goes on and makes me feel most ineffective that I can't carry reforms through, and most unpatriotic.

She was very depressed, and she was finding her bad conscience demoralizing.

It makes one feel set apart from the "home front" war effort, and therefore thoroughly browned off by it—and also that I might as well be hung for a sheep as a lamb, so to speak, whenever the choice presents itself. Why not burn a crust or show a light or turn the second bar of the electric stove on, when I'm all wrong on so many counts already?

Compared with the bulk of London's population, Rosemary Black was privileged. She was a good customer at her local stores, always ready to buy the more expensive tid-bits, and therefore was never forgotten when there were a few extra grams of butter or ounces of meat. She knew nothing of having to stand in line, of the rudeness of shopkeepers, or of the self-satisfied way in which some of them "delight in telling you that there will be no more of this or that until after the war," as one office worker put it.

It was the doldrums of the war, a time when people seemed to be at their worst to one another and when there was no excitement to alleviate the misery, boredom, bitchiness, monotony and spite.

"I had terrible trouble this morning," reported a young woman named Gertrude South. "Trust me to get involved in other people's troubles." A scientific worker who had lived through some of the worst moments of the Blitz in the East End, she was now "tensed up and unsettled." For some time a friend of hers had been feuding with the local butcher.

Yesterday it came to a head. For one thing she's never allowed to have any choice—she gets just a dollop of meat handed out to her. If she dares to ask for anything different, this pig of a man snaps at her. For instance, he insisted that she should have pork again this week, making it the third time in succession, whereas he had other meat in the shop, but not for her. Also he never weighs the meat in front of her, just hands her a parcel for which she pays, cap in hand, like a beggar almost. Another thing, unless she tells him in the morning whether she will be calling for the meat on Friday or Saturday he tells her when she calls for it that it is shut away in the refrigerator and he can't let her have it. Yesterday . . . she felt she should collect the meat and part cook it, as she is going out. It would mean carrying the wretched chop around with her until late at night. She took a few minutes off from work yesterday to arrange to go round to the shop at ten past four in the afternoon, and he refused to let her have it as it was in the safe. She was furious as it would mean her not having any meat at all, but he didn't care.

The friend was too fed up to try again and was prepared to sacrifice her ration for the week, but Miss South offered to go in her place.

So I went into the shop this morning and said I had come for Miss M's meat ration. He at once handed me a parcel wrapped up in a newspaper. I said: "What is that?" He said, in a cocky, take-it-or-leave-it sort of voice: "It's pork." I said: "How much per pound is it?" He said: "Two shillings." Then he seemed to hesitate and stutter and then asked why I wanted to know. I said: "Never mind, you'll soon find out." I've long had the suspicion that he has overcharged her but he would probably have got away with it if he had kept a civil tongue in his head. I said: "I thought loin of pork was one and eightpence a pound." He said: "This is a chop. Mrs. S. (his wife) will tell you the price of it." Mrs. S. looked at the register and said: "One and sixpence" and I paid her with a shilling and sixpence. I then turned to the butcher and said: "I wonder what Lord Woolton would think of shopkeepers like you who make things as difficult as you can for people in business." He and his wife both got into a rage and told me to get out of the shop. I said I was going to find out if he was entitled to withhold a customer's meat at four in the afternoon when he had it on the premises. Also I said if there was anything wrong with the weight and price of the meat he would hear about it.

The redoubtable Miss South marched to the nearest post office, where she had the small packet of meat weighed. It was just under twelve ounces,* wrapped, but she then telephoned the local Food Office and

---

* The meat ration for one person for a week.

discovered that at the prevailing price for pork, the butcher had over-charged by three halfpence.

The local Food Officer was on it like a shot, and an enforcement officer cycled round to see us immediately. He took the chop to the shop and asked the butcher to weigh it, and it weighed only eleven ounces unwrapped. But the butcher said he had only charged me one and threepence, making it right. The officer came back and told us and asked us whether we would come round and challenge the man. I went with him and asked the man why he said he had charged one and three when I had paid him one and six. He absolutely denied it, and I said: "Can you absolutely look me in the face and say you only charged me one and three?"

"Yes."

I said: "How much a pound did you tell me it was?"

He said: "One and tenpence."

I turned to the officer and I said: "That is a lie."

The butcher bridled. "Don't you call me a liar."

I said: "I will because you are a liar."

The officer then asked to see the register, which was written in pencil and quite clearly had been deleted, and the figure three written over it, not even done carefully, so the man is stupid as well as dishonest and disobliging. The butcher denied that he had altered it, and the officer said:

"Don't you call *me* a liar. Already you are accusing Miss South of robbing her friend of threepence. I believe her and I don't believe you."

He then wrote down the particulars . . . and said I would be doing a public service if I attend as a witness if the Food people decide to prosecute . . . Oh dear, my friend and I hope other people in the office will not hear of it, as it makes us seem viragoes to take a man to court for threepence. But it's the principle . . . He has bullied my friend for months and she's a gentle sort . . . Anyway, we have no option. Born under Mars, born under Mars!

But rationing and shortages brought moments of sheer bliss that Britains would never experience in the days of peace and plenty. "I had a new-laid egg sent to me from the country for breakfast," reported a friend of Vere Hodgson. "First new-laid egg I've had for five months. Have given away to a delicate child both my ration eggs during this period. There was an agony of indecision over how to cook it: fried with bacon, omelette, scrambled? Decided that boiling it made it more— *more*. How delicious it tasted as I rolled it round and round in my mouth. . . . A friend of mine when she gets an egg can't bring herself to break the shell, with the result that two have gone bad on her and stank to high heaven when she at last went to use them."

And in her journal Gertrude South told about a family she knew which had spent the bulk of its precious ration points on a can of Bartlett pears. Opening the tin that evening, the mother said to the assembled family, "Now we mustn't talk. Just concentrate on the pears and get the utmost out of them."

This moved Miss South to write: "Are we showing deprivation symptoms? Or are we gluttons?"

In the autumn of 1942, Squadron Leader Geoffrey Page took off from Martlesham Airfield in a Spitfire and led his first low-level daylight raid on the railways and marshaling yards of northern France. He was pleased at the way the plane handled, he was back in his favorite element, and he had never been happier. True, his face still looked as if someone had given it a quick going-over with a blow torch. But part of McIndoe's therapy was to impress upon his Guinea Pigs that looks didn't really matter, particularly to girls; the character and personality of the man behind the face would always come through. "Go out there and mix," McIndoe told his burned pilots. "Pick out the prettiest girl in the room, and to hell with the competition—you'll get her if you want her."

It was true. The Guinea Pigs were not only going back into the world but they were also marrying, and their brides were almost always extraordinarily attractive girls.

Since returning to duty, Page had not seen anything of Richard Hillary, but he kept hearing about him. For one thing his book, *The Last Enemy*, a sensitive study of a young pilot's experiences and emotions, had just been published and was the best seller of the year. But the word was that Hillary was still morose and full of gloom. He had at last persuaded the Air Ministry to let him fly again, and in December he went up to Berwickshire, on the Scottish border, to complete his training. Actually, he was not fit; his new eyelid was still bothering him.

Just before Christmas, Geoffrey Page called Archibald McIndoe at Queen Victoria Hospital in East Grinstead to tell him that he was being transferred to Wittering RAF Station in Sussex, and would henceforth be flying Mustang fighters over France. He had been made an acting wing commander and was delighted with the new American plane. "It's not as sensitive as the Spit or Hurry," he said, "but with hands like mine it's just the job."

Page did not tell McIndoe that both his hands were giving him great pain, as was one of his eyelids. He was flying his Mustang in tandem with another piloted by Squadron Leader Jimmy MacLachlan, who had lost an arm over Malta. In their squadron they were known as "The One-Handed Duet," but they were both masters of their machines and the heroes of the Typhoon fighter pilots who flew cover for them on their low-level raids over France.

Page asked for news of Richard Hillary, and McIndoe told him that Hillary was having trouble adapting himself to night fighters. They both agreed that Hillary had made an unfortunate choice. Though he knew that Hillary would never forgive him, McIndoe was trying to get him grounded; he had, in fact, already written Hillary's commanding officer:

. . . I saw him the other day and was impressed by the fact that his left eye did not appear to be standing up to the strain of night flying, as might be expected, a fact of which Hillary is aware but which I think he is very loath to admit. As you know, he is very able young writer and I feel very strongly that flying under these conditions can only end in one way.

McIndoe asked the CO to send Hillary back to the hospital for further attention, and added:

In the meantime, I do feel if you could with discretion restrain him from further flying it might save him from a very serious accident . . . Would you be so good as to treat this letter as private and confidential to yourself? The feelings of these young men are very apt to be hurt in relation to this vexed question of operations work following an injury. I feel, however, there is a strong case here for intervention.

Evidently the commanding officer did not take this advice seriously. Two weeks later Flight Lieutenant Richard Hillary and his observer took off on a training flight. The plane dived into the ground at the end of the field and both men were killed.

On almost the same day, Wing Commander Geoffrey Page was staggering into bed at Wittering Airfield after a celebration. He had just received news that he had been recommended for a DSO for a series of daring and successful low-level raids over France.

Most Londoners had been walking around like zombies during the fall of 1942, with their hearts in their shabby shoes. Still nothing went right in the war. The Russians were fighting desperately at Stalingrad but looked as if they might be overwhelmed at any moment. British citizens felt not only gloomy about the outcome of that great struggle but guilty, too, because though Allied armies were hold-ing their own in Egypt, they were not yet fighting in Western Europe to take the pressure off their comrades in the East. "One cannot help wondering whether our aim is to let Germany and Russia wear each other down in this gigantic struggle," one man wrote to the newspapers, "and that we are really more afraid of a powerful Russia spreading Communist ideas abroad than we are of Germany itself. I mean by *we* our ruling classes and not the common people, who feel quite differ-ently."

In August more than six thousand Commando troops, most of them Canadians, had attempted a raid on the submarine pens at Dieppe and were driven back with a loss of two thousand killed, wounded and prisoners. The operation was a "fiasco,"* more as a result of delays and poor planning than German toughness. Reading the news, people felt crushed. If this is what happened when a small force raided the Con-tinent, how many years must it be before they dared attempt an invasion in force?

In fact, the survivors (including fifty American Rangers) brought back some valuable lessons—particularly in what not to do—from Dieppe, and these were used to good effect later for the invasion of France. But at the same time, the Dieppe affair provided a useful argu-ment for such advisers of Winston Churchill's as Lindemann and Sir Alan Brooke, who thought it would prove to the Americans once and for all that a second front across the Channel was unthinkable for at least another year.

For women one of the most irritating things was a sudden short-age of hair curlers and sanitary napkins. The prevailing topic amongst the sex was compulsory registration of female labor, and in many cases how to dodge it. It was remarkable how many women suddenly dis-covered invalid mothers and fathers needing their constant care, and how many young married—and single—women found themselves preg-nant within a week or two of registration. The bulk of Britain's women responded readily to the call, but they resented how often they were taken out of admittedly nonessential work and compulsorily directed into even more ineffective occupations, and their loudest grumbles were reserved for the members of their own sex in the labor exchanges who had the power to decide into which jobs they should go and wielded it with bureaucratic lack of feeling. It was reported in the newspapers that one young woman slapped the face of an official who told her,

---

* General Eisenhower's estimate.

"Don't argue with me. You're our property now," and there was much sympathy for her when she was fined for assault.

There was no sympathy at all, however, for the girls who were swarming into London to walk the streets or into the shady clubs rather than face the draft. Police and female military police, called "red caps," began regular checks in Piccadilly and its environs to round up deserters from the female forces and munitions factories.

With plenty of women on the loose, and with British, American and Dominion troops on leave cramming the streets in search of entertainment, London experienced a mounting epidemic of black-marketeering and thievery. There were silk stockings, lipsticks, butter and meat to be bought in the back streets of Soho, but naturally the bulk of London's population did not have the wherewithal to buy them. In any case, one solid achievement of the government was that though rations were small and dull, at least the system allowed a basic diet for everyone and there was no danger of starvation. On the Continent and in Russia, people found dealing in the black market were shot, but this was because the shortages were desperate and men, women and children were dying of starvation because black marketeers had cornered food. In Britain there was never any need for such dire penalties. No matter how many vans were hijacked by gangs in London and the provinces, the ration was always met. It was on the luxuries—cigarettes, liquor, silk stockings, clothing and gas coupons—that the black marketeers did their most profitable business.

But though the people of London were not starving that autumn, they were weary and downhearted. "I'm fed up with the ceaseless gamble of living," a woman complained to a questioner. "There's no let-up anywhere. I leave off work to carry bricks, so to speak. I never get enough sleep."

There was one commodity in London now for which no black market was needed, and that was sex. By this time the city had become a gigantic staging post, and it was bursting with troops waiting for the day when they would be called upon to fight and perhaps die. In the meantime, what most of them needed was women.

Most of the girls flocking into London now were incredibly young —bored schoolgirls from the Midlands and Wales, teen-agers dodging the call-up into the services and factories, deserters from the ATS and the WAAF. The majority ended up in the West End, and their favorite spots for picking up soldiers were the sidewalks around Rainbow Corner (a few yards from Piccadilly Circus), the chief recreation center in the West End for U.S. troops on leave. After darkness, the blacked-out streets were a seething mass of girls and men grabbing at each other, shrieking, shouting, laughing, then pairing off and groping their way to a Soho club or a bomb site in a back street.

Thanks to her "friend" Joey, Jenny Martin never found it necessary to pound the beat along Piccadilly. He had picked her up in a pub in Chelsea one night, and since it was the day she had heard that her husband wanted a divorce, she was in no mood to say no when he asked her back to his flat in Lexham Gardens. After the court had taken away her children, she moved in with him. It was he who took her along to big hotels like the Mayfair, the Dorchester or the Park Lane and drank with her in the bar until a likely customer turned up. One always did. The hotels had a special quota for liquor, and they were always full of officers and U.S. NCOs on leave. The moment one of them responded to Jenny's laugh or glance, Joey would excuse himself and disappear.

Jenny soon discovered that her customers had plenty to give in return. They had brought with them from the United States all those little things that had once been the stuff of everyday life but were now long-forgotten luxuries: fountain pens, wrist watches, cigarette lighters, whole cartons of cigarettes and bottles of whiskey and gin. Thanks to their PX in Grosvenor Square they were the new millionaires, and when they left to go back to their depots a girl might find gifts of clothing coupons and canned food and silk stockings on her mantel as well as money.

One night a shy young sergeant from New Jersey, made bold by drink, insisted that the stockings he had brought Jenny were particularly special, and giggled like a naughty schoolboy as he helped her put them on. They were fantastically sheer and yet somehow more durable than silk, and she kept walking around naked in them, staring at herself in the mirror in narcissistic delight.

"But what kind of silk is it?" she asked the sergeant.

"This ain't silk at all, honey," he said. "It's a new kind of fiber we've invented. It's called nylon."

The next day all Jenny's friends looked in envy at the attractive hose on her slim legs, and the word spread among all the girls to ask their American friends to bring them nylons.

Before long Jenny Martin had more money than she had ever dreamed of, and was seeing a side of London she had not known existed. Joey was not like most men she had heard about who lived on women's earnings. He was kind and easygoing, he only took half her money, and

The Invaders

he let her keep all the gifts except clothing coupons. While she slept during the day, he went off to Soho, where he gambled endlessly with groups of his fellow deserters (he had walked out of Catterick Army Depot in 1939, after two days drilling on the square, and had never been back since). On weekends he went with her to the greyhound races at White City, and he always seemed to know at least one winner. Until she gave up the visits, figuring that it made all of them too unhappy, he even went with her to the two foster homes where they had farmed out her children.

One Saturday, however, when she and Joey were leaving White City, a couple of military policemen suddenly moved in on either side and asked them for their identity cards. Joey showed no sign of panic; he had long since equipped himself with false papers. Unfortunately, by one of those odd coincidences, he had run up against just the wrong M.P. "Haven't I seen you somewhere before?" he said, peering at him. "Yes, by God, I have. Catterick, wasn't it, Joey?"

That night and the next, Jenny Martin stayed away from Joey's apartment in case the police were there, but the night after that she met a woman in the Panama Club in Knightsbridge who said she was the owner of the apartment, and suggested that Jenny take over the lease. When Jenny said it was too big and that the rent might be more than she could afford, the woman gestured to a girl on the dance floor who was lackadaisically shuffling through a striptease routine. "That kid's looking for somewhere to live," she said. "She'll share the place with you."

The stripteaser was billed as "Georgina Grayson," but her real name was Elizabeth Marina Jones and she too was a soldier's wife. It was a name that some months later would become notorious in Britain.

On October 23, 1942, the Eighth Army under the command of General Bernard L. Montgomery launched the attack on Rommel's Afrika Korps in Libya that was to become known as the Battle of El Alamein. During its most decisive phase ten days later, just as the twenty-mile-front artillery barrage lifted and the armored corps began its advance, Winston Churchill was at dinner at Buckingham Palace with the King and Queen and their guest of honor, Mrs. Eleanor Roosevelt.* The PM was gloomy and uncommunicative for most

* They ate a frugal, rationed meal, Mrs. Roosevelt afterward recalled, but dined off ceremonial gold plates.

of the meal until he was called away to the telephone. He returned with a beam on his round red face. The Germans had broken and were on the run; the Eighth Army was advancing in what was to prove its greatest victory.

"We open a second front! Oh, yes, we do!" wrote one commentator. "Libya will be our second front."

By the time Rommel's forces had begun their retreat, first into Libya and then into Tunisia, the great convoys carrying Allied forces under General Eisenhower were on their way to a landing at the western end of Africa, and Operation TORCH had begun. The great squeeze of the Axis forces on that continent was under way.

The objective of Eisenhower's forces was to occupy the French possessions in North Africa: Algeria, Tunisia and Morocco, all of which were in the hands of Marshal Pétain's puppet administration in Vichy. They hoped to achieve the goal without having to fight the Vichy-French armies on the spot, and President Roosevelt had calculated that they had a far better chance of doing so if General de Gaulle and the Free French were not associated with the operation. Therefore he insisted— with Churchill's concurrence—that not only were the Free French forces to be kept out, but that General de Gaulle was not to be told about the invasion until operations had begun. Recently the general had renamed his troops the Fighting French, but at five o'clock on the morning of the landing he was awakened in London and told that this was one operation in which the Fighting French would have no part. According to one source,* his first reaction was to say angrily, "I hope the Vichy clique will throw them back into the sea."

But that night De Gaulle broadcast over the BBC to give his full support to the landing and ask all Frenchmen in North Africa to lay down their arms or join up with the Allies. This was before he learned that Eisenhower and Washington were dealing with Admiral Darlan and a French general who was senior in rank to De Gaulle. General Henri-Honoré Giraud had escaped from prison in Germany, and with Allied approval he now proclaimed himself commander in chief of all the French forces in North Africa. It was a grave threat to De Gaulle's claim to speak for France, for Giraud would command an army almost ten times the force under De Gaulle.

On November 11 De Gaulle attended a meeting of his followers —hundreds of pro-Gaullist Britons tried to get in too—in the Albert

---

* J. R. Tournoux, *Pétain et De Gaulle.*

The Invaders

Hall in London, ostensibly to celebrate Armistice Day but principally to make his position clear. "Today is Armistice Day," he proclaimed, "and it is also the day to celebrate the spirit of Fighting France. From the Fighting French alone will liberation come. In truth, every day France makes a plebiscite in favor of Fighting France. It is toward Fighting France that the nation turns. It is from Fighting France and from Fighting France alone that she expects the direction of her struggle. Therefore we suffer no one to come and divide our country's war effort by any of these so-called parallel enterprises."

Then, from somewhere in the hall a retired French general named Eon rose and read an appeal to De Gaulle. Pointing out that Giraud was his senior, commanded ten times as many men and therefore had the right to lead the French henceforth, he asked De Gaulle to put himself under Giraud's command. He was immediately seized by irate Gaullists and roughly escorted from the hall.

General de Gaulle had made his position clear. No one, no matter what his rank, was going to oust him from his role as the savior of France. It was a warning both to ambitious officers in the French forces and to any Allied heads of state who might be tempted to sponsor them, and it was an attitude of which the British public heartily approved.

"De Gaulle had lunch with our Prime Minister today," wrote Vere Hodgson on November 29. "I do hope they understood one another. I have much admiration for De Gaulle and when he has done all the hard work I don't want to see him pushed out. I heard his clarion voice on the wireless the other day—he is most thrilling. I can well believe what it meant to France when they first heard him in 1940 calling to them."

She had no need to worry. General de Gaulle was soon demonstrating that he knew how to look after himself and the Fighting French.

In January 1943, the Germans in Stalingrad crumbled before the Russian armies and surrendered. Other victories followed. They were by no means decisive, but they gave Hitler his biggest setbacks of the war and were a cause for great rejoicing in Britain.

From the BBC in London went a haunting song to the German people whose words and music so caught the ear of the British public that a translation was made. It was called "The Ballad of the German Soldier's Bride":

And what did he send you, my bonny lass,
From Paris, the city of light?
From Paris he sent me a silken dress,
A dream caress of a silken dress
From Paris, the city of light.

And what did he send you, my bonny lass
From the deep, deep Russian snows?
From Russia he sent me my widow's weeds
For the funeral feast my widow's weeds
From the deep, deep Russian snows.

The words were written by an anti-Nazi emigré named Bertolt Brecht.

But once more Londoners found their mood changing to black depression, for even now, things were going wrong for the Allies. The pincers movement in North Africa had fallen tragically far behind schedule. The Eighth Army was not moving fast enough from the east, and in the west, Vichy trickery had enabled the Germans to establish themselves in Tunisia and to fight back against Eisenhower's armies. In their first major encounter with the Afrika Korps, the battle of Kasserine Pass, the U.S. forces got their noses severely bloodied and had to retreat.

Far from clearing North Africa and the Mediterranean before the end of 1942, as they had hoped, the Allies would need several months to overcome Rommel and his armies. This meant that the bulk of the Allied armies and the ships to supply them were still stuck in the Mediterranean and Africa when they should have been preparing for the invasion of Europe.

Only fanatics and sadists got any comfort from the fact that Germany was now being bombed day and night, and that great cities like Cologne were being smashed beyond recognition. Instinctively, the British knew that wholesale destruction from the air was not going to win a war for anybody; it would only kill men, women and children.

In January 1943 the Germans decided to retaliate and kill some children themselves.

14

Scalded Cats

They were known in the newspapers as "scalded cat" raids because the planes—usually Messerschmitt 110s or Focke-Wulfs—came in at rooftop level under the radar screen in formations of four or six, dropped their bombs on their targets, and streaked for home. The initial attack occurred on January 17, 1943, and the sirens wailed for the first time in several months. There was no rush for the shelters.

On the outskirts of East London, Donald Ketley and his schoolmates saw several of the raids and thought they were the most exciting things ever. "One Saturday," he recalls, "they bombed Romford Gas Works and then passed over our house at what seemed no more than a hundred feet up. They continued towards Ilford, shooting up various areas on the way. But I honestly don't think anyone was very bothered by these terrorist tactics. People became quite adept at diving for cover, though."

Not quickly enough in some cases, however. On January 20, six planes slipped under the radar net and were over East London before the sirens could sound the alert or the barrage balloons be raised. Their bombs hit a school at Lewisham just as one hundred and fifty children and their teachers were assembling for lunch in the main hall. The heavy building disintegrated and buried them under a mountain of rubble. It was a disaster which aroused stronger feelings of sorrow and anger in the East End of London than any single catastrophe during the Blitz. Forty children died, and forty more plus six teachers were injured. Londoners cringed at pictures of frantic parents digging with their bare hands in the debris in the hope of uncovering a missing child. Ten thousand people turned up for the burial ceremony on January 27.

There was another disaster in London, on March 3, and this one too hit the East End hard. Its impact was not quite so widespread because news of it was censored, but word of mouth spread it quickly across the capital and aroused feelings of horror. By this time the raids had become so regular that many people had begun taking to the shelters again, and on March 3 the crowd entering the Underground coincided with the evening rush hour as well as with the sounding of the sirens. At Bethnal Green Station a vast mob of home-going workers and shelterers swarmed down the stairway to the platform under ground. Suddenly at the top of the stairs a woman carrying a baby was jostled by an old man and slipped. She fell into the people in front of her, and they in turn tripped. Soon other people fell. Hearing the sound of screaming and shouting, those down below rushed on ahead and fell themselves, or turned and tried to struggle up to the surface.

The terror took several minutes to build up, survivors said afterward, and then the mass of struggling, screaming, panic-stricken humanity fell upon one another and collapsed down the stairs like a human avalanche into a quivering heap below. One hundred and seventy-eight persons died of suffocation. Up above, the German raiders killed four.

But save for such isolated instances, the "scalded cats" did far less damage than shrapnel from the antiaircraft guns and rockets which London now turned against them.* "Many people have been killed by our shrapnel in the past few days," wrote Vere Hodgson in January. "The wardens begged people to go inside, and on Wednesday, during the daylight raid, people were pushed into Marks and Spencers department store in Oxford Street and made to stay there, as the Hyde Park guns were in full cry. In the park itself the wardens were hastily opening the trench shelters. A friend from our office was there airing a dog, and when the warning sounded everyone scattered. She was in conversation with an old lady who refused to budge. The noise of the guns was really terrible and my friend, Mrs. Winnal, was

---

* Though one isolated bomb on a Hammersmith dance hall later in the year did kill three hundred young people.

really frightened, but she didn't care to leave the old lady alone. They were near Queen Victoria's statue. Poor old Queen. I wonder what she would have said if she had been alive."

"In the early days of 1943, Londoners in the know were still afraid of the future, afraid that we were still in danger of losing the war," says Charles Snow. "Even the Americans, who had come to Britain full of optimism, were disillusioned. They were nursing the bruises they had received from the Germans in Tunisia and beginning to realize what sort of a military machine they were facing. By now they knew that we couldn't match the Germans unless we had an enormous and overwhelming superiority in material. And of course the more percipient realized that the fate of all of us was being decided not in North Africa or over Germany itself, despite our vast bombing raids, but on the battlefields of Russia.

"As for the ordinary Londoners, however, I would say that their feelings were about equally divided between what they were going to eat today and what was going to happen in Britain tomorrow."

Early in February the House of Commons held a debate on what had become known as the Beveridge Plan. It was a blueprint drawn up by a committee headed by an economist and sociologist named Sir William Beveridge for the building of the postwar world in Britain, and it detailed at some length plans for what subsequently became known as the welfare state. The report proposed schemes for education, health service and pensions that would take care of every Briton from the cradle to the grave, and its civilized and egalitarian ideas for bridging the gap between rich and poor caught the imagination of the British public. If this was what Britain was fighting for, the ordinary citizen was all for it.

It was with great reluctance that the government consented to discuss the Beveridge Plan at all, and then it was only because Labour party members of the Cabinet, egged on by their rank and file, insisted. It so happened that Winston Churchill took no part in the debate, for he lay seriously ill with pneumonia in North Africa, where he had met with President Roosevelt at Casablanca in January. His views, however, were widely known and were shared by most of the Tory rank-and-file Members of Parliament: this was a blueprint for Utopia, far too costly to implement, and premature in any case.

"Let's win the war first and talk about the welfare state afterwards," was the burden of the Tory speeches. When the debate came to the vote on February 18, only 119 members, out of a House of over 600, voted for the plan, and they were nearly all members of the Labour party.

It was a serious misreading of the mood of the British people to push the Beveridge Plan to one side so curtly, and civilians and soldiers alike mentally marked it up against the Tories. Snow later remarked, "It's important to remember how idealistic everyone was in those days, despite the rigors and pressures of war. Winston Churchill forgot it, or wouldn't believe it, and look what happened to him."

Also, once more Parliament had voted to prolong itself, and there would be no general election until the war was over. But people were not going to forget. On February 17, Gertrude South wrote: "I am seething over the Beveridge debate, just seething. The same old gang right out of the Ark. Wish Bevin and Co. [the Labour minister] would resign and damn the consequences. Just as important to win a victory here by establishing the principle that the welfare of the people is the first charge on the nation's resources as it is to win the war. Who cares whether we win the war or not if we are going to be saddled with these ninny-hammers [the Tories]. I wanna kill 'em."

Two days later, after the vote, she wrote: "Only 119 against the Government on Beveridge. Mr. Churchill's indisposition was very timely from one point of view, but what an opportunity was lost! How his name might have gone down in history as one of the truly great if he had defied the Tories and come out for the Beveridge scheme. He could do what no other British statesman could do at this juncture. All this talk about cutting our coat according to our cloth my foot! If the war were to last another ten years we should find means of financing it, by hook or by crook. Only when it's a question of raising the standard of life of the people does this niggling cutting-of-coat crop up. What a world!

"Yet it's a glorious day. Real spring. Feel nostalgic and unsettled. One's mind is never at leisure nowadays. I go down the road on a bus four times a day and have been told that the japonica along it is in bloom, yet I have never seen it. What with the stuff over the bus windows and being tensed up inside wondering whether I shall succeed in getting my foot inside a shop before they let the shutters down, or catch trains, etc. . . . More retreats in Tunisia. Feel apprehensive. When, oh when are we going to start winning this bloody war?"

Vere Hodgson was also finding it hard to remain cheerful. She wasn't surprised that Winston Churchill was ill; everyone she knew seemed to be ill. "I think it's the diet," she wrote her relatives in Rhodesia. "Everyone is overtired with all these years of blackout and war and anxiety and domestic difficulties."

There was a song on the radio, however, which made her laugh. Its first lines were: "If you're up to your neck in hot water, be like a kettle and sing." And her boss, Miss Moyes, who never seemed to lose her good spirits, did her best to keep them all cheerful. "I told her this morning that Abyssinia had declared war on Germany, Italy and Japan. 'Why,' she said, 'it's just like a fly putting out its tongue!' "

But for Vere Hodgson, as for most women in London, it was the shopping which depressed her, even when she tried to make light of it. "How shopkeepers have changed," she reported. "In bygone times, the great lady used to ring up her fishmonger and order five lobsters 'and mind they are fresh' or she'd take her custom elsewhere. Nowadays the great lady takes her basket on her arm and goes to the fishmonger and in her most ingratiating voice implores him to send her what he can. And as she departs puts in very sweetly: 'I shall see you at my cocktail party tonight, shan't I? And you'll bring the kippers with you?' "

An announcement in the newspapers in February informed Londoners that canned goods would probably be on sale in the capital again the following week because a convoy had arrived safely from America. On the strength of it, Miss Hodgson opened a can of blackberries for Miss Moyes and herself. "They tasted delicious and we felt fearfully extravagant. It was a bit of our invasion reserve, but as invasion does not seem imminent now I took the risk."

Every Sunday, as always, she would lie late abed and read about the state of the war in *The Observer,* and then would get up to explore London and see what the war had done to it during the week. One day in the spring she wrote:

I came along Tottenham Court Road today and couldn't help noticing how quiet it was. It was like a country town, an occasional bus, a taxi here and there, but practically nothing on the streets. I believe Cairo has all the traffic nowadays. Our roads are wonderfully peaceful, no noise, it's heavenly.

In mid-March she went out to see what was happening to the great campaign to raise money for the war, a government-sponsored propaganda effort called "Wings for Victory" week. That night she wrote a vivid picture of what the West End of London looked like in the fourth year of the war:

Truly, Piccadilly is a thrilling place to walk along. All the uniforms of the United Nations jostle you along the pavements, and since there is no traffic hardly you can walk right round the Circus. Some of the soldiers label themselves POLAND or CANADA but there are lots of them with just emblems on their shoulders. Such varied faces and manners. Girls too in their Service costumes by the hundred. Very few fashionable dressed women, because all the pretty ones are in uniform.

From there she walked to Trafalgar Square, where a big bomber, a veteran of the raids on Germany, had been placed.

Such crowds of people. Men selling flags and bawbees. Music playing and some soldiers in a jeep going round and round the square. I edged my way in and saw the big bomber O for Orange, a Lancaster. It was perched high up and looked very aristocratic. The crowd was constantly moving, so I slithered into the centre of things. Presently I found some firemen selling odd stamps to put on the bomber, so I bought one and with great satisfaction stuck it on. Then I worked my way to the fountain where some air cadets were shouting and enjoying themselves. I found they were trying to raise one million pennies to try and buy a Typhoon [a fighter plane] for Westminster. They paddled around in a rubber dinghy such as wrecked airmen use and you threw pennies to them. Other lads were in rubbers wading about in search of pennies which had gone into the pool. I forbore to give them this trouble but put my three pence into a bag which came round.

With the rest of the crowd, she gaped at a man holding up two precious lemons which, he said, had been brought back on a convoy from Gibraltar. They were to be auctioned off for the war effort in a theatre that evening.

Another bomber was on display in the open space in front of St. Paul's Cathedral in the City, and Vere Hodgson decided that she mustn't miss it, either.

I was fortunate in getting on the bus, because large segments of the British public were of a like mind. It was sitting behind St. Paul's, in all that desolation. Really, looking on it all, you cannot help but think that it was a miracle that St. Paul's was saved. All the buildings have been pulled down right down to the steps of St. Paul's. There's one wall of a little church just a few inches from the edge of the cathedral. I don't know the name of it. . . . This bomber, H for Harry, was a Stirling, a shabby-looking giant. It had been on sixty-two bombing raids, including Berlin, so I bought another stamp for Lucy because I know she would like one to go on in her name.

Scalded Cats

The next day there were rumors in the newspapers that bread was about to be rationed.* That really would be the end, Miss Hodgson felt. How would the poor keep their stomachs full then?

Londoners were in a curious mood that spring. Though they displayed fortitude and indomitability in the face of a gray and unpromising future, they also revealed a considerable amount of prejudice. The privations of war did nothing to increase their tolerance of the minorities in their midst, and a strong strain of anti-Semitism was sweeping through the city. Even kind Vere Hodgson and the civilized and intelligent Rosemary Black were victims of it.

Not that Vere Hodgson did more than express superior, Aryan-like sentiments about her Jewish neighbors. Noting that the tragic accident in which almost two hundred people suffocated in a stampede had taken place at Bethnal Green, she commented: "It's a Jewish quarter, and Jews have a reputation everywhere of scrambling out of danger as fast as they can, and further tending to look after themselves."

Surprisingly, Rosemary Black was much more petulant. After seeing an old Bette Davis film at a West End cinema, she wrote in her diary that night: "I had to wait some time for the others in the cinema foyer, and I was much struck, as often before, by the almost complete absence of English people these days, from the capital of England. Almost every person who came in was either a foreigner, a roaring Jew, or both. The Cumberland [Hotel] has always been a complete New Jerusalem, but this evening it really struck me as no worse than anywhere else! It is really dismaying to see that this should be the result of this war in defence of our country."

But perhaps this was due to the miserable time Rosemary Black was having, for that spring she was almost crippled by an agonizing attack of rheumatism. Still, a Mass-Observation survey taken during this period revealed that despite the news of the persecution of Jews now trickling in from Nazi-occupied Europe, Londoners felt a saddening lack of friendliness toward them. In 1941 a group had been asked about its attitude toward Jews, and the two responses were now compared.

---

* It remained a rumor. Lord Woolton, the Food Minister, threatened to resign if bread was rationed, and managed to keep the supply going somehow, though loaves thereafter seemed to contain an increasing amount of soggy chalk. Ironically enough, bread was never rationed in Britain until after the war.

	1941	1943
Favourable	29%	23%
Half and Half	29%	50%
Unfavourable	27%	13%
Vague	15%	12%

Some of those polled were asked their opinion of their Jewish neighbors, and one of the responses summed up a widespread feeling of smug English patronage:

"They haven't got steadiness, like us. We may be slow but we don't lack courage. The Jews, they're like foreigners—in fact, they are foreigners."

But apparently the attitude of most Londoners toward foreigners in their midst went in inverse ratio to their numbers; the fewer there were of a particular nationality, the more popular they were. Another Mass-Observation survey in 1943 came out this way:

Attitude towards the Dutch

Favourable	73%
Half and Half	4%
Unfavourable	5%
Vague	18%

Attitude towards the Czechs

Favourable	64%
Half and Half	12%
Unfavourable	2%
Vague	22%

Attitude towards the Fighting French

Favourable	52%
Half and Half	32%
Unfavourable	11%
Vague	5%

Attitude towards the Poles

Favourable	27%
Half and Half	39%
Unfavourable	17%
Vague	17%

Attitude towards the Americans

Favourable	33%
Half and Half	44%
Unfavourable	21%
Vague	2%

Scalded Cats

Between them, the Poles and the Americans had more troops in Britain—and more of them visible in London on leave—than all the other Allies put together. The lukewarm attitude toward the Poles may be explained by the fact that their success with women had been considerable, and in the eyes of many English males they were too charming and gallant. There was also the factor that the Poles' attitude toward Russia was almost overwhelmingly hostile, and the British resented this. So far as they were concerned, the Russians were winning the war for them.

The curious thing about the Londoners' feelings toward Americans was that practically everyone, male and female alike, seemed to have a friend in the U.S. forces and showed him off proudly to everyone, but were always criticizing the Americans as a whole. Kathleen Tipper, a secretary who worked at night in the New Zealand Club canteen in the Strand, wrote: "We were very busy tonight. Talked to an American sailor. He is a nice-looking lad who will get on well here. He had such nice manners. I think we can divide the Americans up into two distinct groups. Some have dreadful manners and are rude and uncouth. Yet the rest—and these are most of them—have most charming manners. It is a pity the other, unpleasant ones are agreed upon to be typical."

Americans were now pouring into London in hordes every weekend looking for fun and relaxation, and guests and hosts were eying one another warily. The surprises on each side were often unpleasant. A survey of British feelings toward the American forces asked two questions:

What Are Your Main Reasons for Liking Americans?
  Enterprise
  Energy
  Generosity
  Friendliness
  Fighting qualities
  Technical efficiency
  Intelligence
  Adaptability

What Are Your Main Reasons for Disliking Americans?
  Boastfulness
  Immaturity
  Material and commercial preoccupation

Morals
Accent
Conversational superficiality
Intolerance
Ostentation
Attitude to Negroes
Habit of chewing gum
Overpaid

Simultaneously a cross section of the U.S. forces visiting London were asked their opinions of their English hosts, and almost all of them mentioned the "lower moral standards" of women in the city. Most of them, however, made haste to point out that it was such women who were most likely to consort with foreign soldiers, and that the West End was hardly typical of the country as a whole. However, on other aspects of London life they could be forthright. An English interviewer (who must have translated these conversations freely, for a U.S. citizen would hardly use some of these words) recorded the following:

An American soldier:
Well, I'll be frank with you. I was here in 1937 and the difference in London today is terrific. I mean the difference in the tradesmen, most of all. They used to be proud of their businesses, proud of their craftsmanship, proud of what they were selling. They were much too proud to do you down. That's all gone. They're all on the snatch now. They don't care. I don't care for the attitude of the shopkeepers, the hotel-keepers, the taxi-drivers towards us Americans—they're all as indifferent as hell and apt to do the living lights out of you. The English still think themselves the top dog everywhere."

An American sailor:
"One thing struck me a lot. Your civilians are pretty decent about helping out about money, about the exchange. One of the times one of our boys couldn't figure it out about your money some civilians stopped and helped out, and they've never done one of them a dirty deal yet. But they're slow in giving change in the shops and the shopkeepers are surly. They don't seem to want to serve you. You'd think they wanted to keep their stocks to themselves."

An American airman:
"I think sex morals here are very low, and our boys take advantage of

it. I don't think they respect the women for it. I know it's the worst women who pick up soldiers in any country, but our boys don't see it that way . . . But I don't think you English should blame our boys for being wild. Of course we're wild. We're 3,000 miles from home for the first time in our lives. It's the chance of a lifetime. It's just the same when a British ship docks in a foreign port. They go wild just the same as us."

For most Britons coming in contact with American troops for the first time, what seems to have made the most impact was the deep gulf between white and black members of the U.S. forces. Discrimination against black soldiers by their white comrades did much to influence the reaction of Londoners. The previous autumn* *The Times* had published a letter which had become a talking point in many a British home:

Sir, I am the manager of a snack bar in Oxford, and have had a rather unfortunate state of affairs, which is beginning to exist in this country, very forcibly brought to my notice. The other night a coloured United States soldier came into our establishment and very diffidently presented me with an open letter from his commanding officer explaining that "Pte.—— is a soldier in the U.S. Army and it is necessary that he sometimes has a meal out, which he has, on occasions, found difficult to obtain. I would be grateful if you would look after him."

Naturally we "looked after" him to the best of our ability, but I could not help feeling ashamed that in a country where even stray dogs are "looked after" by special societies, a citizen of the world, who is fighting the world's battle for freedom and equality, should have found it necessary to place himself in this humiliating position. Had there been the slightest objection from the other customers I should not have had any hesitation in asking them all to leave.

I should like to feel that everybody shared my views, as England's reputation for hospitality is in danger of being questioned. Incidentally, the gentleman in question showed his gratitude by a donation of just twice the amount of his bill in the poor box. [Signed] D. Davie-Distin.

Thereafter a wave of warmth toward black Americans and a coolness toward the whites who treated them shabbily seemed to spread over England. At the New Zealand Club canteen Kathleen Tipper noticed how frequently the race problem came up:

* October 2, 1942.

Had an interesting conversation with an American tonight. We discussed the colour question. He said he had no idea of the feeling here before he arrived in England, he had naturally presumed that we had the same ideas as the Americans. He said that until he got to England he had never seen a white girl dancing with a coloured boy, and he didn't like it and that if he married an English girl he would take very good care to investigate her family tree so that he would not find himself the proud father of a black baby. I pointed out that I thought this was far more likely to occur in America, there being so many more black people in that country than there are here. My American friend then said that in America they never intermarried except in the slums, and I told him (with no authority to back up my statement) that although intermarriage of this sort was quite rare in England, it too was usually in the slums of some of our ports. Eileen, who had been listening to the whole conversation with amusement, said that anyway it did not follow that because a girl danced with a coloured American, babies would follow, but the American said, "Why not?" and added, "If the girls go around with the coloured boys, surely they intend to marry them," and this really made us laugh, he was so serious about it all, and really thought that they were after marriage, and he didn't believe that a girl might dance with one of the coloured soldiers in order to show him that we didn't ostracize them here, and his final comment was, "Don't worry, the coloured boys will soon take advantage of this tolerance and you will feel the same way as we do." This conversation was just typical of many I have had recently with those Americans who are willing to talk seriously about the problem.

A few months later she was writing:

We had an unpleasantness here this evening when a young American Negro came in and walked up to the bar to be served. All the Americans there turned away or made loud insulting remarks to him. We were furious and I served him and was rather hurt when he said, "Is it all right for me to come in here?" Anyway, a moment later a New Zealand officer came up and stood next to him and after a few moments the Negro asked him, very humbly, if he wouldn't have a drink with him. We were pleased to see the officer accept and they talked and drank for about half an hour. It showed the Americans up, but they weren't a bit ashamed of their behaviour. We didn't hide our feelings.

At about this time Mass-Observation did a survey on discrimination among American troops. Only 43 percent of those Britons questioned had met black American soldiers, and of these, men outnumbered women 3 to 1. Both sexes were asked the somewhat loaded

question: "Do you think the treatment of American Negroes is just?"
The answers were:

	Male	Female
Just	13%	10%
Unjust	45%	34%
Treatment improving	4%	1%
Not our affair	10%	7%
No opinion	28%	48%

Not that Londoners themselves were immune from prejudice against colored soldiers. A Mrs. May Capper wrote to Mass-Observation in May 1943 to report a conversation she had heard in a fish queue between a "retired-colonel type" and a woman with the "right accent":

Woman: Look, there's a black soldier. No, he's an *officer!*

  Man: Can't be.

Woman: Yes, it is. American probably. No, I think he's French. Senegalese, I expect. Well [with contempt], they can keep him.

  Man: By jove, yes! Mind you, these fellows fight well and they're good fellows in their way, providing they know their place.

Woman: I was talking to some American boys the other day and I said to them: "How do you manage when these fellows get back home? Is there any difference?" and they said: "Well, they know their place. They know they're"—and she turned her thumb down—"and we're"—and she turned it up.

  Man: (with enthusiasm) That's it. The utter rot you hear talked nowadays. As if they were our equals, as if they could be.

Mrs. Capper ended her report with the sentence, "I left the fish queue in order not to say something rude or hit the speakers."

herever he went in Whitehall in the early days of July 1943, Charles Snow could hear the whispers about Italy. The Allies had at last mopped up the German armies in North Africa and were about to land in Sicily, but first the "negotiators" were at work trying to make a deal with Italy, and there were emissaries everywhere covertly tempting Mussolini's cohorts to desert him and take Italy out of the war.

"I thought at the time that they were going about it in an extraordinarily flat-footed way," Snow says, "and I don't think history has proved me wrong. In any case, as far as I and my friends were concerned, at that moment Italy hardly seemed to matter. It was just a side show; the fate of the war was being settled fifteen hundred miles away near Kharkov."

For Snow and the little group of top scientists with whom he was spending most of his hours now, the first half of 1943 had not been as depressing as for most Londoners because they had news—which for security reasons the public could not share—that enlivened their spirits. For over a year Snow had been haunted not only by the fear that Britain would lose the war but by a specter even more terrifying: the atomic bomb with which the Germans might win it. "We had no idea how the Germans had mishandled their research into atomic weapons," he recalls. "We couldn't guess that Adolf Hitler wouldn't have a scientist near him, or even someone who understood scientific developments, with the possible exception of Speer. As a result, no one could get to him and persuade him to back the research and provide the resources necessary to prove that an atomic bomb was possible. Since we didn't know this, there was always the feeling, even when everything was going all right for us, that there might be this horror in the background. None of us expected that the Germans were so bad in atomic research."

Then, in the spring of 1943, trustworthy news had arrived from Germany which convinced them that the Nazis would never produce an atomic bomb, not even if the war lasted another five years,* whereas the Manhattan Project, which eventually produced the Anglo-American atomic bomb, would be under way before the end of the year.

This was indeed heartening news, but for Snow and his friends there was a crucial trial of strength to come before they could really rejoice. While everyone else in London hung around their radios or snatched up the newspapers on July 11 to read about the Anglo-American landings in Sicily, Snow and his closest friend, Professor P. M. S. Blackett, were searching the ticker tapes for news from Russia. The battle of the Kursk salient, the biggest and most savage German assault of the war, had begun north and south of Kharkov on July 5. The

---

* Word reached them from, among others, Professor Niels Bohr, the Danish physicist, who got a message through to London by concealing it in the hollow handle of a door key which the underground smuggled out of Denmark. Professor Bohr and his wife were also smuggled out of Nazi-occupied Denmark, in the autumn of 1943, and he helped build the Allied atomic bomb.

front was two hundred miles from end to end and thousands of guns, tanks and planes were involved. The German army lost nearly six hundred tanks the first day, but it went on bashing its head against the armored Red defenses for ten more days before the blood and pain were too much. On July 15 the great German retreat westward began; Russia had inflicted the most decisive defeat upon an invading enemy since Napoleon's retreat from Moscow.

"I don't think Alan Brooke or any of the other people on the General Staff in London had any idea that it had been the decisive battle of the war," Snow says. "All they were interested in was Sicily and what the Italians would do in Rome. But compared with this, it didn't matter. In Russia the Germans had launched their greatest offensive, and it had been thrown back. If this was the utmost they could do— and it was—then it was clearly the end. We couldn't possibly lose the war now."

When Snow returned to his flat that night, he turned on the news and there it was. After the reports on Sicily came the cursory announcement of a German withdrawal around Kursk.

Elated, Snow sat down to write a note to his girl friend, for he felt he had to share this mood with someone: "Dearest, this is it. This is the end. No, I don't mean between you and me . . ."

He put down his pen here and went into the kitchen to look for a drink, but could find nothing. "It was very difficult to get drunk in wartime," he remarks, "but I felt I must do the best I could."

He went out to a pub behind Dolphin Square and managed to get a couple of drinks, then went on and had two more, and then on again. Just before closing time, when he was feeling very merry, a couple of friends came over and joined him. Noting the warm glow of happiness suffusing his normally owlish features, one of them asked, "And what might you be celebrating, Charles?"

"Victory!"

"Where? Sicily?"

"No," he said, shaking his head hard. "Kursk. The Kursk salient."

They looked at him as if he were mad.

For Rosemary Black the first half of 1943 had been "bloody, bloody, bloody." Her rheumatism had turned the normally active young woman into a miserable cripple racked with pain and always conscious of the lack of heating. She was luckier than most, for she could afford to go out three or four times a week to fashionable West End restaurants and make up on unrationed meals what food she could not get in the shops. Even so she was finding it difficult to stretch her rations; there was never enough milk for the children, and like almost everyone else she hadn't seen an egg for months. To be sure, she found dried eggs to be "wonderful stuff and I do appreciate our good fortune in being so generously provided with it. Unlike Mrs. G. who says that she and her children (both under-nourished and rickety) can't touch it. It never seems to occur to her, if they really are too finicky to eat the dried egg scrambled, to use it in cakes and puddings."

Tea, that perennial English stand-by, was rarer than gold by 1943, and Mrs. Black, who once had drunk it hourly hot and strong enough to stand a spoon in, now preferred coffee—or at least convinced herself that she did. But some of her friends remained addicts: "B. and John rang up for the night. "B., being rather a tea-drinker and always having been a most generous host to me with rationed commodities, I was dismayed to find that I'd let myself run out of tea . . . However, my Wine Society order having been delivered a few days ago, I then had the idea of sending K. to the P.s with the suggestion of trading a half bottle of whisky for a pound of tea—at which J. apparently simply leapt. Presently I began to get conscience-stricken, feeling a pound altogether too much tea to have accepted in return for a mere half bottle of whisky. After all, it's a 4-week ration. But just then J. phoned in a state to say was it really all right, she couldn't help feeling they were profiting madly on the exchange, and so forth! It seems that both parties are equally satisfied."

The "scalded cat" raids affected Mrs. Black badly, particularly as they continued through the spring and summer. It was the noise which troubled her most, though she knew that it came not from the bombs but from the increasing strength of the antiaircraft and the new types of rocket guns. "Each burst of shellfire seemed to thunder and shake the house as only big bombs did in the good old days." She crouched miserable on the floor of her drafty basement shelter (which now had no heat to keep it comfortable) and tried to soothe her two children, who, now that they were older, seemed to have become nervous in a way they never had been earlier. Above all, her rheumatism seemed to have weakened her resolve:

What with one thing and another, I was more shaken than I ever remember being. Both physically and mentally I felt completely incapable of rising to meet any emergency which might occur. Frankly, I was completely limp with terror, and after the all-clear had gone I felt too weak and shaken to so

WILLIAM VANDIVERT—© TIME, INC.

Tottenham Court
Road in September
1940 after a raid,
and exactly one
year later.

HANS WILD—© TIME, INC.

Sunday service held in roofless Church
of St. John, destroyed by a
direct hit just before Christmas, 1941.

MAGNUM PHOTOS—ROBERT CAPA

facing page: September 1943: A vegetable garden grows where bombed buildings once stood in the East End. St. Paul's is in the background.

IMPERIAL WAR MUSEUM

RADIO TIMES HULTON PICTURE LIBRARY

A recruitment poster at a time when women's conscription was still voluntary. Later on, women were drafted.

Pianist Myra Hess gave lunchtime concerts in the National Gallery throughout the war. Her fur coat testifies to the severity of the fuel shortage.

IMPERIAL WAR MUSEUM

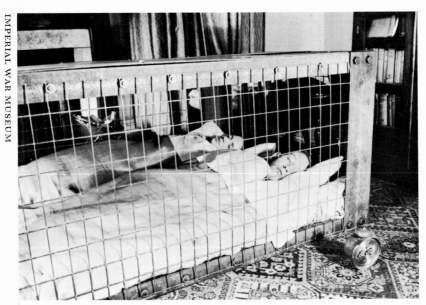

A Morrison shelter (named after the Home Secretary) in use.

RADIO TIMES HULTON PICTURE LIBRARY

General Eisenhower with other members of the Allied Expeditionary Force. *Left to right:* Lieutenant General Omar Bradley, Admiral Sir Bertram Ramsay, Air Chief Marshal Sir Arthur Tedder, General Eisenhower, General Sir Bernard Montgomery, Air Chief Marshal Sir Trafford Leigh-Mallory and Lieutenant General Walter Bedell Smith.

IMPERIAL WAR MUSEUM

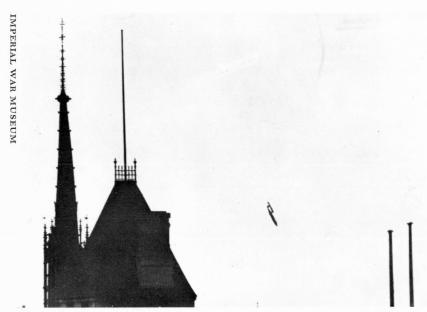

May 11, 1944: A V-1 about to crash in Chancery Lane. Photograph was taken from a Fleet Street roof.

GEORGE RODGER—© TIME, INC.

A rescue squad carries off a woman injured by a V-1 before the dust of the explosion is cleared away.

The terror of the V-2, which was silent, unlike the "buzz bomb," is reflected in the face of this little girl being rescued from her destroyed home.

UNITED PRESS INTERNATIONAL PHOTO

BOB LANDRY—© TIME, INC.

May 8, 1945: Hundreds of thousands of Londoners wait for an appearance of the King and Queen in front of Buckingham Palace on V-E Day.

much as turn over in bed. I don't feel I can *possibly* face up to a renewal of the blitz, if this horror is what the future holds in store for us.

All next day, she felt suicidally depressed and apprehensive, and got no comfort from the fact that "no one else seems to have worried much over the raids which scared the daylights out of me." Asked by her friend Mrs. C. whether she was keeping up her reports to Mass-Observation, she wrote waspishly in her journal:

I used to feel that Mass-Observation, by enabling an increased knowledge of "the will of the people" by the people's representatives and rulers to be known, was making a real contribution to democracy, and that by working for M.O. one was, consequently, playing some part, however small, in improving the democratic system. Nowadays, like Galileo, I care for none of these things. Democracy seems pretty well blown to hell, and really the man-in-the-street's ideas are so bloody silly (no wonder, since they're formed by newspapers and irresponsible advertisements) that I feel this is just as well. How can democracy be any good anyway until a decent and universal system of education makes government of, by, for the people something else than government of, by, for ignorant prejudiced fools? Until such a decent system of education comes into being, to attempt to improve democracy is to ornament a house built without foundations. Anyway, I just don't give a damn.

But even her bad nerves could not last long, and with spring her mood changed:

A lovely day. Things certainly do seem brighter when birds are singing and buds bursting, and the yellow crocuses in front of the kitchen window opening out into quite a good patch of colour in the sun. A great stroke of luck today: the greengrocer let me have a jar of greengages [plums] and promised some prunes later on in the week. Supper with the P.s and Mrs. C. over the canal. They had provided a most terrific blow-out—actual shell eggs and bacon (two rashers, moreover) and tinned apricots . . . To my consternation they then put the frying pan in the sink to be washed up, just as it was, with a good half inch of priceless bacon fat congealing in it. Later P. fell upstairs carrying a full pint bottle of milk of which three quarters spilt—mostly over her. This to me was worse than the burning of a £5 note.

It was a time when people dreamed at night not of wealth or of love, not even of peace, but of food. Just about this time, Hollywood film producers decided to include no more banquet scenes in their films, because the sight of people guzzling on the screen was too much for moviegoers to bear. If she had known about it, Rosemary Black would have approved. In June she wrote:

I had a real hunger-dream last night, of streets lined with greengrocers' shops each with its window fuller of oranges than the last. For some reason I'd had no idea there were going to be oranges, and so hadn't brought out whatever it was that was necessary to buy them—I don't know whether it was coupons or merely cash. I remember feeling fearfully hurt that my own greengrocer, who always looks after me so well, had never thought to send me round any of these miraculously plentiful oranges. I stood dismally on the pavement practically drooling at the mouth as I gazed at the heaven of plenty from which I was so cruelly cut off. When I told B. about this on the phone she said a friend of hers had spoken the other day of dreaming of eating a banana and cream, and having it suddenly snatched away. He awoke weeping like hell!

July 14, 1943, was warm and sunny in London. For the Fighting French it was Bastille Day, and they and their friends danced to the music of a concertina in the mews outside Le Petit Club Français in St. James until well after midnight. But one Fighting Frenchman who was not celebrating the occasion was General Charles de Gaulle. He was fighting for his future, and, he believed, for the future of France.

By this time relations between the general and the leaders of the Western Allies had reached their lowest ebb. Winston Churchill found De Gaulle's arrogant attitude increasingly difficult to stomach, and he had difficulty in keeping his temper when they met. Though he had once been the general's most enthusiastic supporter, he now bitterly regretted recognizing him as the leader of the French. "After all we have done for him," he once said to his son, Randolph, "he has the impudence not only to be ungrateful, but to make it plain that he dislikes everything I stand for."

The PM had already cabled President Roosevelt, who shared his dislike of De Gaulle, to say: "I agree with you that no confidence can be placed in de Gaulle's friendship for the Allies."

In his war memoirs, Churchill was subsequently to claim that he understood why the general acted as he did. "He had to be rude to the British to prove to French eyes that he was not a British puppet," he wrote. "He certainly carried out this policy with perseverance." But the fact remained that he found De Gaulle impossibly rude, arrogant, importunate and monomaniacally ambitious, and like Henry V with Thomas Becket, he must often have wished aloud that someone would rid him of his unruly and unpleasant protegé.

Scalded Cats

If so, someone at the Special Branch of Scotland Yard must have heard him, because it was at about this time that the file on General de Gaulle was sent to 10 Downing Street for his perusal. There was material in it to involve the general in quite a public scandal—or so its compilers suggested.

FDR had no doubts that the Allies should rid themselves of Charles de Gaulle.* He too could not stand the general's high-handedness, but it was not so much his personal arrogance that he disliked as his insistence that France must be treated on exactly the same basis of equality as the United States and Britain. That was not part of Roosevelt's plan. In July *Time* magazine reported that FDR was supporting General Giraud as the leader of the French, mainly because he was a weaker and more amenable character, and that Washington was full of stories attacking De Gaulle's motives and personality.

Pet reporters of the State Department and the White House [reported *Time*] were called in and given confidential tips. . . . Wrote Harold Callender in the *New York Times:* "In the opinion of high American officials General de Gaulle is less interested in helping to win the war than in advancing his personal political fortunes." . . .

Why is the President so set against De Gaulle? Why all the inspired anti-De Gaulle stories? No matter how unlovable a personality, De Gaulle is still, to most living Frenchmen, the symbol of French resistance. What is the President's case against him?

The President's case appears to be this: he is convinced that the solution of European problems will be much easier if its basic lines are established by the three big powers—the United States, Great Britain and Russia. The President wants to assure all European powers, great and small, full inde-

---

* For those who find it difficult to understand why Churchill and FDR were so angry with De Gaulle, it should be pointed out that Washington's policy, with London's reluctant concurrence, was to subordinate De Gaulle to a French soldier much senior to him in rank but far weaker in personality, General Henri-Honoré Giraud. De Gaulle was determined to sabotage this plan, and missed no opportunity to assert himself. At about this time he reluctantly consented to an arrangement by which the French National Liberation Committee was established in Algiers, with Giraud as commander in chief of troops in North Africa and De Gaulle was made head of the forces in West Africa and the Middle East. But it was an arrangement which, De Gaulle made plain, he was going to wreck the moment the opportunity arose.

pendence and freedom. But he believes that they need not all be consulted; their voices would complicate a solution or even make it impossible. For that reason Mr. Roosevelt would prefer to have France absent when those solutions are worked out—in short, not only no De Gaulle but no Giraud.

That Bastille Day, Roosevelt sent Churchill a cable. The exact text has not been—and is not likely to be—released by either country, but its purport was that the U.S. President had learned that the British had a good case for arresting and firing De Gaulle, and urged the Prime Minister to do so.*

Obviously FDR knew about Scotland Yard's file.

After his experiences with Admiral Muselier, Charles de Gaulle had resolved that never again would he let the British authorities be involved in the domestic affairs of the Fighting French forces. Henceforward, he ordered, all arrests and punishment of members of the forces in England would be carried out by the Fighting French themselves. With this goal in mind, he agreed to the immediate expansion of the French intelligence organization (Bureau Central de Renseignements et d'Action), under the overall command of Colonel Passy (code name for Major André Dewavrin). Shortly after the Muselier affair, the BCRA had established its headquarters in a house of several stories in Duke Street, in Mayfair, and in a prison camp near the Free French barracks at Camberley, in Surrey. No details of what went on at either establishment were furnished to the British, but soon the Special Branch at Scotland Yard was tipped off by the SOE (Special Operations Executive) that it should look into the activities of the BCRA. A discreet surveillance was immediately begun, and soon some hair-raising facts emerged.

Duke Street, it turned out, was not only the headquarters of the BCRA but also its chief interrogation center, and the methods used by some of the French officers operating there made even hardened Scotland Yard officers wince. The file accumulated tales of brutal beatings, of terrified witnesses, of savage cross-examinations not only of Fighting Frenchmen, but of other French citizens, including the wives and girl friends of men who had been questioned. There were photographs in the file of men and women bruised and cut in the most peculiar

---

* On July 19, *Time* magazine reported: "From sources as unimpeachable as those which fostered the anti-De Gaulle stories had come many definite reports that Franklin Roosevelt even had won over Churchill to the sacking of General de Gaulle. Twice, it was said on high authority, Franklin Roosevelt had cabled Winston Churchill actually suggesting the arrest of De Gaulle. Churchill refused."

places, and there was an additional dossier on the punishment center at Camberley, where the treatment of prisoners was truly horrifying.

All this might have remained a nasty skeleton in De Gaulle's closet had not the "Affaire Dufour" forced the British into action. Lieutenant Dufour was a young and gallant member of the French army who had been wounded in the abdomen in France in 1940. Upon his recovery he joined the French resistance as an operator for British intelligence inside France, and his enterprise and daring had won him high praise from his superiors in London. When the Gestapo began to close in upon him, he was ordered to England and was smuggled across the French frontier to Spain and then via Gibraltar to London.

Dufour immediately expressed the wish to volunteer for the Fighting French forces, and duly presented himself to General de Gaulle at Carlton Gardens. After signing the controversial oath of allegiance, he put on his new uniform and proudly walked out into the streets of London, happy, free and eager to carry on the fight.

He did not remain free for long. Shortly after his induction, Lieutenant Dufour was asked to report to BCRA headquarters in Duke Street, where two Fighting French intelligence officers were awaiting him. He willingly gave them the information they asked for about his operations against the Nazis in France, but when he was then urged to give full details about all the British agents with whom he had worked in France, the names of his contacts both in France and in London, and the codes he had used, he pointed out that he had sworn an oath of secrecy to the British and could not possibly break it without their permission. "I will leave now and go and ask them," he said.

"That will not be necessary," one of the intelligence officers said. "You will tell us anyway. You are now a member of the Free French forces. As your superior officer, I order you to give me the details for which I ask."

"I cannot break my oath to the British," said Dufour.

"You can and you will," the intelligence officer said.

In the next four days Dufour was alternately coaxed, bullied and beaten. He was struck repeatedly with a steel rod, particularly in the region of the wound in his kidneys. At one point a girl he had met since his arrival in London was picked up at her home and brought to Duke Street, where she was slapped and threatened in front of Dufour. Still he would not tell the BCRA what they wanted to know.

Finally, in a state of physical collapse and in considerable pain, Dufour was hauled before a Free French court-martial on a trumped-up charge and sentenced to a term of imprisonment and reduction to the ranks. He found himself down on his knees in Camberley camp, scrubbing floors, until friends engineered his escape at the end of 1942. The French immediately listed him as a deserter.

All these facts were in a dossier forwarded to Winston Churchill, and in July 1943 a memorandum containing a damning indictment of General de Gaulle's attitude, his antipathy toward Britain and America, and his methods with his own countrymen began to be circulated in certain select circles in London. Its release was said to have been personally approved by the PM himself, and the word was that Churchill now agreed with Roosevelt that De Gaulle must go.

On July 22 Robert Boothby rose in the House of Commons to ask a question, and since most of the Members knew about it beforehand, they crowded into the Chamber to hear the Prime Minister's answer. By this time, Boothby had transferred his admiration from his own Prime Minister, who had admittedly treated him shabbily, to De Gaulle, for he considered the general the apotheosis of statesmanship and heroism, and he was infuriated by the rumors and sly gossip about him which were circulating in London. Hence, Boothby asked Churchill whether he was aware that a memorandum was circulating in London containing the most odious accusations against General de Gaulle, and if so, what steps he was taking to put an end to the spreading of such shocking lies.

To his astonishment and to an audible gasp from other Members, Churchill replied that a memorandum such as the Honourable Member mentioned had indeed been circulated and that he took complete responsibility for it. However, he could only discuss the nature of its contents if the House went into secret session, which would be arranged in the near future.

It seemed that the moment of truth had come: Churchill was ready to tell all. And if he told all, he would undoubtedly ask the House to back him in taking action against the controversial French leader—and that would mean the sack for De Gaulle, or at least withdrawal of Allied support and subsidy.

No word of the scandal appeared in British newspapers, for they were under censorship, but as MPs awaited the secret session, wild rumors suddenly began to circulate in the corridors that the quarrel was going to break into the open, and that the place where it would be settled was not in Parliament but in the law courts. For Dufour had gone to his solicitors and had asked them to take legal action against General de

Gaulle, Colonel Passy and four others for mistreatment and false imprisonment.

Now it was Winston Churchill's turn to feel harassed. Immediately after making his statement in the House he had been assailed by doubts. Even though the general was a thorn in his side, was he justified in treating him so ruthlessly and casting him aside? Moreover, was it politically wise? General de Gaulle was the darling of the British public, who cheered him wherever he went. They would not thank the Prime Minister now if after backing and praising him for so long, he suddenly revealed him as a trickster, a Fascist and anti-British to boot. So he let the days pass without the secret session being called, and when MPs asked about it they were fobbed off with excuses.

But what could Churchill do now? He could not stop the processes of English law. If Dufour insisted on following through with his action, the fat really would be in the fire, and De Gaulle was not the only one who might get burned.

Finally the Foreign Office had an inspiration. Pierre Viénot, Fighting French diplomatic representative in London, was called to the Foreign Office and handed a note about Dufour's proposed legal action. Dufour had, explained the note, "put into the hands of the British [law] courts a complaint for maltreatment against several French officers and against their leader, General de Gaulle. Because of the separation of powers, which in England is absolute, the British Government cannot prevent justice from taking its course. Furthermore, General de Gaulle does not have diplomatic immunity in this country. Perhaps the General could settle the matter by friendly agreement with Dufour? Otherwise, he will be implicated in the trial. We must urge General de Gaulle to attach serious importance to this matter, for a conviction is likely, and would constitute an occasion for disagreeable publicity, particularly in the United States press, with regard to the methods and procedures of Fighting France."*

What happened next is the subject of conflicting stories. There is a firm of solicitors in London which might, if not bound by the laws of the profession, furnish proof that Dufour consented to withdraw his action on payment of damages, doctors' bills and £3,000. On the other hand, General de Gaulle stoutly maintains in his memoirs that he refused to cringe before this blackmail and sacked out of hand those of his advisers who pressed him to settle out of court. What is certain is

---

* De Gaulle, *Memoirs*, Vol. II.

that the case was never heard, the secret session was never held, and that in November 1943, General de Gaulle ousted his rival, General Giraud, and became undisputed head of the Fighting French. On November 22, 1943, the Committee of National Liberation met in session in Algiers. Giraud was co-president with De Gaulle, but De Gaulle's influence over the members was considerably stronger, and on this occasion the Gaullist members knew what they were to do. At the end of the meeting, Giraud was out and so were three of his nominees. As a face-saver, it was announced that General Giraud would continue as military chief, but the Gaullist spokesman added, "For the time being." Everyone knew that the struggle for power was over and that De Gaulle had won.

With the British public, he was more popular than ever. Whenever his lofty figure was seen in London there were scattered cheers and a rush of autograph hunters. "Good old Charley!" the Cockneys cried. But Winston Churchill had other names for him, and they would become even more colorful in the months to come.

no matter how reluctant he still was to risk the inevitable loss of life involved, Winston Churchill realized that there must be an invasion of Europe, almost certainly across the Channel into northern France. At his meeting with Roosevelt in Casablanca in January 1943 he had agreed with his American allies that a landing would be made some time in 1944. Now a new conference had been scheduled ("Quadrant") for August 1943, at which the statesmen, scientists and technical experts would meet in Quebec to discuss with the Anglo-American Joint Chiefs of Staff what was called "the Grand Strategy of Invasion." In London the experts were busy preparing for the conference under the general direction of Lord Louis Mountbatten (then Commander in Chief, Combined Operations) and the watchful eye of his principal scientific adviser, Professor John Desmond Bernal.

Not even the Americans were more eager than Bernal to see an Allied army drive its way into Nazi-occupied Europe. An exuberant revolutionary and unabashed Communist, Bernal was one of those who believed that Russia was taking the brunt of the war and that the Allies were not doing enough to relieve the pressure. But though he was a fervid advocate of a policy of opening up a second front in France, his ideological bias did not blind him to the perils of a cross-Channel invasion, nor to the difficulties of persuading Winston Churchill that it could be done without risking casualties on the scale of another Gallipoli.

One of the negative lessons of the costly and abortive Dieppe raid had been to show Combined Operations Command what they could not and must not attempt in future: an invasion through a fortified port. The defenders would always be able to batter back the assaulting forces, or to hold them up long enough for reinforcements to arrive.

Mountbatten was later to put the situation to be faced in 1943 in these words: "Since we could not capture a defended port in workable state by direct assault, and almost certainly not by any encircling movement within the necessary time, and since we could not maintain ourselves ashore on the coast of France unless we did have the shelter and facilities of a port, we were driven to the conclusion that we should have to bring our own port along with us from England. I cannot claim that this followed inevitably from the lessons of Dieppe, but the germ of this idea sprang from our experience at Dieppe, and it was later put up by Captain [John] Hughes-Hallett [Royal Navy]. From this germ sprang the great prefabricated mobile harbors known as Mulberry A and Mulberry B which made the Normandy landings possible."*

It had not taken long for Hughes-Hallett and the team of civilian technical experts surrounding him to convince Professor Bernal that it was a practicable proposition for an invading army to take its own harbors with it, even across twenty to fifty miles of hostile sea. But it was harder to persuade Mountbatten, and he would have to approve before the proposal could go to Churchill for his sponsorship at the forthcoming Quebec meeting. The trouble was that at this time Mountbatten was obsessed—as was Lindemann—with the scheme called "Habakkuk" which had been proposed as a potential war winner. This was a project to launch a flat floating iceberg 2,000 feet long which could be moved by motor power to different strategic positions and used as a runway for bomber and fighter planes. The iceberg was to be made of a frozen mixture of salt water and wood pulp which had been invented by an eccentric genius named Geoffrey Pyke, and therefore called pykrete. Both Lindemann and Mountbatten knew that Churchill was a dedicated gadgeteer and that "Habakkuk" would appeal to him. In fact, Mountbatten had already sold him on the project by bursting into his bathroom while the Prime Minister was in the tub and dropping first a lump of ice and then a lump of pykrete into the

---

* Hervé Cras, *Les Canadiens à Dieppe*.

steaming water. Churchill's protests were stilled when he saw that the ice melted but that the pykrete floated and didn't sink.

Hence, Bernal had to divert his chief's enthusiasms from floating airstrips and enlist his support for Hughes-Hallett's floating harbors. Only with Mountbatten's support could he begin to work on Churchill.*

The Prime Minister seemed fated to have his wartime ablutions interrupted, for it was in yet another bathroom (in his suite aboard the liner *Queen Mary* on the way to the Quadrant conference) that Bernal demonstrated the special qualities of the floating harbors the British experts had envisioned for the invasion, and secured the PM's promise to back the project at the meetings with the Chiefs of Staff.

During the Quadrant meetings Bernal was asked where in France the harbors would be installed: in other words, where the invading troops would land, for it was the harbors which would now decide the location, and they could go only where there were offshore shoals onto which blockships could be sunk. He knew that certain members of the Joint Chiefs of Staff (particularly air force brass like Sholto Douglas, Commander in Chief, Fighter Command, RAF) favored a landing on the Pas de Calais.† But Bernal also knew that the Calais area was jammed with German concrete and guns, and he agreed with his colleagues who dubbed any landing in that area "Operation Sacrifice." For this reason he was happy to be able to tell the meeting that there was only one beach along the whole coastline of Western Europe from Holland to the Bay of Biscay whose shoals were right for the emplacement of Mulberry harbors. This was Arromanches, in Normandy, and the landing would have to be there and nowhere else.

Back in London an Anglo-American team of experts got down to the job of building what amounted to two satellite towns—towns that would float—in less than nine months. The project involved 70 large and 120 small units, 250,000 cubic yards of concrete, 7,000 tons of

---

* Mountbatten never lost his enthusiasm for "Habakkuk." At Quebec he gave a demonstration of pykrete's remarkable qualities: placing a block of the material and a block of ice side by side in his room in the Château Frontenac, he invited General "Hap" Arnold, chief of the U.S. Army Air Force, to cleave the two with an ax he handed him. Arnold split the ice easily but failed completely with the pykrete. After which Mountbatten triumphantly took out his revolver, and to show pykrete's indestructibility, fired a bullet into it. The bullet ricocheted and narrowly missed Arnold's head as it buried itself in the wall. (See *Mulberry*, by M. Harrison.)

† The distance was short—twenty-two miles—and providing fighter cover would be easier.

steel bars, 65,000 tons of concrete and a labor force which eventually amounted to 20,000 men.*

Winston Churchill and his advisers agreed to a plan for the invasion of France across the English Channel on May 1, 1944. "Mulberry," the construction of the floating harbors to accompany the invading armies, was accepted as an integral part of the invasion plan, and the Joint Chiefs of Staff (in their Directive CCS 307/2 September 1943) accepted the fact that the task facing the Anglo-American engineers who would build the harbors was gargantuan. "The magnitude of the job is unprecedented," they noted, "and it can be accomplished only under the highest priority." They had £10,000,000 to spend, but everything was in short supply: steel, cement, labor, and even space on which to build the caissons, piers, all-steel breakwaters (known as bombardons) and the harbors themselves. One spot thankfully seized upon by the technical experts was Barking Marshes by the Thames, where Lieutenant Davies had exploded the St. Paul's Cathedral bomb in 1940. Soon 3,500 Irish laborers were camped on the marshes and working night and day on one of the harbors.†

Professor Bernal had confided to his friend Professor P. M. S. Blackett that the return to Europe would be across the Arromanches beach. Though he was engaged on his own chores at the Air Ministry in connection with jet engines, some days later Blackett appeared at the Mulberry headquarters in the Metropolitan Hotel on Northumberland Avenue.‡ "I thought you might like to know," he told the astonished, and then grateful, experts, "that France is not where we always thought it was. I have been studying my records and the charts. It is three feet farther away than we have always been told. Look, I will show you"— and he proceeded to demonstrate his calculations. The information was more than welcome; it would be invaluable when it came to dealing with tides and soundings.

Bernal was working on charts and records of his own. His task was to assemble a complete picture of Normandy Bay and all the beaches on either side of it at Arromanches: depth, quality of sand, shingle, mud, and nature of winds and tides. At one point a midget submarine

---

* Report to the Combined Chiefs of Staff, Washington, September 28, 1943. Quoted in Harrison, *op. cit.*

† When the time came, a breach was cut in the Thames bank, the marshes (below Thames level) were flooded, and the parts floated out.

‡ The offices were cramped and had nothing on the door except the number 473; inside was a complete scale model of a Mulberry harbor.

was towed to Normandy, where it lay on the sea bed until nightfall, when its three-man crew rowed ashore and collected samples of sand and rocks, and charted shorelines and underwater obstructions.

Early in December 1943, a row blew up in Parliament and the newspapers when Sir Oswald Mosley, leader of the British Union of Fascists, was released from jail. He had been detained under Regulation 18b since 1940, but in the last twelve months had been allowed to share two cells in Holloway Prison with his wife. Now he was being freed, the Home Secretary, Herbert Morrison, announced, because he was suffering from phlebitis. Public reaction to the announcement in the capital was almost uniformly hostile, and there were cheers when Communist party orators called for a strike to protest the release and shouted, "Why don't they let the bastard die in jail?"

Polly Wright read the news of Mosley's release in her morning paper and at once a memory, the lovely aroma of rich red wine, haunted her. She herself had never seen Mosley in Holloway, for the married Fascists had been given a wing on the far side of the prison where they lived a cozy communal life flapping their hands and kowtowing to their Führer from afar. But one day, after a "big nob from the Government," as the matron called him, had been in to see Mosley—for the British Fascist still had many friends in high places—she saw the fat Mosley "maiden" who now acted as batwoman to the Leader and his wife coming along the corridor with a tray in her hands. She was taking the Mosleys' midday meal to be washed up, and as she passed, Polly smelled its remains. It was a time of great despair when she would have given her all for a great whacking alcoholic drink. By God, she thought, the bastards have actually had wine with their lunch, would you believe it? It was all she could do not to burst into tears with envy and frustration.

But Polly did not begrudge the Mosleys their freedom, for it was hard not to feel sympathy for anyone who had suffered the rigors and humiliations of Regulation 18b. What were people squawking about? If they wanted to keep him locked up, why didn't they put him on trial? But what would they charge him with—wanting Hitler and national socialism to win the war? It was a reprehensible wish, if they could prove he cherished it, but was it to stop people from thinking reprehensible thoughts for which this war was being fought?

"Pardon me for being rude," said Polly Wright, "but may I ask what we are fighting this war for, anyway? Will someone please tell me? Or do I sound bitter?" But she said the words into her mirror in the privacy of her room. Having convinced the authorities at last that falling in love with a Nazi didn't make her one, she had managed to get out of Holloway in late 1942, and she had no intention of being sent back again for spreading gloom and despondency by speaking her stray thoughts in public. She couldn't help smiling wryly, though, when she read in her paper that "Sir Oswald and Lady Mosley were driven away from Holloway by a friend after their release. Sir Oswald will stay with friends in the country to recuperate from his illness and his prison experiences."

The only person Polly had met when she came out of Holloway was a pale man with glittery eyes in a sleek, tight suit. He was waiting for his girl friend, just finishing a stretch for rifling the pockets of a soldier-customer, and those eyes burned eagerly when he saw Polly. "You're a pretty girl," he said. "Got a job to go to, my dear?"

"No."

"I can put you in the way of lots of money, and a good time too. There's lots of lolly around in London these days."

"And lots of people like you too," Polly said. Then she repeated a phrase which she had learned in Holloway, and even he looked shocked when he heard it from such tender lips.

No, there had been no resting in the country for Polly after *her* prison experiences. Her ex-husband had found a room for her in Marylebone and paid the rent on it for three months, and she was grateful to him. Eventually she got a job as a secretary-typist to a small, fat, asthmatic man in Soho who was making a small fortune (which he did not share with her) buying second-hand jewelry and selling it to the big stores. He paid her in cash and she had to lie about it at the Labour Exchange, so she had been "directed" to do twenty-four hours' work a week at a factory in Camden Town making camouflage nets. The rope played such havoc with her hands that she could hardly type the following morning, and she had taken to wearing gloves to conceal the welts. But she got by, and for the time being she shunned company. She never even went near her old pub, The Gluepot, for fear of running into former friends; she didn't think she could face them yet.

For her Christmas meal that year Polly Wright had an omelette made from three black-market eggs, and a quarter of a bottle of whisky. She wondered what Sir Oswald and Lady Mosley were having.

*   *   *

From the diary of Miss Vere Hodgson:

Sunday, December 19, 1943: So we are near to another Christmas of war. This is the fifth, and we are pretty well on our beam ends as far as Christmas fare is concerned. Though we all have enough to eat, there is no chance of turkey, chicken or goose, or even the despised rabbit. If we can get a little mutton that is the best we can hope for.

There are a few Christmas puddings around but not many. However, I managed to get one. This is marvellous because many people have not been able to get any at all. There are shops with three Christmas puddings and 800 registered customers.

The most worrying event of the week has been the illness of Mr. Churchill. He has been taken with pneumonia.*

The shops are full of expensive goods which only munition workers can afford, but no decorations anywhere. The best I've heard are what American soldiers have done for children somewhere. They've given them a great dinner and a Christmas tree and Father Christmas arriving in a Flying Fortress. I've seen very little in the shops except for one wet Saturday morning when I scoured the West End for gents' socks, not utility or wool, and of the prewar length. I found them at last, and I hope they will give satisfaction. Otherwise I give the shops a wide berth.

Won't it be lovely if this time next year there is no black-out. The only worry for us now is coal. It seems as if it is going to be a hard winter, though we have had no snow. There have been a great number of deaths from flu this week and thousands are down with it. In fact, they've had to put off the few passenger trains there are because the drivers and signals-men are down with flu. I hope they run one for me on Thursday [to her home in Birmingham]. It seems the epidemic has now spread all over Europe, and it is like the plague, though a quicker and less unsightly death.

Well, a happy Christmas to all my readers, and also a New Year without the shadow of air raids on our beloved island!†

---

* He had fallen ill after meeting Roosevelt and Stalin at the Teheran Conference, and was recuperating at Marrakech by this time.

† Vere Hodgson sent copies of her diary to relatives in England and various parts of the world.

Part Four

LIGHT AT LAST

15

The Run-Up

It needed a fresh perspective to see London as it was
at the beginning of 1944, for the eyes of Londoners
themselves were strained from four and a quarter years
of war and they had become apathetically unconscious
of the way they and their capital looked. London was
an old Mother Courage of a town: sagging, seedy,
knocked-about, dirty, rheumy-eyed, her face pock-marked, lined, and
furrowed with pain, suffering and deprivation.

But if a Cockney had been asked about his city now, his answer
might have been, "Oh, jogging along, you know, weathering through."
Time had erased peacetime memories with which to compare the city,
and its citizens had learned to live and come to terms with queues, shortages, shabby clothes, overcrowded transportation, underheated rooms,
the blackout,* and the dull feeling even immediately after a meal that
one's appetite had not been satisfied.

During one of his visits to Dublin, Charles Snow found himself
walking down Gresham Street in the bright lights of the Irish capital
sucking on a bar of execrable local chocolate and feeling that man
could hardly ask for anything better in life. He brought back the menu
from the Gresham Hotel to show it to his girl friend, who promptly
burst into tears.

---

* Actually the dimout now, for some amelioration of street lighting had been
allowed in 1944.

But most Londoners had lost the capacity to know what they were missing and what had gone out of the life of the great city. It took foreigners, particularly the Americans now swarming across the Atlantic, to see the capital clear and true.

One such visitor was a young man from South Orange, New Jersey. Private First Class Charles Gillen had come over to Europe with the 28th Infantry Division in the fall of 1943 but he did not get his first leave until January 1944. It was for eight days, long enough to allow him to travel up to London from his camp at Tenby, in Pembrokeshire, on the Welsh border, a journey he would never forget.

A U.S. army truck dropped him one January morning outside a large house in Hans Crescent, in Belgravia, where by now most of the great rows of Regency houses had either been bombed out or taken over as clubs and billets for Allied troops in London. His was manned by the formidable women of the WVS (Women's Voluntary Service), and they gave Gillen his first look at the English class system. "The place was largely managed by women volunteers of the upper middle class," he remembers, "and by one or two titled ladies, and was staffed by working class girls, and the cold and to me rather contemptuous manner in which the former spoke to the latter was quite fascinating because I was used to the belligerently egalitarian attitudes of the States."

He had been advised to take his meals at the Hans Crescent billet because of the food shortage, and had been given ration chits for this purpose. But that would have meant breaking up his trips around the city twice a day, so he either went hungry or made the acquaintance of Lyons restaurants, pubs, fish-and-chips shops and Chinese cafés, where he ate starchily but happily.

"London was my first experience of a foreign city, and it enthralled me with its ubiquitous reminders of its literary greatness: I made a pilgrimage to Keats's house in Hampstead, and visited the literary shrines of Chelsea, and saw Arnold Bennett's house in Cadogan Square close by my billet, and had many other reminders of literary greatness in the London County Council's plaques. London's long history jumped out at a newcomer everywhere, and I made trips to St. Paul's, the Tower (which was closed), the Inns of Court (open), got lost repeatedly in the City but found my way around quite handily in Mayfair, and, of course, went to the House of Commons. The Commons was then *hors de combat,* and oddly enough the thing about the place that intrigued me most was the sight of the empty terrace—you see, I had read several times of the swank of having 'tea on the Terrace.' "

Gillen was very much aware that his wide-eyed appreciation of

London and his enthrallment with its sights and sounds was not always shared by his fellow GIs. At any moment now, they would be on their way across the Channel to butt their heads against Hitler's Fortress Europe, and their mood was to eat, drink and be merry, for tomorrow . . .

"They traveled in packs, and seemed to head straight for the flesh market in Piccadilly Circus, or tried to get drunk on the weak, warm beer (whiskey was practically unobtainable) or to have a black-market meal of steak and eggs, and they shunned the 'Limeys,' regarding them distastefully and disdainfully. This dislike was heartily reciprocated by the English, particularly as the American soldiery was paid on a far more lavish scale than the average Englishman: when a London taxi was hailed simultaneously by an English civilian and an American soldier, the cab driver invariably stopped for the American because he knew he could charge any rate he liked (Americans seemed to consider it *infra dig* to know about British coinage) and that he would be given a lordly tip into the bargain. The boxes in the theaters (to my observation) were almost always filled with American soldiers, usually champing on dead cigars and always exuding an ineffable boredom, while the English in the stalls regarded them resentfully."

January was comparatively warm in London that year and Gillen traveled mostly on the tops of buses.

"Since American soldiers seldom ventured beyond central London, I was often the subject of the curiosity of the 'clippies,' the women conductors of wartime. I went to Wimbledon and Limehouse, Dulwich and Hampstead, Putney and Shepherd's Bush. Everywhere the scenes were somehow what I had expected of them from my reading about London: Lilliputian, or grim, or ornate, and I often felt the 'shock of recognition.' The neighborhoods away from the center were not nearly so crowded as they are today. There were not many men of military age about, and the women were mostly obviously housewives out shopping. The general feeling was one of uncrowdedness. There was comparatively little motor traffic, just the buses and taxis, few civilian cars. There was a prevalent drabness, too—the austerity of wartime, a lack of color and the gaiety of new shop fronts and no street lighting helped to produce this effect. Everywhere the air raids had knocked out houses and big buildings which had not been replaced, producing a gap-toothed effect."

The days of the Blitz were long since over, but the "scalded cat" raids still continued; practically every night of Gillen's leave the air-raid warnings sounded, the searchlights flicked on out of the blackout, and the barrage of guns and rockets opened up. One night, just as he was going down into Knightsbridge Underground Station, the great ring of antiaircraft guns in Hyde Park began shooting just behind him.

"They seemed to be firing some sort of rocket-propelled missile because one felt one's body lifting upward with every round fired; it was a most curious sensation. A little crowd gathered in the area of the station in the hopes of observing something of the action skyward, but the clouds were impenetrable, although the noise was thrilling enough. Just next to me was a couple who seemed to be viewing the spectacle against their better judgment. 'You know,' said the man to the woman, 'this is the way that fifty people were killed in a raid on Battersea— gawking up when a stick of bombs fell on 'em.' I shuddered slightly at the picture this conjured up and then, a few seconds later, I heard a low whistling sound above me. The noise grew rapidly louder; the little crowd of Englishmen around me affected indifference and did not budge, so that I could not possibly be the one to run to shelter. As the screech grew louder I began to tremble and in the crescendo of sound of the last few seconds I was certain that my time had come. Then something hollowly metallic, like a length of pipe, struck the street about a block away, and bounded around with a loud jangling. Apparently I had heard part of an antiaircraft round returning to earth. I was shaken, petrified, but no one around me had turned a hair."

Nearly every night the young American went to the theatre, which was just different enough from Broadway to be fascinating to him. Buskers still plied their trade outside the theatre, entertaining the queue with music or songs or acrobatics, and he found this custom exotic. At the Windmill the girls were still kicking their legs, and the nudes were still valiantly breasting the flood of male stares from the stalls below. Gillen preferred New York burlesque, but there was one revue starring a comedian named Sid Field which he enjoyed hugely. Field won the heart of every GI in the audience in an uproarious skit of a brash American air force officer, a type from whom everyone was suffering in those days.

"One night I went to the Haymarket to see *Love for Love* with Gielgud and (I think) Ralph Richardson. It was a very fine thing, and played with a gloss one seldom saw in New York. About halfway through, two large signs on either side of the proscenium arch suddenly lit up. 'ALERT' they read, meaning that the Luftwaffe was visiting somewhere in the London area. The audience ignored the lit-up signs, the play's cast ignored the signs, and I, in American uniform, could not possibly get up and conspicuously seek shelter in the face of such sang-froid, although the rumblings of the ack-ack were now quite close. It was an impressive show of English coolness and phlegm."

After the theatre, Gillen usually headed for Piccadilly Circus. "The Circus, particularly that part of it around the foot of Glasshouse Street and the foot of Coventry Street, then reminded me of nothing so much as the Third Circle of Hell. You must picture it as almost completely blacked out, although one was allowed to use a flashlight with an anemic bulb and a blue-coated lens. These weak little things cast a sickly dribble of bluish light that had no effect whatever on the inky night. Packed along the sidewalks of the Circus, in what seemed to be thousands, were prostitutes of every age, shape and size, although one couldn't be sure of individual looks because the pitiful flashlight revealed very little even when swept upward closely from toes to head, a procedure most potential customers seemed to be using. One was solicited every few steps, sometimes in the baldest words, sometimes in more genteel phrases like: 'Want to come home with me, love?' One curious thing was this: there were a lot of Continental accents among the English ones, and I had the puzzled thought: Did the whores escape from Europe just to cash in on the Golconda in Piccadilly Circus?"

It was the memory of Piccadilly by day and by night which most haunted Gillen at the end of his furlough. "Uniforms of all the Allied services abounded, a good many new to me, but I was really captivated by the get-up of the British Women's Land Army—brownish jodhpurs stuck into swagger knee-length boots, and a wild sort of Australian big-brimmed hat. I had to inquire as to just what the hell these girls were supposed to be, and after I had been enlightened by one of them I tried to imagine them in this get-up ministering to potatoes, turnips and cabbages.

"The predominating uniforms around, though, were American. The Yanks seemed to just swamp the center of London then, most of them on leave like me, I suppose, but reinforced by the thousands stationed in the 'Little America' around Grosvenor Square or the many other American military establishments around London. I could well sympathize with the natives' resentments and fears in the face of this flood."

But the time was not far off when suddenly the streets of London would empty of this horde, and the transatlantic cry of "Taxi!" would be as rare around Berkeley Square as the song of the nightingale.

And then the natives would miss them.

ondon had no respite from German air raids that spring, and
though in weight and frequency they were nothing like the
brutal and unrelenting attacks the RAF and the U.S. Army Air Force
were now making against German cities, Londoners found them wearing on their nerves and temper. What German bombs lacked in size was
made up in ingenuity. Worst to deal with was the so-called butterfly
bomb which came down in showers and was timed to detonate on impact, by time fuse, or on contact. It was extremely difficult to defuse,
and bomb squads called it "the Beast." A big shower of them could tie
up a whole district for days.

Not many people were killed or injured any more, but the alerts
were of long duration, the antiaircraft barrage was ferocious, and
Whitehall, the City and the House of Commons were taking one more
round of punishment that shattered the last windows and tore bigger
holes in the walls.

"I walked past Westminster Abbey," wrote Vere Hodgson on Sunday, March 5, "and the less said about that the better. It will soon be
all right again, as an army of men were working on it. I did not try to
go to St. James's, as I believe it is rather nasty. I see that Mr. Partridge
[who owned a well-known picture gallery] tried to get into his treasures
when the firemen were pouring water on the place, had an altercation
with the police, and has been fined £75. I am very sorry for him because
it must be agonising to think that your Rembrandts are being soused
with water and you cannot get in to save them."

But it was hard to guess, on such a Sunday morning in the spring
of 1944, that only a few hours before, thousands of shells had been
shot over London's housetops and that a great battle had been raging in
the skies overhead. The streets were full of pedestrians airing their dogs,
and of soldiers on leave. The air was balmy with the smell of spring. In
Hyde Park, at Speakers' Corner, the same crowds hung around the
same orators preaching doom or revolution or obscure religions.

"What are we fighting for?" cried a speaker.

"Spam!" replied someone in the crowd.

"Who are the two greatest men in the world?" asked another
orator.

"Flanagan and Allen,"* a heckler suggested.

It took so little to cheer people up. In March, enough citrus fruit

* A team of stage comedians.

had arrived in Britain for a special issue to be made to shops in London. "There are lemons about!" wrote Vere Hodgson. "I've had an orgy of pancakes.* We haven't had them for years. There are oranges, but I haven't got any yet."

A couple of weeks later everyone in London seemed to have found them, however, and like the stones which were everywhere during a cherry glut in 1941, orange peel now lay in the gutters of Oxford Street and Leicester Square to demonstrate the change in the national diet.

Such luxuries were rare—"The meat ration lasts for three evening meals," Vere Hodgson wrote to her cousin in Rhodesia. "I don't think anyone can make it go further, whatever you have. This covers Saturday, Sunday and Monday. Tuesday and Wednesday I have a handful of rice or macaroni dogged up in some way with curry or cheese. But the cheese ration is so small now that there is rarely any left. Thursday I have an order with the dairy for a pound of sausages. These do for Thursday, Friday and Saturday lunch. They do not, however, taste much of sausage. I understand they are nearly all soya-bean flour and the flavour is nothing much. However, they look like sausages and we pretend they are. Of course a little fish would help a lot but there are always long queues for it and my dinner hour is only one hour and I never have time to wait. But you see, we manage and we are not hungry."

On April 1 the government announced that henceforth all coastal areas along the Channel facing France would be prohibited areas; only people living in seaside resorts and the coastal fringe would be allowed in. Police and military police manned the main-line stations and boarded southbound trains to check the identity of travelers.

On April 17 a young co-ordinator in a munitions factory observed an odd phenomenon when he came up to London. "I have suddenly noticed the *absence* of American servicemen both in buses and the Underground. None of them to be seen in the streets, either. I have quite missed them, being used to seeing many of them in the course of the day."

For some time, speculation about the second front had been a conversational gambit in every pub and restaurant in London. Everybody had a guess about the date and a theory about the landing, and

---

* The English like their pancakes, or crêpes, sprinkled with sugar and lemon juice.

in every group there was always some chairborne belligerent who would say, "I don't understand what we're waiting for. Why don't we just barge in on them and batter our way through to Berlin? That's what the Russians are doing, aren't they?"

But suddenly a restraint seemed to fall upon the armchair strategists, as if the knowledge that the invasion of Europe might really be coming at long last impelled them to face the horrid reality of what it might mean. "The second-front talk buzzes," wrote one woman to Mass-Observation from her home in West London. "Some hope that the present bombing offensive is designed if possible to avoid a really bloody second front. Most think it will be a blood bath."

On March 21 Captain Harry Butcher, the naval Aide to General Eisenhower, had written in his diary: "The target date for Overlord* is May 31, 1944. Will the Channel run red with blood?"

Vere Hodgson wrote: "What I must remark upon is the beauty of the spring in London just now. I suppose it has always been just as beautiful, but it is such a joy to us this year after five years of war that I notice it especially. There are such a lot of lovely prunus trees all in full flower and a wild cherry on the opposite side of the road. It seems like a wedding every time I pass. The plane trees are a golden green just now and my chestnut has all its candles out and the lilacs are coming on fast. It is the best time for London. As I pass the park on the bus, the beauty of the trees is overpowering. They look like the shades of the blessed."

By this time Professor J. D. Bernal, deep in preparations for the landings in France, was a familiar figure at conferences at Supreme Headquarters, Allied Expeditionary Force, in London. On more than one occasion, when he wanted more information about landing hazards, Eisenhower took the professor home with him to his quarters in Kingston Vale, on the far side of Richmond Park. No one now remembered that during the period of the phony war Bernal had refused all except passive help to the war effort, and the fact that he was still a card-carrying member of the Communist party was ignored—that is, by everyone except Security at SHAEF.

One morning early in 1944 Professor Bernal called C. P. Snow at his office in Tothill Mansions. "Bernal wanted a former colleague of his —let's call him Williams—to be attached to him immediately," Snow

* The name for the invasion of Europe.

recalls. "This chap was an expert on solid structures, like beaches, and Bernal needed him for the D-Day preparations. It so happened that Williams was working on something with fairly high priority in another government department, and I knew it was going to be difficult. But I worked at it, and after some pressure I managed to get Williams released and posted to Bernal."

Snow thought no more about it until six weeks later when Lord Mountbatten* telephoned him. He was very angry. "What the bloody hell do you mean," he barked, "not getting Williams transferred to Bernal as he requested?"

"Sorry," replied Snow, "I thought it had been arranged."

"It has not been arranged," said Mountbatten. "Will you look into it? And don't take too long about it," he added. "If you don't get cracking today, I'm going to take it up with the PM tomorrow."

Snow promised to do his best and put down the telephone, puzzled. Then suddenly the reason for the delay hit him. "I rang up the chap who was in charge of security at Supreme Headquarters and told him to come over and see me without delay."

When the security officer arrived, Snow said, "I've just been told from high up that Williams hasn't been allowed to join Bernal at Supreme Headquarters. I want to know why."

The security man hesitated.

"Look," Snow continued, "this matter is going to Winston Churchill tomorrow, so you'd better come clean with me. It's about Williams' security clearance, I suppose?"

The security man nodded glumly.

"What's wrong with him? What have you got against him?"

Once more the man hesitated. "I couldn't possibly tell even you," he said at last.

Snow drew a deep breath. "Look, man," he said, "I've told you already that this matter is going to the PM tomorrow. Bernal has asked for Williams, and what Bernal wants he both needs and gets. If the PM hears we are standing in his way, all our heads will roll. Now tell me: What's the black mark against Williams?"

"Well," said the security man, "it's like this. We've discovered that before the war Williams used to work very closely indeed with a notorious Communist."

---

* Bernal had been Mountbatten's chief scientific adviser until the latter's appointment as Commander in Chief, South-East Asia.

"And who was the notorious Communist?" asked Snow.

"Bernal," the security man replied sheepishly.

Snow, Bernal, Blackett and their friends walked around London that spring with a nasty prickling sensation at the back of their necks, and every time an airplane passed overhead they would look up and stare at it intently. Those acquaintances who remembered Snow's misery during the height of the Blitz put his edginess down to nerves. "He's getting bomb-happy again," they said.

But it wasn't edginess that was causing the scientists, the War Cabinet and Eisenhower and his invasion staff at SHAEF to look overhead during the lovely spring days and nights of April and May. They knew what Londoners did not: that at any moment Hitler's secret weapons—pilotless planes and rockets—might come winging in to spread death and destruction among them.

"It wasn't so bad for the generals and the Cabinet ministers," says Snow, "because although they knew of the menace that was threatening London they were able to talk about it among themselves. We who lived the lives of ordinary Londoners and moved around with ordinary people could not. It was a curious feeling being with friends in a pub at night. Talking about the invasion, they would voice their apprehensions about the slaughter which might soon be facing our troops, and of their own guilt in being safe in London when it happened. And one couldn't succumb to the temptation and say, 'Don't feel guilty. You'll be in a hell of a dangerous spot yourself any moment now. London may be just as bad as the beaches.' "

When would the invasion begin? Everyone was asking the question. In pubs, people laid bets; factories ran sweepstakes on the exact time. In London there was no doubt in anyone's mind that it must be a matter of days rather than weeks. Uninterruptedly, in the warm May sunshine or the cool blue night, bombers flew low over the rooftops on their way to smash the railway communication centers in France and Germany. Foreign diplomats had been officially informed that until further notice they would neither be allowed to travel in or out of the United Kingdom, nor send messages to their governments in code.

The only American troops left in London were chairborne types, and they had no desire to eat, drink and be merry. All the troops had gone south to rendezvous with the invasion barges, and the "Piccadilly commandos," the whores, were not the only ones in London who would miss them. The great city went about its daily business with its mind on other things, and waited and waited and waited.

Charles de Gaulle was in Algiers and in a state of cold anger with Winston Churchill. The ban on the transmission of coded diplomatic messages from London included the representatives of Fighting France, and, not without reason, he considered this a deliberate insult to himself and his organization. Was he not to be trusted?

As far as Churchill and Roosevelt were concerned, he was not. Their relations with the general had gone from bad to worse, and they now considered him not only arrogant and unco-operative but unreliable as well. FDR in particular felt this so strongly that in the days before the invasion he would not willingly have trusted De Gaulle with the name of his third cousin, and he had instructed Eisenhower that when D-Day came he was welcome to use every French soldier he wished—except De Gaulle. He was to be kept out of it.

On May 24 the House of Commons held a debate on foreign affairs. Churchill made the main speech of the day, and within minutes after he had finished the Lobbies and the smoking room were buzzing with comment. To everyone's surprise the Prime Minister had warmly praised General Franco's Spain for its neutrality in the war, and had spoken of France and of De Gaulle with a coldness which was almost palpable. Friends of the general among the MPs were either furious or distressed, not least Robert Boothby, who considered Churchill's cavalier treatment of the French leader to be little short of scandalous. But it was Harold Nicolson who rose to reply to the Prime Minister:

"It seems to me and many Frenchmen that the United States Government, with His Majesty's Government in their train, instead of helping the French and welcoming them, lose no opportunity of administering any snub which ingenuity can devise and ill-manners perpetrate. I hope that the Foreign Secretary [who was due to speak after him] will go further than the negative and even ungracious statement made on this subject by the Prime Minister. It is most unwise, most weak and most ill-informed of the United States Government to refuse to accord any special recognition to the [De Gaulle] National Committee and Provisional Government. I am convinced that this is a grave error of policy."

Whether or not this rebuke hit home, Churchill realized that he may have gone too far in making his dislike of the French leader so publicly plain. On June 3 he sent his own aircraft to Algiers to bring the general back to London, and the following day De Gaulle joined him on a special train drawn up at a siding near Portsmouth. Here, close to General Eisenhower's headquarters, Churchill and several of his ministers, including Anthony Eden and Ernest Bevin, were waiting for the invasion to begin. *

The meeting between the two leaders began badly and ended worse. When De Gaulle entered Churchill's suite he found the South African premier, Field Marshal Jan Smuts, with him. A few months previously Smuts had delivered a much-publicized speech in which he called France a "third-rate power" and suggested that her only chance in the postwar world lay in joining the British Commonwealth. For this reason De Gaulle now refused to shake his hand.

Soon Churchill and the general were quarreling bitterly, much to the embarrassment of the others present. Churchill was urging De Gaulle to bend a little, to go to the United States and talk to Roosevelt, to make concessions in order to secure American support for his administration. De Gaulle was haughtily insisting that he didn't care what the Americans did or said because he was France, and all Frenchmen would recognize him as such. He launched into a bitter attack on U.S. policy and its insults to him and his country. "How do you expect us to come to terms on this basis?" he asked.

"And you! How do you expect that the British should take a position separate from that of the United States?" Churchill blazed back. He drew an angry breath and then said words that De Gaulle would always remember, words that would color Anglo-French relations in the postwar world for as long as De Gaulle was in power.

"We are going to liberate Europe," said Churchill, "but it is because the Americans are in agreement with us to do so. This is something you ought to know: each time we have to choose between Europe and the open sea, we shall always choose the open sea. Each time I must choose between you and Roosevelt, I shall always choose Roosevelt." He glared at the frigid Frenchman and then turned away.† Invasion

---

* Originally the invasion force was scheduled to sail early in the morning on Sunday, June 4, but was delayed because of the weather. That is why Churchill had arranged the meeting with De Gaulle on the fourth, so that he could present him with a fait accompli.

† The embarrassment of the Englishmen present may be gauged by the fact that afterward Ernest Bevin, Minister of Labour, came up to De Gaulle and said that Churchill had spoken "on his own initiative and not at all in the name of the British Cabinet."

was only a matter of hours away, but no one suggested that De Gaulle remain on the special train and see the great armada set off for France. The General returned to London that evening.

Chief Inspector Reginald Smith had been called to Scotland Yard from his office in the East End in mid-May where he was told the approximate date of D-Day. He didn't really need to be told how imminent the invasion was; for several weeks now thousands of men had been working around the clock on the great green flats of the Barking Marshes, building something called Mulberry harbors. The need for them was so urgent that workers were not even allowed to stop for air raids.

Ships and landing craft were assembling in the Royal group of docks all through May, and by the end of the month every landing stage and inlet was jammed with them. Then the convoys began coming in, bearing troops by the thousands. Most of Canning Town had been destroyed as a result of the Blitz, and what few houses remained had been knocked down by the street-fighting school which had been established there and in Silvertown. Tents were erected in the ruins and barbed wire rolled around the perimeters of the camps. Over the Whitsun weekend, May 27–29, one of the largest contingents of British troops arrived from Scotland and the north of England, and these were shepherded into the West Ham football stadium. As in all the other camps, barbed-wire fences were set up and sentries posted, and the troops cut off from the civilian world outside. Which was how the trouble began.

On June 1 the soldiers were divided up into groups and addressed in turn by their respective commanding officer. They were told that they would be going to France "any day now," and given a rough idea of the nature of their task and the area of their landing. Afterward the groups were allowed to come forward to study maps of the Ouistreham beaches in Normandy to which their tank landing craft would be carrying them. Then they were told to line up before their supply sergeants, to be issued, and sign for, their first payment in French money. * Some of the NCOs were issued escape kits which showed routes through France to the Spanish frontier, to be used in case they found themselves trapped behind the enemy lines, along with various intriguing articles

---

* These "invasion francs" were the subject of a bitter quarrel between the U.S. military, which had printed them and decided their rate of worth, and De Gaulle, who had not been consulted.

and information put together by the U.S. intelligence service. After all this the troops were assembled at mid-field and addressed by an army chaplain, but his gloomy tone of voice and even gloomier forecast of the "perils that lie ahead for all of us" drove the soldiers off in the direction of the canteens in search of a soothing drink and a smoke. By seven o'clock on the evening of May 28 the beer had run out and there was not a cigarette to be had in the stadium. Angry soldiers who approached the supply sergeants were told in no uncertain terms that this was Whitsunday weekend and that all NAAFI (the British equivalent of a PX) depots were closed. No one thought of ordering extra supplies.

With the prospect of a dry, smokeless and confining weekend facing them, several score D-Day soldiers did the logical thing. They crept past the sentries and crawled under the barbed wire; they snipped their way through it; they climbed on each other's shoulders and leaped over it. Some of them, who knew the ground and had smuggled themselves into the stadium as kids to see matches, now tunneled their way out. Soon every pub in the vicinity was filled with British troops clamoring for drinks and smokes and offering to pay in French francs, which the barmen were accepting as souvenirs.

When the news reached him, Inspector Smith was at Wanstead Police Station looking over three members of the Luftwaffe. The Nazi fliers, who had been shot down in a raid on the marshes, not only refused to answer questions, as was their right, but were deliberately baiting the British with what would happen to them when the invasion began— *if* it began. Smith, who was feeling edgy, had to control himself from punching the most insolent one in the nose. When at last his office reached him and told him what had happened at West Ham Stadium, his first reaction was to think, "My God, this could wreck the invasion!"

It wouldn't do that, but it might put invaluable information into the hands of a spy if the troops were allowed to go on roaming around East End pubs. God knows what they would start blabbing if they got drunk—and drunk was what they seemed bent on becoming.

"But what could we do?" he said later. "By this time everybody from Montgomery on down was telling us to get those soldiers back inside the stadium. My office had already been on the job, and the bulk of the AWOLs had returned quietly. Only about thirty remained, but they were carousing in pubs as widely apart as Limehouse and Canning Town and were in no mood to respond to the orders of the military and civilian police who had been sent to round them up. Their attitude was that if they were going to die on the beaches tomorrow, they might as well get

The Run-Up

drunk on the streets of London tonight—and no snotty policeman was going to tell them otherwise. The army was all for getting tough and strong-arming them back to the stadium, but in the circumstances that seemed to me to be the height of folly, for it would not only attract attention but cause bitterness through the camp just when spirits needed to be high."

Luckily, in Canning Town Police Station the inspector found the man who turned the trick for him. He was an old retired police sergeant who had rejoined the force as a volunteer for the duration. He had sons of his own in the services, he had been used to dealing with people in trouble all his life, and he was known to have a way with him. "If you'll just give me a truck and a driver, sir," he said, "I think I can get the boys back for you. No rough stuff, either."

Smith decided to try him, and the old sergeant departed on what he was afterward to describe as the "longest pub crawl of my life." Methodically he went from bar to bar, and wherever he found soldiers gathered, raucously singing together, he joined them, sang along with them, drank with them, listened to their complaints, and then sweet-talked them back to the stadium.

By five o'clock the next morning not only had the sergeant retrieved all the escapees, but there were six more men in the stadium than before the troops had made a break for it; these half-dozen soldiers on legitimate leave had fallen for his persuasive line and decided to come along. They had to be held in custody until the D-Day barges were scraping the beaches of Normandy. So did a couple of East End pub keepers, but when they were released they were allowed to keep the invasion francs with which they had been paid.

A few days before D-Day a full-dress meeting of the Cabinet Committee was held in the Hole in the Ground, Whitehall. Anybody who had anything to do with the intelligence services and had been involved in the invasion preparations was summoned to attend. In turn the heads of the different branches read out reports from their agents inside occupied Europe, but there were no surprises until Rear Admiral Edmund Rushbrooke, Director of Naval Intelligence at the Admiralty, rose to his feet. On this occasion a young assistant, Ian Fleming, sat on one hand, and on the other one of his brightest female aides, Joan St. George Saunders. Throughout the meeting, each of them had difficulty in suppressing their excitement, for their chief had startling information to reveal.

As everybody knew, Rushbrooke began, in the neutral capital of Lisbon there was a certain Czechoslovak whose code name was Radek and who was a spy for the Germans.

"Oh, Radek!" said someone along the table. "No one pays any attention to him!"

Indeed they didn't—neither his German masters nor the British counterintelligence services in Lisbon, who intercepted and read his messages to the Abwehr in Berlin—for Radek never seemed to get anything right. He moved around in the foreign colonies of Lisbon and was always to be seen at the right—as well as the wrong—parties, but what he put into his secret cables was pure trash. Everybody in London had long since decided that the Germans only kept Radek on because he had a relative somewhere in the Abwehr organization; certainly by now they must have learned to discount anything he reported.

Now, however, Admiral Rushbrooke proceeded to read to the Cabinet Committee the breakdown from naval intelligence's agent in Lisbon of Radek's latest cable to his masters. As he read, a stillness fell over the room, for the message purported to reveal the date of the Allied landings in France and the nature of the invasion. Specifically, Radek reported:

1. The Allied forces would make a feint attack in the region of the Pas de Calais, but their main landings would be in Normandy, in the neighborhood of the Ouistreham beaches ("where King Henry the Fifth and his English army landed").

2. The invasion would almost certainly occur between the dates of June 4 and June 7, 1944, because this was the only period when the tides would be right.

3. Airborne forces would be used to secure the two flanks of the invasion area, probably dropping on the Orne River and Canal to the east and the Cherbourg peninsula to the west.

Through the deathly silence which followed Rushbrooke's reading, someone said, "My God, the only thing he's forgotten are the Mulberry harbors!"

"Well, gentlemen, what do we do?" asked the admiral.

Ian Fleming said, "We can hardly call off the invasion, can we? Or change it around."

Joan Saunders suggested, "Radek's been wrong so many times before that Canaris * is bound to think he's wrong again. I don't think he'll even bother to pass the report on to Hitler." †

---

* Admiral Canaris was chief of the Abwehr (German military intelligence).

† Joan Saunders was right; Radek's report was ignored.

Everybody around the table nodded vigorously. In the circumstances, it was the only thing to do.

"There's just one thing," Mrs. Saunders added. "Don't you think we ought to put Mr. Radek out of harm's way? Just in case he gets things right a second time?"

Everyone at the table looked at her as if she had suggested something terribly ungentlemanly.

The six weeks before D-Day were among the happiest of Polly Wright's life, mainly because she had fallen in love again.

One night in mid-April, sick of sitting around in her bed-sitting room, bored with her own company, too fidgety to sit through a movie, unwilling to enter a strange pub, she decided to brave The Gluepot. She had not felt up to risking snubs from the pubkeeper and her old friends since her release from prison, but now the need to see a familiar face, even if its expression was hostile, drove her to Mortimer Street.

She need not have worried. The pubkeeper greeted her with a broad smile and a gin-and-tonic, as if she had never been away. Dylan Thomas, his red lips buried in the foam of a large beer, slammed down his glass and rushed forward with a great shout. "Polly, my love, my beautiful, my fairy's child!" he cried, folding her in his arms. "What *have* those brutes been doing to you?"

He drew her into a throng of people around the bar—musicians, painters, soldiers, British, American, Canadian—and when the pub closed they all moved on to someone's apartment in a mews behind Broadcasting House. Apparently this was the usual procedure, because they had all brought some kind of bottle along with them, and the drinking went on amid fumes of smoke and torrents of talk all night long. No one mentioned the war. Everyone pressed drinks on Polly and put their arms around her, and somehow it was warm and affectionate rather than lascivious when they embraced her. Through the haze the face of one particular man kept swimming in and out, looking owlishly concerned for her, making sure she was never without a drink or a cigarette—and the next morning, when she awoke in a strange, enormously comfortable bed, it was to find his face bending over her, smiling now, but still owlish. "I had to bring you here," he said. "I didn't know where you lived, and I thought you needed a little help. Here, drink this."

He handed her a fizzing Alka-Seltzer, and though she didn't need it because she'd never had a hangover in her life, she found herself drinking it and staring at him over the glass. When she put it down, she felt under the bedsheets and found that she was still in her pants and bra.

The owl-faced man was a war correspondent. He told her that he had just come back from Italy, where he had been covering General Mark Clark's Fifth Army, and was now "waiting for a new assignment." But later when she looked in one of the closets for her dress, she found a uniform hanging there with the insignia of a paratrooper on the shoulder just below the war correspondent patch. He only shrugged his shoulders when she asked about it. "It was just one of those things I fell into when I got drunk," he said.

Over breakfast of a luxury she hadn't experienced for a long time —tomato juice, eggs and canned bacon, lots of toast and butter and American coffee—she decided that she liked this man a great deal—so much so that she thought she had better tell him about herself before someone else did. The story about the German, about 18b and about Holloway poured out of her.

"Actually, I know all about it," he said. "But I'm glad you told me yourself. I can't tell you how sorry I am. It isn't fair. It's a bloody horrible world—especially for women."

He reached over and took her hand, and suddenly she was crying and he was embracing her, and then they were in bed making love.

They made love—oh, how they made love—but in between they did everything together. It was simple enough to get leave of absence from her jewelry dealer boss; he didn't mind as long as she promised to come back and as long as he didn't have to pay her. Getting out of the camouflage-net job was more difficult, but her new friend solved the problem by finding a doctor friend who produced a medical certificate giving her a month's health leave.

The two of them wandered around London hand in hand in the spring sunshine. They sat on the grass at Lord's Cricket Ground and watched the match. He put on his uniform, waved a pass and took her down to forbidden Brighton, the resort on the Channel whose shore was covered with tank traps and minefields and barbed wire, but there the restaurants were full of fresh fish and there seemed to be no scarcity of food or drink. They went to concerts; they dined at the Ritz and the Savoy and the Berkeley and the Dorchester, and she was introduced to Duff Cooper and Ambassador Winant and Robert Boothby and Edward Murrow. They danced to Carroll Gibbons and his orchestra and then sat down to watch in admiration as two slim U.S. sailors and their WAAC partners jitterbugged.

The Run-Up

The days went by so fast that April and May disappeared, and then June was upon them. Still they never talked about the war. The only time it had come up was when she asked him what his next assignment was likely to be, and he had replied, "Some boring story with the RAF, I expect."

Early in June her friend received an enormous supply of clothing coupons from his friends at the War Office, more of them than the average British family got in one year. He had already provided her with six pairs of nylon stockings he had somehow obtained from his American friends. Now he took her on a round of the shops, buying her dresses, coats and everything she needed to restock her frayed and shabby wardrobe.

But it wasn't the clothes she loved, it was him, and she loved him most when she was wearing no clothes whatsoever.

On the morning of June 2 the telephone rang. Dawn had just broken, but Polly had fallen asleep only a few minutes before. She barely felt him get up and go into the other room to answer the ringing, and then she was asleep again.

An hour later she rolled over and reached for him, but there was no one there. She listened for sounds in the bathroom; there were none. She got up to look, and as soon as she entered the next room she saw the note by the telephone. "Darling Polly," it said. "I didn't want to wake you but I had to go. Thank you, my love, for everything. Please stay in the flat for as long as you like. The lease runs until the end of the month." Underneath the note was his emergency ration book and the rest of his clothing coupons.

A few days later she read her friend's story of the Allied parachute landing in Normandy, but she never saw him again. It was a long time before she could bring herself to use the clothing coupons.

16

The Last Straw

From a report by L. N. Adamson, factory manager, to
Mass-Observation, on June 6, 1944:

At 7 o'clock this morning I switched on the wireless
and then I heard what sounded to me like the beginning
of our great invasion of the Continent, but I wasn't sure.
During the hours of darkness we had been much disturbed
by the constant drone of our bombers, and with the coming of first light
this increased in intensity. It is not often I see Mosquito bombers, but they
were travelling to the unknown horizon in great numbers. I wondered why.

I did not think much about the subject until coming to the office I again
switched on the wireless and heard the Belgian Prime Minister speaking to
his country in French, and he was telling them not to take any hasty action,
but to await events. Then I knew that the great day had arrived. Later of
course I followed the official communiqué which gave the greatest news the
world has ever known: the free nations of the world, coming from England,
had landed in France to liberate their countries. All my work today has seemed
so unimportant and inconsequential: the petty telephone calls from irate
customers about delivery of goods, the attendance at a meeting to hear yet
another person talk about postwar planning, and so on. The fact that up to
the present I am not taking part in this momentous affair is particularly
irksome, and I have a feeling of suppressed frustration . . .

In my carriage this morning was a woman talking to a friend about
her son who had recently been killed at sea. She did not (as the papers would
say) feel proud of him; she only said: "There is an emptiness with me all the

time, for Gerald will not come back." This "emptiness" will soon be multiplied a thousand-fold, for great victories and banner waving successes are not without cost. I have no faith, and never have had, in a rapid Nazi collapse. Germans do not show fight and then run away. All through the war they have fought to the bitter end and they will again.

From the diary of Vere Hodgson:

JUNE 11, 1944:   I turned on the 8 A.M. news on Tuesday morning and pricked up my ears as I heard the man say with a voice of suppressed excitement that the Germans were fighting invasion barges in the Channel. I didn't think they would speak like that on our wireless if there were not something in it, so I took it as certain. Later people came in to say that Eisenhower had spoken on the radio to say that the invasion was on. We listened to every scrap of news all day. At nine o'clock when the King was to speak we were all agog. His speech was nice and sincere and, just like him, he brought the Queen in a lot and told us all to pray.

It is one man's vision which has brought this about. In those awful days Mr. Churchill was the only one who could see the comeback, and knew that if only we could hold on we had the power to beat them.

"We are most happy to salute great Marlborough's great heir, who never, amid catastrophes more awful than those which beat about the heads of a Job or a Lear, lost faith or nerve or grip. [The invasion] was the result of the design of grand strategy which Mr. Churchill adopted four years ago, to which he clung with stubborn faith when it seemed little more than a visionary dream, which he pressed through with a single-minded energy and persistence regardless of peril, defeat, pressure from abroad or clamour at home. The 4,000 ships and 11,000 planes which carried the gigantic Anglo-American-Canadian army to France were, four years ago, one man's vision and would never have become reality but for the man's undaunted faith and creative energy."

So says my newspaper, the *Observer*, today and let not future ages forget it.

From the diary of Harold Nicolson, MP:

JUNE 6, 1944:   I go down to the House, arriving there about ten to twelve. When I enter the Chamber, I find a buzz of conversation going on. Questions had ended unexpectedly early and people were just sitting there chatting, waiting for Winston. It was an unusual scene. He entered the Chamber at three minutes to twelve. He looked as white as a sheet. The House noticed this at once, and we feared that he was about to announce some terrible disaster. He is called immediately, and places two separate fids of typescript on the table. He begins with the first, which is about Rome.* Alexander gets a really tremendous cheer. He ends with the words: "This great and timely operation," stressing the word "timely" with a rise of the voice and that familiar bending of the two knees. He then picks up his other fid of notes and begins: "I have also to announce to the House that during the night and early hours of this morning, the first of a series of landings in force upon the Continent of Europe has taken place . . ." The House listens in hushed awe. He speaks for only seven minutes and then Greenwood follows with a few words. We then pass to the Colonial Office estimates in the Committee of Supply.

In the days after D-Day the weather was terrible, and everyone in London, slopping through the rain, gazing up at the dark clouds, was depressed. They pictured the men fighting their way through the Normandy mud under fire from Rommel's guns and tanks, deprived of air cover by the low clouds. Although they were told that the campaign was going well—actually, the Germans never at any moment showed themselves capable of driving the liberating armies back into the sea—Londoners were nevertheless itchy and nervous. They had long been schooled to expect Allied setbacks and swift German ripostes, and they could not convince themselves that all was proceeding without a hitch. "Just you wait," they were saying in the pubs. " 'E'll 'it back. 'E won't take it lying darn, 'Itler won't."

But except for those in the know, few Londoners guessed that when they came, the reprisals would not be against the troops in Normandy but against themselves.

Harold Nicolson felt that General de Gaulle was in a remarkably agreeable mood in the days after the invasion of France. His colleague Robert Boothby did not agree; he found the French leader an angry and unhappy man, and thought he had good reason.

Nicolson dined with De Gaulle on June 9, and when he asked him about the war, the general replied that he thought it was going well, "beyond our hopes. This is the last year of the war. The war will be

---

* Allied troops, under the overall command of General Sir Harold Alexander, had entered Rome on June 5.

over before Christmas." Later in the evening, however, when Nicolson asked De Gaulle to make a grand gesture and bring part of his government-in-exile to London from Algiers, he refused peremptorily and launched into an attack against Eisenhower and the United States. He was returning to North Africa, he said, and wanted no more of London.

Robert Boothby, on the other hand, knew that De Gaulle's dearest wish was not to return to Algiers at this moment but to set foot on native soil, to be part of the struggle for liberation. The young MP thought it outrageous that an edict from President Roosevelt, which had been willingly accepted by Winston Churchill, should prevent the Frenchman from doing so. What right had the Americans to insist that the general did not represent France, that his presence there would "muddy the waters," when there was every indication from the territories that had already been liberated that it was De Gaulle whom most French men and women were waiting to see?

Boothby decided that the situation was intolerable. He canvassed the opinions of his colleagues in the House and came to the conclusion that most of them agreed with him. Forbidding De Gaulle's return to his own country was an outrageous interference with his rights, and something had to be done.

Churchill was mysteriously absent from London, and when Boothby approached government leaders to express his dissatisfaction, he was fobbed off with such remarks from the party whips as, "The Yanks don't want him there, and that's it, old boy." Or "Winston knows best, and Winston doesn't want him in France."

Irked by these hackneyed responses, Boothby decided to draw up a list of names of Members who would support him in a motion recommending that General de Gaulle, head of the Provisional Government of the French Republic, commander in chief of the forces of Fighting France, be allowed to set foot at once in his native France to join his fellow citizens fighting to liberate their country. He collected sixty names, but he had no real intention of submitting the proposal as a serious motion until he learned why Winston Churchill was not available. The PM was on a trip to the Normandy beachhead with the Chief of the Imperial General Staff, Field Marshal Sir Alan Brooke. What particularly infuriated Boothby and his friends was the fact that Churchill had taken with him Field Marshal Smuts, the South African leader who had sneered at France a few weeks back. To have chosen him as a companion instead of the French leader seemed to be a calculated insult not only to De Gaulle but to all French citizens. In light of this news, Boothby put his motion down on the order paper when he arrived at the House on June 12.

The next day, as he was drinking a brandy after lunch in the smoking room of the House, Boothby heard that Churchill was back in London. Not only that; the Old Man was on his way to the House. Someone had dared to wake him from his customary afternoon siesta to tell him about Boothby's motion, and he was coming down to do something about it.

Those Members who saw him will always remember Winston Churchill's face that afternoon. It was strained and dark with anger. With legs slightly apart, like a sailor on the deck of a rocking ship, he strode across the smoking room until he reached Boothby's table and stood over the young Scotsman. "You will withdraw your motion!" he said in a loud voice.

"I will withdraw it if you will allow the general to go to France," Boothby replied. "Not unless."

For a moment it seemed as if Churchill was going to lose control of himself. His face went purple with fury. He lifted his arm and clenched his fist as if he were about to bring it down on Boothby's head. "Oh God, no!" someone exclaimed in the sudden hush.

The PM went rigid, and then slowly dropped his arm to his side. In a quiet but emotional voice, he said, "There are political reasons why he cannot go. But you will withdraw your motion just the same. Otherwise I shall move that the House go into secret session, and then I will tell the House why De Gaulle cannot go."

"In that case," Boothby conceded, "I must withdraw my motion. Its only motive is to ensure that the matter is debated in public."

"Yes," said Churchill, "and that I will not allow. So withdraw it." He turned and stalked out of the room.

Shattered by Churchill's blind fury, Boothby sat staring into his drink, unconscious of the buzz all around him. He reflected that he had never seen Winston Churchill so near to losing all his composure. It has gone on too long, he thought. It is breaking too many men. It is time this war came to an end.

Finally he rose from the table and walked out to tell the Speaker and his friends that he was withdrawing his motion.

But twenty-four hours later, word reached De Gaulle that the ban on his movements had been lifted. He left for his homeland in a French destroyer, and on June 14 he set foot on French soil for the first time since the collapse of his country.

t 2:35 A.M. on June 16 the air-raid sirens wailed over Banstead Common on the southern outskirts of London, and L. N. Adamson rolled over, groaned, and tiptoed out of bed so as not to disturb his wife. But she had been awakened too. "Don't forget your helmet, dear," she said.

Adamson dressed, put on his tin hat and padded out into the cool blue darkness toward the ARP post where he was a warden. As he walked, he noticed a small glow in the eastern sky streaking toward him at a slightly downward angle. Ah, he thought, a Nazi plane on fire. Then the engine spluttered and suddenly stopped, and the glow disappeared. Good, the damn thing was coming down. A few seconds later there was a fearful explosion. Bombs on board, Adamson decided. By this time he had reached his post, and he instructed the warden on duty to send a "crashed aircraft" report to Control, and then telephoned the fire brigade. With two other wardens he set out for the scene of the crash, each of them carrying a spade in case the German pilot proved obstreperous.

But when they reached the spot there was nothing to see except a shallow crater, a few bits of wreckage, and three long curious bits of metal. The site was a stretch of open field, so there were no civilian casualties.

Puzzled, Adamson phoned the Home Guard and told them to look out for a German pilot and his crew. Then he returned to his ARP post, peering suspiciously at passing pedestrians for Germans in disguise.

Once back at the post, however, real trouble began. "More and more of these 'crashed aircraft' came over," he wrote later, "and it began to dawn on our feeble intelligence that we were faced with something entirely new. I called out every available man and woman and settled down to deal with the new menace. We made a hurried search at the post for information about these things and any instructions, but couldn't find much of value. True, we had a few meagre details but very little. All the time these instruments of destruction were skidding across the sky and coming down and then blowing up. The mid-day paper then told us what it was. Incidentally, the speed is announced as 200 miles per hour. What rot. At least 400 miles per hour would be nearer. It was a blow when the alert was still on at 6:30 A.M., but I had to go off to work, and so left fresh wardens to deal with the remainder of the raid.

The Last Straw

"This is something we definitely hadn't bargained for, but no doubt our defences will soon find the answer.

"P.S. I have forgotten all about our invasion of France."

When Adamson realized that at last Hitler's secret weapon had begun to hit London, he was alarmed. "I don't mind admitting that for a moment my knees shook and I was scared stiff," he said.

But in a way he was relieved, as were most other Londoners at first when they discovered that this asthmatic crate weaving across the sky was the devastating weapon that would bring them to their knees.* There were jokes on the radio, and ruder ones in the pubs. In the beginning the newspapers all called them robot bombs, then robots, then doodlebugs, before finally settling for the German name, V-1. Earthier citizens called them the Farting Furies.

At this time most buzz bombs were fired on London from camouflaged launching sites in the Pas de Calais area, and as they trundled across Kent and Sussex, which became known as Bomb Alley, RAF fighters and antiaircraft guns did their best to explode them in the air. But their success was not spectacular, and the bulk of them got through. They were even exciting at first, though they kept on coming day and night. "Today I have really seen one," wrote Vere Hodgson on July 7. "It was in this wise. As I got the meat at the butcher's the alert went. I walked back to the flat, deposited my goods, and, as I could hear nothing, I walked down to the Sanctuary. Halfway down the road I heard a thrum-thrum, but as it was a long way off I didn't pay much attention. However, a platinum blonde on the other side of the road lifted her head from reading a letter and called out to me: 'Can you see it?' I said: 'No,' so she said: 'Come over here.' I crossed and sure enough right over our heads was a horrible black thing. It seemed three inches over our heads. It gave me quite a turn. The platinum blonde pursued her way unperturbed, still reading her letter."

Warrant Officer R. H. Reynolds of the U.S. Army (promotion had been rapid for him in the past twelve months) was in his new billet in Sussex Place, Paddington, when he saw his first buzz bomb.

"There were twelve of us in the billet, and we were upstairs when we heard what we thought was a low-flying plane," he recalls. "We ran to the window and caught a glimpse of it flying over. The sound was like an outboard motor, and we thought it was crippled. We saw

---

* For several months, Hitler had been threatening to launch a "secret weapon" against the British.

flames shooting out of the back end and figured it was a Jerry in distress. We yelled, 'We got that one!' as it went over and out of sight. Then we heard the explosion and felt sorry for the homes it had dropped on in Paddington. Next day we got Churchill's announcement of the flying bomb, or V-1. Ours had come over about 9:05 p.m., and we could always expect one at that time in the evening.

"Next day at work everybody was talking at once and we cocked our ears, stood still, and waited as each came toward us. It was suspense, as we didn't know when the engine would cut off or in which direction it would glide. The whole summer we sweated them out, and I have to admit they were diabolical and made you cringe. At first sign of their approach you could see everybody's eyes look at each other, and if it got too close we'd get up and stand in the hall away from the flying glass."

After ten days of almost continual alerts and the strain of always having to keep an ear cocked, the nerves of most Londoners changed for the worse. Those who could afford it started to leave the city again for the West Country, as they had during the Blitz. Those who stayed behind again began flocking to the Underground shelters. By now conditions there were better; small cubicles had been rigged up, and playrooms for children, as well as regular canteens with tea and hot food.

"Life is one long air raid," wrote Vere Hodgson. "Things go bump in the night and frequently for most of the day. I sleep on the ground floor of the office now. The doodlebugs keep coming and one listens fascinated as they pass over one's roof, praying that they will go on but feeling a wretched cad because you know that means they will explode on someone else. No sleep at all. As a result, I feel pretty cheap today."

She set down a list of buildings which had been hit by the V-1s: the Regent Palace Hotel in Piccadilly Circus, Selfridge's in Oxford Street, Barker's store in Kensington, and innumerable places in the East End, which as usual was hardest hit.

"A Canadian soldier came in the other day," Vere Hodgson wrote. "He saw a bad one last week. A doodlebug came down just beside Adastral House [the Air Ministry] in Aldwych. As he turned the corner, the Canadian saw it come down and half a dozen WAAFs who had been working on the top floor and had put their heads out of the windows to see the beastly thing had been drawn out by the blast, and bodies flew through the air. They were killed on the pavement, whereas if they had thrown themselves on the floor they would have been all right. Those who stayed inside were unhurt."

The Last Straw

It was examination time in London's schools. "I feel so awfully sorry and sad for children having to take their exams in these conditions, sitting in air-raid shelters all night and unable to concentrate the night before they take their papers. Poor kids. Rotten."

The atmosphere of London had changed within a fortnight. The excitement over D-Day had disappeared, and when people talked about the campaign, it was to say, "Why the hell doesn't Monty get on with it? What's he waiting for?"

British troops under General Montgomery were being held up on the left flank of the invasion, and did not seem to be able to break through the German lines defending the Pas de Calais. And the Pas de Calais was a goal every Londoner wanted the Allies to reach, so that the V-1 launching pads could be destroyed.

Theatres stayed open, though the "Alert" placard was now up permanently. The chorus girls at the Windmill Theatre still went through their routines, and the customers still thought they were marvelous. A U.S. air force pilot, Major Carl Greenstein, came down on leave with his crew at about this time, and together they went through the routine of buzz bombs (which really unnerved them), Piccadilly commandos ("dogs"), back-street Soho clubs (where liquor made them ill before they could get their hands on the hostesses). But it was the Windmill show that lingered longest in their memories. "The girls were real pretty—*all* of them," Greenstein recalls.

For people living in the great capital, however, it was a time of irritability, tiredness and apprehension. There was little of the camaraderie of the Blitz; people snapped at one another, jumped queues and jostled one another in the streets. They were always staring upward and flinching at odd noises, and visitors noticed that many of them could be seen talking to themselves as they walked along the streets. Everyone had the great fear that one of the monsters would descend from the sky and kill them now, just when the end of the war was in sight. It was a thought too awful to contemplate, but contemplate it they did until they were all exhausted.

On June 19, 1944, Mrs. Jenny Martin was charged at Bow Street Magistrates Court with "receiving clothing coupons, petrol coupons, cigarettes, liquor and other uncustomed goods, knowing them to be stolen."

Somehow Joey had got out of the military prison to which he had been consigned and returned to London. He had tried to move back into his old apartment and take Jenny on again as his protegée, but he had been dissuaded by her current boy friend, a supply sergeant in the U.S. Army. Joey had retired to nurse his wounds and resentment, and an anonymous tip to the police had followed. They had raided the flat in Lexham Gardens and taken Jenny into custody after finding a stock of goods from the U.S. Army PX.

The probation officer read out Jenny's history to the court, and the old story of the neglected children, the miscarriage, and the "temptations of London for a young and pretty girl" rang out once more for the benefit of the magistrates. But Jenny knew that she hadn't a chance. She had been dressed in her smartest clothes when the police took her in, and she had the look of possessing all the things that were now beyond the reach of the ordinary Londoner: lipstick, nylon stockings, expensive shoes and an elaborate hair style.

The magistrates talked among themselves about putting a stop to the "illicit activities" and "immoral goings-on, particularly with foreign soldiers" that were turning London into a "city of shame." The case was good headline material, and Jenny knew she was in for it. There was a slight rustle of applause from the people in the courtroom when she was sentenced to twelve months' imprisonment.

But in a way, Jenny was lucky; the next day the apartment in Lexham Gardens was hit and damaged by a V-1. Elizabeth Marina Jones, who was also living in the apartment, was doing her striptease act at a club in Carnaby Street when the explosion occurred, but she decided that London was becoming too hot for her and left for her home in Neath, South Wales, taking with her the stock of canned goods, cigarettes and nylons that were trophies of her stay in London.* She was luckier than Jenny Martin; when Welsh police asked her how she had acquired them, she replied that they were gifts from "my friends in the U.S. Army," and they left it at that.

Elizabeth Jones stayed in Wales for six weeks, and then boredom drove her back to the capital. This time she too would end up in court, but on much graver charges than living on the favors of U.S. soldiers.

For the Ketley family, on the edge of the East End, the V-1s came as a complete surprise. One night they were all in the Morrison shelter in their living room when Donald's mother woke them and said

---

* How they escaped the police raid, no one seems to know. Possibly she kept them at the club.

something strange had happened. Mr. Ketley told his wife she had been having a nightmare, but suddenly they heard an airplane pass low over the house, and shortly after its engine stopped came the explosion.

The Ketleys found the V-1s much harder to bear than the Blitz because they never knew what the missiles were going to do. "You would be lying there at night and hear the characteristic throbbing of the engine," Donald recalls. "If the thing stopped, then the thing might come down right then and there, or it might glide down to some place a mile away. I remember one whose engine cut out right over our house; we could hear it gliding—a strange noise almost like the beating of a large bird's wings. We lay rigid, hardly breathing, but it continued on its way and perhaps a minute later we heard the muffled boom as it hit the ground."

Unless the cloud ceiling was very low, the bombs could be seen coming over Chadwell Heath during the daytime. "People ignored them," Donald recalls, "unless they were coming directly towards them. We were at a pub one evening which was next to a transit camp for U.S. troops. Now and then a V-1 would come over a mile or so to the north or south. When this happened, the troops, who had just arrived from the U.S., would make a wild dash into the shelters across the street. Everybody else thought this was hilarious."

By this time, Donald's father was working in the Royal Victoria Docks in East London, and this was a prime target for the new weapon because it was from the Pool of London that most of the supplies for the armies in France were being dispatched, and the docks were packed with ships. According to government statements, the secret weapon was only an "instrument of terror," sent over to drive Londoners to distraction while killing as many of them as possible. But though a large number of them continued to land in civilian areas,* the Germans were guiding many of them to the docks and doing great damage there. In a space of four weeks no fewer than one hundred and thirty-nine V-1s landed in the Royal Docks group target zone.

From his office window, Mr. Ketley could look down on a railway yard that was usually full of munitions trains, and he constantly worked with one ear cocked. Hearing a missile on one occasion, he stepped out of the office to see it coming right at him. He began running toward the shelter in the basement of a nearby warehouse with a feeling that the

---

* Of the 6,725 V-1s observed over England between June and September, 3,500 were destroyed by gun, fighter-plane and balloon defenses; 2,340 reached London; and, in all, 5,475 civilians were killed and 16,000 injured.

flying bomb was chasing him. He made it just as it exploded, but fell down the stairs, breaking his ankle. The V-1 hit a munitions train but miraculously only struck the last few cars, which contained not explosives but food. However, they were aflame and the fire was creeping toward the explosives when a dock policeman dashed out and uncoupled them, and the rest of the train drew away to safety.

During those summer weeks, several ships were sunk by the flying bombs. In September came V-2, the rockets. One of the first homed in on the Royal Docks and couldn't have picked a better target; it smashed into the Bascule Bridge connecting East Ham and Canning Town with North Woolwich. There were few casualties because there were few people and houses in the area, but its destruction imprisoned a vast number of ships loaded with heavy equipment for Normandy inside the docks.

For the next forty-eight hours, while rockets continued to come down, the Royal Engineers struggled with the tangled mass of steel clogging the passageway to the river and sea. They worked with acetylene torches throughout the night to chop up the debris and drag it clear of the channel while the loaded convoy waited to get out and commanders in France screamed for supplies. Three days later they were on their way.

C. P. Snow hadn't minded the V-1s ("You could always dive beneath a table or something like that") but he loathed the second vengeance weapon. "The rockets frightened me much more than the others. Quite unrealistically, in fact. As you know, if one had been hit by a rocket one wouldn't have known anything about it. Most people took them more calmly than I did. This was purely subjective. They hadn't a big-enough warhead to be really dangerous, but somehow the idea that fate was above one without one knowing anything about it—that I found disturbing."

Donald Ketley thought so too. He had long since lost the feeling that the war was a great lark, but it was only when the rockets descended that he became aware of the possibility of death. "Before that," he said "I always felt that one could get into a shelter when a raid started or a V-1 was coming, and the chances of getting killed were small—in fact, nonexistent from a boy's point of view. With the V-2s there was no question of getting into a shelter. If they were near enough you could hear them enter the upper atmosphere but that was no more than a few seconds before they hit the ground, so all you could do was attempt to ignore them. Probably the worst damage to our house was done by a V-2 which hit the railway near Chadwell Heath Station one Saturday morning. Fortunately the rocket fell behind an embankment. I was in the kitchen facing the railway. The embankment caused the blast to be diverted upwards so that only the upper part of the house was damaged, except for the wall between the kitchen and the living room, which cracked right through—and in those days they made internal walls of brick rather than cardboard. It was the only structural damage the house ever suffered. Fortunately for me the kitchen windows held—they were covered with a kind of glued-on net which was enormously effective."

One morning on his way to work, Mr. Ketley passed a house where a V-2 had just landed. The warhead had not exploded and the bomb had buried itself upright in the garden. The man of the house was standing open-mouthed in his doorway, staring in amazement at the enormous, gleaming tower which had suddenly appeared in his yard. Donald's father always laughed when he recalled the expression on the man's face.

But he had another rocket story that was not so humorous. One evening he ran to catch a bus, but just missed it. He took the next one, and a mile down the road was halted by a traffic jam. A V-2 had dropped in the road and completely destroyed the bus he had just missed.

The Ketleys found the V-2s unsettling and depressing. Like all other Londoners, they were exhausted, sick of the war, wondering whether it would ever end, and growing old with worry and the frustrating round of everyday living. "Do you realize," said Mrs. Ketley one day, "that our Donald is thirteen years old and has never flown a kite?" In their part of London kite flying was prohibited as part of the defense regulations.

One Sunday that autumn the family walked up onto the plateau above Chigwell and looked back down on the huge black-and-gray mass that was London, with the silver thread of the Thames winding through it. It was a quiet day. It was also a day when the Germans were intensifying their rocket attacks on the capital, and the Ketleys must have seen more than twenty landing in puffs of smoke and flame. "You could hear the explosions," Donald remembers, "now close, now far, now somewhere in between, like muffled drums. Before, one had felt always like a participant in a battle, but the lack of antiaircraft fire or fighter planes during the V-2 period gave the rockets an aura of invincibility. People became more on edge, more irritable than they'd ever been. In part this was because the war had been going on for so long, but I think it was also the nature of the V-2s. They were cosmic terrors."

Mr. Ketley held his wife and son by the hand as they gazed down on the vast gray landscape before them and listened to the drums of the rockets. "You know," he said at last, "if the Germans had had those things in 1940, I think we might have cracked."

Slowly, oh, so slowly, the war was being won. Paris was liberated in August. Without much hesitation the French people acclaimed General de Gaulle as their leader, and America and Britain had no option but to accept him as such. Past quarrels were pushed under the diplomatic carpet, but they were not forgotten, and they were not forgiven by De Gaulle.

The Russians slogged into Poland and the Balkans. The British at last captured the missile sites in the Pas de Calais area, but both V-1s and V-2s kept coming from Holland, and there was no respite for the people of London. At the height of the summer they were being killed at the rate of 130 a day, and thousands of houses were damaged every twenty-four hours by the terror weapons. In the autumn the slaughter slackened off, but still the ugly menaces came trundling over London or swooping out of the sky night and day, and though the bangs were less frequent, life was no less frightening.

But the war was ending. In September the government announced that the Home Guard would be disbanded. There was a final parade in Hyde Park, at which King George took the salute, and then the part-time soldiers put away their rifles, looked nostalgically at the broom handles and muskets with which they had prepared to defend their island kingdom in 1940, and went back to their offices and factories. For many of them, things would never be quite the same.

That autumn also, the blackout was officially relaxed somewhat. Lights did not immediately spring up and bathe the great city in midnight sunshine, but it meant that blackout curtains did not have to be pinned up so rigidly, and that some pale illumination could be cast on the chipped sidewalks. Soldiers in search of fun in the West End could now actually see the painted faces of the "Piccadilly commandos" without shining a flashlight on them, and it did not seem to cause any slackening in trade.

Surprisingly, not everybody welcomed the end of the blackout. Mary Lelean, a young member of the ATS, heard nothing but grumbles at her depot in Kensington. "Lighting conditions along Knightsbridge and Kensington Road are such that the Albert Hall is now surrounded by light after being surrounded by gloom for all these years," she wrote on November 8, 1944. "The stretch of pavement from the corner to the door of our billet is shining bright and completely deserted. Ever since the ATS descended upon this quiet Kensington backwater at the beginning of the war, countless swains of all nationalities have bidden a fond farewell to their khaki-clad Juliets along this strip of pavement. Now the lights have gone up along this paradise, and the couples will be forced to seek some less public rendezvous for their goodnight kisses. Among many of the girls in my unit the lifting of the black-out at this particular spot is most unpopular, and they say so with feeling."

General de Gaulle had forecast that the war would be over by Christmas, but of course it was not; instead, the Germans counterattacked in the Ardennes and the Battle of the Bulge began.

No one in London seemed surprised that the war dragged on. It had lasted so long that by now they found it impossible to imagine existence without it. Christmas 1944 was marked by a killing cold spell which covered the streets with snow and numbed their spirits. Disillusionment and hopelessness were specters at Christmas dinners in the capital, and though most households managed to get hold of a chicken or rabbit for the feast, there wasn't much else to go with it. The extras announced for the holiday by the Ministry of Food were confined to one extra half pound of margarine and one of sugar. There was no canned fruit, no reduction of points on the purchase of the rarer foods, no oranges or lemons. In addition, many pubs, which had taken to closing early anyway because of lack of liquor, used Christmas as an excuse to close all day.

It was the most miserable Christmas of the war. All the fine hopes of the summer, when the Allied armies had landed on the Continent, had faded. Five years of marginal diet, bombing, defeats and humiliations, conscription, and the increasing regimentation and degradation of life in a great city in wartime had sapped the strength and optimism of seven million people.

On December 22, 1944, one reporter for Mass-Observation wrote:

My landlady said, "I've never heard as much grumbling as I've heard this year." Her husband: "You can't wonder at it. This is the worst Christmas we've had. I think so many people were counting on the war being over that it's fallen flat now. People are sick of the war. You can stand it so long but there comes a time when you can't stand any more."

They were not just sick of the war; they were sick of everyone connected with it, including Winston Churchill. All over the country there were signs of discontent with the government in power, and a surging feeling that it must be changed. "No one should have been surprised," Robert Boothby said. "These were the same old MPs who had been elected before the war began. Every six months from the date when Parliament should have been prorogued they had voted themselves extensions of power. They themselves may have chosen to forget that they were the same squalid lot who had appeased with Chamberlain and fawned before Hitler, but the people hadn't. Now that the war was coming to an end, they wanted them out."

Of course Winston Churchill was not tarred with that brush; his fighting spirit was still admired everywhere. But the majority of people did feel that he was an old Tory taskmaster who could lead them in war but would never learn the civilized ways of the kind of peace of which they were dreaming. They looked forward to a world where there would be no more war, no more unemployment, no more exploitation, to what they were increasingly calling the welfare state. They sensed that Churchill was looking not forward but backward to the kind of privileged world he had known all his life. They resented it when he warned them that a welfare state could not simply spring into being, that it must be worked for and paid for.

Just before Christmas the Labour party held its annual conference, and its leaders, Attlee, Bevin, Morrison—all members of Churchill's coalition cabinet—found themselves harassed by the rank and file and told to get ready for the political battle to come. The sooner the coalition was ended and a general election called, the better, in the opinion of the rank and file. Attlee stiffly retorted that there could be no thought of a break in the coalition until the war was truly won.

The Tories were restive too, and they did not have the same compunction about breaking up the coalition. Already the party managers were working on a plan for an election the moment the war was over. Then they would ride to victory on the shoulders of Winston Churchill, the man who had won the war. Even the strongest of the appeasers hoped to be returned to Parliament on Winston's coattails.

There were no political polls in those days, but if the Tory managers had read the reports that were currently flowing into Mass-Observation, they might have seen that it was not going to be quite that simple. The first trickles of the anti-Tory tide that would soon engulf even Winston Churchill were already audible, for British voters were determined on a change in the coming days of peace.

If peace ever came.

17

Permission to Grumble

The first few weeks of 1945 were, as Vere Hodgson put it, "thunderingly cold," and since gas and electricity were in desperately short supply there was little they could do to get the ache out of their bones. Every day over the radio and in the newspapers came descriptions of new conquests and more Nazi retreats, but it seemed that as long as one German remained with a gun in his hand, the war in Europe would go on and London's own ordeal would continue.

"Just as all these wonderful sounds were coming over the air," wrote Vere Hodgson, "behold I heard a rocket bomb drop in the distance. It was a long way away but it was there to remind us that there are still some very unpleasant things about and that *the war is not over.*"

Life was particularly hard for her at this moment because her doughty and beloved Aunt Nell, who had stayed alive just to hear that the hated Hitler was beaten, lay dying in the hospital. On February 1 Vere Hodgson was allowed to see her. "She looked very, very ill and grey. They said she was in great pain. I kissed her and she opened her eyes. I told her that the Russian Army was rushing for Berlin, and the old spirit flashed out in her joy. But she was too tired to talk."

Two weeks later she was dead, and Vere Hodgson wept. "We are pushing the Germans from our side, and the Russians from the other," she wrote in her diary on February 18. "It is like a giant nut-cracker. But it is all a long time, and I had prayed earnestly that dear Auntie would survive to the Peace. We had planned such a party. She and I. We were going to put on our best frocks and drink the health of England and Mr. Churchill in great style. But now that little party will never take place."

While people waited for peace to come, small changes in the stodgy diet made life bearable. An issue of oranges helped to appease the desperate need for sweetness. When Vere Hodgson passed Ponting's, the department store, she noticed "enormous queues of women. I asked what they were there for, and I was told: *sheets*. There had been an advert that the Government had released some sheets, and so short is everyone that the women were there at 5 a.m. There were not hundreds but thousands. The police were controlling the queues. Some of the happy buyers got in my bus. They did look pleased."

Aside from the war news, which many Londoners only glanced at nowadays, the big story was a murder trial. A U.S. paratrooper and an eighteen-year-old blonde were in the dock at the Old Bailey, charged with killing a taxi driver.

The girl was Elizabeth Marina Jones, the striptease dancer whom Jenny Martin had lived with in Lexham Gardens.

The trial of Elizabeth Jones and Private Carl Gustav Hulten in January 1945 was reported in British newspapers and talked about by the British public as if it were the most sensational crime of World War II. For several days it drove the war news off the front pages, for it seemed to contain every element which would confirm ordinary people's worst suspicions about the decadence in the wartime West End: a gun-toting paratrooper, on the run from the U.S. Army, who boasted of heading a black-market gang in Soho, and who, after shooting his victim in the back, had remarked, "People in my profession are used to things like that"; his striptease girl friend who had deserted her soldier-husband for a good time in London—plus the background of the sinister underworld of black-marketeering and illicit sex through which they had moved.

In actual fact, however, two more pitiable and mediocre people charged with a major crime have rarely come before a British court.

Far from being an exotic gun moll thriving on the thrills of criminal life, Elizabeth Jones had been a failure at everything she tried. As a stripteaser she was a clumsy amateur, hired only because all the professional show girls were now dancing for ENSA (the British USO). She had finally lost her job because of a disfiguring rash on her body. And, as Jenny Martin had learned when they shared the flat in Lexham Gardens, she was a failure in sex as well. Not even her husband, whom she had married when she was on leave from an approved school (for delinquents), had slept with her, and men never came back to her twice. Even Hulten, frightened away by the rash, had never slept in the same bed with her.

Their crime was equally mean and sordid. These two were no thrill-seeking, wartime Bonnie and Clyde. In the six days that their association lasted, they knocked a girl off a bike and stole her handbag for ten shillings and some clothing coupons, beat another girl over the head with an iron bar and threw her in the river after taking five shillings, the only money she had,* and murdered the taxi driver for four pounds, a fountain pen and a wrist watch. They even lacked the dignity of loyalty; in court, each tried to escape the consequences by blaming the other.

The trial aroused a vindictive streak in the public, and there were howls of disapproval when the jury found them both guilty but recommended that Hulten should be hanged and the girl reprieved. Women in an arms factory in Scotland threatened to go on strike if Elizabeth Jones was not sent to the gallows. Hundreds of other members of her sex bombarded the Home Secretary—in whose hands her fate lay—with letters urging him not to exercise his right of clemency. The trial seemed to unleash a pent-up resentment against all those who had "done well" out of the war, particularly girls who had dodged the draft or the strains of coping with rations, coupons, points and taking care of families.

But perhaps the most extraordinary comment came from George Bernard Shaw, who wrote a letter to *The Times:*

> We have before us the case of a girl whose mental condition unfits her to live in a civilised community. She has been guilty of theft and murder; and apparently her highest ambition is to be what she calls a gun moll . . . She has earned her living as a strip-tease girl, which I, never having seen a strip-tease act, take to be a performance as near to indecent exposure as the police will allow, though after 20 years' observation of sun-bathing I find it difficult to imagine anyone being entertained by the undress that would have shocked Queen Victoria.
>
> Clearly we have either to put such a character to death or to re-educate her. Having no technique of re-education immediately available, we have decided to put her to death. The decision is a very sensible one, as the alternative is to waste useful lives in caging and watching her as a tigress in the zoo has to be caged and watched.

---

* She managed to struggle ashore and was taken to a hospital by a passer-by.

Aside from blithely ignoring the fact that clemency had been rec-ommended by the jury, it turned out, on further reading, that GBS's letter was an attack on hanging as a method of execution and a plea for the establishment of the gas chamber as the means of getting rid of murderers.

In spite of overwhelming public opinion in favor of her execution, Elizabeth Jones was finally reprieved,* but she was kept waiting to know her fate until the last minute, as if the government, reluctant to cheat the public and the gallows of a victim, wished to torture her.

Private Carl Gustav Hulten was hanged at Pentonville Gaol on March 8, 1945. Curiously enough, though many women demanded that Elizabeth Jones be hanged, no one exulted at his execution. Many a British soldier resented the success that U.S. troops were having with their wives and girls, but not to the extent of wanting to see them hanged, even as a symbolic act.

The case produced a rash of articles about wartime morals, good-time girls, the rise in illegitimate births and the alarming increase of venereal disease. One school headmistress wrote to Mass-Observation giving details of forty girls and boys at her school whose mothers were having affairs or had given birth to illegitimate children. "I talked about it to our school nurse," she wrote, "and she said: 'You're telling me! Every week we have a policeman searching our pre-natal records to see if they can discover who abandoned a newborn baby in a ditch or in a pond, or tried to dispose of the effects of an abortion.' "

There was always one subject that could distract Londoners even from crime and sex, and that was the weather. They had become more con-scious of it than ever during the war, because when the moon was shin-ing the blackout was less of a hardship, when it was dry they didn't have to worry about the holes in their shoddy shoes and the patches in their raincoats, when it was warm they didn't have to shiver because of lack of fuel. All winter they had stumbled because clouds covered the moon, had been soaked by rain, and had suffered through spells of biting cold. Now, toward the end of March, the weather suddenly changed, as it can only in England, and with it the public mood. "There are many things to say," reported Vere Hodgson on Palm Sunday, March 25, 1945. "First of all *the weather*. It has been marvellous all week. Never can we

---

* She was sentenced to life imprisonment, which can be anything up to twenty years. She served ten years.

remember such a March, and we shall *pay* later on. Yesterday was the hottest day in London in March for half a century. The sun blazed down from a cloudless blue. I went out without a coat and even then was too warm. It was glorious. Now it has clouded over, but I do hope it won't affect the armies."

It did not. The stirring in Londoners' blood may have come not only from the weather but from a precognitive realization that at long last the ordeal of war was coming to an end. On March 25 a rocket dropped on what was described in an official British communiqué as "waste ground in Southern England." The waste ground was, in fact, Hyde Park, and the rocket just missed Speakers' Corner and took down most of the remaining windows in the houses and hotels of Park Lane. The following day a rocket demolished the Whitfield Tabernacle in Tottenham Court Road. No one knew it at the time, of course, but it was the last enemy explosive to hit London.*

"*No bombs . . . ain't it lovely?*" reported Vere Hodgson on April 11, 1945.

The ordeal was over. There would be no more nights of waiting for the swish of high explosive, the sudden cough of a V-1 engine or the crunch of a rocket hitting a neighbor's house. Still, how could anyone know that it was really over, that it wasn't just a lull, that Hitler didn't have another engine of terror waiting to strike?

Nevertheless, in walking the streets of the capital in those spring days, one could almost feel the smile opening on the face of London.

"Well, what sort of a night did you have last night, Mrs. Murgatroyd?"

"Slept like a log, love. And in my own bed too. It's hard to believe, ain't it? Haven't snuggled up to me old man in our own double bed since 1940, straight we haven't."

"Hope you didn't get up to any mischief, Mrs. Murgatroyd."

"Why, Mr. Brown! Don't you know there's a war on?"

On April 12, 1945, President Franklin D. Roosevelt died, and probably no American can comprehend how broken-hearted the British were to hear the news. The voter is apt to see the politician in his own statesmen. Churchill was always a Tory to the British, but they had never

---

* Since September the previous year, 750 V-1s had been spotted, of which 79 reached London. In the same period, 1,100 V-2 rockets were observed, and 518 reached London. The V-2s killed 2,724 civilians and injured 6,000.

thought of Roosevelt as a politician. He was a world statesman, a liberator, a man they had hoped would be in the forefront when they marched into the brave new postwar world. His death before he could see the victory he had helped to achieve hurt them deeply.

"I don't think I have ever seen London quite so devastated by an event," Charles Snow recalls. "Even my slatternly old landlady was crying. The Underground was full of tearful faces—far more than if Winston had died, I'm sure."

Vere Hodgson wrote: "It's a black day for all of us. What a shock it was when I hopped out of bed and found the *Daily Telegraph* all in black and the terrible announcement. Then I heard a bit of the wireless and really I shed tears, because it will make it harder for Mr. Churchill. They got on so well and I am afraid Stalin is a hard nut to crack and a very different mentality . . . Anyway, thank you, Mr. Roosevelt for all the help you gave us, and the way you helped us in those dark and lonely days of 1940."

The House of Commons adjourned for the day on April 13, the first time it had ever done so for the death of a foreign statesman. All over London people walked around as if they had suffered a death in the family.

Soon, to add a sickness to their sorrow, came news of the overrunning of the concentration camps in Germany, and then the newsreel pictures to confirm the unbelievable evil of the enemy they had been fighting.

A Mass-Observation correspondent went to see the films of Belsen at a cinema in the West End. Arriving at the end of a cartoon—a Donald Duck short—he sat through the regular news feature. The atrocity film came at the end.

"The audience was intensely still throughout the latter film," he wrote. "No words were spoken. There were occasional sniffs, as of people restraining tears but blowing their noses, and several sounds of sharp in-breathing, particularly as the skeleton-like bodies of those still just alive were shown. A very large number of the audience got up and went out at the end of the film, and from overheard comments ('Don't let's stay for this—I don't want to see it' and 'Let's go now') I got the impression that many found it distasteful to see a Donald Duck film immediately after the horror film. They filed down the staircase fairly silently; in the case of five couples, the men were holding the women by the arm or half supporting them; one woman, about thirty-five, was covering her eyes with her hands; several others were dabbing their eyes or using their handkerchiefs. Several men blew their noses violently."

It was too much to bear. People were tired. It had gone on too long.

o Londoners, May 7, 1945, was the messiest day of World War II. They knew that the war was over but nobody would make it official and no one quite knew what to do.

From their cellars most of the big stores had dug out the flags of all nations. The sidewalks of the West End were suddenly alive with street vendors selling paper hats, favors, rattles and whistles of a kind which hadn't been seen since 1939. Everybody knew that Hitler and Goebbels were dead, and that somewhere on Lüneburg Heath, German generals had signed an armistice with Field Marshal Montgomery. The stage was set for the signature of unconditional surrender at General Eisenhower's headquarters in Rheims.

But the English are a formal people; they do not like to celebrate something, even a victory, until it is official—and peace was not official yet, for there had been no announcement.

V-E DAY MAY BE TOMORROW the newspaper headlines said, but nobody could be certain, so crowds began converging on the capital in preparation for the celebration.

An unexcited expectancy was the dominant mood [a Mass-Observation survey reported], coupled with the usual uncertainty and confusion. The knowledge that the dates, and perhaps also the length, of their V-E holidays depended on the official announcement was probably most important of all in maintaining people's interest in the matter.* The official announcement was, after all, a technical matter. Everyone knew that the European war in actual practice was an affair of the past, and all that remained now was, it was hoped, the experiencing of some dramatic moment when the transition from official war to official peace might be felt and recognised.

On May 7, people went to work uncertain whether tomorrow would be a holiday or not. Newspaper headlines continued to trumpet GERMANY SURRENDERS, but as a female bus conductor remarked, "It's neither one thing nor the other, is it?"

The pubs were full and pubkeepers suddenly seemed to have

---

* The government had promised to make the official end of the war with Germany a paid holiday.

discovered extra supplies of drink. Attempts to start mass celebrations were discouraged, however. A Cockney group which started to dance to the tune of "Knees Up, Mother Brown" in Trafalgar Square were stared at as if they were dancing on a grave, and soon they became self-conscious and stopped.

The next day, May 8, it was official. "The war is over," announced Vere Hodgson. "Churchill says so."

That afternoon a vast river of Londoners flowed down the Strand and the Mall, through Trafalgar Square into Whitehall, where it had been announced the Prime Minister would speak. At three o'clock the great bell of Big Ben struck and over loudspeakers a voice proclaimed that the Prime Minister was coming.

He appeared alone on a balcony of the Ministry of Works and looked down upon the pulsating sea of people below him. A great cheer rose, and then a sudden and heart-catching quiet. There had been no silence like it for more than five years.

"People hung on to every word he said," Vere Hodgson remembered. "When he told them that as from midnight hostilities would cease, there were loud cheers and a waving of hats and flags; and then a louder cheer when he said: 'The German war is therefore at an end.' People began to cry and laugh and cheer at the same time. Mention of Eisenhower's name and 'our Russian comrades' started more clapping. He ended his speech with 'Advance Britannia,' and the buglers of the Scots Guards sounded the ceremonial cease-fire. Then the band struck up the National Anthem, and looking round I saw everyone, young and old, civilians and soldiers, singing with such reverence that the anthem sounded like a sacred hymn."

Wild celebrations began all over London. Now when people danced "Knees Up, Mother Brown" and the "Lambeth Walk" in the streets, everybody joined in. A British sailor, an American GI and a Pole did a strip-tease in Piccadilly Circus. A young blonde did the same in the fountains of Trafalgar Square, and was much more popular. A U.S. paratrooper, his face covered with lipstick, passed along Oxford Street thrusting his cheek toward every passing pretty girl and saying, "Please add to my collection."

They did. Nobody said no to anybody in London on May 8, 1945.

But there were many who eschewed the crowds and tried to be alone or with their families. Young John Hardiman had gone off to school to take part in the celebrations, but George and Ellen stayed home and listened to Mr. Churchill on the radio. "Thank God it's all over, George," Ellen said. Simultaneously they looked at the picture of their daughter, Sheila, on the mantelshelf and then she began to cry.

Chips Channon was where one would have expected him to be on such an auspicious day: the Ritz Hotel. It was "beflagged and decorated: everyone kissed me, Mrs. Keppel, the Duchess of Rutland and Violet Trefusis all seized me alternately."

Wing Commander Geoffrey Page, now an assistant air attaché at the British embassy in Washington, was in Hollywood, taking time off to woo the beautiful daughter of a movie actor, and she would shortly become his wife.*

William Hutchins was happily in bed with Marlene, his new wife, for May 8 was the day that had been chosen, quite fortuitously, by London bus drivers to strike for better pay and working hours.

Jenny Martin was also in bed, fast asleep, in her new flat in Shepherd's Market; she would need all the rest she could get, for V-E Day would be a tiring day for members of her profession. Still, as she often reminded herself these days, it was better than jail.†

On V-E night the Ketleys left their house on Chadwell Heath and walked through the fields to a pub at Chigwell. While Mr. and Mrs. Ketley went inside to get their drinks, young Donald sat in the garden. He remembers the moment well. There were a lot of people in the pub, a beautiful old hostelry dating back to Charles I, "but it was not a rejoicing crowd. Rather, one had the sense of people relaxing, getting their breath back after having run a long, long way. Two RAF trucks drove into the parking lot and disgorged a group of aircrew and WAAFs who laughed and horsed around as they went into the pub. I watched them and felt very happy. Towards the end of the war, the thing that had really bothered me was that I'd get killed before I'd ever had a girl. Like everybody else that night, I could think about the normal pleasures of life again."

Far below, in a pattern of shimmering light that was suddenly brighter than the stars above, a London newly released from the blackout lay before Donald. It glowed and sparkled, and he stared at it, fascinated. For the first time in his life he realized that London was a city of light.

* * *

---

* At the end of his last tour of duty, Page was posted by the Air Ministry to Washington and sent around the United States to lecture on the RAF's part in the war.

† Jenny Martin had earned a remission of her sentence for good behavior in prison.

"And so it all ends," wrote Vere Hodgson, "and the long nightmare I have recorded in these pages is over. Our great city is sadly broken and her wounds are dire, but she lives. All we can say is *thank God*, and I can get along to St. Paul's or Westminster Abbey or somewhere like that and tell him so. I shall go and represent Aunty Nell, who, I know, would have gone to one of them, and give thanks for all the family for this great deliverance. As Mr. Hillyard says, we have been spared the worst in this country. We have not had to take part in a Resistance Movement and see German soldiers marching through our streets. We have not starved. We have not been herded into gas ovens. We have seen our beloved London stand up and take it."

A space in her diary followed, and then she wrote: "I see that Parliament's first act after the end of the war in Europe has been to rescind the Bill making it a punishable offence to spread gloom and despondency. So great was our danger in certain years that we were forbidden to look miserable. Now we can be as unhappy as we please. Freedom is returning."

EPILOGUE

On July 5, 1945, the British public went to the polls for the first general election in Britain in ten years. The Tories were convinced that they would ride to victory in the slipstream of Winston Churchill's glory. Even Labour party leaders did not think they had any hope of winning in face of the Prime Minister's overwhelming prestige.

Neither side had any inkling of the way the minds of the British voters were turning. People were looking forward to a brave new world of peace and light, and they did not believe that an old belligerent like Winston Churchill could play a useful part in it.

So he was dismissed. To the amazement of both parties, Labour was voted into power by 393 seats to the Tories' 213. Clement Attlee took Churchill's place as the head of the British government and went to Potsdam to deal with Stalin and Truman in the first great conference of the postwar world. A new era had begun, but it would not be as rosy and warm as British voters hoped.

Winston Churchill, the old warrior, retired to lick his wounds. But when his friends suggested that he was a victim of base ingratitude, he shook his head. He would not have such a charge leveled against his beloved countrymen. Ingratitude? "Oh, no," he said quietly, "I wouldn't call it that. They have had a very hard time."

WHERE ARE THEY NOW?

What has happened to the people in the twenty-six years since the end of World War II? Here are some details:

Mrs. Rosemary Black still lives at the same house in Maida Vale, London.

John Desmond Bernal is Professor of Crystallography at Birkbeck College, University of London.

His friend and collaborator, Patrick Maynard Stuart Blackett, strong opponent of the Allies' policy of obliteration bombing, is now Professor Emeritus and Senior Research Fellow at the Imperial College of Science and Technology in London. He was made a Companion of Honour in 1965.

Robert John Graham Boothby is now Lord Boothby of Buchan and Rattray Head, a member of the House of Lords, and a well-known figure in British public life.

Sir Henry ("Chips") Channon is dead. His son, Paul, has taken his place as Tory MP for Southend-on-Sea.

Commander Peter Victor Danckwerts, who won the George Cross for bomb-disposal work during the Blitz, is now Shell Professor of Chemical Engineering at Cambridge University.

John Henry Leslie Bernard (Jack) Davies, who wrote sketches for a number of West End revues during the war while serving in the RAF, is now a screen writer (*Those Magnificent Men in Their Flying Machines*) and lives in the South of France.

Squadron Leader Al Deere, Battle of Britain pilot, is now an air commodore in the RAF.

John James Donald, pacifist, conscientious objector, worked on the land later in the war. I have since lost track of him.

Robert Elvins, newspaper copyboy who went to Dunkirk, joined the army, served in the Middle East, and emigrated to Australia after the war.

Commander J. H. ("Dick") Fordham, London fire chief who was made a CBE (Commander of the Order of the British Empire) for his work during the Blitz, is dead.

Charles Gillen, who saw London in its weariest days in 1944, but saw it through the fresh, eager eyes of a newly arrived GI, is now a writer and lives in South Orange, New Jersey.

George Hardiman retired in 1965 because of ill health and lives with his son John, John's wife and two children in Epping, Essex. Ellen Hardiman died in 1963.

Vere Hodgson now lives in Church Stretton, Shropshire, on the border of Wales, and teaches English to Italian students.

Colonel (later Brigadier) Leslie Hollis, aide to Winston Churchill, was later knighted for his war services. He is now dead.

Mrs. Elizabeth Humphreys still lives in southeast London.

Elizabeth Marina Jones, Carl Gustav Hulten's girl friend and accomplice, also found guilty of murder, was reprieved at the last minute and sentenced to life imprisonment. She was released in the 1950s and is now married and living in Wales.

Donald Ketley, who saw wartime London through the eager eyes of a growing boy, now works as a research chemist in Columbia, Maryland. His father still lives not far from their old home in Chadwell Heath.

Professor F. A. Lindemann (later Lord Cherwell), Winston Churchill's friend and passionate apostle of obliteration bombing, is dead. So is the professor who opposed him, and lost, Sir Henry (later Lord) Tizard.

Jenny Martin has remarried and lives in Brighton, Sussex.

The Very Reverend Walter Robert Matthews has now retired as Dean of St. Paul's Cathedral but still lives in London. He is eighty-nine.

Archibald McIndoe was knighted after the war for his services to surgery. He died in 1960, but the Guinea Pigs Club still thrives.

Police Constable David Meade of Limehouse Causeway now teaches school in Cheshire, Connecticut.

Robert Mengin was awarded the Croix de Guerre and the Légion d'honneur for gallantry in combat later in the war. Afterward he was offered, and refused, service under De Gaulle. He became a journalist and lives in Paris.

Henry Moore, OM, lives and works at Hoglands, Perry Green, Much Hadham, Hertfordshire—the farm he rented during the war and afterward bought—and also in his studio at Fortei di Marmi, in Italy.

Herbert Morrison, MP (later Lord Morrison of Lambeth), is dead.

Sir Oswald Mosley and his wife, the former Diana Mitford, live in France.

Admiral Emile-Henri Muselier, French Navy, died in France in 1960, his quarrel with General de Gaulle unresolved. He wrote a book about his bitter experiences at the General's hands: *De Gaulle contre le Gaullisme.*

Robert Nichols, armaments worker, is retired and still living in Eltham, East London.

Geoffrey Page married the daughter of the late Nigel Bruce, the screen actor. He is the father of two children and lives in Switzerland, where he represents aircraft companies.

Phil Piratin, Communist, MP for Stepney, is now a member of the Central Committee of the British Communist Party. His fellow worker, Tubby Rosen, still lives in the East End.

Pfc. (later Warrant Officer) R. H. Reynolds teaches social studies in Fairfield, Pennsylvania, and lives in Gettysburg.

Joan St. George Saunders left the Admiralty at the end of the war when her husband, Hilary St. George Saunders, became Librarian of the House of Commons. He died in 1951. She now runs a research agency for writers and speakers.

Commander Reginald K. Smith, CVO, KPM (King's Police Medal), is now retired and lives at East Dene, near Eastbourne, in Sussex.

Charles Percy Snow (now a baron, Lord Snow, and member of the House of Lords) was the Labour party's chief spokesman on science and industry in the Upper House during the 1960s, but did not allow this to interrupt his principal occupation, the eleven-volume sequence of novels, *Strangers and Brothers*, which he completed in 1970 with the final volume, *Last Things.* He lives in Eaton Place, London, with his wife, Pamela Hansford Johnson, the novelist.

Polly Wright is believed to be living in Birmingham.

BIBLIOGRAPHY

Since there are hundreds of books dealing with World War II which mention some facet of life in London during 1939–45, it is possible to give only a limited list of them here. Among the official volumes I have used are:

Central Statistical Office, *Statistical Digest of the War*. London: His Majesty's Stationery Office, 1951.

Collier, Basil, *The Defence of the United Kingdom*. HMSO, 1957.

Court, W. H. B., *Coal*. HMSO, 1951.

Ferguson, S. M., and H. Fitzgerald, *Studies in the Social Services*. HMSO, 1954.

Hammond, R. J., *Food*, Vol. I, *The Growth of Policy*, and Vol. II, *Studies in Administration and Control*. HMSO, 1951 and 1956.

Hancock, W. K., and Margaret Gowing, *British War Economy*. HMSO, 1952.

Hansard, House of Commons debates, 1939–45.

A History of Combined Operations: Amphibious Warfare Headquarters. HMSO, 1956.

Inman, P., *Labour in the Munitions Industries*. HMSO, 1957.

Jackson, W. Eric, *Achievement: A Short History of the London County Council*. London: Longmans, 1965.

McCallum, R. B., and A. Readman, *The British General Election of 1945*. London: Oxford U. Press, 1947.

Ministry of Information, *Front Line*. HMSO, 1942.

O'Brien, T. H., *Civil Defence*. HMSO, 1955.

Postan, M. M., *British War Production*. HMSO, 1952.

Savers, R. S., *Financial Policy*. HMSO, 1956.

Select Committee on National Expenditures (reports 1939–40). HMSO, 1940–43.

Titmuss, R. M., *Problems of Social Policy*. HMSO, 1950.

A selection of books by a widely differing range of authors, in all of whose narratives I have found some interesting accounts of wartime life in London, is given below. I would emphasize that it is a purely personal selection.

Banks, Sir Donald, *Flame Over Britain*. London: Low, 1946.

Beaton, Cecil, *The Years Between —Diaries 1939–44*. London:

Weidenfeld & Nicolson, 1965 (New York: Holt, 1965).

Bedford, Duke of, *A Silver-Plated Spoon*. London: Cassell, 1959.

Blackstone, G. V., *A History of the Fire Service*. London: Routledge & Kegan Paul, 1957.

Boothby, Robert, *I Fight to Live*. London: Gollancz, 1947.

———, *My Yesterdays, Your Tomorrows*. London: Hutchinson, 1962.

Bowen, Elizabeth, *The Heat of the Day*. London: Cape, 1954.

Brockway, Fenner, *The Bermondsey Story*. London: Allen & Unwin, 1949.

Bryant, Sir Arthur, *Turn of the Tide*. London: Collins, 1957 (New York: Doubleday, 1957).

Bullock, Alan, *The Life and Times of Ernest Bevin*, Vol. II, *Minister of Labour 1940–45*. London: Heinemann, 1967.

Bullock, John, *M15*. London: Arthur Barker, 1957.

Butcher, Harry C., *My Three Years with Eisenhower*. London: Heinemann, 1946. (New York: Simon & Schuster, 1948).

Calder, Angus, *The People's War*. London: Cape, 1969 (New York: Pantheon, 1969).

Channon, Sir H., *Chips: The Diaries of Sir Henry Channon*. R. Rhodes James, ed. London: Weidenfeld & Nicolson, 1967.

Churchill, Winston S., *The Second World War*, Vol. I, *The Gathering Storm;* Vol. II, *Their Finest Hour;* Vol. III, *The Grand Alliance;* Vol. IV, *The Hinge of Fate;* Vol. V, *Closing the Ring;* Vol. VI, *Triumph and Tragedy*. London: Cassell, 1948–53 (Boston: Houghton Mifflin, 1948–53).

———, *War Speeches*. 3 vols. Charles Eade, ed. London: Cassell, 1951–52 (Boston: Houghton Mifflin, 1953).

———, *Secret Session Speeches*. Charles Eade, ed. London: Cassell, 1946 (New York: Simon & Schuster, 1946).

Clark, Ronald W., *Birth of the Bomb*. London: Phoenix, 1961 (New York: Horizon Press, 1962).

———, *The Rise of the Boffins*. London: Phoenix, 1962.

———, *Tizard*. London: Methuen, 1965 (Cambridge, Mass.: The M.I.T. Press, 1966).

Clostermann, Pierre, *The Big Show*. London: Chatto & Windus, 1951 (New York: Random House, 1952).

Collier, Richard, *The City That Would Not Die*. London: Collins, 1959. (New York: Dutton, 1960).

Coote, Colin, *Companion of Honour*. London: Collins, 1965.

Cras, Hervé, *Les Canadiens à Dieppe*. Paris: Editions France Empire, 1953.

Cudlipp, Hugh, *Publish and Be Damned!* London: Dakers, 1953 (Philadelphia: Saunders, 1954).

BIBLIOGRAPHY

Deacon, Richard, *A History of the British Secret Service*, London: Muller, 1969.

De Gaulle, Charles, *War Memoirs*, Vol. I, *The Call to Honour, 1940–42*. London: Collins, 1955 (New York: Viking, 1955); Vol. II, *Unity, 1942–44*. London: Collins, 1959 (New York: Simon & Schuster, 1959); Vol. III, *Salvation, 1944–46*. London: Collins, 1960 (New York: Simon & Schuster, 1960).

Driberg, Tom, *Beaverbrook*. London: Weindenfeld & Nicolson, 1956.

Eisenhower, Dwight D., *Crusade in Europe*. London: Heinemann, 1948 (New York: Doubleday, 1948).

Farrer, David, *The Sky's the Limit*. London: Hutchinson, 1943 (Toronto: Ryerson, 1944).

———, *G for God Almighty*. London: Weidenfeld & Nicolson, 1969. (New York: Stein & Day, 1969).

Firebrace, Sir Aymler, *Fire Service Memories*. London: Melrose, 1949.

FitzGibbon, Constantine, *The Blitz*. London: Wingate, 1957; republished 1970 (*The Winter of the Bombs;* New York: Norton, 1958).

———, *The Life of Dylan Thomas*. London: Dent, 1965 (Boston: Little, Brown, 1965).

Fleming, Peter, *Invasion 1940*. London: Hart-Davis, 1957 (*Operation Sea Lion;* New York: Simon & Schuster, 1957).

Foot, Michael, *Aneurin Bevan*, Vol. I. London: MacGibbon & Kee, 1962 (New York: Atheneum, 1963).

Galland, Adolf, *The First and the Last*. London: Methuen, 1955 (New York: Holt, 1955).

Gardner, Brian, *Churchill in Power*. London: Methuen, 1968 (Boston: Houghton Mifflin, 1969).

Gowing, Margaret, *Britain and Atomic Energy 1939–45*. London: Macmillan, 1964 (New York: St. Martin's, 1964).

Graves, Charles, *The Home Guard of Britain*. London: Hutchinson, 1943.

———, *Londoner's Life*. London: Hutchinson, 1944.

———, *London Transport Carried On*. London: London Passenger Transport Board, 1947.

———, *Off the Record*. London: Hutchinson, 1942.

———, *Women in Green*. London: Heinemann, 1948.

Harrison, Michael, *Mulberry*. London: W. H. Allen, 1965.

Harrod, Roy F., *The Prof.* London: Macmillan, 1959.

Henry, (Mrs.) Robert, *London Under Fire.* London: Dent, 1946.

————, *The Siege of London.* London: Dent, 1946.

Herbert, Sir Alan Patrick, *Independent Member.* London: Methuen, 1950 (New York: Doubleday, 1951).

Hillary, Richard, *The Last Enemy.* London: Macmillan, 1942 (*Falling Through Space;* New York: Reynal, 1942).

Hodson, J. L., *Through the Dark Night.* London: Gollancz, 1941 (New York: Ryerson Press, 1941).

Hollis, Sir L. and J. Leasor, *War at the Top.* London: Michael Joseph, 1959.

Ingersoll, Ralph, *Top Secret.* London: Partridge, 1946 (New York: Harcourt, 1946).

Izzard, Molly, *A Heroine of Her Time.* London: Macmillan, 1969.

Jackson, Stanley, *The Savoy.* Muller, 1964 (New York: Dutton, 1965).

Jasper, Ronald C., *George Bell: Bishop of Chichester.* London and New York: Oxford U. Press, 1967.

Kordt, Erich, *Wahn and Wirklichkeit.* Stuttgart, 1947.

Lafitte, François, *The Internment of Aliens.* London: Penguin, 1940.

Martin, Kingsley, *Editor.* London, Hutchinson, 1968.

Matthews, W. R., *St. Paul's Cathedral in Wartime.* London: Hutchinson, 1946.

McLachlan, Donald, *Room 39: A Study in Naval Intelligence.* London: Weidenfeld & Nicolson, 1968 (New York: Atheneum, 1968).

Mengin, Robert, *De Gaulle à Londres.* Paris: Editions de la Table Ronde, 1965 (*No Laurels for De Gaulle;* London: Michael Joseph, 1967; New York: Farrar, Straus, 1966).

Monckton, Walter, *Memoirs.* London: Weidenfeld & Nicolson, 1969.

Moran, Lord, *Winston Churchill: The Struggle for Survival 1940–65.* London: Constable, 1966 (Boston: Houghton Mifflin, 1966).

Morgan, Guy, *Red Roses Every Night.* London: Quality Press, 1948.

Mosley, Leonard, *Faces from the Fire* (biography of Sir Archibald McIndoe). London: Weidenfeld & Nicolson, 1962 (Englewood Cliffs, N.J.: Prentice-Hall, 1963).

Muselier, Emile-Henri, *De Gaulle contre le Gaullisme.* Paris: Editions du Chene, 1946.

Nicolson, Harold, *Diaries and Letters*. Nigel Nicolson, ed. Vol. II, *The War Years, 1939–45*. London: Collins, 1967 (New York: Atheneum, 1967).

Orr, Sir J. B., and D. Lubbock, *Feeding the People in Wartime*. London: Macmillan, 1940.

Orwell, George, *The Collected Essays, Journalism and Letters of George Orwell*. 4 vols. Sonia Orwell and Ian Angus, eds. Vol. I, *An Age Like This, 1920–40*; Vol. II, *My Country Right or Left, 1940–43*; Vol. III, *As I Please, 1944–45*. London: Secker & Warburg, 1968 (New York: Harcourt, 1968).

Pawle, Gerald, *The War and Colonel Warden*. London: Harrap, 1963 (New York: Knopf, 1963).

Philby, Kim, *My Silent War*. London: MacGibbon & Kee, 1968 (New York: Grove, 1968).

Rawnsley, Cecil Frederick, and Robert Wright, *Night Fighter*. London: Collins, 1957 (New York: Holt, 1957).

Reading, the Marchioness of, *It's the Job That Counts*. Speeches as chairman of the WVS (privately published, 1954).

Reynolds, Quentin, *Only the Stars Are Neutral*. London: Cassell, 1942 (New York: Random House, 1942).

Robertson, Ben, *I Saw England*. London: Jarrold, 1942 (New York: Knopf, 1941).

Sansom, William, *Westminster in War*. London: Faber, 1947.

Snow, C. P., *The Light and the Dark*, London: Faber, 1947 (New York: Scribner, 1961).

———, *The Masters*. London: Macmillan, 1951 (New York: Scribner, 1960).

———, *Science and Government*. London: Oxford U. Press, 1960 (Cambridge, Mass.: Harvard U. Press, 1961).

———, *Strangers and Brothers*. London: Macmillan, 1951 (New York: Scribner, 1960).

———, *Time of Hope*. London: Macmillan, 1951 (New York: Scribner, 1960).

Stanford, Captain Alfred, USNR. *Force Mulberry*, New York: Morrow, 1951.

Strachey, John, *Post D*. London: Gollancz, 1941 (*Digging for Mrs. Miller;* New York: Random House, 1941).

Thompson, Laurence, *1940*. London: Collins, 1966 (New York: Morrow, 1966).

Thompson, R. W., *The Yankee Marlborough*. London: Allen & Unwin, 1965.

Thomson, George Malcolm, *Vote of Censure*. London: Secker & Warburg, 1968 (New York: Stein & Day, 1968).

Thomson, George Pirie, *Blue Pencil Admiral*. London: Low, 1947.

Tournoux, Jean-Raymond, *Pétain et De Gaulle*. Paris: Librairie Plon, 1964 (New York: Viking, 1966).

Trevor-Roper, H., *The Philby Affair*. London: Kimber, 1968.

Turner, Ernest S., *The Phoney War on the Home Front*. London: Michael Joseph, 1961 (New York: St. Martin's 1962).

Villefosse, Louis Héron de, *Souvenirs d'un marin de la France Libre*. Paris: Editions du Chene, 1947.

Wheeler-Bennett, Sir John, *King George VI: His Life and Reign*. London: Macmillan, 1958 (New York: St. Martin's, 1958).

Winant, John G., *Letters from Grosvenor Square*. London: Hodder & Stoughton, 1947 (Boston: Houghton Mifflin, 1947).

Wood, Derek, and Derek Dempster, *The Narrow Margin*. London: Hutchinson, 1961 (New York: McGraw, 1961).

Woolton, Earl of, *Memoirs*. London: Cassell, 1959.

INDEX

ABOUT THE AUTHOR

Though LEONARD MOSLEY was born in Manchester,
England, he has known London well ever since he can
remember. As a war correspondent during World War II,
he covered the campaigns in India, the Middle East, Italy
and Germany, but he was in London and on the cliffs of
Dover during the Battle of Britain, and he returned
periodically to the capital throughout the Blitz.

On D-Day, 1944, Mr. Mosley dropped by parachute
into Normandy with the 6th British Airborne Division
and reported the capture of the vital Caen bridges. He
arrived back in London just in time for the bombardment
of the city by Hitler's V-1s and V-2s.

For his work as a war correspondent, Mr. Mosley was
twice mentioned in dispatches and made an officer of
the Order of the British Empire. He now lives in the south
of France.

71- 90469

940.5342
M   **Mosley, Leonard,** 1913–
              Backs to the wall: London under fire, 1939–45.   [1st,
         American ed.]   New York, Random House,
         [c1971]

              xiii, 430 p.   illus.
%   Illus. on lining papers.
             Bibliography: p. 405–410.

                    STATE LIBRARY OF OHIO
                         65 S. FRONT ST.
                    COLUMBUS, OHIO 43215

         1. World War, 1939–1945—Gt. Brit.—London.   I. Title.

         D760.8.L7M63   940.53421   73–577573
         ISBN 0–297–00271–6   MARC

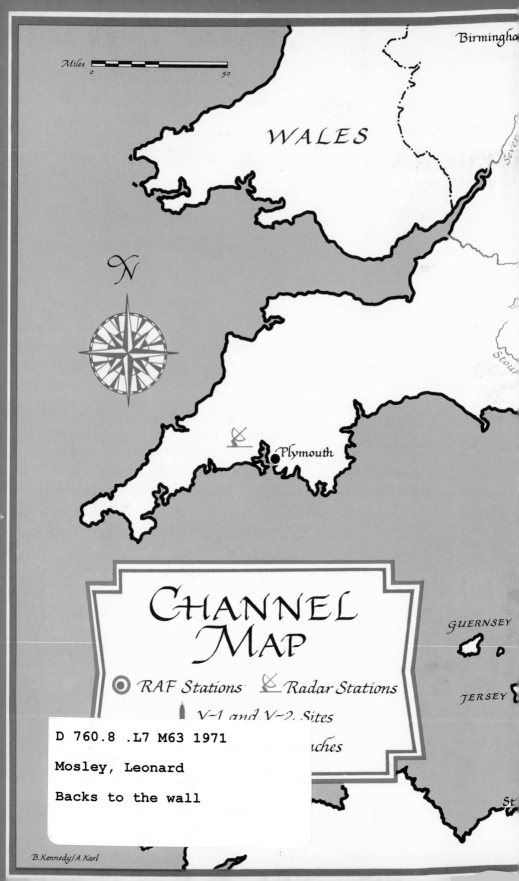

Miles 0 50

WALES

Birmingham

Severn

Stour

N

Plymouth

GUERNSEY

JERSEY

St

CHANNEL MAP

◉ *RAF Stations*   ⚔ *Radar Stations*

   V~1 and V~2 Sites

   ...ches

D 760.8 .L7 M63 1971

Mosley, Leonard

Backs to the wall

B.Kennedy/A.Karl